Understanding
Psychology

Understanding Psychology

C.B. Dobson, M. Hardy, S. Heyes
A. Humphreys, P. Humphreys

Oxford University Press

Oxford University Press, Walton Street, Oxford OX2 6DP

Oxford New York
Athens Auckland Bangkok Bombay
Calcutta Cape Town Dar es Salaam Delhi
Florence Hong Kong Istanbul Karachi
Kuala Lumpur Madras Madrid Melbourne
Mexico City Nairobi Paris Singapore
Taipei Tokyo Toronto

and associated companies in
Berlin Ibadan

© by C.B. Dobson, M. Hardy, S. Heyes,
A. Humphreys and P. Humphreys 1981

Reprinted 1982
Reprinted 1983 (twice)
Reprinted 1985
Reprinted 1986
Reprinted 1987
Reprinted 1988
Reprinted 1990
Reprinted 1992
Reprinted 1993
Reprinted by Oxford University Press 1995

ISBN Paperback 0 297 77872 2

Printed in Great Britain by
Butler & Tanner Ltd
Frome and London

Contents

14 Social perception 376

Self-perception
  Social theories of the self
  Contributions from depth theorists
  Stability and change in the self-image
  Maintaining and stabilizing the self-image
  Individual factors *Misperception*
  Selective interaction Response evocation
  Selective evaluation of the other person
  Selective evaluation of the self Affective congruency
  Social factors *Roles Constancy of interaction*
  Changes in the self Age
  Occupation
  Highly significant others
  Self-actualization and the integrity of the self
  Measuring the self-concept The interview
  Rating scales The checklist Q-sorts
  Unstructured and free-response methods
  Projective techniques

Interpersonal perception
  The intuition model Innate perception
  Global perception Immediate perception
  The inference model Associations *Induction*
  Construction Analogy Authority Identifications
  Content Non-verbal communication

Further reading

15 The psychology examination 411

The format of practical reports
  The title
  The summary
  The aim of the experiment and its background
  The conditions
  The subjects and experimenters
  The apparatus
  The method
  The results
  The treatment of results

Preface

This book is written specifically to cover the GCE A-level psychology syllabus. The motivation for writing it arose out of our experiences of teaching the Associated Examinations Board syllabus on psychology, when we found that no suitable textbooks existed other than large American glossy editions which did not always contain the depth or breadth of content demanded by the syllabus. We hope that this book will also prove to be useful for the new A-level psychology syllabus to be introduced by the Joint Matriculation Board.

Inevitably, a book of this size cannot hope to include full details of such a wide range of research effort. Consequently we would advise teachers to use this book as the basis of their teaching, but in conjunction with other more specialized sources as appropriate, and a list of relatively easily available resource books and articles is provided at the end of each chapter. The chapter on the biological bases of behaviour is markedly longer than the others, and this is not by chance. Physiological psychology is an important part of Option 1 of the AEB syllabus, and our experiences suggest that many students and some teachers express concern about the level of difficulty of some standard physiological psychology textbooks.

While this book is obviously intended for students of GCE A-level psychology, because of the overlaps with many first-year university and polytechnic courses we feel that it will prove to be a very useful primer for first- and perhaps second-year undergraduates, as well as for education and para-medical students.

We should like to thank the Associated Examining Board for permission to quote an extract from the current A-level syllabus.

Manchester, March 1980

C.B. Dobson
M.R. Hardy
S.W. Heyes
A. Humphreys
P.W. Humphreys

1 Understanding psychology

What is psychology?

Readers of this book will have different ideas of what psychology is. Some will believe that psychology is the study of the mind; some will think of psychologists studying rats in mazes, children, or the effects of maternal deprivation, or conducting laboratory experiments with drugs and electrodes; some people will come to psychology expecting it to explain to them why others behave as they do, to help them with their own relationships with their children, parents or friends, or to help them understand problems such as mental disorder or deviance; and others will simply want to know 'how to win friends and influence people'. Can psychology possibly be all these things, or are people mistaken in their expectations? The simple answer is that psychology is all of these things, and more. The main aim of psychology must be to increase our understanding of man and his complex behaviour, and psychologists have as many contributions to make to our self-knowledge as there are different aspects to man himself.

Most introductory textbooks get around the difficulty of defining psychology either by saying that psychology is a very complex discipline and cannot be easily categorized, and by offering a very simple, limited definition (such as William James's 'Psychology is the science of mental life', which was fine when it was first offered in 1890 but is somewhat inadequate in describing psychology in the 1980s); or by saying that psychology is so difficult to define satisfactorily that it is a waste of time to try. It seems to us that the difficulty is rooted in the nature of language. Very few words indeed have simple, one-entry definitions in a dictionary: the majority have a number of alternative meanings. Brown and Herrnstein (1975) illustrate this point with the example of the word 'board' which has at least four quite different meanings: we can talk of a plank of wood, the meal or meals offered at a guest house, an aggregate of company directors, or the act of going onto a ship. It is difficult to imagine anyone getting them confused in the normal course of conversation. If writers persist in considering 'psychology' as a monolith, a unified structure, rather than merely a word, we should not be surprised that no single statement will satisfy all its meanings and applications. This way of looking at the problem can be traced to the philosopher of language, Ludwig Wittgenstein (1953), who talked of certain concepts belonging to a 'family', which is like a rope of many strands, none of which runs through its entire length. We would ask you to bear this analogy in mind as you read the following outline of psychology. Only in this way can any definition of psychology make sense, for no single one can be an accurate description of all aspects of the subject at all times.

The working definition we would offer is that psychology is the scientific study of behaviour and experience. It involves observation and experimentation, the establishment of facts, and the employment of theories which make sense of these facts. In accordance with this definition we shall now introduce you to some of the material which you will meet in the rest of the book. We shall do so by looking at the *methods* and *content* of the selected areas. Our aim in doing this is twofold: first, to give an indication of the rich and varied mosaic that is psychology today, and secondly to consider that old chestnut of which examiners are so fond, is psychology a science?

Methods of psychology

In many ways scientific psychology was made possible by the writings of the eighteenth-century philosopher Auguste Comte who, incidentally, is also credited with the founding of sociology. Comte's philosophy, *positivism*, advocated the study of man by the methods of science. As Miller (1966) explains, positivism provided the intellectual atmosphere for the emergence of a scientific psychology in Europe in the second half of the nineteenth century, greatly aided by the publication in 1859 of Charles Darwin's *Origin of Species* which, through the theory of evolution by natural selection, established the common heritage of man and the lower animals, and hence showed man to be a member of the animal kingdom. A case could no longer be logically denied for applying the methods of the established sciences such as physics and chemistry to the study of man. Positivism, then, created the desire to study man scientifically, the theory of evolution justified such a study and, approximately a hundred years ago, modern psychology was born. The nineteenth century saw physicists such as Weber and Fechner, and a host of physiologists including von Helmholtz and Wundt (who was responsible for opening the world's first formal psychology laboratory at Leipzig in 1879), addressing themselves to psychological problems – at this stage, almost exclusively in the field of perception. What scientific techniques did they bring to psychology? The answer is, the experiment.

The experiment

The simplest version of an experiment is what John Stuart Mill called the '*rule of one variable*'. Let us consider an example. Imagine we prepare two samples of the same chemical: we put them in separate containers, labelling one A, the other B. We apply a flame to the substance and observe (from a safe distance) that they do not ignite. We then leave the contents of container A (the so-called *control condition*) unchanged, but add a new substance (x) to the contents of container B (the *experimental condition*). If we then treat the two containers in exactly the same way as previously (that is, held in a flame of the same intensity at the same distance and for the same period of time), and B then catches fire, we are left with the inescapable conclusion that it was the addition of x which caused B to become inflammable. This is the only logical conclusion because the two conditions are identical, and are treated identically, in all respects except for one solitary difference. Hence any differences in outcome must be directly attributed to the sole difference between the conditions.

It was a challenge for the positivists to apply similar scientific experiments to man. But it may be objected that people are not like chemicals: how can we say that two people (even identical twins) are the same, and will react to a situation in the same way? Surely a science of man, as opposed to a science of inanimate matter, is out of the question because of this. This objection, which concerns the individuality of people, is not the impasse that it may appear: we simply modify the experimental procedure so that we study *groups* of subjects rather than just comparing Fred with Jim. In this new procedure we assemble two similar groups, call the one the experimental group and the other the control, and then proceed exactly as before. An example may well be of value – an experiment to see if consumption of alcohol affects people's memories.

Stating the hypothesis

Our first step is usually to formulate a *hypothesis*, that is, a testable statement which we then aim to verify or refute. Hypotheses take one of two forms: *experimental hypotheses*, which predict that there will be a reliable difference between the two groups of subjects (in our experiment, consumption of alcohol *will* affect performance), or *null hypotheses*, which predict that there will be no reliable difference between the performances of the two groups (in our experiment, alcohol will *not* affect memory). Note that the scientist does not have to worry about guessing whether there will or will not be a difference between the groups: a hypothesis is simply a statement to test, not a statement of belief. The most important factor is that after the experiment has been carried out, we should be able to say unequivocally whether the hypothesis has been proved or disproved. It should be worded precisely and without ambiguity, and we should be quite clear what we mean by all the terms included.

Take the example 'A deprived upbringing will detrimentally affect intellectual attainment in later life'. What is meant by 'a deprived upbringing' (impoverished home life, absence of mother or father, lack of good schooling?); 'intellectual attainment' (the job a person has, his score in an IQ test, his ability to do crossword puzzles?); and 'later life'? The experimenter as scientist must *operationally define* all the terms in his hypotheses. By this we simply mean that all the terms must be defined by some observable operation or criterion (for example, the psychologist usually defines a person's intelligence by his score in an IQ test). Thus, to come back to our example, we must operationally define 'consumption of alcohol' and 'memory recall'. We could define the former as, say, the drinking of three standard measures ($3 \times 1/6$th gill) of whisky within a period of not less than five minutes and not more than twenty minutes; while the memory recall could be defined as a subject's ability to recall random letters or numbers read to him at one-second intervals in groups of three to ten digits.

Selecting the subjects

We have pointed out that experiments in psychology generally require the study of groups rather than individuals. So we begin to undertake the actual experiment by obtaining *subjects*, that is, people who will participate in the experiment. At this stage we have to think ahead and ask ourselves, when the experiment has been conducted and we have analysed our results, to whom do we want to apply our conclusions? Do we want to be in a position where we can say, 'The recall ability of my friends is adversely affected by alcohol'; or 'The recall ability of the students of my college is adversely affected by alcohol'; or 'The recall ability of the people of my town is adversely affected by alcohol'; or 'The recall ability of women is adversely affected by alcohol'; or 'The recall ability of members of the Liberal party is adversely affected by alcohol'? The group of people to whom we wish to generalize our results constitutes our *population*. It is nearly always impossible to include all members of the population in our experiment and so we settle for studying a *representative sample*. We should thus work in the same way as an organization such as NOP, which carries out opinion polls in the build up to a General Election: they do not ask everyone in the country how they intend to vote, only a sample of the voting population. If the sample is a sound one it should reflect the balance of opinion in the country as a whole, and the results can be generalized to the relevant population (in this case, all the voters in the UK). It may help to think of the ideal relationship between a population and a sample as that between two photographic prints of different sizes taken from the same negative: they have identical features but the one is smaller than the other.

The simplest and probably most widely used technique for drawing a sample from a population is that of *random selection*: everyone has an equal chance of being selected and selections are made in a purely chance, unbiased way. Pulling names out of a hat, or picking, say, every tenth name from an electoral register would constitute a random sample (although the second one would provide a random sample only of a voting population).

We should note at this point that many psychological experiments do not make clear the limitations of their applicability. It has been estimated that nearly 90% of psychology experiments use American college or university students as subjects. This is perfectly acceptable as long as it is made clear that the results obtained apply only to such groups. Unfortunately, this is rarely done, and one is led to believe that the results apply to much larger and less specialized populations of people. Clearly a rule of scientific procedure is being disregarded.

Allocating the subjects to the conditions

It is fundamental to the experimental method that our groups of subjects should be, if not identical, then at least highly similar to each other. If this is not the case we have a *confounding influence*, and our results are invalidated. In order to reduce the likelihood of biased allocation of subjects, experimentalists generally use three methods: (1) *independent subjects*, in which subjects are allocated randomly to the groups (for example, by picking names out of a hat); (2) *matched subjects*, in which subjects are given a pre-test, and arranged in equal-ability pairs, and then split so that one of each pair goes into one condition and his matched partner into the other; and (3) *repeated measures*, in which an individual participates in both conditions (in our example, each subject would perform a memory task sober *and* after drinking three whiskies, thus acting as his own control). The relative merits and limitations of these techniques are discussed in statistics books such as Robson (1973) and Miller (1975).

Carrying out the experiment

Having stated our hypothesis, gathered our subjects, and allocated them to the experimental conditions, we can now carry out the experiment itself. Subjects should be carefully instructed in what will happen in the experiment and what part they will be expected to play. Instructions should be precise, straightforward and honest. The last criterion is important: some experimenters may consider deceiving their subjects to further the cause of their experiments. The whole question of deception and the general ethics of the way subjects are treated in psychology experiments was brought to crisis point by the work of the American social psychologist Stanley Milgram (1963, 1964, 1965), who encouraged subjects to believe that they were causing great distress, pain and possibly even death in an experimental partner (see Chapter 10). In response to this Cook *et al.* (1972) drew up a code of practice, *Ethical Standards for Research with Human Subjects*, to prevent a repetition of such experimentation.

If we return to the demands of science, rather than ethics, an important requirement is that all subjects are given identical instructions. To this end most psychologists read the instructions to subjects from a printed sheet, or play them to them from a tape. This can give the impression of unnecessary formality or woodenness on the part of the experimenter, but it is important, otherwise we again risk violating our guiding rule of one variable. If, in our experiment, one group is given a good, precise explanation of what its members are to do and is consequently well prepared and motivated to concentrate and try hard, but the other group is given a rushed and garbled set of instructions which serves only to confuse its individual members and causes them to lose interest in the task, another potential confounding variable is introduced which, once again, will prevent us from pinpointing the cause of any difference that emerges between the groups' performances.

As well as similarity of instructions, we have to ensure that there is a similarity of conditions and assessment. Both groups should be studied in the same physical and psychological environment, at the same time of day, and so forth, and they should be assessed on an objective criterion which cannot be affected by changes in the mood or whim of the experimenter (that is, the experiment must be open and fair so that any bias, conscious or unconscious, on the part of the experimenter cannot affect his assessment of performance).

The guiding principle is thus very simple: we need to ensure that in absolutely all respects except one the groups are identical. In particular experimenters should check composition of groups; conditions of experimentation; and assessment of performance. The name given to the one difference between the groups (that is, what we are studying) is the *independent variable* (IV). In our experiment the IV is alcohol consumption. The name given to our measurement of its effect (the outcome or results) is the *dependent variable* (DV) – in our case, the numbers of digits that are recalled from a memory test. The sole aim of all experiments is to see if the IV affects the DV (in the case of our experiment, does alcohol affect memory recall?)

Analysing the results

Let us imagine that we have carried out our experiment and found
that the subjects performed as follows:

No-drink group	Drink group
8	7
8	6
9	6
7	5
7	4
6	5
7	6
8	7
5	7
7	6
6	9
8	5
7	5
10	4
7	6
7	4
5	3
8	7
9	7
7	5
8	6
6	5
7	7
8	4
7	5

Does our hypothesis 'Alcohol will affect memory ability' stand or
fall? Simply by looking at these lists of figures it is almost impossible
to say. The psychologist solves the problem by totalling the numbers
of digits recalled by each subject (here, out of a maximum of ten) and
dividing this figure by the number of subjects in the group, thus
producing what a statistician calls an *arithmetic mean average* (or
'average' to non-statisticians!) for each group, so that he can see
which one has done best. Here the total number of correct responses
by the 'drink group' equals 141; by dividing this by 25 we find the
average for the group is 5.64 correct responses per subject. The total
for the 'no-drink group' is 182, producing an average of 7.28 correct
responses per subject.

Thus we see that the sober group did better. Is this the end of it? Unfortunately, no: we need to be confident that our result was a reliable one (that is, if we repeated the experiment time and again that we would keep obtaining the same direction of difference between the conditions). Just as in tennis, for example, even a good player may experience 'off-days' or apparent bad luck against a poor player, so in an experiment all the chance or luck factors can, in a one-off situation, 'fall' for one of the conditions. It is improbable, of course, but not impossible: if a group of one hundred people simultaneously tossed a coin, it *could* come down heads for all of them, even though whether a coin lands face-up or -down is chance-determined. So the experimenter must ask whether the observed difference in a particular study is a genuine one, or a 'freak' (that is, produced by chance alone). To answer this he applies a *significance test* to his results. If it transpires that the odds that chance factors caused the difference exceed 1 in 20 – **p**, probability, $= 0.05$ – we reject the null hypothesis and state that the difference is a real (non-chance-determined) one (by tradition this is the risk level used in most social sciences); in other words, we conclude that the iv is affecting the dv. To return to our example, if we find that the difference between our sets of scores is statistically significant (that is, that the odds of it occurring by chance are greater than 1 in 20) we would conclude that alcohol does affect memory.

The experiment is held in the highest esteem by mainstream psychologists, as it can be seen as a microcosm of science itself. Establishment psychologists such as Donald Broadbent (1964, 1973) and H.J. Eysenck (in almost innumerable articles) argue that the employment of the experimental method offers the main hope for the advancement of psychology as a science, and indeed for its continued existence as a viable and useful analytical perspective. Certainly its employment over the past seventy years or so has greatly influenced the shape and development of psychology; the field of learning has probably been characterized more than any other by an almost exclusive usage of the technique (see Chapter 3). The movement reached its zenith in the 1930s and 1940s with the work of Clark Hull (1943). Hull's writings probably represent psychology's closest approximation to classical physics and chemistry. By a rigorous application of the experimental method, testing hypotheses and formulating operational theories, Hull hoped to develop a formal mathematical model which would ultimately predict all learning behaviour. Despite a lifetime of dedicated research Hull's ambitions were not realized, and psychology has never since tried to imitate the natural sciences quite so single-mindedly or uncritically, for although the experimental method is arguably the psychologist's most powerful tool (the only one enabling him to explain events in cause-and-effect terms), it does have a number of drawbacks, which effectively mean that psychology will never be characterized by just one methodology.

Criticisms of the experimental method
Dehumanization
It has been frequently argued that placing a person in a foreign environment, such as a laboratory, and exposing him to strange events or stimuli and asking him to respond by performing an alien task, depersonalizes and dehumanizes the subject (some writers argue that usage of the term 'subject' instead of 'person' illustrates the experimenter's attitudes). Heather (1976) claims this has resulted in a 'mechanistic' view of man: 'He is regarded as something passive and inert, propelled into motion only by the action of some force, either external or internal, upon him.... Human beings continue to be regarded by psychologists as some kind of helpless clockwork puppet, jerked into life only when something happens to it.' This view, for its own part, would be strongly attacked by writers such as Broadbent, who would claim that only by taking a detached, 'objective' and impersonal view of man can we gain understanding. Such writers point to the outstanding track record of the experimental method in the natural sciences, such as physics and chemistry, as proof of the method's success and effectiveness.

It would be misleading to suggest that we can decide by any simple yardstick which viewpoint is right and which wrong: the issue is a fundamental and deep-lying one which underpins entirely different perspectives within the overall framework of psychology. We can only reiterate one of our original points about the multi-faceted nature of the discipline, and remind you of Wittgenstein's analogy of the rope of many strands.

Distortion of behaviour
Critics of the experimental method argue that the controlled or contrived situation gives a false and misleading impression of how

people behave in real-life situations. To quote Heather again, 'Psychologists have attempted to squeeze the study of human life into a laboratory situation where it becomes unrecognizably different from its naturally occurring form.' This is exactly the problem which confronted zoologists studying the behaviour of animals in artificial environments such as laboratories and zoos. Here it resulted in the founding, in the 1940s, of a new perspective, *ethology*, in which biologists study animals in their natural habitat (see Chapter 9). Some psychologists at that time, such as Brunswik (1944), argued for a similar adaptation in psychology, but it is only in recent years that consistent and effective attempts have been made. In particular, social psychologists have made increasing use of field studies and natural observations to help them understand such phenomena as attitude change and prejudice (see Chapter 13).

Expectancy effects
Not only does the experimental *situation* affect a subject's behaviour, but, in addition, it has been clearly demonstrated that his *perception* of the experiment and his vested interest in his performance will further distort his behaviour. As Swingle (1973) puts it, 'An individual may act in a way he thinks the experimenter wants him to act, or in a way he feels normal people should act, but not in the way he would behave were he unaware that his behaviour was being observed.' Orne (1962) set subjects a series of exceedingly boring and frustrating tasks (such as presenting them with 2,000 sheets of random numbers, asking them to add up 224 pairs of numbers on each sheet and then immediately tear the sheet into at least 32 pieces before tackling the additions on the next sheet), and found that if merely asked to perform such a task they would refuse but if it was stated that the task was part of an experiment they would often agree and, furthermore, having agreed to participate did so with such zeal and dedication that the experimenter frequently had to intervene and put an end to their labours, for they showed no signs of doing so themselves, and were still diligently tearing up the slips of paper after five and a half hours. It appears that subjects display what Orne calls *'demand characteristics'*: they want to be 'good' subjects, perform well and please the experimenter. The very nature of the situation seems to engender the belief in a subject that he is being 'tested', he then feels that he must give a good account of himself, and this in turn tends to produce a feeling of personal

involvement and commitment to the experiment, and the subject tries hard to 'make the experiment work'. Thus the behaviour of subjects in experiments is not typical of their normal behaviour.

Furthermore, the behaviour of the experimenter can be a further source of bias. We have already talked about how an experimenter can deliberately falsify or 'rig' an experiment, and how ignorance of basic techniques can also destroy the accuracy of any experiment, but Rosenthal (1966) has shown how even the best intentioned, knowledgeable and well-meaning experimenters can bias their results. Rosenthal carried out the following experiment using hundreds of his students as experimenters. One group was told that they would be studying a strain of 'bright' rats, while a second group of student experimenters was told that their rats were 'dull'. When asked to observe the performance of the rats running mazes and report back it was found that the first group of experimenters reported significantly better performances than those working with the 'dull' rats. In reality, there had been no difference between the two so-called 'strains' of rats: both had been taken at random from the population of ordinary rats used in the psychology laboratory. The only difference had been in the expectations of the experimenters, and this had been strong enough to produce the apparent variability in performance.

Moreover, when an experimenter is working with *human* subjects his expectancies may feed back to the subjects and thus further exaggerate the effect, for they may anticipate how they are expected to perform by 'reading' the experimenter's behaviour towards them. It is obvious that an experiment constitutes a social situation, and here the psychologist is faced with problems that do not confront physicists or chemists. It has led writers to talk of the 'social psychology of the psychology experiment'.

We may summarize Rosenthal's work on experimenter effects into three main points:

1 The experimenter's expectations may work for or against the 'favoured' condition, for if he is aware of his potential bias he may well over-compensate to counteract any imagined bias.
2 First impressions tend to exert a considerable influence: experimenters who obtain good data at the beginning of data collection continue to see good results in later performances, whereas experimenters who obtain bad data at first continue to find such results later on.
3 The bias which Rosenthal observed was not caused by cheating or falsify-

ing the data; rather it was due to the experimenter's unconsciously reinforcing 'appropriate' behaviour with facial expressions such as smiles or frowns,
and other non-verbal cues (see Chapter 14). Rosenthal emphasizes that
experimenters in his study were unaware of their own behaviour and its
effects.

We want to make it quite clear that subject and experimenter
biases affect not only the experimental method, but almost all the
techniques used in psychology. Less 'objective' methods such as the
clinical interview and the structured introspection technique used by
the currently fashionable phenomenologists (see Chapters 8 and 14)
are far more prone to biases than experimentation; for example, one
of the severest criticisms levelled against psychoanalysis is that the
analyst can interpret *any* event in a way which supports his beliefs.
So should we not admit these incapacitating distortions, cut our
losses and write off the whole enterprise of psychology? Fortunately
the answer is no, for there exist two simple remedies which counteract subject and experimenter effects.

First, subjects can only behave in a 'desirable' manner if they
know what the appropriate behaviour is, so by ensuring that they
cannot know whether they are in the experimental or control group
we eliminate the possibility of demand characteristics. For instance,
in our earlier example of the effect of alcohol on recall, subject bias
would have occurred if the subjects in the control group, realizing
that as sober subjects they would be expected to perform better than
their intoxicated counterparts, had tried harder on the memory task.
Similarly, the experimental group subjects might act the part of how
drunks should perform, to fulfil their perceptions of the experimenter's expectations. To avoid this, we can treat the 'drink group' as
before but now ensure that the subjects in the control condition are
required to consume equal volumes of an inert liquid (called a
placebo) which is indistinguishable from spirit but is in fact non-
alcoholic. By doing this the subjects will be unable to identify which
group they are in, and consequently cannot adjust their behaviour
accordingly. This is called the *single-blind technique of control*.

Secondly, in a similar manner we can prevent experimenter bias
by keeping the experimenter in the dark as to which subjects are in
which group. All that is needed is for an assistant to dispense the
drinks and keep a note of which subjects receive whisky and which
the placebos. He will only disclose this information to the experimenter after the experiment has been carried out and the results

recorded. This technique is called *double-blind*, because neither the experimenter nor the subject can know who is in which group.

Biased sampling

We have mentioned earlier that a substantial proportion of psychology experiments utilize American college students as their only subjects, but tend to generalize their results implicitly to 'universal man'. The reasons for the heavy reliance on student subjects are easy to appreciate – they constitute a ready and captive pool of bright young adults – but this does not excuse some psychologists' failure to specify fully the limitations of their studies.

Another problem is that psychologists frequently do not determine their sample themselves: they work with self-selected groups of subjects, or volunteers. Ora (1965) has shown that volunteers cannot be regarded as a typical sample of people. Amongst other things he found that they tend to be abnormally insecure, dependent upon and influenced by others, aggressive, neurotic and introverted. Again, this does not constitute a problem as long as results obtained from volunteer subjects are generalized only to other volunteers or potential volunteers, but it is not acceptable to generalize such results to wider, more diverse populations.

A related problem concerns the use of animals as subjects in psychology experiments. Many areas of psychology make extensive use of rats, chimpanzees and pigeons in their research – so much so that Eysenck, a fervent supporter of behaviourism, which is so disposed to using animals as almost to ignore human subjects on occasions, anticipates such criticism by giving one of his more recent books (1977) the title, *Psychology is about People*. There are many sound reasons for using animals in psychology experiments (see Chapter 9), but we must, again, be extremely careful in stating the limitations of generalization. Here the problem can be biased sampling in the widest possible sense, for example where a sample of rats is used to represent the population of all living creatures, including *Homo sapiens*. Clearly rats are not typical of all forms of animal life, and it is quite unforgiveable to apply findings from such research to human beings without further study, in which a sample is drawn from an appropriate population of men and women. Studies of rats tell us a lot about rats themselves and may suggest things about humans, but inferences should not be drawn directly from rodents to man.

The nature of statistical inference

It has been pointed out that statistical significance tests are applied to experimental results to see if we should attribute any differences to chance factors or whether there is a genuine difference between the performances of the control and experimental groups. The criterion we usually apply is that if the odds of chance factors causing the difference exceed 1 in 20 we reject this as the likely cause and say that the IV is affecting the performances, but it *could* be chance-determined: it's not impossible, only unlikely. By using odds of 20:1 as the cut-off point we are setting up a situation in which, on average, 1 in every 20 experiments which is accepted as showing an experimental effect (that is, experiments in which the null hypothesis has been rejected) is a fraud. This is the risk that experimenters take. The only certain way to check their conclusions is to re-run their experiments to see if the same results are obtained, but it is difficult to replicate studies exactly in all respects, and many experiments are by their very nature only possible on a one-off basis (many depend, for example, on the total näivety of the subjects). So the experimenter has to put his reputation on the line and risk making a wrong statement about the outcome of his study. The risk is equivalent to the gambler who plays Russian roulette with one bullet in an (imaginary) twenty-hole chamber. He puts the gun to his head knowing that he has just one pull of the trigger: the odds are heavily in favour of the hammer hitting a blank, but he also knows that it might be the bullet. He has no way of knowing, and neither has the experimenter. And just as the gambler's luck will eventually run out if he repeats this chancy exercise often enough, so our experimenter will, sooner or later, be caught out and unknowingly make an incorrect assertion. The problem is that we do not have the same dramatic proof when the experimenter is caught out as we do with the Russian roulette gambler. If one takes twenty accepted, but unreplicated, sets of results, it is likely that one of them is a fraud, but impossible to know which one.

The correlational method

Despite the drawbacks of experimentation, most psychologists would argue that it is their discipline's most powerful technique, the one which gives maximum control and objectivity, and the greatest capacity to deduce causal explanations of phenomena. However, there are many occasions when psychologists either choose, or are forced, to employ other methods. There may be ethical or practical reasons why an experiment cannot be used, or the experimental method may not be suitable for certain areas of study within psychology. In a substantial proportion of such cases the technique of *correlation* is employed. This consists simply of assessing the strength of the relationship between two or more observed variables, and dominates the areas of psychology concerned with individual differences (see especially Chapters 6 and 8).

It should be clearly understood at the outset that, strictly speaking, correlation is not a method: it is a technique of data analysis. To illustrate this, imagine that we wish to know whether smoking cigarettes affects health. We could conceivably set up an experiment along the lines that we have previously outlined: we could draw a sample from our specified population and allocate the subjects in a reliable manner to either an experimental or control group. The experimental group would then be required to smoke, say, twenty cigarettes per day for the duration of the experiment, while members of the control group, on the other hand, would be prohibited from smoking at all. Note that in accordance with our sacrosanct rule of one variable we must ensure that they are equally balanced in all other respects (age, sex, occupation, personality variables, and, of course, previous smoking history). Clearly there would be severe problems of a practical nature in trying to carry out such an experiment; for instance, how could we ensure that the members of the group behaved as they were supposed to, smoking or not smoking to order; how long would the experiment have to last for the influence of smoking to show itself – five, ten, thirty years; how could we possibly maintain contact with and monitor subjects over such a long period; and how could we prevent possible subject bias, for the use of placebo cigarettes would be expensive and cumbersome? Above all, there is a moral constraint. It is hardly ethical to enforce smoking with all its possible effects on people who would otherwise not engage in such behaviour. Thus, in practice, such an experiment would not be carried out. The researcher would use the alternative technique of correlational study. In this particular case the researcher would simply observe a group of subjects and record their behaviour. He would ask subjects how many cigarettes, if any, they smoked, and he could see if this correlated in any systematic way with some reliable measures of health, for example, days lost from work due to lung or chest disorders, incidences of relevant cancers (such as those of the lungs or throat), or general fitness (this could be assessed by a doctor, or our researcher requiring subjects to perform some task like running on the spot or up and down stairs).

Note that the researcher would make no attempt to control the situation: he would simply observe what we might term nature's distribution. We would not even have two distinct groups, but subjects allocated along a continuum (no cigarettes, through to the heaviest consumption of cigarettes in the survey). It should also be noted that, in correlational studies, the researcher often does not come into direct contact with his subjects at all. In this particular case he could simply enlist the help of doctors in recording the smoking behaviour of their patients and correlate these with eventual mortality rates. Furthermore, there is often no need for the researcher to have to arrange for measures to be taken at all; they may have been already recorded for some other reason and he can simply carry out a *post-hoc* (after-the-event) analysis.

Imagine that you want to see if couples who marry at a young age tend to be more prone to divorce than couples who marry in their mid- and late twenties, or later. Clearly, an experiment is out of the question, so an obvious solution would be a correlational analysis, and here the figures are even recorded for us in official Government statistics, and the researcher simply has to apply his statistical technique. The end product will be a number between 0 and 1; the closer the number is to 1 (which indicates perfect co-variance), moving away from 0 (which indicates no relationship between two variables), the stronger is the relationship between the two variables. The value of a correlation is determined by - in this case - calculating the correlation between the ages of the younger partners in a number of marriages and the lengths of those marriages in years. The value should then be looked up in a 'Significance of correlations' table to see if the relationship is a reliable (non-chance-determined) one. Readers wishing a fuller explanation of the procedures and logic involved should consult Crocker (1969).

We should note that sometimes there is a + sign in front of a correlation coefficient, and sometimes a − sign. This tells the direction of the relationship: + means the variables move together (as one increases, the other increases too, as with height and weight); − means that as one increases the other decreases, as with the age of a car and its value. In the examples that we have considered in this section, our relationship between earliness and length of marriage would be positive (the lower the marriage age, the shorter the duration), whereas the relationship between smoking and health would be negative (as smoking increases, health decreases).

Just as there are drawbacks to the experimental method, so correlation has its limitations.

Criticisms of the correlation
Causality
The major constraint of the correlation is that no matter how strongly related two variables are, we cannot imply a cause-and-effect relationship between the two. This is because there will have been no control in the situation, no equivalent of the experiment's rule of one variable; for example, in the case of cigarette smoking and health, the tobacco companies are quick to point out that although there may be a strong inverse relationship between smoking and health, we cannot, on the basis of a correlational study alone, assume that smoking is causing health deterioration. They say that smoking may be just one of a number of factors which go with bad health. Heavy smokers may have a greater tendency to have jobs involving dusty, smoky or dirty working conditions, they may have poor eating and drinking habits, anxious or neurotic personality dispositions, and so on, so that bad health may be associated with all of these factors in the people that we have studied; so how can we know which one is directly affecting health? The answer is we cannot. All that we can say is that some factors seem to go together; we cannot imply causality.

Extrapolation
It is always dangerous to generalize beyond the range of our data, but especially so when using the correlation. Imagine that we were collecting data on the IQ scores of schoolchildren, and we found that there emerged a strong positive correlation between IQ and height (the taller the child, the higher his IQ). Given the parameters of our population (schoolchildren), it would be easy to explain this relationship: obviously both height and IQ are closely related to a third factor, age. As children grow older they grow taller, and practice effects at intelligence, aptitude and streaming tests could raise their Intelligence Quotients (see Chapter 6). If we failed to mention

these limits of our study sample, however, it is easy to imagine headlines in the press: 'Psychologists show that tall people are brighter.' Thus we can see the dangers of generalizing beyond one's data range and taking results out of context – known as *extrapolation*.

Linear relationships

Correlations deal only with linear relationships; that is, they can only successfully quantify relationships where the factors co-vary in a consistent manner, either increasing together, or decreasing together. However, many perfectly sound relationships exist which are curvilinear. For example, social psychologists have shown, when studying the efficiency of groups, that when we add members to a group of, say, four or five who are engaged in solving problems, the group becomes more efficient, solving problems in less time: 'More heads make light work.' However, beyond a certain size the group begins to become unwieldy, and the advantages of more people working on a problem are cancelled out by problems of communication and division of labour problems as the group finds it necessary to break into factions. Eventually, if we continue to add members to the group, it will actually begin to decrease in efficiency ('Too many cooks spoil the broth'), and we see what economists call the Law of Diminishing Returns coming into operation. A pictorial representation of this would show a sound relationship (it would be possible to say exactly how efficient the group would be for a given membership), but it would be non-linear. If we calculated a Pearson's Product Moment or Spearman's rank order correlation it would equal 0, because the first part of the curve would give a coefficient of $+1$, the second a coefficient of -1, and the two taken together would cancel each other out to give an end product of 0. Thus the researcher might be tempted to believe, if he looked no further, that there was no relationship between the factors – which could hardly be less true. Researchers working with correlational analysis should therefore always double-check by displaying their data in a graphical form.

We have said that correlation is not so much a method, but more a data assessment technique. If data are not obtained from experiments, what methods do psychologists use to produce them? Two of the most common methods are *psychometrics* and *observation*.

Psychometrics

Psychometrics literally means measuring the mind, but in modern psychology it has become the generic term for the development and administration of tests. Psychologists have developed a dazzling range of tests to measure such attributes as intelligence (see Chapter 6), personality (see Chapter 8), attitudes (see Chapters 12 and 13), and the self-concept (see Chapter 14). Such instruments are used extensively not only in academic psychology but also in industry, education, the medical and clinical world and many other areas. As Miller (1966) points out, tests began by testing aptitudes, classifying interests and evaluating achievements; 'Now they can pigeonhole your personality, assess your emotional stability, your masculinity, your imagination, executive potential, chances of marital bliss, conformity to an employer's stereotype, or ability to operate a turret lathe. Whatever you do there seems to be a psychological test you should do first.' To give an idea of the scale of operations, he estimates that in 1960 alone 130 million psychological tests were given to American schoolchildren. Organizations such as the National Foundation for Educational Research at Windsor have been formed specifically to develop and supply tests to qualified researchers such as psychologists, clinicians and academics.

The history of psychological testing can be traced back to Francis Galton (1869, 1883). Kirby and Radford (1976) say, 'What Galton did ... was to claim a new territory for scientific inquiry; to explore much of it himself, developing new theories and techniques on the way; and in so doing to give us a new view of ourselves. On this view, every ability and trait of man is amenable to measurement.' If it was Galton who launched the movement of psychological testing, it was the Frenchman Alfred Binet who ensured its prominence by developing the first IQ test (see Chapter 6). Once IQ testing was established as a military selection procedure in World War I, the psychometric movement never looked back, and today it is one of the most productive and influential areas of psychology, with hundreds, perhaps thousands, of researchers dedicated to developing new testing procedures and exploring the uses and limitations of existing ones: 'The psychometric industry is a bit like the car industry. It has its standard models that go on seemingly for ever, and it has its nine day wonders; it has its economy products and luxury products' (Kirby and Radford). For examples of these in the fields of individual differences and attitude scaling see Chapters 6, 8, 12 and 14.

But why do some tests seemingly go on forever, whilst others are, to mix the metaphor, like ships passing in the night? What distinguishes a good test from a bad one? Tests are usually judged on three criteria.

Reliability

For reliability, read consistency. In order to be of any use a test must be a consistent measuring device. An IQ test would be worse than useless if a person scored, say, 120 on the test one day and then, when he re-sat it a month later (by which time he would have forgotten the answers but would probably not have changed very much in terms of his intellectual ability), he scored only 75. Imagine the consequences if such an unreliable and variable test were used as an 11 + examination or a criterion for job selection. Such a test would have no stable discriminating value at all, and would be an extremely misleading and dangerous tool.

Validity

A test is valid if it measures what it claims to measure. This may sound rather strange. How does it apply, for example, to IQ tests of the kind we have just considered? IQ tests are designed to measure *intelligence* – which Heim (1970) defines as 'the ability to grasp at essentials and to respond appropriately to them'. Intelligence is emphatically not the same thing as knowledge or education; intelligence tests tend to consist of abstract reasoning items, rather than questions such as 'Who wrote *Paradise Lost*?', because such knowledge questions do not measure intelligence. (Reliability and validity are discussed more fully in Chapters 6 and 13.)

Standardization

Standardization refers to the establishment of a set of *norms*, or typical values, for the test. If a person scores 115 on a particular IQ test, what does this tell us? By itself, practically nothing; we need to put his performance into context, and consider how other people have fared on the test; and obviously it is only useful to compare the score of an individual with those of comparable others – people of a similar culture, socio-economic class, occupation, sex, and so on (in fact, Chapter 6 explains that with a test mean of 100 and standard deviation of 15, our individual's score of 115 puts him in the top 16% of the population). Thus, norms have to be established for a number of appropriate sub-groups. Imagine Sally, a sociable and confident twenty-eight-year-old, fills in a copy of the famous American personality test, Cattell's 16 PF (see Chapter 8). She finds that she has a *raw* (unadjusted) score of 15 points on the 'reserved' – 'outgoing' dimension. As with the IQ score earlier this tells nothing in itself: we need to interpret the score via a set of appropriate norms. Now let us say that Sally has a vague appreciation of this exercise and looks up her score in a table of standard scores which she sees lying on the table. It tells her she is only slightly more outgoing and participating than the 'average' person. She is surprised by this as she thinks of herself as a real extravert. She tells the psychologist who supervised her performance on the test and he explains that the table of norms which she has just consulted were based on the scores of American male college students. Thus although Sally is outgoing compared with other British women in their late twenties she appeared to be relatively reserved because she was comparing herself with American teenage college boys; hence the necessity always to use the appropriate set of norms.

Unfortunately, it is not quite that simple. Often tests may not have been standardized against an appropriate population; for example, British norms for the 16 PF were only published some fifteen years after the introduction of the test, and psychologists in this country wishing to use the test before then had to interpret their subjects' scores against American norms. In other instances, tests may have been standardized only for children, the educationally subnormal, or one sex, whereas a researcher may wish to use the test for a different group. This will clearly limit the value of his study. Finally, differences between English and American terminology and idiom must be carefully noted and allowed for.

Criticisms of the psychometric method
Despite the enormous contribution made by mental testing and measurement, both to psychology and to society at large, psychometricians have been subjected to more scathing criticism than any other workers in psychology. In fact, it may be the size of its contribution that has made psychometrics so visible and open to attack. Whereas the nature of scientific experimentation may be of only passing interest to most readers, almost everyone has actually

completed an IQ test or personality inventory at some stage in his life, and may well have gained or lost a job, or had his educational career decided, on its outcome. This can often lead to biased or prejudiced criticism, and this is not appropriate to consider here. There are, however, a number of informed criticisms of the method.

A static and mechanical view
The loudest and most persistent criticism of psychometrics is that tests portray humans as static and fixed. Critics argue that they give the impression that a person's IQ or personality profile is a rigid, unchanging attribute of that person, like his name or sex. In actual fact, of course, this is far from the case. All the characteristics that psychometric tests measure – intelligence, personality, attitudes, interests, and so on – go through numerous changes during an individual's lifetime. Researchers who create the impression that test scores give permanent descriptions of individuals can actually bring about this permanence; for example, when a youngster performs poorly in an IQ test at school it is all too easy to label him 'slow' or 'dull' and for the teacher to adjust his behaviour to him accordingly (this was demonstrated by the 'Pygmalion in the classroom' study by Rosenthal and Jacobson, 1968). This teacher reaction can, in turn, convince the child that he is what the teacher believes him to be, and so he may resign himself to a life of non-achievement – all this on the basis of test results ascertained over a short period of time early in life.

It is evident that as well as attributing permanence to test profiles, tests also implicitly assume a mechanistic view of man. By this we mean not only that people are talked about and described as objects, but also that they are assumed to act in a consistent and predictable manner. Little account is taken of the fact that Jack may, for example, tend to 'go along' with other people and conform to their views on certain occasions, but, on other occasions (for example, when an issue in which he has very strong personal beliefs is involved), he may contradict his usual behaviour and stand firm against the views of his disagreeing friends (see Chapter 10). Tests tend to assume that behaviour is determined by personal rather than situational factors. This is frequently a mistaken view.

Rigidity
Psychoanalysts and other depth psychologists frequently complain that tests can only give general, and consequently imprecise, pictures

of people. They point to the fixed structure of tests, and argue that what is needed is a flexible approach to the study of man, in which the method is adaptable to the individual under study. A majority of these critics would argue that only the interview and the case study (see later in this chapter) can meet these demands, but an inventive compromise was provided by George Kelly (1955). Kelly's Role Repertory Test (discussed in Chapter 8) allows the researcher to identify each individual's unique way of perceiving and judging the world and then to structure these perspectives into a uniform testing procedure. Thus, each individual is required to carry out a pre-determined task, such as judging or responding to a number of events or people, but the frame of reference that he is able to use is totally his own.

Creation of concepts

One of the classic criticisms of the psychological testing movement is that by measuring something a *concept* develops to account for what is being measured. The argument runs that many of the concepts that have developed out of psychometric assessment cannot be justi-fied in any theoretical terms. The most widely quoted example is that of intelligence. In 1904 the Minister of Public Instruction in Paris set up a commission to help identify what we would now term educa-tionally subnormal children so that they could be placed in special schools. One member of the commission, Alfred Binet (already men-tioned), became quickly dissatisfied with what he believed to be time wasted, as members tried in vain to satisfactorily define what they were to study, namely the nature of intelligence. His approach was to go out into the schools and try thousands of questions on the children to see which ones discriminated the pupils rated by the teachers as intelligent, from those rated unintelligent. Those ques-tions which did not reliably discriminate were rejected: those which did were retained for inclusion in a battery of items which became the first IQ test (see Chapter 6). Thus intelligence was defined in terms of performance on the test, not by any abstract or theoretical conceptualization. This led to the famous statement made by a psychologist when asked to define intelligence: 'Intelligence is what an IQ test measures.' Many writers believe that it is profoundly wrong to work backwards from a measurement to a concept in this manner. They argue that it is like inventing the notion of height to justify the existence of a ruler. We are left with the unanswerable question, are there such things in the real world as intelligence and extraversion *apart* from their existence on pieces of paper called psychology tests?

The lack of explanatory capacity
Psychometric assessment only measures or describes: it makes no attempt at explanation. It is one thing to be able to describe someone as intellectually retarded, neurotic or having a positive self-esteem, but it is quite another to explain why this is so. Explanation is therefore left to the likes of experimenters and clinicians.

Observation

The final method for collecting data (which may then be statistically treated) is observation. In this context we use the term to mean watching and recording, and it constitutes the main method of the other two behavioural sciences, anthropology and sociology (psychology being the third member of the trio). Observation may be structured or casual, and we can subdivide the approach according to the degree of structuring.

The survey
The survey technique, which may be defined as gathering information by questioning a large sample of people, falls rather awkwardly as a method between psychometrics and observation, in that it often consists of asking people to respond to a pre-determined and highly structured questionnaire which could be regarded as a test, and yet the term 'survey' is usually taken to refer to the exercise of *gathering* the data, especially the selection of respondents. Thus the work of opinion pollsters around election time is clearly an exercise in sampling procedure rather than psychometrics: the onus is on questioning a representative sample of the voting population, not the questions asked (there is frequently only one, 'Which party would you vote for if there was a General Election tomorrow?'). In psychology, the distinction is less clear-cut; for example, if we are conducting a survey to assess attitudes of racial prejudice (see Chapter 13), the actual construction and phrasing of the questions become extremely important.

One of the most influential surveys of post-war social science was carried out by a research team from Indiana University headed by Alfred Kinsey (1948, 1953), the first major survey of human sexual behaviour. 6,200 American men and 5,800 American women were asked up to 521 questions, many of which were highly detailed and personal in nature, classified into nine categories: social and economic data; marital histories; sex education; physical and physiological data; nocturnal sex dreams; masturbation; heterosexual history; and animal contacts. Each of the categories was further subdivided into smaller units. For example, category 7 (heterosexual history) was subdivided into twelve smaller categories: pre-adolescent play; pre-marital petting; attitudes on pre-marital relations; experience in pre-marital coitus; marital intercourse; extra-marital relations; post-marital intercourse; intercourse with prostitutes; coital techniques; contraceptive history; group heterosexual activities; and heterosexual prostitution (the subject as prostitute). Furthermore, these secondary classifications were themselves subdivided into third- and fourth-order groupings. For example, Category 7, sub-category 5 (marital intercourse) was divided into first experience: age of each spouse, virginity of partner, speed of orgasm, physical satisfaction and lapse between marriage and first coitus; frequencies: maximum ever and means at various periods, and relation of sexual and marital adjustments.

The results were collated, tabulated, categorized and cross-related in 162 tables and 173 figures (1948), covering every aspect of sexual behaviour. Kinsey also discusses the degrees of variability where relevant; for instance, it was found that the average rate of sexual outlet for males was approximately three times per week, but this single figure disguised an amazing range of differences between individuals.

The survey is an extremely useful and widely used technique for gathering information. Social and developmental psychologists, in particular, find it a valuable technique; see, for example, the classic survey on child-rearing techniques by Sears *et al.* (1957) in Chapter 11. However, again there are criticisms.

Criticisms of the survey
Truth distortions
The main drawback with surveys is that they usually concentrate solely upon verbal reports, not actual behaviour. Most survey researchers, like Kinsey, go to elaborate lengths to minimize the possi-

bility of subjects' lying, and develop ways of detecting it should it occur, but such techniques can never be entirely fool-proof. We should realize that what people say does not necessarily equal what they do (see the study by Kutner *et al.* (1952) in Chapter 12). Even if the subject has every intention of being honest, the truth may still be distorted because of a number of different factors:

1 If subjects are required to report some aspects of their past behaviour, we cannot attribute absolute reliability to their recollections of events. Memory distorts in a number of complex ways (see Chapter 4).

2 If subjects do not understand what information is required from a question, or have a different understanding of the key word in a question, they will not be able to answer truthfully. To stay with our example of the Kinsey report, if the researcher asks a subject 'How many times per week do you experience sexual outlet?', he may think only of intercourse, not knowing that the interviewer includes masturbation in the term.

3 When discussing experimentation we introduced the notion of demand characteristics (that is, the subject's acting in a way which he hopes will please the experimenter). The same can happen in the survey: the respondent may give the answers that he thinks will please or impress the interviewer. It is not easy to cancel out or allow for this, because different subjects may have different ideas of what the 'desirable' answer is.

4 It is quite possible for the researcher to influence the subject by subtle non-verbal cues as to how he should respond. The survey technique is further complicated by the fact that several interviewers are normally used, and they may all be causing the results to be biased, but not in any one consistent direction which could be later statistically adjusted out.

Non-participant observation
Sometimes the researcher just watches, either in the field (the natural environment), in a laboratory or other artificial environment, or by means of some kind of recording, such as videotape. There are many reasons why he may opt for this minimally controlled method. He may be studying new areas of research and seek only to identify the important elements in a behavioural sequence, as with the pioneering work of researchers such as LaBarre (1964) and Eibl-Eibesfeldt (1972) in the field of non-verbal communication (see Chapter 14). He may feel that only in a 'free', non-controlled situation will behaviour appear in its true form (see the work of ethologists such as Lorenz and Tinbergen, who observed the behaviour of animals 'in the wild' in Chapter 9). It may be that for practical or ethical reasons, the only way to glean information on a particular topic is to

observe the results of naturally occurring events; for example, our understanding of the importance of learning in the process of perception has been greatly aided by the work of Von Senden (1932), who gathered together descriptions of people who had been born blind and who later in life had successful eye operations which gave them sight at a time when they could verbalize the experience. Similarly (see Chapter 5), physiological psychologists are greatly indebted to the study of brain-damaged patients in their search for an understanding of the mechanisms of the human brain. Obviously, such information could not be gathered by any enforced method.

Yet another reason for using observation is the simple one that all the researcher wants to do is to describe something, and the event is such that observation is the only possible study method. For example, the husband-and-wife team of William Masters and Virginia Johnson (1966) carried out an observational study of sexual behaviour. Whereas Kinsey worked with verbal reports, Masters and Johnson devised an elaborate technique of observing sexual performance, employing sophisticated physiological apparatus to supplement their direct observations.

Social psychologists, in particular, have developed a number of different classification systems for structuring observations on a predetermined basis. One of the best known is Moreno's (1953) sociogram which enables the observer to describe pictorially interactions between group members.

Criticisms of non-participant observation
Causality
As with all non-experimental analyses, we cannot imply cause-and-effect relationships, however much we are tempted to do so. If we observe that people who work hard do well at school we cannot say that the relationship is a causal one because there is no isolation of variables (we cannot be sure that the hard-working and lazy people we observe are comparable in other respects, such as intelligence and home background).

Observer bias
Observation, especially unstructured observation, is more prone to potential observer bias than any of the other methods that we have considered so far. Experimenters and psychometricians have the benefit of objectively defined and easily measurable categories of

appraisal, often tied in with the use of mechanical apparatus such as reaction timers, and pre-determined criteria of evaluation, such as pass-and-fail or standardized scores. Unstructured observation, such as that found in ethology, is far more open-ended. This affords greater flexibility, but at the price of far greater subjectivity, and possible observer bias. Even in structured observation this is still a problem; for example, in Moreno's sociometric categorization the observer still has to decide what constitutes an interaction during his period of observation. Such a problem does not trouble the marker of personality or IQ tests: he simply has to count ticks and crosses. Structuring of observations reduces the possibility of observer bias, but cannot eliminate it. The philosopher P.B. Medawar (1963) points out there is no such thing as unprejudiced observation. We all see and interpret what we see differently, largely as a function of earlier experiences.

Subject bias
If a person is aware that he is being observed, will he behave naturally? Most of us would say that he probably will not. Observation may well increase the likelihood of self-consciousness or exhibitionism in those under observation. Clearly this can only be resolved if we can observe subjects without their knowledge. Two techniques are used to this end (we should not, however, ignore the question of ethics: is it 'proper' to study people without their awareness of permission?). The first technique is the employment of two-way mirrors, but this is somewhat restricted in its usage as behaviour can only be studied in this manner in a pre-arranged, fixed location, usually a laboratory. We suppose psychologists could take the practice into the 'field' and hide behind bushes or around street corners, but one rarely hears of this. The second technique for preventing the subject knowing he is under observation is participant observation.

Participant observation
With this kind of observation, the participant observer becomes a part of what he is studying – usually a social or industrial group – and observes from the inside. For the practice to achieve its aim of accuracy it is important that the other members of the group accept the newcomer as a genuine member and are not aware of his true function. A number of studies have been carried out in this manner, for example Patrick (1973) on street gangs in Glasgow, Lupton

(1963) on the social relations of workers in an engineering work-shop, Festinger *et al.* (1956) on an 'End-of-the-World' group, and Frankenberg (1957) on a small Welsh village. The most famous participant observation study, however, is William F. Whyte's (1955) study of an Italian slum gang in Boston. Whyte learnt Italian, and after joining the gang participated in all its activities, including gambling and some shady political electioneering. Such activity can enable the researcher to make penetrating observations of social phenomena and affords a useful understanding more than almost all other methods, but, once again, there are drawbacks.

Criticisms of participant observation
Causality
See above.

Recording the data
Even given the benefit of micro-tape-recorders, it is very difficult to keep a record of what is happening and still participate in the activities. The participant observer rather 'blows his cover' if he keeps getting out his notebook to make entries. Frankenberg, in his Welsh village study, got around the problem by the selection of his role in the community: he played the part of Secretary to the Football Club and this justified his attending meetings and 'taking minutes'. Opportunities such as these are, however, rare.

Observer bias
It is extremely difficult for observers, who have to behave as fully fledged and participating members of groups, not to be become involved but to maintain a dispassionate and neutral perspective. Whyte said, 'I began as a non-participating observer. As I became accepted into the community I found myself becoming almost a non-observing participator.'

The case study

A nineteenth-century philosopher, Windleband, introduced the terms '*idiographic*' and '*nomothetic*' to distinguish between analyses of individuals and of groups, respectively. The techniques that we have examined so far tend to concentrate on a group perspective (nomothetic analysis). What price the individual in psychology? Certain extremely influential writers have used the case study (which we may define as the detailed description, usually built up on interview data, of one individual) as their psychological tool. One complete branch of the discipline, psychoanalysis, uses only this method. The case study differs from the nomothetic methods that we have considered so far not only in that it concentrates on individuals, but also that the end product is almost always qualitative (verbally descriptive), not quantitative (numerical). Therefore unlike all the other methods it does not lead to statistical analysis.

The first branch of modern psychology which made exclusive use of the case study was the psychoanalytic movement founded by Sigmund Freud in Austria around the turn of the century. Freud, a doctor of medicine, worked with patients on an individual basis and recorded his 'data' in the form of detailed case histories which gave him the material for his profound theories on the nature of the personality (see Chapter 8). His most widely known case studies are probably those of Anna O. (a colleague's patient who stimulated his original interest in the unconscious mind), Little Hans, and himself. Following the death of his father and his subsequent confusion of emotions in 1897 Freud decided to apply his analytical techniques to himself (and for the rest of his life spent the final half-hour of each day in self-analysis). He concentrated particularly on two crucial, emerging elements in his theory, the interpretation of dreams and infantile sexuality. The process was extraordinarily demanding and often painful, but he emerged, as Jones (1964) in the definitive biography of Freud says, 'serene and benign ... henceforth free to pursue his work in imperturbable composure'.

Another very eminent psychologist who subscribed totally to the idiographic method was G.W. Allport. He argued (1961) that psychology must concentrate upon the individual, not the group – on uniqueness, not commonalities. His case studies differed greatly from Freud's in accordance with his very different view of the nature of personality (see Chapter 8), and it is probably reasonable to say that Allport wanted psychology to be the science of the biography. Critics argue that this is best done by literature and historians, and psychologists should leave well alone. This is not to say that we as psychologists cannot learn a great deal from the biography; for example, in the area of handicap the detailed study of the massive difficulties of the so-called 'elephant man', Joseph Merrick, whose hideous deformities made it impossible for him to walk the streets of nineteenth-century England, gives us great insight into the human condition. Allport was adamant that psychology could only advance by concerning itself with the individual study. Kirby and Radford (1976) say, 'Perhaps alone among psychologists, he was keen that psychology should learn from literature, where we see depicted traits, characterological self-sufficiency and the sustained interest in one person at a time.'

More conventional, mainstream psychology has not been averse to consideration of the case study when it has had an obvious contribution to make; for instance, Gregory and Wallace (1963) made a detailed case study of a fifty-two-year-old blind man, S.B., who gained his sight following an eye operation (see Chapter 2), which tells us a good deal about the gradual and often unexpected manner in which we come to perceive visually. A number of case studies have helped us understand the role of early experience in determining intelligence. The latest and possibly most dramatic of these (Koluchova, 1972) concerns two twin Czech boys whose mother died shortly after childbirth. When the boys were one year old their father re-married, and then six years of appalling cruelty and neglect began for them. Their stepmother, 'a selfish, aggressive woman', kept the boys locked away in an unheated closet or the house cellar, and they were frequently beaten with a rubber hose-pipe and hit about the skull, leaving their scalps badly scarred. They were not discovered by the authorities until they were seven years old, suffering from acute rickets, severely withdrawn, with poor motor co-ordination and with an IQ level of three-year-olds. They were taken into care and eventually, at the age of nine, fostered out. With a caring and loving new family and special schooling the progress of the boys was remarkable: by the age of fourteen their IQs had risen from the low 40s (on their discovery) to 100 (normal functioning), and they showed no signs of maladjustment or personality disorder – a remarkable testimony to the plasticity of the human being.

Criticisms of the case study
Generality
By its nature and definition, the case study applies only to its single subject and should not be generalized to others. It is not so much a sample of one, but rather a population of one: the study is descrip-

tive, and valid only for its subject. For many psychologists this is an unacceptable and debarring limitation.

Inaccuracy of recall

Most case studies are compiled from retrospective data: the subject is asked to recall certain elements of his past life. But how reliable is an account based solely on the memory of the subject or people who have known him? In terms of reliability and objectivity it hardly matches the data of the experiment or test. (An interesting point is that Freud recognized the limitations of memory recall, but turned this to his advantage by studying *why* subjects 'forgot' certain events in their lives. He argued that forgetting, rather than being a process of passive decay, can be the active, but unconscious, suppression of certain memories, so that although they still exist they cannot be brought into consciousness.

Subjectivity

It is extremely hard for biographers to be totally dispassionate and neutral towards the people they study. Furthermore, they are confronted with the additional problems of inclusion and interpretation: how do they decide what to include and what to omit from the vast amount of information that can be ascertained about the life of an individual, and how do they interpret all the pieces of separate information so as to compose an integrated picture of their subject? The problem of subjectivity is one of the greatest criticisms of psychoanalysis, for Freud, as analyst, acted as sole recorder and arbitrator in his patients' case studies.

From this chapter so far it must be clear that psychology is a multimethod discipline. Which method is used by a particular psychologist for a particular piece of research depends upon several factors. Ideally it should be determined by the criterion of suitability: the researcher should look at the problem he is investigating and check the appropriateness of each method to its study, dispassionately assessing the plausibility of using each. In practice this rarely happens. Most psychologists have a preference for using a particular method, and if a problem they are considering researching cannot be studied by their preferred technique the usual response is to discard the problem by saying that it is 'irrelevant', 'metaphysical' or 'of no importance', or to distort it so that it does 'fit' the method. Although regrettable, this tendency to bend problems to fit pre-elected methods rather than using the full range of techniques is hardly surprising. Today specialization is the rule in most professions and sciences; for example, a surgeon who has developed a new technique in micro-surgery will seek out problems to which he can apply his method, not vice versa. Certainly, for the student it is important to ensure that in any experimental course he is not restricted just to experiments, just to case studies, and so on. He should want to experience the full range of psychology's methods (see Chapter 15).

Methods have certainly influenced the direction and shape of psychology's progress just as much as the problems it studies. However, this is not to say that psychology cannot be described by reference to its subject-matter.

The subject-matter of psychology

We do not feel it necessary to consider the subject-matter of psychology in detail in this introductory chapter; that is the concern of the remainder of the book. All we wish to do is to offer a brief overall view of what psychologists have chosen to examine.

Behaviour and experience

In our earlier definition of psychology (see page 2) we said that it is the 'scientific study of behaviour and experience'. The usual distinction between these two is that behaviour is external, while experience is internal. This is somewhat misleading because we classify the work of physiological psychologists (Chapter 5), who study 'under-the-skin' structures and processes such as those of the nervous systems and the endocrine system, as behavioural, and yet most people would think of the functioning of the cortex, for example, as being an internal event. Probably a more helpful distinction is therefore the criterion of accessibility: behaviour (whether external or 'under-the-skin') can be *directly* observed (albeit with the occasional aid of machinery, such as EEG readings to help us observe the 'behaviour' of the brain); whereas experience can only be *indirectly* observed (either by introspection, if we are talking about our own experiences, or by verbalization, if we are concerned with the experience of others).

The first branch of scientific psychology to emerge concentrated upon experience, and could truly be called 'the science of mental life.' It consisted of the efforts of Wundt and his colleagues at Leipzig in the 1880s and 1890s to train subjects in structured introspection, to turn inwards into their world of mental experience and report what they perceived.

The Leipzig school was trying to map out the shape and boundaries of our inner world, but there were many problems: despite its laboratory setting, how could any discipline based upon individuals' uncheckable subjective reports be scientific? Perhaps the method, laboratory experimentation, was right but the subject-matter was wrong.

In 1913 the American John Watson published a paper which changed the focal point of psychology from experience to behaviour. He opens by saying, 'Psychology as the behaviourist views it is a purely objective experimental branch of natural science. Its theoretical goal is the prediction and control of behaviour. Introspection forms no essential part of its methods, nor is the scientific value of its data dependent upon the readiness with which they lend themselves to interpretation in terms of consciousness.'

Watson's behaviourism captured the imagination and the pursestrings of American psychology and dominated psychology there almost totally until the early 1960s, concentrating particularly upon learning and conditioning (see Chapter 3). European psychology (excluding that of Britain, which tends to follow American trends rather than those in say France or Germany) never really lost faith in the study of experience. In Germany, Gestalt psychology was founded in 1912 and continued the pioneering work of Wundt in perception (see Chapter 2). In Austria, Freud founded psychoanalysis, which rendered previous concepts about personality obsolete (see Chapter 8), and a Swiss biologist named Jean Piaget (see Chapter 11) studied the cognitive development of his own children, and in the 1920s began to develop a theory of mental growth which became probably the major focus of psychological research in the psychology of the 1970s, as Britain and America began to turn back to the analysis of experience after a gap of some fifty or so years.

It is fashionable today to criticize behaviourism, and its later formulation, S–R psychology, as being mechanistic, and as ignoring or being unable to deal with many of psychology's greatest concerns, but without its advent it is doubtful whether psychology would be as well established academically as it is today. Whatever limitations the behaviourists imposed upon themselves by choosing to deny any reference to mental experience, there is no doubt that they established many procedural techniques, methods and pieces of apparatus which have benefited the science. As we shall see in the next section, it is far easier to justify behavioural psychology as being scientific than it is to make out a case for a science of experience.

Is psychology a science?

In recent years a number of philosophers such as Karl Popper (1945, 1959, 1972), Thomas Kuhn (1970) and P.B. Medawar (1963) have considered the question of whether psychology can be considered a science. In the limited amount of space available here we can do no more than scratch the surface of this complex and controversial argument; if you wish to consider the propositions in more detail you should refer to the works in their original form. For our analysis, we have taken three criteria that may help us label psychology as scientific or non-scientific: subject-matter, method, and use of theory.

Subject-matter

When modern psychology was founded just over a hundred years ago as the science of mental life, many observers, while being impressed by the attempt of the Leipzig school at putting psychology in a laboratory and structuring its method of introspection by the careful training of subjects, were of the opinion that psychology could never be truly scientific because of its subject-matter – mental life. How could we check the truth of what subjects were telling us? How could we be sure that they were not simply seeing what they had been told to see? How could a difference of opinion be resolved when the object of study could not be observed directly? It seemed as though the very subject-matter of psychology as it was understood at the turn of the century prevented its entry into the sciences. Kant (1902) believed that because of its concentration upon mental events and concepts, 'empirical psychology must always remain outside the rank of a natural science properly so called'.

The standing of psychoanalysis must be even more precarious, being concerned as it is with the unconscious mind, which the subject himself is unable to see. The unconscious mind, strictly speaking, exists only as an inferred construct, created and described by the analyst. Little hope for science here!

The founding of behaviourism changed the picture dramatically, altering the subject-matter of psychology from experience to behaviour. Behaviour is open, observable and can be accurately measured. In terms of the subject-matter criterion, psychology has not been as scientific since behaviourism began to wane seriously in the 1960s. A good deal of current psychology is characterized by the perspective of phenomenology (see Chapters 8 and 14). Phenomenology was founded by Husserl (1859–1938), and, very simply, it states that to understand a person we have to see the world through his eyes. The approach argues that we all live in our own subjective worlds, and that the ways in which we think and behave can only be understood by reference to each individual's unique set of perspectives. The recent popularity of the approach is largely attributable to the work of Kelly (1955).

So psychology is turning back to experience as its chief subject-matter. Many psychologists argue that we should never have allowed the hard-line 'scientificism' of the behaviourists to seduce us away from the subject's 'true' reference, mental life. This may or may not be true; what we can be sure of is, as we have said before, that a study of experience fits far less comfortably into the traditional model of science than a study of behaviour.

A corollary of the re-emergence of the psychology of experience in recent years has been a trend away from nomothetic studies and greater concentration upon the idiographic. This has implications for science too. As we have already mentioned, Allport contended that if psychology concerns itself, as he believed it should, with the individual rather than the group, it could not be scientific, for, he argued, science is concerned with the general, not the specific. Kirby and Radford deal with this assertion by quoting Popper (1945), who distinguishes between the historical sciences (which include history, biography and some personality research) and the generalizing sciences (which include the natural sciences and related subjects). 'The ultimate aim of science', they say, 'is not to establish *general* or any other kind of laws, but to establish (or at least to approach) the truth - what is, was and always will be the case' (our italics).

Method
We have little to say in this section as we have dealt with the methods of psychology earlier in the chapter. Our main concern here is with the objectivity of the methods, and hence of psychology as an

aspiring science. Generally speaking, the methods which have greatest control and structure, especially the experiment, can be said to be
reasonably objective (that is, dealing with 'facts' uncoloured by the
researchers' feelings or opinions), whereas the unstructured methods
of observation, such as participant observation and psychoanalysis,
are most prone to subjectivity. However, we should appreciate that
it is quite unrealistic to talk of any observation's being totally objective and value-free. We are talking about degrees of objectivity and
subjectivity, not absolutes. Popper (1972) claims that observation is
always pre-structured and directed. To demonstrate the impossi-
bility of pure observation he asked a group of physics students to
take paper and pencil, observe, and write down what they observed.
The students asked what they were to observe. It is obvious that the
initial instruction in totally open: undirected observation cannot be
followed. The idea that the scientist sees all and is equally prepared
for all observations is misleading; it is just as much a nonsense in
physics as it is in psychology. One of the traditional yardsticks of
science, observational objectivity, has been shown by the recent
philosophers to be a non-starter.

However, before we leave the realm of data gathering (subject-
matter and methods) we need to consider briefly one further area –
that of verifiability. In talking earlier about the nature of the experiment, we discussed hypotheses (statements of outcome) which the
experimenter verifies or refutes, and emphasized that these should be
clearly and unequivocally defined in operational terms: there should
be no room for ambivalence. Not all branches of psychology have
this characteristic of being objectively verifiable, and consequently
cannot be classified as being scientific.

One of Popper's best-known contentions concerns verifiability
and refutability. He argued that it is all too easy to look and find
support for our ideas and beliefs, as Marxists, Freudians and Chris-
tians, for example, do: 'Once your eyes were ... opened [to the belief]
you saw confirming instances everywhere: the world was full of
verifications of the theory. Whatever happened always confirmed it.
Thus its truth appeared manifest; and unbelievers were clearly
people who did not want the manifest truth; who refused to see it,
either because it was against their class interest, or because of their
repressions which were still 'un-analysed', and crying aloud for
treatment [1972].' For such believers, truth is a matter of belief and
conviction. Science must be more demanding, and Popper's solution

is to look for refuting evidence rather than verifications. He says (1959), 'Observations, and even more so observation statements and statements of experimental results are always *interpretations* of the facts observed; ... they are *interpretations in the light of theories.* This is one of the main reasons why it is always deceptively easy to find *verifications* of a theory, and why we have to adopt a highly critical attitude towards our theories if we do not wish to argue in circles: the attitude of trying to falsify them.'

This brings us to our final criterion of science.

The use of theory
In our original definition of psychology we said that we seek to establish, by the use of observation and experimentation, facts about behaviour and experience which can be explained by theories. It is not sufficient to simply record data and establish facts: we need to interpret them and explain what they mean. Cohen (1968) says, 'Properly speaking, the word psychology should perhaps refer to ... theoretical perspectives, however provisional they may be, rather than to assemblies of factual information. On this view, the task of psychology is primarily to systematise the facts, to give them order and meaning, thus enabling us to understand, and possibly to predict, human behaviour.' As we have just emphasized, such theories should be testable, and the emphasis should be on disproving rather than proving them.

The formulation of theory is the final stage of the classical scientific procedure: observation–facts–theory. Medawar (1963) indicates the mysticism and reverence with which some regard the process when he describes it as follows: 'It starts with simple observation – simple, unbiased, unprejudiced, naive, or innocent observation – and out of this sensory evidence, embodied in the form of propositions or declarations of fact, generalizations will grow up and take shape almost as if some process of crystallization or condensation were taking place. Out of the disorderly array of facts, an orderly theory, an orderly general statement will somehow emerge.' Medawar is highly critical of such a view, seeing it as naïve and illogical. Popper offered the following procedural model as more appropriate: (1) the problem (usually a refutation of an existing theory or prediction); (2) the proposed solution or new theory; (3) the deduction of testable propositions from the new theory; (4) testing or attempting to refute by, amongst other things, observation and experimentation; and (5) establishing a preference between competing theories.

The last point has been emphasized by the philosopher in the history of science, Kuhn (1970). He believes the role of theory to be absolutely central to the definition and state of science. He claims that a subject can only be rightly considered a science if a majority of its workers subscribe to a common global theory or perspective, which he calls a *paradigm*. Examples can readily be seen in the natural sciences; for example, nearly all biologists believe in the theory of evolution, and this acts both to unite their field – and consequently to differentiate it from others – and to define the work that biologists should engage in – exploring and establishing the fine details of evolutionary procedure and history.

Kuhn proposes three historical stages in the development of a science – pre-science, normal science and revolution. In pre-science, the subject has no paradigm, no global uniting belief; it only becomes a science when someone proposes a perspective or theory which seems to explain the facts and difficulties of the past, and unites the field. The names of Newton in physics and Darwin in biology come readily to mind as examples. The establishment of a paradigm leads to a settled state of normal science, in which the researchers dedicate themselves to exploring the parameters of the paradigm and filling in all the small detail. This stage lasts until such a time as the established paradigm is challenged by a newcomer and is defeated. This stage, revolution, is usually relatively brief in comparison to the other two; an example is when Einstein revolutionized physics with his Theory of Relativity. This leads back to normal science, when settled work proceeds as before but with the new paradigm holding sway.

In psychology the closest we come to paradigms are levels of explanation.

Levels of explanation
There are many different ways of explaining the same facts or observations in psychology. You will hardly fail to notice these as you read the subsequent chapters of this book. Let us take the example of a kiss. We could describe this act in a number of ways: some psychologists would describe it in behavioural terms (physical or physiological), whereas others would do so in terms of mental experience (feelings, thoughts and emotions). Furthermore, if we

wanted not only to describe the act but also to explain it there are
quite a number of ways in which we could do this. We could offer an
explanation which reduced the act to nervous and muscular activities (*reductionism:* see Chapter 5); we could offer an evolutionary
explanation, which would explain why we kiss in terms of its past
survival value (primate mothers chewing up food and passing it
from their own mouths to those of their offspring); an explanation
could be offered in terms of the current situation (the presence of a
sexually attractive person), or of the conditioning history of the
kisser (whether he had been previously rewarded or punished for
kissing, or whether he associated kissing with happy or sad events);
or we could try and explain the behaviour in psychoanalytic terms
(attraction towards a mother substitute) or in terms of social factors
(social etiquette, or wanting to be accepted or admired by fellow
group members). And so on.

In our opinion psychology is not at present characterized by a
paradigm. No one level of explanation, or school of psychology, as
they were once called, can successfully embrace all that psychology
studies. Brown and Herrnstein (1975) say

Each school has had certain phenomena with which it was maximally comfortable: psychophysics for structuralism; dreams and psychopathology for
psychoanalysis; all the phenomena of conditioning for behaviourism; perceived movement for Gestalt psychology; cognitive development for
Piaget's psychology; conformity and obedience for social psychology, and
so forth. The schools lost their adherents by attempting to fit their concepts,
with much stretching and straining, to all psychological phenomena.

It would therefore appear that psychology, according to Kuhn's
criterion, is still pre-science. Popper is not so pessimistic, and believes that many branches of the subject fulfil the criteria of relative
objectivity, generality, accessibility and refutability. Allport's (1947)
criteria also fit psychology quite successfully. He says that science is
defined by its aims, which are 'understanding, prediction and control
above the levels achieved by unaided common sense'. It is with these
aims in mind that we introduce you to the science of psychology.

Further reading

Anderson, B.F. (1966), *The Psychology Experiment: An Introduction to the Scientific Method*, Brooks/Cole

Broadbent, D.E. (1964), *Behaviour*, Methuen

Burns, R.B. and Dobson, C.B. (1981), *Experimental Psychology*, M.T.P.

Fransella, F. (1975), *Need To Change?*, Methuen

Hardy, M. and Heyes, S. (1979), *Beginning Psychology*, Weidenfeld and Nicolson

Hyman, R. (1964), *The Nature of Psychological Inquiry*, Prentice Hall

Kirby, R. and Radford, J. (1976), *Individual Differences*, Methuen

Miller, G.A. (1966), *Psychology: The Science of Mental Life*, Penguin

Popper, K. (1972), *Conjectures and Refutations: The Growth of Scientific Knowledge* (4th ed.), Routledge and Kegan Paul

Robson, C. (1973), *Experiment, Design and Statistics in Psychology*, Penguin

2 Perception

The framework of perception

It is perhaps apt that having defined psychology as a behavioural science we should begin our investigation of its subject-matter with perception. Not only was perception the area which attracted the attention of the German physiologists who were the founding fathers of scientific psychology, but it is also the precursor to much of our behaviour (without a stimulus there is rarely a response).

A major difficulty confronting students beginning the study of perception lies in accepting that there is a problem to investigate at all. Sense organs such as the eyes and ears may tend to be regarded as apertures, admitting external information, like direct channels allowing light or sound into the brain. Many liken the visual apparatus to a camera; a shutter opens, light enters the black box to be received by a 'recording' surface like a film, and a photograph is made. This chapter aims to correct this mistaken and inappropriate analogy.

A most interesting feature of the perceptual system is that it is interpretative. Did you notice the repetition of the word 'the' in

1.

Figure 1? We frequently see what we expect to see, rather than what is actually there. Photographs revealing weird perspectives of subjects, such as disproportionately large hands or feet, result when taken too close to the subjects, or from an unusual angle. The point is that *we* never saw it that way, but the unthinking, non-correcting camera recorded it without the adjustments that we unconsciously make. Whether or not it is true that the camera cannot lie, the eye certainly can and frequently does.

This chapter concentrates almost exclusively on visual perception, though it has long been accepted that there are five human senses – sight, smell, touch, taste and hearing. However, unlike many other animals, humans are predominantly visual creatures, and Dodwell (1966) reports an estimation that 'well over' 90% of information about the world is received through the visual sense. Brunswik (1952, 1956) proposed a model of perception which related the role of perception to an individual's overall behaviour.

The term *'central'* refers to events within the individual, *'proximal'* to events at the boundaries of the individual, and *'distal'* to events or phenomena with which he is not in immediate contact, that is, objects or events 'in the outside world'. Figure 2 is a flow diagram showing time from left to right, so that events occur in the order **c-b-a-0-A-B-C**. Consider the following dramatic example. A couple arrive home after an evening out, and the husband opens the door to see a fire in the hall. Thinking quickly, he recognizes that the outbreak is small and localized and that he should be able to deal with it himself. He does this by using the fire extinguisher kept in the car, and the damage to their property is minimal. This example can be examined in terms of the Brunswik model. Before entering the house, the husband knows the perceptual characteristics of fire – how it looks, smells, sounds and so on – so there is a perceptual interpretation, previously acquired through experience, already present in his brain. This is level **c**, and though it may appear rather simple, it can be complicated, by the distortion or bias of these rules for the interpretation of stimuli in many ways, such as by emotion, motivation and expectation, as we shall see later. Level **b** is the existence of fire in the hall of the house before the man is aware of it, while level **a** is when he opens the door and light from the fire reaches his eyes and stimulates the photo-receptive cells which convert the light waves into electrical impulses. The final perceptual stage, level **0**, is when the brain reconstitutes and interprets the image and the

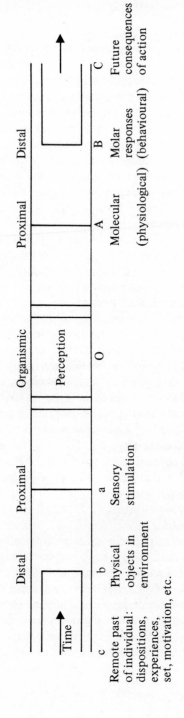

2. Brunswik's model of perception

man 'sees' the fire. The remainder of the diagram demonstrates the continuity between perception and behaviour. Level **A** indicates that before an individual can actually be seen to behave or respond, there is frequently physiological preparation. In the tense situation of our example there would probably be increases in adrenalin, heart-rate, muscular tension and so on, before overt action began (level **B**). The 'under-the-skin' preparatory behaviour is called *molecular* (and is fully discussed in Chapter 5), while the overt behaviour is *molar*. Level **C** is self-explanatory, and in this example might include strong emotional reaction to the episode, the carrying out of repairs, greater attention to fire precautions generally, and perhaps increased perceptual awareness of fire (recognizing and reacting to fire more rapidly than before).

For the remainder of this chapter we shall, perversely, work through the left half of the model backwards, beginning with the proximal, or physiological, aspects of perception, including a brief account of the structure and function of the eye and some examples of how perception is adjusted to meet specific needs. For example, it is more useful for humans to see objects rather than sensations, and although your retina is currently registering a white rectangle and a series of small black shapes in front of you, you perceive a book. Following this, the role of emotion and motivation in perception will be discussed. The proximal level of analysis, concerned as it is with the structure and function of the sense organs and their relationships with the appropriate regions of the brain, is primarily the concern of the biologist and the physiologist, while distal analysis – the world of objects – is for the physicist. The level of perception which most concerns the psychologist is level **c** in the Brunswik model, the level of experience and cognition, and the discussion in this chapter will reflect this weighting.

Proximal analysis
Just as humans are bodily different from other animals, so too are their eyes unique. Most living creatures are sensitive to light, though not all possess eyes, and certain stages of the evolution of the eye can be identified when examining increasingly complex creatures, though there is no direct correspondence between the general position of an animal on the evolutionary scale and the sophistication of its eyes. Although humans may be seen as the pinnacle of evolutionary development, their eyes are not among the most highly devel-

oped. However, while in most complex animals the relationship is often that of complex eye to simple brain, in humans, though the eye is not especially complex, the brain is the most highly developed of all brains, and we are able to feed it with relatively unprocessed 'raw' information which it can then process at a higher level. Animals possessing simpler brains need this processing to be performed by the eye itself.

Details of the structure and functioning of the human eye are given in Chapter 5, but it must be noted that the role of the rods and cones in perception is important, since these photo-receptive cells are part of the brain itself; they are an out-growth reaching into the eye-ball. They have the critical function of translating light waves into the only language the brain can understand – neural impulses – and this has intriguing implications of which most people are unaware. Look away from the page for a moment at some nearby object, maybe a picture on the wall, or a table, or someone's face. You see the colour, the texture, the character, just as though you are looking 'out' through your eyes and into the world around you. The reality is very different. Light comes *in* to us, and we do not see *out*, though we have the impression of being in touch with the world 'out there'. In the literal sense there is no picture inside our heads that we view, for pictures are made up of light, and there is no light inside our brain, nor are there any sounds. Our brains are dark, silent structures, although we 'see' pictures and 'hear' music. In the case of vision, the visual cortex of the brain interprets the electrical impulses sent to it by the retina, and re-constitutes them into an *illusion* of pictures. Perception uses the medium of electricity, not colour.

Distal analysis
This area of Brunswik's categorization is probably least confusing if thought of as concerned with how closely a perception fits the 'external reality', in other words the extent to which **0** (the perception) = **b** (the object in the outside world). It is a measure of the accuracy of perception in its representation of the physical world at which we look. A camera-like perceptual system would physically reflect the geometry of the objects perceived, but perception is active and interpretative, and not a purely receptive process of absorbing sensations and faithfully reproducing them inside our heads. If it were so, we would not see illusions or hallucinations, or overlook objects which we are seeking. Three-dimensional perception would not occur, for

depth perception is a function of the system's efforts to read more into the data than is directly provided by the senses.

It is now appropriate to introduce an important definition of perception which acknowledges its interpretative role. Gregory (1966) says: 'Perception is not determined simply by ... stimulus patterns; rather it is a dynamic searching for the best interpretation of the available data.... It seems clear that perception involves going beyond the immediately given evidence of the senses.' He goes on to say that perception consists of attempts to interpret the data received from the senses so that what is perceived is not the data, but the interpretation of it ('a perceived object is a hypothesis, suggested and tested by sensory data'). This concept of perception is extremely important and requires close attention.

Perception is an active system, converting a world of sensations into a state of awareness of the world around us. Perception of a painting such as the 'Mona Lisa' is not merely in terms of a collection of colours and textures, but an organization and interpretation of them as a familiar face, the beauty of the mouth and eyes. Incoming sensations are organized and interpreted as perceptions of objects, for we learn by experience that the world is made up of objects and that sensations such as colours and smells are merely the means by which they are made available for perception.

Distal analysis is concerned with assessing how 'successful' our interpretations are: how close is the relationship between the object of perception and the perception itself. Sometimes in attempting to provide a working and functional picture of the world, the perceptual system will erroneously interpret the data, and lead to a misperception of the object. There are many reasons for incorrect interpretations, and some of the most interesting ones are connected with motivation and *set* (see p. 62). The old adage 'Love is blind' appears to have some validity, as some studies of lovers' perceptions have shown. People tend to see their loved or desired ones as being taller, slimmer, more facially attractive, and having better figures and physiques and fewer blemishes or imperfections than is actually the case (as judged by neutral evaluators). We see what we want to see, rather than what is actually there, and 'rose-coloured spectacles' are the effects of motivation upon the interpretation of information from the sense organs. Further illustrations of the interpretative errors due to motivation, emotion and set will be given later, but it should be remembered that discussion of such errors is only half the story. In interpreting sensory data so that a functional picture rather than a sensory picture of the world is built up, the perceptual system only rarely makes errors, and perceptions usually *add* usefully to the original. James (1890) said that the world of the baby is one of 'booming, buzzing confusion', and it may be helpful to think of the difference between the perceptual world of the baby and that of the adult as that between 'raw sensory data' in the infant and the same sensory data meaningfully organized and interpreted in the adult, and clearly the latter system is far more functional and useful than the former.

Depth perception

Two frequently discussed illustrations of 'successful' perceptual interpretations are those of *depth perception* and the so-called *perceptual constancies*. Both clearly show enhanced and enriched versions of what is given by the sense organs, and both constitute complex fields of study, though an outline of depth perception only is possible here.

The retina is a two-dimensional surface, yet the world is perceived in depth. A look around your immediate environment now should produce a 3-D perception, yet in reality it could be likened to a painting on a piece of canvas. There is no depth at the sensory input level, yet the perception is not one of a flat, uni-distant picture. Why? The answer is that images given by the senses are interpreted, and that by the careful scanning and 'reading' of certain cues, the pictures are blown out, as it were, into the third dimension. The cues which give information about the relative distances of the constituent parts of the picture are usually divided into two categories – *monocular cues* (those accessible to the single eye) and *binocular cues* (those which depend upon the interaction between the two eyes).

Monocular cues
Monocular cues include the following:

Perspective
There are several factors involved in perspective, and they may be seen in Figure 3.

3. *Perspective in 'The Annunciation' by Crivelli* (by courtesy of the Trustees of the National Gallery, London)

Decreasing size We learn that the size of the image made by an object is not constant. Watching a figure walking away demonstrates the simple geometry of the stimulus situation: as the distance of the figure doubles so the image on the retina halves. At a distance of three metres the retinal image is twice that at six metres. Perception 'compensates for this, and the figure is perceived as being the same size, irrespective of distance, and not as alternately growing and shrinking in size as he walks around. Gregory (1966) illustrates the magnitude of this effect (called *size constancy*) with a simple but striking demonstration. A strong retinal after-image can be obtained by, say, looking at a photographic flash. Re-focusing the eyes on a nearby surface such as the palm of the hand, and then looking at a distant wall, shows that the after-image clearly increases in size with distant focusing. Since the retinal image is obviously fixed in size, it

4. Size perception as influenced by conditions of viewing

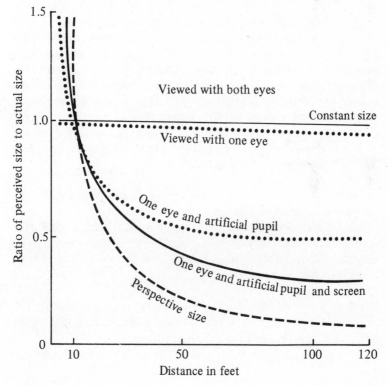

must be the perceptual processing apparatus which is responsible for the adjustment.

Figures judged more distant in Figure 3 are considerably smaller in terms of their *actual* size in the photograph; therefore the retinal size of a figure or object, especially if a familiar figure or object, is a good indicator of its distance away, with distance being directly related to retinal size. However, retinal size alone is insufficient for unerring judgement. Holway and Boring (1941) asked subjects to estimate the size of a number of discs at a variety of distances down a narrow hallway. Results showed that estimates of the size of the discs under normal conditions (i.e. with both eyes) slightly over-compensated for retinal size decreasing with distance, and consequently over-estimated the disc sizes. Judging with only one eye was more accurate, the under-estimating being only slight. More importantly, if other sources of information, such as surrounding objects and other cues to distance, were not available, subjects were decidedly less successful in their estimates. Subjects asked to judge using only one eye looking through a screen with a small hole placed near the eye, and later with the addition of a second screen, so that subjects could see only a limited area when looking through both peep-holes in alignment, showed practically no depth perception. Making appropriate allowance for the size of objects shrinking with increasing distance was minimal, and subjects reverted to estimations based purely on retinal size, so that they were unable to differentiate between small discs quite close to them and large discs shown at a greater distance. Cues other than decreasing size are necessary for depth perception (see Fig. 4).

Height in the horizontal plane One way in which artists successfully create the impression of distance is by placing objects that are 'more distant' higher in the picture than 'closer' ones. Inspection of Figure 3 will confirm this. Objects below our line of vision seem to go *up* into the distance, whereas objects above our line of vision seem to go *down* into the distance.

Gradient of texture Another cue used in depth perception is perception of the coarseness of texture of close surfaces, and of the finer and less coarse texture of more distant surfaces.

Clarity
Perception of the sharp details of an object prompts the judgement
that it is relatively close, while if the impression is less precise and
reveals only more gross characteristics, it is judged to be more distant. This is because air is not a perfect conveyor of light, and detail
is lost with distance. In Figure 5, note the loss of clarity and detail as
the buildings recede into the distance.

Superimposition of objects
All distance cues are used in conjunction with each other, and it is
artificial to talk of one being more important than another, but this
cue does override others if they contradict it. Note in Figure 5 that
the car in the foreground appears to 'block' part of the view of the
car 'behind it'. This is a strong cue to attributed distance. The
buildings closest to the photographer make it impossible to see *all*
aspects of the buildings behind them. Thus, we learn by experience
that if one object blocks part of the view of another, it is likely that
the former is closer. Perceptual psychologists are notorious for
manipulating situations to deceive observers, and the following is a
fine example (Krech and Crutchfield, 1958). In Figure 6 two ordinary
playing cards are held on stems at different distances from the
observer. Even when judged against a plain dark background (to
eliminate other depth cues), and using only one eye (to eliminate
binocular cues), subjects invariably report the card on the right to be
closer to them. The effect is facilitated by retinal size difference; in
other words, the closer card makes a larger image. This judgement
will be confirmed if the nearer card blocks the view of part of the
distant card. If, however, as in **B**, a corner of the near card is cut
away so that from his pre-arranged viewing angle the observer sees
C, he will report that the right-hand card, although much smaller, is
closer to him. Superimposition will over-rule contrary evidence from
many other cues such as retinal size, height in the horizontal plane
and clarity, even when all combine unanimously in their opposition.

Light and shadow
Patterns of shadows are important in judging distance or depth, and
though shadows are recognized as not being part of their objects, they
do contribute information about the objects. Deductions about depth
using perception of shadows as cues are based on the usually correct
assumption that light comes from above. Altering the light source
to cast different shadows can significantly affect depth perception.

5. *A view illustrating superimposition of objects* (courtesy of Magnum Photos, Inc.)

6. *Interposition and relative size as cues in perception of distance* (after D. Krech and R. S. Crutchfield (1958), *Elements of Psychology,* Alfred A. Knopf, Inc; reproduced by permission)

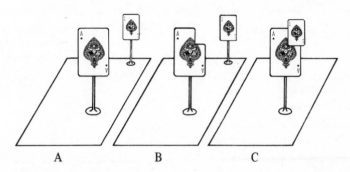

A   B   C

Movement

The technical name for this factor in depth perception is *motion parallax,* and refers to the observation that close objects appear to move relatively quickly whereas those at a greater distance are slower. In attempts to judge the distance of an object, a subject will frequently move his head to produce 'movement' in the object, though perhaps unaware of the reason for this.

Accommodation

Chapter 5 draws attention to the way in which the lens of the eye changes shape to help focus images of objects from varying distances onto the retina. Many muscles in the body contain receptors which provide information about their activity, and it is possible that such receptors in the ciliary muscles which tighten and relax the lens could provide information about the distance of the objects being perceived. This information would be useful only up to a distance of about seven metres, since lens accommodation is negligible beyond that.

Binocular cues

Binocular cues are available because of the interaction between the two eyes, such as:

Retinal disparity

Because the eyes lie in separate sockets in the head, they do not each receive exactly the same view of objects before them. Moreover, the

closer the object, the greater the *retinal disparity* or difference between the two images. Hold the spine of a book towards you at half
an arm's length. By closing your right eye you will see the spine and
part of the left face of the book, but by closing your left eye you will
see the spine and part of the right face of the book. The difference is
less marked if viewed from a greater distance, so an important depth
perception cue is that the greater the difference between the images
presented by each eye when looking at the same object, the closer the
object is.

Convergence

This is a cue from the muscles which turn and direct the eyes. For
objects more than about twenty-five metres distant, the lines of
vision of the two eyes are parallel, but for closer objects, the eyes
must converge, and the closer the object, the greater the convergence. Try the child's game of taking a vertical finger closer and
closer to the face of another, and watch the eyes 'cross' as they
converge to their fullest extent. The *convergence cue* is the feedback
given by the sense organs in the responsible eye muscles, about the
extent to which the eyes have to converge to focus upon an object.

   The convergence and retinal disparity cues are used in combination to determine the distance between objects. When viewing two
objects at four and six feet, for example, the retinal disparity from
the observer's viewpoint is quite large; but if the observer is thirty
feet away from the two objects, the disparity will be much less.
Consequently, the objects will appear to be closer together if retinal
disparity alone is used at this distance. The brain overcomes this
problem by considering small disparities as indicating larger differences in relative distance between objects, when the convergence cue
indicates that the eyes are focused on objects further away from the
observer.

   Due to the use of all these monocular and binocular cues, a flat
retinal image can be translated into a more useful and functional 3-D
perception of the world (the physiological mechanisms which under-
lie this process are discussed in Chapter 5). Our proximal analysis
has shown that perceptions can represent the outside world more
accurately than if the raw information provided by the sense organs
was merely accepted as it was. In terms of Brunswik's model, **0** is the
same as **b**, whereas sometimes **0** is not the same as **a**. In seeking to
supplement and interpret sensory inputs, however, wrong conclusions

and inappropriate interpretations may be made. Moreover, psychologists can rig the odds in special ways to increase the likelihood of perceptual errors, to provide considerable insight into the ways in which the perceptual system works.

Selective attention

Whatever the image projected on the retina, there is no absolute guarantee that it will be perceived in its entirety. Large parts of visual images falling on the retina are coded by the retinal receptive fields and are transmitted along the optic nerve to the brain, but do not seem to be processed any further. Moreover, the brain appears to be able to 'direct its attention' to any part of the visual image, which is processed in great detail.

It seems that this ability to 'concentrate attention' on particular parts of the visual field is necessary, because the human visual perceptual system appears to have limited capacity for fully processing information. Early experiments concentrated on the 'span of attention' – how much information we can take in and process at a glance. The findings were that this was a surprisingly small amount: Kaufman *et al.* (1949) reported that the maximum number of dots which could be counted accurately when exposed for 200 milliseconds was only approximately 7.

Consequently, the perceptual system must select information for full processing. In order for something to be fully perceived, the image must be coded at the retina, and this coded image must be accepted by the brain. There are several 'rules of thumb' by which we can predict whether or not a stimulus will be accepted by the brain. Note that these rules apply to all the senses, not just vision. Certain types of stimulus, by their very nature, are more likely to make us pay attention to them.

Intensity
The more intense a stimulus is (the brighter the light, the louder the noise), the more it will cause us to attend to it. If two stimuli are competing for attention, the more intense of the two will get it.

Contrast
Sudden changes in the intensity of a stimulus will gain attention. A loud noise, after a while, becomes less noticeable. If the noise

suddenly stops, attention is focused on the absence of noise: we hear a 'deafening silence'.

Repetition

The more a stimulus is repeated, the more likely it is to gain attention.

Movement

We tend to be very sensitive to movement, particularly within our visual field (perhaps the remnant of pre-human survival abilities). Thus an illuminated advertisement with moving lights gains more attention than a static display.

All these factors (known as external factors) cause us to pay attention to them, but what exactly is attention; how is it caused?

Broadbent (1958) believed that we have a kind of central filter – allowing some information signals to pass through, but inhibiting others. This view is now regarded as being rather limited: how does the filter know which signals to pass and which to stop? Anne Triesman (1969) has proposed the *attenuator theory* which seems to be gaining general acceptance. Information which has the required physical characteristics, for example a sound of low pitch, or the image of something which is moving, is allowed to pass through the filter/analyser and into the cortex unhindered; but non-essential information is attenuated, weakened. In this weakened form the information reaches the higher processing centres in the cortex. These processing areas are also pre-programmed to respond to certain stimuli, even if they are in an attenuated form. As an example, imagine yourself at a party, with its confused babble of talk. Somebody at the other side of the room mentions your name, and the chances are that you will hear it (the *cocktail party syndrome*). All the confused babble of sound is being attenuated by the attenuator, but when your name is mentioned, even though it reaches the cortex in an attenuated form, it stimulates the pre-programmed cortex, and you become more alert and start seeking more information – looking for the person who mentioned your name, for example.

Broadbent's theory (see Fig. 7) can explain several phenomena associated with attention. It shows that different types of stimulus (sound, light, touch and so on) can be dealt with by the same mechanism. It demonstrates how, from a mass of different stimuli, those which have most relevance to the organism are selected. It explains

7. Broadbent's model of attention

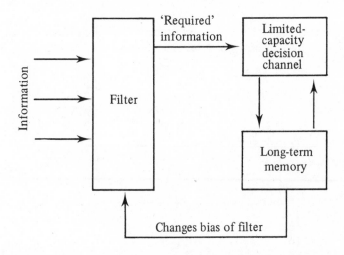

how the type of information to which we attend can be changed: the 'decision channel', in conjunction with long-term memory (LTM) storage, can feed back information to the 'filter', in order to change its bias. For instance, if you had just met a new girl- or boyfriend, their name would be processed by the decision channel, and presumably put into long-term storage. Links from LTM to the filter would then give the filter a new bias: it would now allow stimuli containing their name through. Similarly, if you were hungry, the filter's bias would be changed so as to pass information about food. When you had eaten, the preferential treatment for food stimuli would be stopped. In addition to biases produced by motivation, emotion and set, or expectation, the filter has a permanent bias towards novel stimuli – possibly an ability which has survival value, whereas a stimulus which is repeated will tend to be 'filtered out' after a while. The attention system responds to new stimuli, even if a succession of them are presented. The permanent bias of the filter also extends to external factors (intensity, contrast and so forth).

However, Broadbent's theory has one important failing: it cannot explain the cocktail party syndrome. Your name, spoken from the other side of a crowded room, is not intense enough or repeated enough to get through the filter's permanent bias for external factors. Why, then, is it not filtered out? Broadbent's theory states that the selective filter's bias can be changed by the decision channel and LTM. But even if this is so, how does the selective filter recognize the stimulus? Surely the processing or understanding of stimuli must occur after the filter? We cannot process all the stimuli we receive, so the filter has to cut some out: the filter itself cannot process the stimuli.

8. Triesman's model of attention

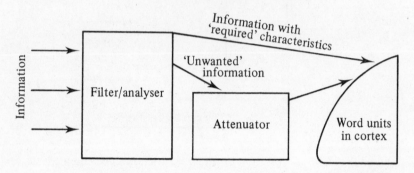

Triesman's theory (see Fig. 8) can explain all that the Broadbent theory does, and also the cocktail party syndrome. In an experiment carried out by Triesman (1960), separate messages are fed through earphones into separate ears of a subject, and the ends of the messages are switched over, for example:

Left ear: He felt somewhat ill window
Right ear: She sat looking out of the at ease

The subject's task is to shadow (that is, repeat immediately afterwards) the message coming into his right ear, so presumably the message coming into the left ear is not attended to. Broadbent's theory predicts that the subject would say 'She sat looking out of the at ease', but in fact subjects usually 'switch' ears at the end of the speeches, so that the message makes sense. The fact that subjects can pick up the odd word from the other ear suggests that the attention system cannot be a simple stop/go mechanism, as Broadbent proposed. Broadbent believed that the filter lay at the edge of the nervous system, but this cannot be so: this type of filtering seems to depend on meaning, so must occur higher up in the nervous system.

Triesman believes that the filter does play a part in attention, but is not as important as Broadbent suggests. The analysis performed by the filter is quite simple: it analyses simple physical characteristics of the stimulus only – pitch, location, volume and so on. Certain information (of a certain pitch or volume, for example) is allowed to pass through unhindered for further processing, but all the rest is attenuated. This attenuated information is allowed to pass to the cortex in its new, weakened form. So the cortex receives two sets of information: first, a limited amount of full-strength signals which have the required physical characteristics, and secondly, much attenuated information.

Triesman believes that the cortex itself is where the full processing occurs. The non-attenuated information is processed most fully, but there are also in the cortex 'word units' (which could be imagined as being like cell assemblies). These word units are very sensitive to particular sorts of information. They will respond to such information, even if it reaches the cortex in attenuated form. One's own name, for example, would reach the filter/analyser, and because it was mixed up with the background noise in the room it would be passed through to the attenuator, and would reach the word unit section in attenuated form. Even in this weakened form, however, the appropriate highly sensitive word unit would pick it up and 'amplify' it ready for further processing.

Broadbent's and Triesman's theories of attention suggest ways in which we select information from among the wide array of stimuli which affect our senses every second of the day. This selected information has now to be processed further, and these processes are examined in the next section.

A definition of perception

It should now be clear that the perceptual system is not passive and purely receptive, but active and interpretative. Level c in Brunswik's model (p. 45) shows that into any perceptual situation we take with us a head full of knowledge and past experiences, and this level of analysis is that of 'interpretative perception'. Level b represents the world of physical objects and events, accessible via their sensory properties; level a is the way in which sense organs receive and translate sources of energy into appropriate forms; and level c refers to the factors which aid understanding and give meaning to the information received. It might seem that this level of analysis should appear *after* the proximal events, since they only come into play after the signal has been received and a perception is being structured. However, the model is a time flow-chart, and the c-level factors are present in the receiver *before* the arrival of the stimulus. In scanning the symbols on this page, the rules for translating them into meanings are already available in your head, held in readiness as interpretations into which stimuli 'fit'.

Gregory's definition of perception as 'a dynamic searching for the best interpretation of the available data' can now be more fully examined, and we can see what happens as perception goes beyond the evidence given. Barber and Legge (1976) argue that 'Perception involves the operation of the senses and is effected in the shadow of the expectations, hopes, fears, needs and memories that make up our internal world'. It is this internal world, as opposed to the external physical one, that is dealt with at level c.

Different writers tend to employ different terms in discussing these internal determinants of perceptions. Helmholtz (1867) uses the term 'umbewusster schluss' to describe the unconscious testing of data for exactness-of-fit into pre-existing interpretations. Woodworth (1947) talks of 'trial and check', while Gregory (1966) calls it 'hypothesis testing'. In describing or classifying the different internal determinants of perception, some writers study emotional factors, others motivations, and yet others examine expectancy. Bartlett (1932) writes about 'schemata' and Allport (1955) introduced the term *set*. We may say that despite the plethora of different terms, they are all essentially describing much the same events, and here the term set will be used, partly because it can conveniently subsume many separate categories, and partly because its very name indicates its nature.

Set as an umbrella

Allport (1955) introduced the term *set* as meaning a perceptual bias or predisposition, and claimed that motivation and emotion do not directly influence perception themselves, but do so indirectly by influencing sets. This at once identifies two of the determinants of set as being motivation and emotion. An individual's set is like the athlete who gets set to run at the sound of the starting pistol – his set includes both the readiness to hear the pistol and the readiness to leap forward into the race. Perceptual set affects attention, increasing the likelihood of picking out certain stimuli, and the way in which the signals are interpreted. Just as the pistol shot has a 'priority channel' for the runner, over-riding other stimuli to gain immediate access to consciousness, so do certain perceptual inputs have priority from the sea of stimuli that surround us, depending on perceptual set. Similarly, the interpretation of a signal may be decided before it is actually received, just as the athlete knows beforehand what he will do as soon as the pistol fires – it would be very surprising to see him rise slowly from his block with an air of puzzlement and then decide to begin running!

The distinction made between set as picking out certain high-priority stimuli and set as determining interpretations follows that of Vernon (1955) when he observes that sets work in two ways: (1) they produce a condition of expectation in which the observer knows what to look for – what particular data to select from the incoming flood – and (2) they help him to know how to deal with data – how to classify, understand and name them and draw from them the inferences that give meaning to perception. The experimental evidence on set can thus be divided into these two aspects – set as a selector, and set as an interpreter.

Set as a selector
The cognitive, c-level factors clearly act as a selector, determining which stimuli of many will be attended to, and the direct effect of motivation can clearly be observed. Cannon (1929) talks in terms of *homeostatic drive theory* (see p. 175) as identifying a number of biogenic drives (hunger, thirst, warmth, and possibly sex) which, if they become noticeably disequilibriated and demand satisfaction, tend to build up short-term perceptual biases predisposing behaviour relating to drive satisfaction. In our society sex is a strong attention-gainer because of its traditional suppression. Satisfaction of hunger and thirst drives are rarely problematic, but sexual drive is socially more difficult to indulge, increasing the likelihood that this drive will be disequilibriated more often than the others and that a perceptual bias towards attending to and seeking out sexual objects will be more prevalent.

Gottschaldt (1929) showed subjects a complex figure, and then asked them to find it when it was hidden in a larger, more complex masking figure. With practice they found it more often, more rapidly, and in different masking configurations. Hanawalt (1942) demonstrated the durability of this effect in a similar experiment by post-testing subjects three years later. He found that the time taken to isolate and identify the masked figures had reduced even further.

An early study by Kulpe and Bryan (1904) demonstrates the power of motivation in selective attention, and oblivion to those aspects of the situation we are not set to observe. Three-letter syllables such as

X D R

were exposed *tachistoscopically* (that is, for very brief periods of time, in a machine known as a tachistoscope) to three groups of subjects. Group A were instructed to report the letters seen; group B the colour of the letters; and group C their spatial arrangement (such as XD R, X DR, XDR and X D R). Most subjects were unable to recall presentation details for which they had not been set, and group B, for instance, could not name the letters just shown them. The implications of such findings are considerable when one considers the importance placed upon eye-witness recollection as court evidence, and the likelihood that observers only notice those aspects for which they are motivated, set or emotionally predisposed to select.

Cultural influences affect set as a selector too. Pettigrew, Allport and Barrett (1958) showed photographs of members of different races to groups of white South Africans (some English-speaking and some Afrikaans-speaking), to Indians, Africans and to 'coloureds' (mixed white and African), in a binocular tachistoscope or stereoscope. Different pictures were presented to the two eyes – a member of one race (European, Indian, African or 'coloured') to one eye, and a member of a different race to the other eye. Results showed that each group of subjects was most accurate in picking out its own members, but Afrikaaners significantly differed from other groups by differentiating their judgements more sharply into Europeans or Africans, with few intermediate judgements of Indians or 'coloureds', indicating that they exaggerated the differentiation between whites and Negroes.

Solley and Murphy (1960) draw attention to the functions of sets, which, if defined as perceptual predispositions affected by motives, emotions, experiences and expectations, will clearly have numerous and wide-ranging functions. They list four functions of expectancy:

1 It narrows the possible modes of action, just as choice reaction time between two alternatives is quicker and more efficient than reaction time between ten alternatives.

2 It sometimes makes more likely the behaviours which will bring us into contact with the goal-objects to which needs direct us.

3 Expectancy may be directly self-rewarding – just as it is pleasurable for a child to entertain an expectancy of Father Christmas.

4 Expectancy facilitates the endurance of hardships before reaching goals, preparing us not only for the good but also for the bad.

Set as an interpreter

As already discussed, there is no one-to-one correspondence between objects as registered by sense organs and the final perception of those objects (for example depth interpretations and adjustments). Similarly, there may be little agreement between the nature of objects in the external world and our internal perception of them (as with illusions and hallucinations). All the set influences in this interpretative process can be identified.

Motivation has a direct influence on perceptual interpretation. Individuals enduring situations of extreme physical stress and hardship may hallucinate objects as they seek relief. The man crawling through the desert under a blazing sun 'sees' an oasis before him when in reality all around him is sand. Motivation effects (the disequilibriation of the biogenic drives of hunger and thirst) cause dramatic and futile misinterpretation of incoming information, and sand and shadows are perceived as water and trees. A number of studies have been concerned with the effects of food deprivation on perception. Sandford (1936) deprived subjects of food for periods of up to four hours, and then showed them ambiguous pictures. As the period of food deprivation increased, so did the tendency to 'see' food or food-related objects. In a follow-up study a year later he increased the food deprivation period to a maximum of twenty-four hours and obtained similar results, together with a waxing and waning of the frequency with which food or food-related objects were reported which accorded with the subject's usual eating cycles: there was a more marked effect at times when the subject normally ate. Gilchrist and Nesberg (1952) found that hungry and thirsty subjects perceived pictures of food and drink as being brighter than pictures of other objects, and that the estimates of brightness increased steadily until a period of eight-hour water deprivation had been reached. Subjects were then allowed to eat and drink as much as they pleased, and their estimates of the brightness of the food and drink pictures immediately fell to the base levels recorded at the beginning of the experiment.

Many studies of the effects of motivation and emotion on perception have been concerned with children, probably because such effects appear to be more dramatic and marked with these subjects, and it has been termed *altruistic perception*. Bruner and Goodman (1947) found that poor children have a greater tendency to over-estimate the size of monetary coins than wealthy children. This was also demonstrated by Lambert *et al.* (1949), who divided seventy-one nursery-school children into experimental and control groups. Subjects were asked to turn a handle to obtain a poker chip, and the experimental group could exchange these for sweets but not the control group. At first, both groups over-estimated the size of the poker chips (measured by having the children adjust a spot of light till it appeared the same size as the chip when viewed from a few feet away) by approximately 5%. This remained constant for the control group, but rose to 13% for the experimental group. Solley and Haigh (1958) studied a special kind of anticipation in children – the excitement of Christmas. Children aged between four and eight were asked to draw pictures of Santa Claus periodically during the month before Christmas, and for two weeks afterwards. As Christmas approached the children drew Santa as bigger, nearer and with a more elaborate costume and a larger bag of toys. After Christmas, the drawings became smaller and the bag of toys shrank to nothing.

The role of expectancy in interpreting stimuli is illustrated by Minturn and Bruner (1951), who presented a series of numbers sequentially to one group of subjects while to a second group they exposed a series of letters. When the figure

was shown to the first group they perceived 13, but the second group reported B. A control group who were given a mixed series perceived the ambiguous figure as B or 13 with equal frequency. A similar experiment by Siipola (1935) gave a series of words and letters to one group of subjects so that they came to expect animal words, and a different series to a second group which led them to expect nautical terms. The first group perceived 'sael', presented tachistoscopically, as 'seal', while the second group perceived it as 'sail'. All subjects were then given skeleton words such as 'oat' and asked to fill them out to make other words. The animal group tended to produce such words as 'goat' and the nautical group 'boat', though neither group could explain why they had done so, demonstrating the unconscious and powerful influence of factors which have been grouped together under the term 'set'.

Reward affects perception in adults as well as in children, and Schafter and Murphy (1943) showed that subjects perceived a previously rewarded perception more rapidly than a previously punished one. The experiment was concerned with the perception of two juxtaposed faces (see Fig. 9). Whenever **A** was shown, the subject was rewarded with money, but when **B** was shown, money was

9. *The effect of reward and punishment on perception of juxtaposed faces*

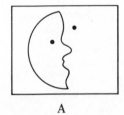 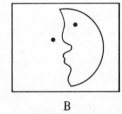 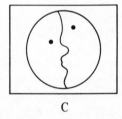

A   B   C

withdrawn as punishment. He was encouraged to learn to name and recognize these faces, though no attention was drawn to the fact that one earned reward and the other punishment. Finally, when **C** was presented, it was found that the rewarded face was perceived more than the punished one.

Interpretative sets are influenced by motivation, by expectancy and by reward and punishment; the role of emotion has been shown to be important too. Lazarus and McCleary (1951) examined the emotional effect on perception caused by punishment. Subjects were given an electric shock when presented with certain nonsense syllables, and their galvanic skin responses were recorded as a measure of anxiety. (The galvanic skin response, or GSR, is the electrical resistance of the skin. The greater the amount of sweat produced, the lower the skin's electrical resistance. An increase in anxiety produces more sweat, so the skin's electrical resistance, measured by a small battery-powered device, will decrease, and thus provides a fairly reliable indicator of anxiety level.) Subsequently, these syllables, along with other neutral syllables, were briefly exposed tachistoscopically, and although subjects failed to *consciously* perceive many of the syllables which had previously been followed by an electric shock, they did give an appreciable galvanic skin response to them. It appears that recognition occurs before a perception comes into conscious awareness, and that in this case a stimulus with painful associations was sometimes anticipated before it was fully perceived.

A well-known group of studies on the effects of emotion on perception are those on so-called *perceptual defence* and *perceptual sensitization*. Perceptual defence was first put forward by Freud as a mechanism whereby individuals protect themselves from potentially disturbing events by failing to perceive them at a conscious level; it is an example of a *defence mechanism* (see Chapter 8). The classic findings of Bruner and Postman (1947) are that there is a reliable difference between the times taken to recognize ordinary words and those of sexual or otherwise taboo words, when presented tachistoscopically. Some studies have shown recognition of taboo words to be faster, displaying perceptual sensitization, and others showed a slower recognition effect or perceptual defence. There has been considerable criticism of these studies, and it has been argued that in the perceptual defence experiments, subjects do perceive taboo words as quickly as non-emotional words, but may be too embarrassed to report them without hesitation to the experimenter. Bitterman and Kniffin (1953) found no perceptual defence effect if subjects were allowed to write down what they perceived, rather than reporting verbally. When presented at threshold level, words may only be perceived in fragments, from which their true identity is guessed; for example, a subject may see 'Ele–ant' and correctly guess 'Elephant'. It is understandable that he would be less willing to make a guess at a taboo word under normal conditions. It is also argued that some subjects may believe that such taboo words would not be used in scientific experiments' and may thus think that they were mistaken in their perception and not report it. Also, the level of familiarity with the taboo words may vary between subjects, and may not be as rapidly recognized because of lack of familiarity: 'Several of the words used were sexual slang words, such as "balls" and "screw"; and whether or not observers are familiar with them must depend on their particular social experience' (Vernon, 1962.)

These criticisms demonstrate the difficulty of separating such processes as perception, learning, memory and socialization. Although this book contains separate chapters on each of these topics, this is only done to simplify communication with the reader; in reality all of these factors continually interact to have an effect on behaviour.

An illuminating investigation of perceptual defence and sensitization was made by Carpenter *et al.* (1956). Adults were asked to complete sentences relating to sex, hostility or feelings of inadequacy, and their responses were classified as to whether they showed sensitivity (characterized by preoccupation, over-reaction and so on) or repression (characterized by blocking, avoidance and other symptoms). It was found that subsequent exposure to words relating to sex and hostility produced more rapid perception than did exposure to neutral words for those subjects who had been classified as sensitizers, and less rapid perception by the repressers. There was no reliable effect for words relating to feelings of inadequacy. Repressers apparently protected themselves by blocking perception of emotionally threatening words. A further convincing demonstration of this effect was given by McGinnies (1949), when subjects' psychogalvanic responses were recorded as sexual and taboo words were exposed tachistoscopically. Not only were subjects slower to perceive the taboo words, but for these the psycho-galvanic response was higher than for neutral words, indicating that the subjects' arousal levels had increased. This is further evidence that words can be recognized before they reach consciousness, as is the evidence of Dixon (1958), who found a psycho-galvanic response to sexual words which could not have been consciously perceived because they were presented subliminally, or below the absolute threshold for perception. (The concept of perceptual defence is also discussed in Chapter 4 in relation to memory.)

Other studies have investigated the effect of emotional and individual differences on perception. Eriksen (1951) showed that aggressive subjects were quicker to perceive pictures showing aggressive acts than were low-aggression control subjects. Those similarly identified as having a strong 'success and mastery' desire perceived words related to success at a lower level of illumination than did subjects with a lesser drive (McClelland and Liberman, 1949). An interesting study by Eriksen and Brown (1956) asked subjects to estimate how well they thought they would do in a particular perceptual task. After completing it, half were told they had done better than they predicted, and half that they had done worse. A series of words were then presented, four of which related to success ('excellent', 'succeed', 'perfection', 'winner'), four to failure ('unable', 'failure', 'obstacle', 'defeat') and four to striving ('improve', 'achieve', 'strive', 'compete'). The success words were perceived more quickly by the 'success' group, and the failure words more quickly by the 'failure' group, though there was no significant difference between the groups with regard to the striving words.

Set in hypothesis testing

In considering set as an interpreter it must be remembered that between the reception of a stimulus and its conscious appearance as a structured perception there is a short, but very active, stage of what Woodworth called 'trial and check' and what Gregory (after Bruner and Postman) has termed 'hypothesis testing':

> When a new percept is in the making – when an obscure stimulus complex is being deciphered or when the meaning of a cue or sign is being discovered – an elementary two-stage process is observable. It is a trial and check. The trial stage is a tentative reading of the sign, a tentative decipherment of the puzzle, a tentative characterization of the object; and the check phase is an acceptance or rejection, a positive or negative reinforcement of the tentative perception [Woodworth, 1947].

It is now possible to understand fully what Gregory means by 'We may say that a perceived object *is a hypothesis*, *suggested* and *tested* by sensory data' (our italics). The vital fact for this discussion is that the *order* in which the hypotheses are put up for trial to check their interpretative viability is determined by sets. Referring to one class of sets (those caused by expectancy), Solley and Murphy (1960) say: 'Strong perceptual expectations provide a sort of right-of-way into consciousness by determining which structures and meanings will be tried first.' The influence of sets can thus be seen at the very core of the making of a perception.

A well-known example illustrating the role of set in hypothesis testing is the Ames distorted room. The room was cleverly constructed by Ames (1952) so that when viewed with one eye from a particular point, it appears as a normal room. In reality the left wall is considerably longer than the right, and the floor slopes down into the far left corner. The most interesting feature of the room is

10.*The Ames distorted room* (courtesy of Eastern Daily Press, Norwich)

not that it is possible to present a retinal image which fools the eye, but what happens when people or objects are placed in the far corners.

People in the room appear strange, one being extraordinarily large and the other abnormally small. The figure demonstrates that perceptual inputs are *interpreted*, and that in this case we come to the wrong conclusions. Past experience teaches that two main causes of large discrepancies in retinal sizes are that the objects are themselves grossly different in size – one a giant, the other a dwarf – or that one of them is located at a greater distance away than the other from the observer. Either or both may be causing the discrepancy, and here we make the wrong interpretation and are fooled. We are 'tricked' because the construction and painting of the room make it appear as an ordinary room, and we thus expect and conclude that it is a rectangular shape with the implicit corollary that the back wall is flat, and hence the people are equidistant from us. The hypothesis of different distances is therefore rejected, leaving the deduction that the people are markedly different in size. The 'wrong' hypothesis has been tried, checked and accepted.

Another clever device constructed by Ames was his rotating trapezoidal window. This is a flat, non-rectangular window-like object which has shadows painted on it and is rotated on a central spindle. The illusion it creates as it rotates constantly in one direction is one of oscillation, and the 'window' appears to turn in first one direction and then the other. Again, we adopt an inappropriate interpretation, believing the object before us to be an ordinary rectangular window angled away from our line of vision, because expectancy and past experience have offered an inappropriate hypothesis which has been accepted. The most dramatic part of this demonstration comes when a metal tube is placed through the 'window', and as the two rotate together strange perceptions occur as the bar's movement (which we see and perceive correctly) appears to contradict the movement of the window (which we misperceive). Subjects frequently report feeling anxious and upset when shown this demonstration, as if they could not really believe what they are seeing, but the explanation is that they do not possess the sets necessary to fit the perceptual information.

Engel (1956) actually shows hypothesis testing working in an experiment in which two figures are presented tachistoscopically, a naked person to one eye and the same person clothed to the other eye. Some subjects reported seeing the naked figure 'getting dressed', others saw the clothed person do a 'strip-tease'. Avoiding speculation on why some saw the naked figure first and others the clothed figure first, it appears that under these conditions the hypothesis testing was so active that apparent movement was seen, and there was a rapid shift in hypotheses, only finally ending in a stabilized perception. Hypothesis testing can be demonstrated by concentrating on Figure 11. Here both possible interpretations of the figure (a vase and two faces) are equally good and likely, so that perception alternates between the two, as first one hypothesis, and then the other, is entertained.

Finally, a note about the rigidity of sets and their resistance to removal. Blake and Vanderplas (1950) presented words very quietly to subjects, at barely threshold levels, and repeated them at gradually increasing volume until they were correctly perceived. If a subject misperceived a word at low levels of stimulation (for example, if he heard 'turn' for 'learn'), it needed much louder presentation for

11. *A vase or two faces?*

him to perceive it correctly and reappraise his perception than it did for subjects who had not made the initial error. Once having decided on what we are perceiving, we are set to continue perceiving it in that form, which is resistant to change.

Morgan and King (1971) note, significantly, that of all the factors determining perception, set is probably the most important. 'It is mainly our sets and expectancies that direct and order the successions of our perceptual experiences. Without them, perceiving would be largely at the mercy of random fluctuations in the environmental stimuli.'

The nature/nurture debate on perception

Philosophers since earliest times have considered the question of whether our behaviour develops as a result of experience, or whether it arises fully formed without the need for environmental stimulation. When experimental techniques developed, psychologists too began to debate this problem. One group, the empiricists, believed that behaviour develops as a result of the effects of the environment, while their opponents, the nativists, believed that environmental factors play little or no part in development. In modern times, very few psychologists take extreme empiricist or nativist positions, most believing that both innate and environmental factors are necessary for normal development. However, some debate still continues over the relative importance of these factors, and this section examines some of the research which has been carried out in the field of perception. It is an area of research which is rich in different types of study design, and will also serve to highlight some of the problems of methodology and interpretation which are found in many areas of psychological research.

Deprivation studies
If a subject is isolated from visual stimulation from birth, and is then exposed to it for the first time in adulthood, will he be able to perceive normally? Empiricists would argue that he will not, since he has had no visual experience, and must begin to learn to perceive. Nativists, on the other hand, would argue that having been deprived of visual stimulation will have no effect, since perceptual abilities are innate. Many studies have been carried out on animals, and a few have been conducted on humans who have gained their sight for the first time in adulthood.

A.N. Riesen (1950) deprived two chimpanzees of light for the first sixteen months of life, except for several forty-five second intervals of light per day, required for feeding purposes. When tested at sixteen months, the chimpanzees showed pupil constriction to light, and could be startled by sudden intense illumination. They did not, however, blink when threatening movements were made towards their faces, or show any interest in their toys unless they happened to touch them with some part of their bodies. One of the chimps was then exposed to limited amounts of light until twenty-one months of age, and developed normal object recognition. The other, who was kept in the dark until thirty-three months, developed inferior object-recognition abilities. When placed in normal light, his perceptual abilities improved slightly, then declined. Weiscrantz (1956) discovered that these visual problems were probably caused by the failure of the chimpanzees' retinas to develop the normal number of retinal cells. This seems to indicate that light is necessary to allow the normal physiological development of the eye and visual pathways.

Riesen reared another chimpanzee in a transluscent mask, which allowed only one and a half hours per day of diffuse and unpatterned light to enter the eye, for the first seven months of its life. This chimpanzee also displayed inferior perceptual abilities. For example, it took six days of receiving two electric shocks per day from a yellow and black striped disc, before it even whimpered when the disc was shown. These results suggest that light is necessary for normal visual development, but also that patterned visual images are required too, and demonstrate the need for environmental stimulation in the development of perception. However, a two-day-old infant chimpanzee who was given practice at avoiding the shock disc had still not developed avoidance behaviour after one month. This suggests that some kind of maturational process may also be involved, since the infant had had more experience of the disc than the seven-month-old chimps. It should also be noted that Riesen's experiments were often carried out on single subjects. Although this does not invalidate them, it could make generalization of the results less valid, particularly if the attempt is made to relate the findings to humans.

Hubel and Wiesel (1962) found similar effects to Riesen's, in cats who had been reared in full or partial blindfolds. Examination of the connections of the retinal cells showed that their *receptive fields* (see p. 190) had not developed normally. Blakemore and Cooper (1966) examined the effect on cats' receptive-field development of rearing them in an environment, actually a large drum, which allowed them to see only vertical lines. On testing at maturity, such animals would reach out to touch a moving pointer held vertically, but would not do so if it were held horizontally. Tests showed that only receptive fields which responded to vertical lines had developed, and that the cats were 'blind' to horizontal lines. However, this result does not show conclusively that line recognition develops solely through environmental action: it may be that receptive fields for all angles of line are present at birth, and that those for horizontal lines are 'taken over' by the vertical fields.

Held and Hein (1965) investigated the effects of deprivation on kittens' abilities to guide their movements through vision. Their apparatus (see Fig. 12) gave both kittens the same amount of the same type of visual experience. However, the 'active' kitten could move itself around, and its movements were transmitted, through a series of pulleys, to the 'passive' kitten. The kittens were given three hours of exposure to light on the apparatus each day, for several weeks. When tested for 'paw-eye co-ordination', it was found that the 'active' kittens were markedly superior; for example, after thirty hours' exposure, all the 'active' kittens would show visually guided paw placement – that is, if gently lowered towards the ground, they

12. *The apparatus used by Held and Hein* (from R. Held,
     'Plasticity in sensory-motor systems'; copyright © November
     1965 by Scientific American, Inc. All rights reserved)

would show the response typical of normally reared kittens, that of
extending the paws. None of the passively reared kittens showed this
ability after thirty hours' exposure.

There exists, however, a problem of interpretation with these deprivation studies. We cannot say for certain that deprived animals
do not perceive, only that they do not *behave* as if they perceive.
Their perceptual processes may indeed have developed in the absence of patterned light stimulation, but because these abilities have
not become linked to the animals' behaviour, they are not evident to
the experimenter. Psychology has been defined as the scientific study
of behaviour and experience. In this case, the behavioural aspects
seems to have been studied well, but, in the case of animals at least,
we have not even begun to study their experience of visual life.
However, studies of humans who have been deprived of visual
stimulation and who can talk may give some insight into human
experience of perception, since an adult who has been blind from
birth and then gains sight can describe what he sees.

Gregory and Wallace (1963) reported the case of a man whom
they called S.B., who received sight after a corneal graft operation at
the age of fifty-two.

When bandages were first removed from his eyes, so that he was no longer blind, he heard the voice of the surgeon. He turned to the voice, and saw nothing but a blur. He realised that this must be a face, because of the voice, but he could not see it. He did not suddenly see the world of objects as we do when we open our eyes.

But within a few days he could use his eyes to good effect. He could walk along the hospital corridors without recourse to touch – he could even tell the time from a large wall clock, having all his life carried a pocket watch with no glass, so that he could feel the time from its hands. He would get up at dawn, and watch from his window the cars and trucks pass by. He was delighted with his progress, which was extremely rapid.

When he left the hospital, we took him to London and showed him many things he never knew from touch, but he became curiously dispirited. At the zoo he was able to name most of the animals correctly, having stroked pet animals and enquired how other animals differed from the cats and dogs he knew by touch. He was also of course familiar with toys and models. He certainly used his previous knowledge from touch, and reports from sighted people to help him name objects by sight, which he did largely by seeking their characteristic features. But he found the world drab, and was upset by flaking paint and blemishes on things. He liked bright colours, but became depressed when the light faded. His depressions became marked, and general. He gradually gave up active living, and three years later he died.

His judgements of size and distance were good, provided that he was familiar with objects; and he could recognize objects visually if he had had experience of them by touching them while blind. However, he seemed to have great difficulty in identifying objects visually if he had not touched them. A year after the operation, he was still unable to draw the front of a bus, although the rest of the drawing was well executed.

Although such studies permit at least a little investigation into the experience of visual life, they do not much help to solve the nature/nurture debate. Adults gaining their sight are not the same as babies, all of whose sensory systems may be undeveloped. Adults have other well-developed senses, such as hearing, touch and smell, to give them clues. In addition, adults' previous learning may hinder visual learning, because people tend to find it easier to use the system they already know than the one they do not. Gregory and Wallace's subject continued to prefer to use touch to vision. Finally, the emotional disturbance experienced by some of the subjects may affect their perception, and thus make the results unreliable to an unknown extent.

Readjustment studies

The logic behind these studies is that, if it is found to be possible to learn to perceive the world in a different way from normal, then this suggests that perception can be learnt.

Sperry (1943) rotated the eyes of salamanders through 180 degrees, so that images on the retina were upside down, compared with the normal eye. Animals treated in this way would, when presented with stimuli moving upwards, move their heads downwards. Such animals either had to be force-fed, or fed in the dark, as they did not show any reduction in these inappropriate movements over time.

Hess (1956) put prisms on chickens, which shifted the image by seven degrees either to the left or to the right. Chickens wearing left-shifting prisms always pecked to the left of the grain they were looking at, and showed no signs of being able to readjust to the shift produced by the prisms.

The evidence from animal studies suggests that they are not very adaptable to changes in the visual image, but experiments with humans seem to show that humans may indeed be capable of readjustment. This points up one of the dangers of extrapolating evidence from animal studies directly to humans. Stratton (1897) wore an inverting telescope on one eye, with the other eye covered (wearing inverting lenses on both eyes is too much of a strain, particularly to the eye-movement muscles). At all times when he was not wearing the lens, he covered both eyes. Over the eight days of the experiment, Stratton found that he gradually came to notice the inversion of his visual world less and less. For example, on the fifth day he reported that he could walk around in his house without bumping into furniture, and noted that when he was moving, his surroundings looked normal, but if he stopped and concentrated on looking at them, they appeared to be upside down. His body, too, appeared to be inverted, but Stratton reported that he automatically tended to 'ignore' this misleading information, and to rely instead on the sense of body feeling (*kinaesthesis*) which was of course unaffected by the lenses.

J. and J.K. Peterson (1938) used inverting lenses on both eyes, and found broadly similar results to Stratton's, except that the degree of readjustment was not as great. Also subjects re-tested with the lenses after a lapse of eight months immediately showed the changes to movements which had developed in the original trials.

The investigations of Stratton and the Petersons suggest that perception in humans may be modifiable, but they also leave an element of doubt. In the Petersons' work, even fourteen days' exposure to an inverted world did not produce full adaptation. In addition, there appears to be the possibility that what was learnt was not a new way of perceiving the world, but a new set of body movements which were applicable to it.

However, Kohler (1962) carried out an investigation which does demonstrate some adaptation. He wore goggles in which the left half of each lens was red, and the right half green. At first, his visual world looked red when he looked to the left, and green when he looked to the right. After only a few hours, this apparent division was no longer so noticeable. After a few days, when the goggles were removed, Kohler found that each time he turned his eyes to the left, the world looked green – the complementary colour to that of the goggles. This adaptation must have been by the brain, because the lenses were static, and Kohler's eyes could move freely, hence the lens colours were rarely on the same places on his retinas. These brain-induced after-images suggest that the brain had been 'cancelling out' the artificial colours produced by the goggles by 'injecting' the complementary colour, which was seen for a short time after the goggles were removed.

That humans can learn to perceive is by no means proved, and even if it were, it would not solve the nature/nurture controversy. These experiments were all carried out on adults, and to show that an adult's perceptual system can learn is by no means the same thing as saying that a baby's perceptual system has to learn.

Neonate (newborn) studies

Despite their inability to talk and describe their experience, it seems logically necessary to study the perception of infants in order to produce evidence with which to silence the debate. But even here, there are problems. First, there is the problem of 'experience versus behaviour' which bedevilled the animal deprivation studies. Secondly, there is the problem that if infants do not show a particular perceptual ability, this does not prove that such abilities have to be learnt: some abilities may not be present at birth, but develop some time afterwards through the action of genetic 'time-switches' involved in maturational processes. Finally, it seems that 'perception' is not a single ability; rather it is a series of abilities, for example the ability to perceive colour, shape, distance and movement, to recognize objects, and so on. It is possible that some of these abilities may be largely innate, while others are largely due to the effects of experience. To ask whether perception is innate or learnt is thus too general a question; we must specify just what aspect of perception we are considering.

Remember that William James had described the perceptual world of the neonate as 'one blooming, buzzing confusion'. Some recent work, however, suggests that infants are by no means as incapable as had been thought. The 'classic' experiment in this field was conducted by Gibson and Walk in 1960 (see Fig. 13). A baby was placed on the central plank and its mother called to it alternately from the 'deep' and 'shallow' sides. The infants used as subjects, who were aged between six and fourteen months, would crawl to their

13. Gibson and Walk's visual cliff apparatus

Shallow side   Baby   Deep side

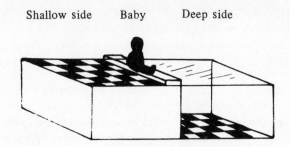

mothers over the 'shallow' side, but would not move over the 'deep' side. Occasionally babies would fall onto the glass over the 'deep' side; they would then show no fear until they looked down. They were obviously relying on visual information to such an extent that it overrode touch information. It seems then that if infants of this age fall down steps and off chairs it is not because they do not see the depth but because they have yet to develop adequate control of their movements.

Other animals tested on the visual cliff all similarly demonstrated an ability to judge depth. Day-old chicks never strayed onto the 'deep' side, lambs and kids placed on the 'deep' side refused to stand, and kittens either froze or circled backwards aimlessly. Rats, however, based their depth perception more on touch than vision, and showed no preference for either the 'deep' or the 'shallow' side. When their whiskers – their main touch sensors – were trimmed, they were forced to use vision, and also refused to move onto the 'deep' side.

Gibson and Walk suggest that the main way in which depth is detected in this experiment is through motion parallax (see p. 55). These results suggest, but still do not prove, that depth perception is innate in humans: the babies were aged between six and fourteen months, and may have been able to learn depth perception during that time.

Bower (1966) gave some indication about whether size constancy (see pp. 51–2) was innate or not; his experiment neatly contrasts the predictions of nativists and empiricists. An empiricist would argue that an infant would respond to the size and shape of objects

14. General layout of Bower's experiment

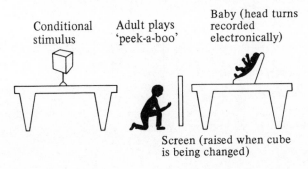

as these images appeared to his eyes and would not show perceptual constancy, because he would not yet have had time to learn it. A nativist, on the other hand, would argue that because perception is innate the infant should show perceptual constancy.

In Figure 14 a two-week-old baby is placed on the table in a comfortable cot from which he can see an object. He comes to learn that if he turns his head to one side he is rewarded by an adult playing 'peek-a-boo' and tickling him. This is called *operant conditioning* (see p. 91). Once the baby is conditioned to pay attention to the stimulus object in this way the stimulus can be changed, and the number of head turns can then be used as a measure of how similar he considers any new stimulus object is to the one he has been conditioned to look at. Using the different-sized cubes shown in Figure 15, placed at their stated distances, Bower found that the infant responded most to the cube of the same size as the original cube, even when it was moved further away than it had been during the conditioning trials; next most prefered was the cube which was the same distance away as the original cube but a different size; and the least preferred was that which was a different size and at a different distance, even though this projected the same retinal image as the original object.

Empiricists would predict that the order of preference for the test stimuli should be: most preferred, stimulus 3; next preferred, stimulus 2; and least preferred, stimulus 1. Nativists, however, would predict the reverse order: 1 most; then 2; and 3 least. In fact, the nativist predictions were firmly upheld by the results of the experiment, suggesting that the baby already had size constancy.

15. The stimulus figures for size constancy used in Bower's experiment

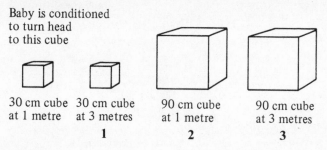

Baby is conditioned
to turn head
to this cube

30 cm cube	30 cm cube	90 cm cube	90 cm cube
at 1 metre	at 3 metres	at 1 metre	at 3 metres
1		**2**	**3**

The fact that the baby was able to recognize the original cube at a different distance also suggests that it had some form of depth or distance perception, as well as size constancy. If the empiricist view had been correct and the baby in the experiment had chosen the ninety-centimetre cube at three metres, this would have given the same retinal image as the original cube; that it did not, therefore, gives strong support to the nativist view.

There are several experiments which show that babies can distinguish patterns and that they prefer some patterns to others. In 1961, R.L. Fantz found that a bull's-eye pattern was preferred to stripes, checks and geometrical shapes, and that a drawing of a human face was preferred to all these patterns, and to a jumbled-up drawing of a face (see Fig. 16). Babies aged between one and fifteen weeks prefer to look at relatively complicated patterns: they are perhaps innately 'programmed' to look at face-like patterns more. However, this experiment has been criticized because the human face was more complicated than the geometrical patterns, and the babies may have preferred the complexity to the 'meaning' of the pictures. The babies still preferred the organized to the scrambled face, though there is the possibility that this was more evident in the older neonates than in the younger.

Using the same procedures as outlined earlier, Bower (1966) showed that eight-week-old babies could already make use of a sophisticated perceptual rule, the *continuation rule*. This rule helps in the interpretation of objects with broken contours, and works on the basis that if the contours on each side of the break have the same orientation, they should be treated as the same contour. Thus in

16. Face shapes of the type used in Fantz's experiment

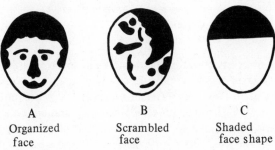

A	B	C
Organized face	Scrambled face	Shaded face shape

Figure 17 the triangle with the bar across it should be regarded as a triangle, if the baby possesses the continuation rule. Once the babies had been conditioned to respond to the top figure, they were shown the four lower figures, and the number of head turns to each of these figures again used as a measure of how similar to the top figure the babies perceived them to be. The results were clear. All the babies preferred figure A, suggesting that they had the continuation rule, since it is unlikely that they had had any experience of triangles before.

An interesting study, also by Bower (1977), shows how babies develop their abilities to reach out to grasp objects. Such an activity requires two main abilities: to locate both the object to be grasped and the baby's own hand; and to monitor the movements of the hand towards the object, which requires the baby to pay attention to both object and hand at the same time. Bower used some babies

17. *The stimulus figures used in Bower's study of the continuation rule* (after T. Bower, *The Prceptual World of the Child*, p. 43, in

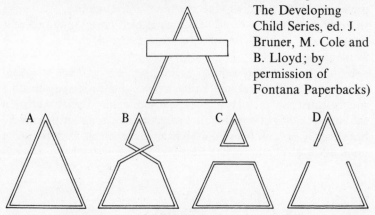

The Developing Child Series, ed. J. Bruner, M. Cole and B. Lloyd; by permission of Fontana Paperbacks)

We see the top figure as a triangle covered with a bar — like A rather than B, C or D. So does an eight-week-old baby.

aged less than five months and some aged seven months, and got them to wear prisms which displaced the image of the object in the same way as in Hess's experiment on page 78. When not wearing prisms, the under-five-month-old babies had great difficulty in monitoring their hand movements: whenever their hands came into their field of vision this apparently distracted their attention and the movement would stop, until they became 'bored' with their hands and noticed the object again. When wearing prisms they reached out towards the displaced image of the object, and not towards the object itself. Having failed to touch it, they pulled their hands back and tried again and again, becoming more frustrated with each try. It seems that they could not attend to both their hand position and the position of the object simultaneously. Seven-month-old babies, by contrast, when wearing the prisms, started to reach out in the wrong direction but quickly changed the path of their hands, to perform a smooth reaching operation which gained them the object. The change in direction of their hands seemed to occur when the image of the hand entered the visual field. These results seem to demonstrate that at some time, roughly between the ages of five and seven months, babies develop the ability to attend to two objects simultaneously. Note the word 'develop': we cannot say 'learn', because it may be that this presumably brain-mediated ability is the result of the maturation of the baby's brain. Because the ability was apparently not present before the age of five months does not necessarily mean that it has to be learnt.

Conclusions

The evidence presented so far gives a confused picture. Some results apparently support the nativists, and some the empiricists, but many experiments have drawbacks or shortcomings which mean that we cannot place too great a reliance on them. This sort of finding is common to many of the nature/nurture debates: there is a great deal of evidence, but no answers. At least partially, this seems to be a result of the question 'Is behaviour (or perception) innate or learnt?' Most psychologists now agree that both factors are essential; to overstate the point somewhat, isn't even our ability to learn (though not what is learnt) innate? If the ability to learn is innate, where does this leave the nature/nurture debate? Many people now refer to the question of whether an ability is innate or learnt as a 'non-question', a question which is not amenable to a solution.

This area of research has also thrown up some interesting methodological considerations. Notice how the type of study used seems to give consistent answers. Thus deprivation studies seem to support the empiricists, while neonate study results emphasize innate abilities. This has made any attempt at an answer even more difficult, and has required that a wide range of different experimental techniques be employed. The same effect, incidentally, is also found in studies of brain function, on page 173.

Finally, it should perhaps be pointed out that although this chapter has concentrated almost exclusively on the perception of inanimate objects, much of this discussion can be applied to the perception of human beings. The perception of ourselves and others is considered in Chapter 14, and the perception of other people's words and deeds has an important part to play in *conformity* (see Chapter 10) as well as attitude formation and attitude change (see Chapters 12 and 13).

Further reading

Bower, T.G.R. (1977), *The Perceptual World of the Child*, Fontana/Open Books

Gibson, J.J. (1950), *The Perception of the Visual World*, Houghton Mifflin

Gregory, R. (1977), *Eye and Brain* (3rd ed.), Weidenfeld and Nicolson

Gregory, R. (1970), *The Intelligent Eye*, Weidenfeld and Nicolson

Solley, C.M. and Murphy, G. (1960), *The Development of the Perceptual World*, Basic Books

Vernon, M.D. (1962), *The Psychology of Perception*, Penguin

3 Learning and conditioning

An area of psychology which has also been particularly influential in the development of the subject as a science is the model of basic learning called *conditioning*. *Classical conditioning* was established by the Russian psychologist Ivan Pavlov and was, at one time, the fundamental unit in behaviourism. Some thirty years later it was challenged for supremacy by the introduction of *operant conditioning* by B.F. Skinner. This paradigm has been applied in such forms as behaviour modification and programmed learning. The second part of this chapter deals with more complex forms of learning and the factors affecting learning.

The human ability for learning underlies behaviour throughout life, and the amount learned by any individual during his lifetime is very great. Learning may be defined as a relatively permanent change in behaviour, caused by a reorganization of habits, skills and tendencies which already exist. It therefore follows that changes in behaviour due to maturation, or to injury such as brain damage, cannot be defined as learning.

As mentioned above, the simplest kind of learning, conditioning, or *response learning*, has two distinct types, classical conditioning and operant conditioning. However, these can only inadequately explain more complex types of learning, and indeed some psychologists argue that even in classical conditioning what is learned is not merely a response to a stimulus, but an anticipation of a stimulus, and that it is the anticipation which produces the response, rather than the stimulus. Other learning theories have been proposed which attempt to explain human learning more satisfactorily than either classical or operant conditioning.

Classical conditioning

Although this theory is usually attributed to the Russian physiologist Ivan Pavlov (1911), it was actually first used by E.B. Twitmeyer in 1904, and it is sometimes referred to as *Pavlovian conditioning* or *respondent behaviour*. Classical conditioning is exclusively concerned with *reflexes*, or automatic behavioural responses which are triggered by specific stimuli. A common example is the knee-jerk reflex, which will only occur in response to the particular stimulus of a tap on the knee. Once the knee is tapped the reflex cannot be prevented, but occurs quite automatically. Other types of reflexes include eye blinks, pupil contraction, salivary reflexes, and many more.

Pavlov used the salivary reflex in his conditioning experiments. The reflex is triggered by the sight or smell of food, and is an automatic response to such a stimulus. The term '*response*' refers to any action on the part of an organism, including movements, thoughts or glandular reactions, which is the result of receiving a stimulus. Humans display the salivary reflex response when, for example, passing a baker's shop makes the mouth water.

The salivary reflex response is an *unconditional response*, that is, a natural response, because it is triggered by an *unconditional stimulus* – a natural stimulus, such as food.

18.

Food   ⟶   Salivation
(unconditional stimulus)   (unconditional response)
UCS   UCR

Pavlov used dogs as experimental subjects, and began sounding a buzzer immediately before food was presented to the animal, thus pairing the buzzer stimulus with the food stimulus.

19.

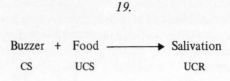

Buzzer + Food   ⟶   Salivation
CS   UCS   UCR

The buzzer is termed the *conditional stimulus* (CS) because it only produces the response of salivation on condition that it is paired with the food stimulus.

However, Pavlov found that after several pairings of the buzzer and the food (CS and UCS), the buzzer alone would trigger the salivary response. At this point, the salivation (formerly the UCR) then became the *conditional response* (CR), because it was a response to a conditional stimulus.

20.

Buzzer   ⟶   Salivation

CS   CR

The whole process is summarized in Figure 21.

21. A summary of Pavlov's conditioning process

UCS   ⟶   UCR

CS + UCS   ⟶   UCR

CS   ⟶   CR

Note that in classical conditioning, the process depends on the pairing, or association, of the UCS with the CS, and that the CS will only trigger the response if it is *contiguous with* (paired, or associated with) a natural UCS.

Pavlov also found that the basic conditioning process could be made more flexible by *generalization*. Other stimuli, if they are fairly similar to the original CS, will elicit the CR; for example, a buzzer with a slightly higher or lower pitch than the original, or perhaps a tapping noise, will probably elicit the salivary response in the example outlined above. In effect, the animal is able to generalize the response to different stimuli. Animals may also be taught to 'choose' between stimuli, to *discriminate*, by conditioning them to choose. If presentation of food is paired with presentation of, say, a circle shape, the animal becomes conditioned to salivate at the appearance of the circle. However, it may, and usually does, generalize the response, so that although perhaps originally a white circle was presented the animal also responds to other coloured circles. The animal can be conditioned to discriminate between these circles, to choose only the white one, by *reinforcing* only the presentation of the white circle stimulus – the other coloured circles are not reinforced by the accompaniment of food, and salivation at their appearance soon stops. Discrimination is a procedure frequently used in studying perception in animals. To check that an animal can perceive a triangle amongst several other shapes, it is first conditioned to salivate at the presentation of a triangle, and any generalization 'cut out' so that the animal responds to triangles only. Then the triangle, in turn with other shapes, is presented to the animal, and if it salivates only on the presentation of the triangle, then clearly it can discriminate between that shape and others.

The process of 'cutting out' unwanted generalizations or previously acquired conditioned responses is called *extinction*. If the conditioning procedure is altered so that the CS is repeatedly presented, but without the UCS, then the strength of the CR is gradually reduced until it does not appear in response to the CS. However, extinction is not a complete erasing of the CR but rather a learning to inhibit it – a new learning, in addition to the original conditioning. *Spontaneous recovery* of the initial CR is sometimes observed if, after extinction followed by a period of rest, an animal is again presented with the CS. Furthermore, re-conditioning is more rapid than the initial conditioning procedure, after a CR has been extinguished. Neither of these would be true if extinction was a complete erasing of the original conditioning.

Applications of classical conditioning

Eysenck (1965) lists cases of neurotic behaviour which have been cured by variations of classical conditioning. In one case a man's impotency was a reaction to a particular pattern of wallpaper. If the stimulus can be removed – as in this case, by changing the wallpaper – the reaction can be removed too. Another means of curing neurotic reactions is by de-conditioning or *desensitization* techniques, which in effect are extinction procedures. By presenting milder forms of the stimulus and allowing the patient to accustom himself to it gradually, usually in conjunction with some method of relaxation technique, it is then possible to gradually make the stimulus more and more like the original neurosis-producing stimulus. Eventually the patient becomes de-sensitized to this stimulus, the reaction is lost and the neurosis cured.

An alternative procedure based on conditioning is called *aversion therapy*, and is used to treat such problems as drug-addiction and alcoholism. The aim is to get the patient to develop an adverse reaction to the stimulus, and uses the vomiting reflex. An emetic such as apomorphine is used as the unconditional stimulus, and produces the unconditional response of vomiting. The emetic UCS is then paired with the conditional stimulus (alcohol, drugs or whatever is appropriate for the problem), and the two acting together produce the UCR of vomiting. Eventually, alcohol alone will produce the CR of vomiting. This vomiting is associated with alcohol, but note that it is *reflexes* which are conditioned – the patient cannot stop himself vomiting. Though he may realize that it is the emetic which causes the vomiting, the association between the UCS and the CS is automatic, and thinking about it cannot stop it.

It is possible that many 'irrational' emotional reactions to stimuli may be conditioned responses, perhaps learned before language was sufficiently developed in an individual for him to label and rationalize such learning. Some psychologists propose that such conditioning underlies that part of the mind often called the 'unconscious' (see Dollard and Miller, 1950).

It should be noted that in discussing classical conditioning, the correct term is condition*al* stimulus, condition*al* response, uncondi-tion*al* stimulus, and so on. Some textbooks use the word condi-tion*ed* instead, but this is a result of a mistranslation of Pavlov's original reports, which were written in Russian.

Operant conditioning

This type of conditioning relies not upon reflexes built into the organism, but upon behaviour emitted by the organism. It deals with the conditioning of behaviour, the shaping of behaviour, and its basis is the Law of Effect, first proposed by E.L. Thorndike in 1911 – acts which are rewarded (reinforced) tend to be repeated: acts which are not reinforced tend to die out.

B.F. Skinner (1938) was the psychologist who developed operant, or instrumental, conditioning, even developing machines for oper-ant conditioning which have been named 'Skinner boxes' after him. The experimental animal, when placed in this box, has to press a lever to obtain reinforcement in the form of food. In any situation an animal has a certain repertoire of behaviours which it displays, and a rat, for example, when placed in a Skinner box usually displays a pattern of exploratory behaviours such as scratching at the walls, sniffing, looking, moving around, and many others. Inside the Skinner box is a lever which, when pressed, opens a food-tray. In the course of its exploration, the rat will accidentally press the lever, and food will be presented. Pressing the lever is an accidental response, while the sight of the lever (a natural stimulus) is the unconditional stimulus. The UCS is the precursor of several responses, one of which is the accidental pressing of the lever, and this is immediately reinforced. This pattern of events leads to the sight of the lever becoming a conditional stimulus, and pressing it a conditional response. Eating the food remains the UCR, because it remains a natural response.

22.

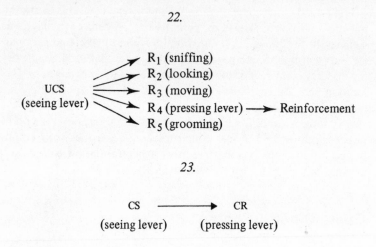

23.

Each time the rat presses the lever it is given food, so that pressing the lever is reinforced by the presentation of food. The animal comes to associate pressing the lever with receiving food, and after several presentations of reinforcement the rat presses the lever much more frequently than it did formerly. A typical bar-pressing graph (see Fig. 24) would show this increase in frequency, and perhaps extinction of the response if the CS was no longer presented, followed by spontaneous recovery (see the earlier discussion under classical conditioning).

Though the two types of conditioning can appear confusingly similar in some ways, they are, in fact, quite distinct. Responses learned via classical conditioning are *elicited*, triggered by specific stimuli. Responses learned via operant conditioning are sponta-

24. A typical bar-pressing graph

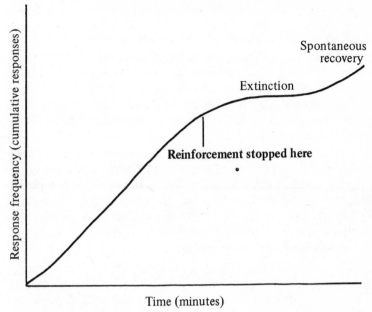

neously *emitted* responses, which act or operate on the environment in some way, and which are sometimes labelled as operant behaviour. Only after this spontaneous emission is an operant behaviour manipulated to increase or decrease its frequency of occurrence.

Responses made during classical conditioning are automatic, relatively fixed reflex responses to the UCS, while the responses made during operant conditioning may be much more varied and not initially closely related to the UCS. For example, the UCS may be seeing a lever, while the response to be reinforced could be running, pressing, sniffing, hopping, or something else.

In classical conditioning the conditional stimulus is the specific stimulus required for the reflex response, and is presented at intervals decided by the experimenter, in order to trigger the response. In operant conditioning the CS remains present all the time – part of a total situation – and it is the organism or subject who initiates the operant behaviour. In classical conditioning the UCS is itself the reinforcement, presented *before* the CS (for example, food presented before the buzzer), but in operant conditioning the reinforcement is presented *after* the cs, and is used to pick out one action from the animal's spontaneous behaviours and to ensure that it is repeated more frequently than his other behaviours. Finally, in classical conditioning the ucs is always paired with the cs, despite anything the subject might do – in other words the reinforcement (the ucs) is not contingent upon something the subject does. In operant conditioning the reinforcement *is* contingent upon the subject's behaviour, and operant conditioning is sometimes called *instrumental conditioning* because the subject himself is instrumental in obtaining reinforcement.

As in classical conditioning, if reinforcement ceases after the initial conditioning procedure the conditional response eventually dies out, but displays spontaneous recovery after a short rest period. However, in operant conditioning the rate at which a response extinguishes can be influenced, by altering the ways in which the reinforcement is presented. These different ways are called *schedules of reinforcement*, and are listed below:

Continuous reinforcement
This is the method used when setting up the conditioning procedure. Every desired response is reinforced, though if reinforcement is stopped extinction occurs fairly quickly.

Fixed-ratio reinforcement
The selected behaviour is not reinforced every time, but only after a fixed number of times – perhaps every third or fifth or tenth time, and so on. Pigeons in a Skinner box have been known to respond to an FR of 1:1,000 (that is, one reinforcement per 1,000 responses). This schedule gives a high rate of response, and displays fairly rapid extinction.

Fixed-interval reinforcement
The selected behaviour is reinforced after a fixed period of time, provided at least one desired response has been made during that time. This results in a slow rate of response, often only one response per period, with the animal often making a response only in the last few seconds of the period. In an FI 2 schedule, reinforcement would be made every two minutes, for example. Fairly rapid extinction is characteristic of this schedule too.

Variable-ratio reinforcement

Reinforcement is given after an *average* number of desired responses, for example a VR 10 schedule is one in which, on average, every ten responses gains one reinforcement. The actual reinforcement does not arrive on every tenth response, but there will be three reinforcements given in thirty responses. This schedule produces a steady rate of response, and the conditioning is resistant to extinction.

Variable-interval reinforcement

Reinforcement is given (say) every five minutes on average, though not on every fifth minute. A VI 5 reinforcement schedule would therefore include three reinforcements, though not given at the five-, ten- and fifteen-minute intervals. This schedule produces a steady rate of response, though not as frequent as the VR schedule, but resistance to extinction is very high.

It should be clear that in planning reinforcement schedules, sudden switches in reinforcement patterns must be avoided. One could not change from a continuous reinforcement schedule to, say, an FR 1,000 schedule in one leap. The process would have to be a gradual one from stage to stage, moving from continuous reinforcement to perhaps an FR 5 schedule, then on through other intermediate stages such as FR 10, FR 20, FR 50, FR 100, FR 200, FR 300, FR 500, and so on, up to FR 1,000.

All the schedules of reinforcement detailed above are to be found in general use, and though only applicable to one particular response, this response can be far more complex than a simple lever-pressing behaviour. Skinner, for example, has taught (or more properly 'conditioned') pigeons to play ping-pong, and to act as pilots in rockets. Such results are obtained by using the technique of *behaviour shaping*, reinforcing a subject's *successive approximations* to the desired behaviour.

Operant conditioning selects particular actions and, by reinforcing them, ensures that they are repeated. Once a particular action is conditioned, the animal tends to use it as the basis of its behaviour and elaborates on it, and behaviour shaping can be developed from this. For example, if we wish to condition a pigeon to turn around full-circle in a left-hand direction, then at first any movement the pigeon makes to the left would have to be reinforced. Once conditioned to make this leftward movement the pigeon will elaborate upon it, perhaps pecking at the floor, or fluttering its wings, or moving its head a little further to the left. Only the latter response would be reinforced, to produce two conditioned bits of behaviour – one, the pigeon turning perhaps fifteen degrees to the left, the second turning another twenty degress or so, so that with two reinforcements the pigeon has been conditioned to turn thirty-five degrees to the left. If we continue only to reinforce further movements which take the pigeon further to the left, eventually it will turn full circle. The whole process may take only thirty minutes or so. This is the principle underlying the more complex behaviours which Skinner conditioned. Behaviour which seems to be leading towards the required final behaviour is reinforced, so that the behaviour is repeated and expanded upon, gradually approaching the final type of behaviour required. In effect, each successive bit of behaviour approximates to the final type of behaviour required.

It was mentioned earlier that, as in classical conditioning, both extinction and spontaneous recovery occur in operant conditioning. In classical conditioning, extinction could be produced by removing the UCS (the reinforcer). The same procedure applies in operant conditioning, although removing reinforcement completely after, say, a VR 5 schedule will not extinguish the response as quickly as removing the reinforcer after an FR 5 schedule. And since extinction of the conditioned response occurs, so also can spontaneous recovery occur. Clark Hull, a leading behaviourist, proposed 'formulae' which he hoped would predict when a response would be made, and help to explain why spontaneous recovery occurs (see Fig. 25).

25. Clark Hull's formula

$$\text{Probability of response} = \text{Drive strength} \times \begin{array}{c}\text{Number of}\\\text{previously}\\\text{reinforced}\\\text{responses}\end{array} - \left[\text{Reactive inhibition} + \text{Conditioned inhibition} \right]$$

(Tend to *increase* probability of response)   (Tend to *decrease* probability of response)

Generalization can also occur, that is, the response can be made to stimuli similar to the original ones. The rat in the Skinner box, for example, may have been conditioned to press the right-hand lever, but may sometimes generalize the lever-pressing response to the left-hand lever. Discrimination can be achieved, and can overcome generalization, using the same principles as those in classical conditioning. An animal can be taught to discriminate between situations in which it will be reinforced for pressing the lever and those when it will not; for example, it can be conditioned to press the lever only when a little light above it is on. Try to work out the conditioning procedure which would achieve this.

Escape and avoidance learning

Reinforcement need not necessarily be limited to the presentation of positive reinforcements, such as the provision of food. *Negative reinforcement* – the removal of an unpleasant stimulus as soon as the required behaviour is achieved – can be an extremely effective conditioning technique. It is often confused with punishment, but the two are quite distinct. A negative reinforcement is applied to all actions except the required one, so that when the unpleasant stimulation stops, the animal's behaviour which caused it to stop is reinforced. Punishment, however, is an aversive (usually painful) stimulus, applied to a wrong response, not to all incorrect responses. Negative reinforcement is the removal of pain, while punishment is the infliction of pain. Skinner's attitude is that negative reinforcement is far more effective in conditioning than is punishment. (For a fuller discussion, see Borger and Seabourne (1966), *The Psychology of Learning*, pp. 39–44.)

Learning which is brought about by negative reinforcement is termed *escape learning*. If an animal is made to stand on an electrified grid and given a shock, and if it jumps or runs away from the grid when the shock stops, the animal learns to escape. Escape behaviour is reinforced by the cessation of the painful stimulation. However, this type of learning can only deal with very simple types of behaviour, since because the painful stimulation produces large emotional responses in the animal, it is unlikely to try to do anything other than escape. It is possible to develop more sophisticated behaviour by this method of conditioning – a type of behaviour called *avoidance learning*. If a warning buzzer is sounded a few seconds before the shock, or other negative reinforcement, is presented, the animal associates this signal with the shock. If in the interval between the buzzer and the shock the animal accidentally displays or approximates to a desired piece of behaviour – which might be

26. The formula for avoidance behaviour

Buzzer ⟶ Shock ⟶ Escape (animal gets away from shock)

Buzzer ⟶ Shock ⟶ Lever-press ⟶ Termination of shock

Eventually leading to:

Buzzer ⟶ Lever-press

pressing or moving closer to a lever, or any other behaviour specified by the experimenter – the shock is stopped. The chosen behaviour is therefore reinforced, and if necessary it can be shaped more precisely (see Fig. 26). Once avoidance behaviour has been established, it is very resistant to extinction, more so even than VI schedules. This form of learning is called avoidance learning because the animal learns to make a particular response in order to avoid a particular stimulus.

Secondary reinforcement

In most of the examples dealt with so far, food is involved as the reinforcer: it is the main, or *primary*, *reinforcer*. However, if another stimulus is paired with the primary reinforcer this second stimulus then acquires reinforcing properties itself. In the Skinner box, when the animal makes a correct response a food-tray 'clicks' into position with an audible click-sound. This sound becomes associated with food, since every time the animal hears the click food appears. Eventually the animal will perform the response required and accept the clicking noise alone as a reinforcer; that is, the click will have become a *secondary reinforcer*. Note, however, that secondary reinforcers are not usually as effective as primary ones, and will rapidly extinguish unless paired with a primary reinforcer. Behaviour in everyday life is often associated with one type of reinforcer or another, although these are seldom allocated in such a purposeful or controlled manner as in the Skinner box. The influence of this, almost accidental, conditioning on the process of socialization is discussed on pages 332–41; more formally controlled applications are considered below.

Some possible reasons for extinction

Perhaps the most obvious explanation of extinction is that, just as the reinforcing of a response increases the performance of that response, non-reinforcement will decrease it. Cognitive processes are thought to be the basis of this process. If a subject can perceive that a previously reinforced response no longer gains a reinforcement, the response will stop. Thus if the experimental situation is changed, for example by turning on a light in a Skinner box when reinforcement ceases, extinction is speeded up. In effect, anything which helps the subject to notice that reinforcement has ceased will speed up extinction. Conversely, any manipulations of the environment which prevent the subject noticing the lack of reinforcement will slow down the extinction process. This is what may happen in schedules of reinforcement. Imagine two separate rooms, A and B, each with a coffee machine. The coffee machine in room A always works correctly when a coin is inserted, but the machine in room B only works occasionally. The inhabitants of each room are not in contact with each other, and know only about the machine in their own room. Unknown to all of them one day both machines simultaneously break down. Which machine will be used most before the inhabitants realize that it has broken down? The inhabitants of room A will realize fairly quickly, for their machine has always worked properly before. The inhabitants of room B, however, have been used to their machine working only intermittently; consequently it will take them longer to realize that the machine has stopped altogether. The inhabitants of room B are, in effect, on an intermittent (VI or VR) schedule, and their behaviour is slow to extinguish. The inhabitants of room A are on continuous reinforcement, and their behaviour extinguishes quickly. Thus the perception that reinforcement is no longer available is an important factor in causing extinction.

The problem with cognitive explanations, though, is that they do not go far enough. Why should perception of non-reinforcement cause extinction? A hypothesis was put forward by Amsel (1962) which may shed some light on this problem. Imagine yourself again in room A with the 'continuous reinforcement' coffee machine: if you put in a coin after it has broken down, and do not receive coffee, how do you feel? In such circumstances, most people seem to feel a sense of frustration. But the inhabitants of room B will not feel so frustrated, because of the intermittent workings of their machine prior to its breakdown. Amsel believes that non-reinforcement leads to frustration, and it is this frustration response which inhibits the normal response and causes it not to be performed.

Amsel's experiment consisted of a simple maze with two goal boxes. Rats had to run down the first alleyway, and would receive food in the first goal box. They then had to run from there along a second alleyway to the second box to receive more food. Food was available in the second box on all trials, but was only available in the first box in 50% of the trials. These rats, compared with a control group who were reinforced in both boxes each time, showed significantly faster running in the second alley. Furthermore, they ran faster in the second alley when there was no food in the first box than they did when there was. How are these results to be explained? Amsel believes that non-reinforcement in the first box led to a build-up of frustration. He likens a frustration response to the response to an aversive stimulus: the rat attempts to get away from it. Consequently, if no food in box 1 causes frustration, the rat will run faster away from it, toward box 2. When next put into the first alley, although the rat will still run towards box 1, it will do so more slowly, since it associates box 1 with frustration, and the frustration response partially inhibits the running response towards the source of frustration.

Possibly both of these theories are correct. It may be that a non-reinforced animal perceives that reinforcement is not available; this causes frustration responses, which begin to inhibit the previous response, so that the animal slows its rate of performance, and, when enough frustration has built up to 'cancel out' the previous response, it extinguishes it.

Gray (1971) suggests a physiological mechanism for this system. He proposes that the reward system (see p. 185) also mediates active escape from punishment – in other words, that the same system is responsible for the effects of both positive and negative reinforcers. In addition to this system he postulates what he terms a 'stop' or 'frustrative non-reward' system. This inhibits both punished responses and those responses which were previously reinforced but are no longer. Just as the 'go' system equated pleasure/reward and relief/escape, so the 'stop' system mediates both fear and frustration responses. When the 'stop' system is firing, a characteristic EEG rhythm of 7·5–8·5 Hz is found near the hippocampus, and is known as the *hippocampal theta rhythm*. This firing can be strengthened by electrical stimulation at the same frequencies, or inhibited by using higher-frequency electrical stimulation or by an injection of the drug amylobarbital. Stimulation of the theta rhythm speeds up extinction, because in effect it stimulates the 'stop' system. Inhibition of the rhythm slows down extinction.

Interestingly, when a rat on continuous reinforcement had its hippocampal theta rhythm stimulated on 50% of the trials, the conditioned behaviour was more resistant to extinction than responses on a normal continuous reinforcement schedule. This seems to be because, on half of the trials, the 'stop' system was artificially activated, mimicking non-reinforcement, and the animal was in effect put on an intermittent schedule. Conversely, if the rhythm was inhibited on non-reinforced trials on an intermittent reinforcement schedule, the resultant behaviour extinguished as quickly as behaviour was established under normal continuous reinforcement. This was because the non-reinforced trials would normally have triggered the 'stop' system, but artificial inhibition of it prevented such trials having any effect.

Extinction, then, does not seem to be a passive affair: it appears likely that the subject's perception of non-reinforcement is important. And on a physiological level extinction does not seem to occur as a result of the waning of the reward system activity, but as a result of the increase in activity of the frustrative non-reward system.

Applications of operant conditioning

The efficiency of operant conditioning as a learning technique depends largely on the fact that required behaviour is reinforced *immediately*. There are two main applications of operant conditioning which make good use of this immediacy of reinforcement - *programmed learning* and *behaviour therapy*. In both cases the situation is carefully structured so that the subject is encouraged, usually unconsciously, to make certain responses, and of these the required responses are immediately reinforced and therefore repeated more often.

Programmed learning

The shaping of human behaviour is in some ways easier than the shaping of animal behaviour, because humans can be given quite complex instructions so that their initial repertoire of behaviours, from which certain responses will be selected for reinforcement, can be much nearer the required goals. For humans, too, the range of reinforcers is much wider, and can include more subtle ones than can be used with lower animals. In a learning situation, the knowledge that a correct response has been made, showing understanding of the problem, can, by producing a sense of satisfaction, of self-achievement, be reinforcement in itself. Knowledge of the correctness of a response may be given by a teacher, or the student can assess his own performance.

Learning involves a change in behaviour. 'Good' or efficient learning is measured by the range of behaviour that can be produced by the new knowledge, and the wider the range of behaviour, the better the learning. Operant conditioning, in the form of programmed learning, gives 'bits' of information and conditions the student's behaviour, so that the conditioned behaviour shows evidence of the understanding of the new information. Correct behavioural responses are reinforced, and therefore become more frequent.

27. Extract from a linear programme, teaching classical conditioning

Frame 1	When we eat some things, saliva comes into our mouths. We say the food makes our mouths _____ .	
Frame 2	The food is a *stimulus* which makes us salivate. When light is shone into our eyes we blink. Light is a *st* _____ which makes us blink.	**Salivate**
Frame 3	When we touch a flame, we jerk our hands away. The stimulus which makes us move our hands is _____ .	**Stimulus**
Frame 4	Light stimulates our eyes to blink; food stimulates our mouths to provide saliva; a flame stimulates our hand to move away. Light, food and flame are all examples of a _____ .	**The flame** (*or* **pain**)
Frame 5	When we salivate, or blink, or move our hands away from a flame, we call those actions *responses*. So the blinking of an eye when light shines on it is called a _____ .	**Stimulus**
Frame 6	A stimulus, such as a flame, causes a _____. we move our hands away quickly.	**Response**

Frame 7	A flame is a _____ and causes us to make the _____ of moving our hands away.	**Response**
Frame 8	When we take our hands away we don't have to think about it: we do it automatically. An Automatic response like this is called a *reflex response*. Salivating when we see food is also a _____ .	**Stimulus, response**
Frame 9	The reflex response to the stimulus of the flame is for us to _____ .	**Reflex response**
Frame 10	This response can also be set off by other things. For example, an electric shock also causes us to withdraw our hands. An electric shock is a _____ which leads to a reflex response.	**Move our hands away**
Frame 11	However, we can also use completely articifial stimuli, and get them to set off the reflex response. A tap on the forehead normally won't make us jerk our hands, so the stimulus of the tap on the forehead is an _____ stimulus, in this case.	**Stimulus**

A learning programme has to predict behaviour: it has to know at which points a student may go wrong. This problem can be greatly reduced by breaking down the information into very small steps or *frames*, each of which requires a correct response before the next step is presented. If the steps are small enough, the possible number of responses will be limited, usually to one correct response, and a programme which allows only correct answers is called a *linear programme*, because the frames are in a straight sequence. A piece of information is given and immediately tested, and the student then moves on to the next information or test frame. Figure 27 is an example of a linear programme, teaching part of a psychology course on classical conditioning. Expose the first frame and answer the question, then expose the second frame, which gives the answer. Next, read the information given in the second frame and answer the question, and moving on to frame 3, check your answer.

A more complex but more flexible type of learning programme is the *branching programme*. Unlike the linear programme, this allows

incorrect responses and can attempt to rectify the fault. It asks
questions, like the linear programme, but gives several alternative
answers, such as:

A 'stimulus' is
(1) a drug
(2) anything affecting an organism's senses
(3) a knock on the knee-cap
(4) the things an organism does.

If the student responds correctly by choosing alternative (2), he is led
on to the next frame in the programme. If, however, he chooses
incorrectly, he passes on to extra, *remedial frames* which explain why
his response was incorrect and repeat and re-test the information
already given. For example, if a student chooses (4) in the above
frame, the programme will lead him to:

(4) the things an organism does.
   No – what an organism does is called its 'behaviour' or its 'responses'.
Anything which affects, or 'stimulates', an organism's senses is a stimulus.
   Now move back to the original question and proceed.

The branching programme therefore allows wrong answers, but
helps the student to correct his mistake and requires him to re-test
himself on the question which he first answered incorrectly. If he
answers all the test questions correctly he is allowed to 'skip' the
remedial frames. This technique of inserting remedial frames into a
programme is known as *skip technique*.
   The operant conditioning basis of programmed learning is clear.
To increase the likelihood of the correct answer being repeated, it
must be reinforced.

28. *Illustration of the operant conditioning basis of programmed
   learning*

Question ⟶ Answer ⟶ Reinforcement:
  CS   CR   'Correct'

In linear programmes, the question is so structured that only one
correct response is possible, as above, and the student is reinforced
by being informed that his answer is correct. In branching programmes, however, the structuring is different.

29.

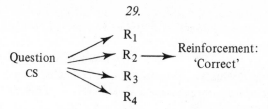

Leading to:

30.

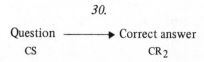

Responses R_1, R_3 and R_4, when chosen, lead the student to the remedial frames which explain his mistake and refer him back to the original question. Thus a correct answer is reinforced immediately, while an incorrect answer is rectified.

Both linear and branching programmes are available in book form. Usually, however, programmes are run on teaching machines, and while linear programme machines are very simple and inexpensive, branching programme machines are more sophisticated and expensive. There are also computer-run programmes called *adaptive programmes*, which are self-adjusting according to the level of attainment of the individual student, and are sometimes known as PASK programmes. There are programmes available which are even simpler than linear programmes, known as PRESSEY programmes, which are objective-answer (one-word answer) tests, usually in the form of sentence completion or filling-in of omitted words. For example:

A conditional stimulus, when paired with an unconditional stimulus, acquires the power to evoke the ——.
(*unconditional response*)

Though programmed learning is based on the principles of operant conditioning, there are some differences between the two which need consideration. For example, though reinforcement of the desired response features in both, in operant conditioning studies the experimental animal can have its drive to respond increased - perhaps by starvation beforehand to increase its hunger drive - so that food becomes a very effective reinforcer. In programmed learning, such reinforcements are less appropriate, with praise, or knowledge of the correct answer, acting as the reinforcer, and it is not possible to strengthen the 'praise drive' by deprivation beforehand. Operant conditioning usually involves a single, repeated response, such as lever-pressing, which is frequently reinforced, while in programmed learning, each response is usually reinforced only once or twice, and many different responses (or answers) are required. The schedules of reinforcement which are so effectively used in operant conditioning are much more difficult to apply in programmed learning, because so many different answers are required from the subject, though it is possible to re-test after a time interval (with FI or VI schedules).

The relative effectiveness of programmed learning compared with other approaches also warrants consideration. Programmed learning is one of several approaches to learning, which include lectures, discovery methods, indoctrination, tutorials, seminars, and so on. Any evaluation of programmed learning must involve the evaluation of the programmes used, since a teaching-machine is only as good as its programme, just as the lecture method is only as good as the lecturer. A further problem occurs because in measuring the amount learnt, examinations are generally used, and it is by no means certain that these do measure all the learning which has taken place. Deficiencies in evaluative techniques make it more difficult to measure the effectiveness of programmed learning.

Despite these problems, there have been attempts to measure the relative efficiencies of programmed learning and more conventional teaching. Cavanagh (1963) performed what are known as the cohort studies, investigating and comparing programmed learning and conventional teaching in the education of technicians in the services. The main findings may be summarized as follows:

1 Achievement with programmed learning was similar to that with conventional instruction, and students from both groups did equally well.
2 Students educated by programmed learning mastered the material in a significantly shorter time than conventionally taught students.
3 Retention and recall of learnt material was better after using programmed learning than after conventional teaching.
4 Teaching-machines were more effective than scrambled texts.
5 There was some evidence that the advantages of programmed learning are more pronounced with the more intelligent student.

These findings appear to suggest that programmed learning is a teaching and learning approach which should be more widely available in education. It has several other advantages, not the least of which is that results are fed back very promptly, often with a 'pat on the back', so that a build-up of misunderstanding is prevented. Programmes are also thoroughly tested in practice before students are exposed to them, with the sequencing and size of steps carefully controlled. They can relieve teachers of routine teaching chores, making more of his time available for work with individual students, and they are very suitable for homework and for self-marking assignments. Programmes usually run at the student's own pace, neither so fast that he becomes confused, nor so slowly that he becomes bored, providing him with individual attention and tuition. Teaching-machines do not get tired, or ill, or bad-tempered, but maintain a constant quality of instruction, and can easily provide a record of a student's errors, so that his progress over a period of time is clearly visible. It is possible that curiosity about teaching-machines is also an aid to motivation, at least initially.

However, despite all these advantages there are disadvantages. One of these is expense, especially for the more sophisticated machines, and for the programmes, which take a long time to write and check. Another is that teaching-machines do not generate an 'atmosphere of learning', and some students find their impersonality disturbing. The programmes are relatively inflexible in that they cannot take account of students' interests in related topics, and cannot recount personal experiences or reminiscences of a process being taught. Nevertheless, the possible uses of programmed learning are very varied. They can be used for revision purposes, as a means of practical application of previous teaching and learning. They provide a means of repeating poor work for remedial purposes, or of making up work missed by absence from classes. Some minority subjects may not justify the appointment of teaching staff, but could use programmed learning as an alternative teaching method. Such methods could also play a part in education in developing countries which have insufficient numbers of trained staff, and in the problem of re-training older people in new skills, a need which is becoming increasingly evident in industrialized societies.

Behaviour therapy

This technique aims to modify or control the overt behavioural symptoms resulting from a patient's disorder. Studies of experimentally induced neuroses in laboratory animals provided evidence that the acquisition and removal of abnormal psychological reactions could be mediated by operant conditioning. The classical conditioning technique of desensitization has already been discussed, and though the distinctions between classical and operant conditioning are often blurred in behaviour therapy, in general classical conditioning tries to establish the emergence of a *new* reaction (which may then be reinforced), while operant conditioning tries to change the rate of occurrence of an *already existing* response (which may then be shaped to establish another response).

An important application of operant conditioning has been in the development of the 'token economy' system. It is very desirable, but not always practicable, that in operant conditioning the desired behaviour should be reinforced immediately. Clearly, patients in a psychiatric ward would demand enormous nursing effort to observe and immediately reward desired behaviours each time they occurred, but a 'substitute' reward in the form of a 'privilege' token helps to overcome this problem. Behaviour meriting the reward of, say, a bus-trip or a visit to the shops would gain, instead, a token entitling the patient to such a reward at a certain convenient time.

Isaacs *et al.* (1960) report the use of operant conditioning in the modification of the behaviour of a schizophrenic who had been silent and immobile for twenty years in a hospital. Beginning by increasing the frequency of his slight eye movements (by holding a packet of chewing gum near his face till his eyes moved towards it, then giving him the gum), the therapy continued with shaping techniques, until eye *and* lip movements preceded reinforcements. Further shaping eventually elicited the use of some meaningful vocalizations. More recently such techniques have been used to help develop speech in autistic children. The cause of autism remains uncertain, but its symptoms include total unresponsiveness to the environment and a marked lack of interaction with others. Operant conditioning techniques have been used to help such children to speak. Building on their few existing vocalizations – moans, grunts, screams – these are at first reinforced and then shaped, using food or some prized activity as the reinforcing agent. It may be difficult to find such an agent, since praise and loving contact are not reinforcements for such children. Via shaping techniques they may learn to string words together into phrases, but though it is relatively easy to establish the use of single words, their more complex use is difficult to achieve. It may be necessary to train parents to use operant conditioning too, to provide intensive and continuous use of the operant conditioning techniques.

Miller and DiCara (1969) found that operant conditioning could influence reflexes as well as non-reflexive or voluntary behaviours, though it had previously been thought that involuntary responses such as heart-rate, blood-pressure and intestinal contractions were amenable only to classical conditioning. To check that such responses were operant-conditioned, and not merely reflecting some conscious motor relaxing and contracting of muscles to control the involuntary responses in turn (as some yogas can do), they paralysed rats by using a curare-type drug. This eliminated the use of food or water as reinforcements, and instead used the direct electrode stimulation of the *hypothalamus* or *pleasure centre* of the rats' brains (see p. 184). Desired responses such as the raising or lowering of the heart-rate or blood-pressure was reinforced by stimulating the pleasure centre, and produced positive results. Such evidence is the basis of *biofeedback techniques*, which are now marketed or used medically for humans. For people, however, the reinforcing agent is the self-knowledge of being able to achieve such conscious control of physiological processes.

Complex learning

The types of learning dealt with so far, classical and operant conditioning, are sufficient explanation for many simple behavioural responses, and are largely concerned with very simple 'bits' of behaviour such as salivation or lever-pressing. However, there are more complex forms of learning which occur – even more complex than *habits*, two or three actions chained together. However tempting it might seem to think of learning as being just chains of responses or reflexes – and there is a theory called the *chain response*, or *reflex, theory* of learning – this is by no means adequate to explain all learning. Restle (1957) demonstrated this in an experiment in which he trained rats to run a maze, in order to reach food at the 'goal'. According to chain response theory, a rat learns the specific muscle movements that must be made in order to reach the goal. The completion of each movement leads to the performance of the next, and the mastery of the maze simply consists of learning each of the muscle responses and chaining them together. Because this theory proposes that a rat learns muscle movements rather than the geographical characteristics of the maze, it predicts that a rat would have to relearn the maze if it was required to swim rather than to walk to the goal. Restle tested this prediction by flooding the maze immediately after the group of rats had learnt to run it, but found that they swam to the goal with no more errors than when they had walked. This evidence weakens the validity of the chain response theory, though it may still hold in some cases. Tolman (1948) proposed that when an animal learns a maze, it learns the *signs* of 'what leads to what'. This *sign-learning theory* holds that the animal develops *expectations* that one stimulus will be followed by another when in the maze. These expectations are cognitive ones, with the animal developing a primitive kind of perceptual or cognitive map of the maze in its brain – an understanding of spatial relationships which is much more flexible than learning a chain of bodily responses. If the maze is altered slightly, the animal can use an alternative route to the goal because of this internal map. Many other changed-response experiments support the general conclusion that what is learnt is a perception of relationships between situational stimuli, rather than a chain of bodily responses or reflexes.

Considerable experimental evidence also exists for a type of learning called *latent learning*. One example is Tolman (1930), who investigated the effect on animal learning of not providing reinforcement. He found that if rats were put in a maze which contained no food, such non-reinforced animals did not appear to learn as rapidly as reinforced animals, though they freely explored the maze. However, post-testing of this group of non-reinforced rats, this time providing food as reinforcement, showed that they learnt as well as or even better than the always-reinforced groups. The non-reinforced group, while in the maze without being reinforced, must have been acquiring their 'internal maps' of the maze but not displaying this learning by their behaviour at this time. This latent learning was not used, or displayed in behaviour, until appropriate reinforcement was introduced, when it had the effect of accelerating the rats' performances compared with the control groups. It seems, therefore, that learning can take place without the behaviourist idea of reinforcement being necessary, though such learning is only brought into use when reinforcement is available. Learning when actually used, or displayed in behaviour, is properly called *performance*.

Humans exhibit similar learning mechanisms if put into maze-learning situations, but there are some important differences. One is that humans can use *verbal aids* to construct a 'formula' for the maze, for example, 'right, left, left, left, right, right'. Furthermore, humans have memory of the maze and, if asked, can draw a map of it after learning it. This is *recall memory*, whereas rats probably only have *recognition memory*: they can recognize an area of the maze when they come upon it, but do not possess a full cognitive map.

The types of learning discussed so far might be called *trial-and-error learning*, in which the organism makes numerous responses, some of which are incorrect. The learning process appears to be a reduction in the number of errors made, until all the responses which remain are the correct ones, and this is achieved by the animal associating a particular stimulus with a particular response. Thus trial-and-error learning is also known as *stimulus-response learning*, or *S-R learning*. Partly as a reaction against this emphasis on S-R learning, Gestalt psychologists developed a theory of *insight learning*. Kohler (1925) used chimpanzees in a series of experiments designed to demonstrate this type of learning. Perhaps the best known of these experiments is that in which Kohler placed a chimpanzee named Sultan in a cage, with a piece of fruit placed outside the cage, just out of reach. Inside the cage was a stick, and the only way for Sultan to reach the fruit was by using the stick to extend his own reach. Kohler claimed that Sultan solved the problem through insight. He tried first to reach the fruit by hand, but seeing that this was impossible he sat down and gazed around him. Suddenly he went over to the stick, picked it up and then completed the task of retrieving the fruit, having apparently organized the whole solution cognitively in the brain. The main stages in learning with insight seem to be: (1) an initial helplessness or inability to deal with the problem; (2) a pause in activity; and (3) a sudden and smooth performance of the solution.

In humans, insight learning takes the form of those 'Aha!' experiences; a sudden solving of a problem when 'the light dawns' or one feels 'Oh, I see!' There seem to be several underlying principles of insight learning, summarized below:

(1) Insight depends on the arrangement of the problem - all the tools, processes, and so forth necessary for the solution of the problem must be available. In animals this means available within vision of the animal, but in humans they can be 'available' mentally. Insight is essentially the reorganization of the problem.

(2) In trial-an-error learning the solution comes gradually, as associations are made and errors eliminated. In insight learning, the solution 'appears' suddenly, and it can be repeated immediately. The Gestalt view of trial-and-error learning is that it involves a series of small insights.

(3) A solution learned by insight can be applied to new situations much more flexibly than trial-and-error learning, because it involves no S–R bonds but is a cognitive process, an understanding of the relationship between things.

However, the Gestalt theory of insight learning, like the Gestalt theory of perception, appears to explain one unknown quantity by reference to another. What is 'insight'? Gestalt psychologists say that it is 'organization of the whole situation', but they do not explain how or why this occurs. Some experimenters attempting to duplicate Kohler's work have found that some solutions applying insight to problems were quite wrong, yet were still repeated by subjects. In addition, Birch (1945) found that insightful behaviour in animals could only be evoked after considerable preliminary training in simpler tasks. Harlow (1949) provides similar evidence in his work on the development of *schemata* or *learning sets*, in which the animal apparently 'learns how to learn'. He tested the discrimination abilities of monkeys using a variety of tasks, and found that even though the tasks were dissimilar, some transfer of learning seemed to be occurring. The monkeys had to learn to discriminate between geometrical shapes (for example, triangles and circles), and Harlow found that though the stimulus shapes were changed between trials, to include examples of other geometrical shapes, the monkeys made far fewer mistakes in the later trials. It seemed that they had learned more than just to discriminate between circles and triangles: they had learnt to become adept at discrimination problems which involved other geometrical shapes too.

Transfer of learning, or transfer of training, is an important aspect of learning processes. Learning to perform one task may influence performance of another (and indeed this is an essential presupposition of most educational practices). This process of inter-problem influence may be *positive transfer*, in which performance of one task helps, or has a positive effect on, performance of another task. An example might be that learning to ride a bicycle makes learning to ride a motor-cycle easier. In some cases, however, learning task A may interfere with the learning of task B: learning to drive on the left-hand side of the road may interfere with, or have a negative effect on, learning to drive in a country which uses the right-hand side of the road.

Several factors affect transfer of learning, including that of learning set discussed above. Bruce (1933) demonstrated that similarity of stimuli and similarity of response influence transfer, and whether positive or negative transfer occurs between two tasks depends on the relationship between the stimuli and the responses involved in the tasks. Learning to perform a single task could be shown in S–R terms as

31.

$$S_1 \longrightarrow R_1$$

No transfer is possible here, since only one task has been learnt. However, if the subject is then given a second task to learn, which involves making the same response but to a different stimulus, this will correspond to

32.

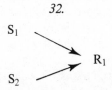

Having learnt the original response, R_1, the subject can make it to the new stimulus, S_2 – he can, in effect, perform two tasks after having learnt only one. This is positive transfer.

However, if the second task which the subject has to learn requires a different response to be made, but to the same stimulus as in the first task, negative transfer can occur.

33.

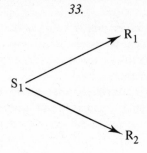

Negative transfer occurs because not only does the subject have to learn a new response, R_2, to the original stimulus, but he also has to unlearn R_1.

A third factor affecting transfer of learning is the use of mediating responses. One of the main differences between animal and human learning is that humans are able to use language as a mediating response. This is a response which acts as a go-between for stimuli and responses, helping to make the response to the stimulus. For example, imagine that you have to learn a list of ten objects. Think of the numbers 1 to 10, and try to think of a 'picture' word which goes with each number (for example, 'one'-'sun', 'two'-'shoe', 'three'-'tree', and so on). Now take the list of objects which have to be learnt and relate each one in turn to the picture you have in mind for each number. Object number three (tree), for example, may be a pen. You might visualize a pen as a tree trunk with branches growing out of it. Such an unusual sight is easy to remember, so that when someone asks what object number three was, your thought processes are: 'Three – tree – with a pen for a trunk – pen is the answer.' In this case the word 'tree' acted as a mediating response, helping you to give a new response ('pen') to an old stimulus ('three').

The principles of transfer (although not named as such), were the basis for the old concept of a classical education, that is, the study of Latin, Greek and logic. The belief was that the logical, deductive form of these subjects would be transferred to the rest of the students' intellectual activities, but it quite ignored the need to emphasize the similarities between the subject and the situations to which it was hoped the principles would transfer.

Factors affecting learning

One obvious factor influencing learning is that of the retention of learned material in memory, and the following chapter deals with this in detail. Here the discussion is restricted to other factors which are important for learning.

Learning is measured through performance of the learned task, with measurements usually displayed as learning curves which show how the learning is progressing. As learning proceeds, the number of errors normally reduces, so that if the number of errors are plotted

34. A typical graph for the process of learning

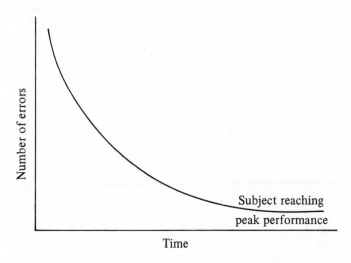

against time, a typical downward-sloping curve is obtained (see Fig. 34).

Alternatively, the number of correct responses may be plotted against time, to produce a typical upward-sloping curve (see Fig. 35).

35. An alternative graph for the process of learning

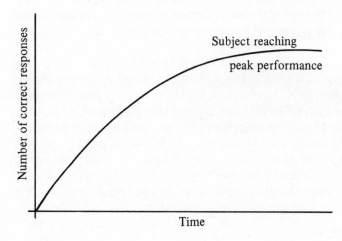

Both these graphs are *learning curves*. In Figure 27, a levelling-off of the curve may sometimes be seen, to produce a plateau, which means that the subject's performance is temporarily not improving. There appear to be two main causes of this. The first is a change in the type of skill being learnt. For example, in typewriting the plateau marked **A** in Figure 36 may be caused by reaching the limits of speed using two fingers only to type. Performance begins to improve again, at **B**, when the subject begins to use all fingers and thus increases speed again.

36. A graph showing a plateau in learning

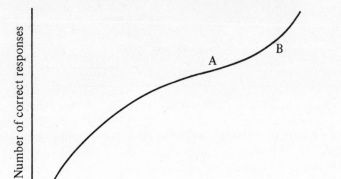

Secondly, the same effect on a learning curve may also be produced by *reactive inhibition*, which is an effect in the nervous system similar to muscular fatigue, where continued activity causes a build-up of inhibition, resulting in a decrement in performance. The levelling-off in performance reflects as a plateau in the learning curve, but a short rest pause allows the inhibition to dissipate and performance once again improves.

McGeoch and Irion (1952) showed that *distributed practice*, or practice periods with short periods of rest between them, is a much more efficient means of learning than continuous practice. Massed or continuous practice may produce reactive inhibition, and the rest periods in distributed practice help to prevent this, or to dissipate any that has built up, though the length and frequency of practice and rest periods are important. Practice periods should be short, but not so short that learning is broken up into meaningless units

(Kimble, 1949); nor should they be too long, as this allows the subjects to forget some of what they have learnt (Lorge, 1930).

Knowledge of results or feedback of information is important in learning, especially in learning sensorimotor skills. Lack of knowledge of results is, in effect, removal of *external feedback*, and the controlling of the skilled process depends on adequate feedback of the effects of motor activity. Baker and Young (1960) showed that a group of subjects asked to learn a task, estimating the length of lines, without any feedback of information, learnt very little, if anything at all. A second group of subjects who were given feedback learned to perform the same task normally.

Active involvement with the material to be learnt helps the learning process, and recitation is far more efficient as a learning aid than is reading and re-reading. Gates (1967) showed that if 80% of study time is spent reciting, more and better learning is produced than by reading 100% of the time. The meaningfulness of the material to be learned is also a factor influencing learning; and material that is meaningful, related to knowledge already possessed, is easier to learn than completely new material. A passage of prose is much easier to learn than the same number of words taken at random from the dictionary.

Learning may proceed either by learning the whole block of material required, or by breaking up the big block into smaller sections. There seems to be no definitive answer as to which is most efficient, but McGeoch and Irion (1952) provide some general rules, summarized below:

1 If material is very long, or easily split into sections, use the *part method*.
2 Part method gives feedback of results more quickly than the *whole method*, and is a more varied and therefore more interesting method.
3 If material to be learnt is meaningful as a whole, that is, if it 'hangs together' well, as a poem perhaps might, then the whole method is more efficient.
4 If the learner is highly intelligent, the whole method generally seems to be more effective.

Experiments performed by Hostetter (1970) seem to suggest that spaced practice allows time for material to be absorbed into memory storage. This process takes time, and possibly involves DNA or RNA protein changes in the brain itself, which is provided in distributed practice. Massed practice, however, does not permit such time and may therefore be less efficient than distributed practice.

As in conditioning, the presence or absence of reward can affect learning. Generally, reward is more effective in promoting learning than is punishment, since the latter only represses undesired responses, giving no clue to the learner as to which of his responses is correct. Reward 'picks out' desired responses and has the effect of informing the subject whether he is progressing along the right lines or not. McVicker Hunt (1963) proposed two distinct types of reward termed *intrinsic* and *extrinsic*, or internal and external. Intrinsic, internal rewards are produced within the individual, such as feelings of satisfaction and pleasure, while extrinsic rewards are external, such as food, water and money – the rewards usually associated with conditioning. A person may be either extrinsically or intrinsically rewarded, and it is possible that the former may lead to the latter. A subject extrinsically motivated to perform a task, perhaps with money as a reward, may gradually become so proficient that he derives intrinsic rewards from his new-found abilities. It should be noted that extrinsic rewards, although effective, may lead to the subject's working solely for that reward, particularly if it is very large. Intrinsic reward may be roughly interpreted as 'interest', and is generally regarded as being more subtle and effective as a reward than extrinsic reward.

Although reward is more effective in promoting learning than is punishment, the latter does have some effects on learning. It tends to repress an undesired response, but it does not extinguish it, and when punishment is effective, it is because it represses an incorrect response long enough for the organism to try an alternative response, which may be reinforced. Estes (1970) demonstrated this temporary repression of responses in an experiment in which he conditioned rats to press levers, and then ceased reinforcement. Group B rats were left to extinguish their responses normally, but the rats in group A were given electric shocks as punishment for pressing the lever, for the first few times only, after reinforcement had ceased. Figure 37 shows that group A rats made fewer 'wrong' responses in the first few minutes after reinforcement ceased, but their response rate increased again after the shock was turned off, and they eventually made as many total responses as group B. Punishment may reduce the number of undesired responses for as long as it is practised, but response rate returns to a higher level unless an alternative response is reinforced in the meantime.

Learning is a central concept for many psychologists, and most

37. A graph showing the temporary repression of responses

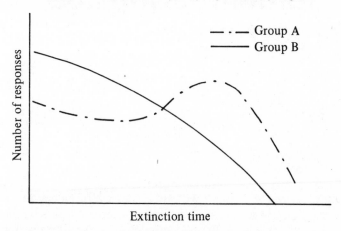

chapters of this book deal with it in one way or another. Its influence on behaviour is often contrasted with that of genetics, as shown in the discussions of the nature/nurture debate in Chapters 2, 5, 6 and 7, and the concept of instinct in Chapter 9. It can, however, be affected by hereditary factors, because selective breeding experiments can influence rates of learning (see p. 205), and some animal species have a tendency to learn particular things at specific times of their lives, as demonstrated by the study of *imprinting* (see p. 287).

As we have seen, in the early models of scientific psychology a simple S–R approach dominated the field. Chapter 2 examined how stimuli are perceived, and this chapter has detailed the S–R model of learning. In more recent years psychologists have placed more and more emphasis on what happens *between* the stimulus and the response, that is, on factors within the organism itself. The next chapter considers one of these factors, *memory*, without which learning would be impossible.

Further reading

Hilgard, E.R. and Bower, G.H. (1975), *Theories of Learning* (4th ed.), Prentice Hall
Rachlin, H. (1970), *An Introduction to Modern Behaviourism*, W.H. Freeman and Co.
Walker, S. (1975), *Learning and Reinforcement*, Methuen Essential Psychology Series

4 Remembering and forgetting

When we speak of memory we tend to think of it as one process, whereas it is possible to recognize at least three different systems. One system, known as *sensory information storage*, retains for a fraction of a second sensory material which has been directed at a particular sense organ. Another system is concerned with *short-term memory*. Here, information is encoded and held for several seconds or minutes for immediate use, or is prepared for permanent storage in the *long-term memory*, the third of our storage systems.

Sensory information storage

This system gives an accurate account of the environment as experienced by the sensory system, and lasts for only several tenths of a second. When we receive a visual input, its image remains with us for approximately 0.5 of a second – slightly longer than the actual input. This visual image is referred to as the visual sensory information store. A vital feature of this sensory information store is that far more information is retained there than is actually recalled at a later stage, giving rise to the supposition that the sensory store has only a limited capacity. It will retain information for a very short period of time, during which it will select the material it wishes to retain.

It is possible to demonstrate that the sis holds more information than is actually used at later stages by reference to an experiment which follows the work of Sperling. A card, consisting of nine letters arranged in three rows of three letters, is presented to a subject for a period of fifty milliseconds. He is then asked to report on the number of letters he actually read. For the majority of people, this number would be about five.

It is possible that the subject sees all nine letters, but about half of them are forgotten almost immediately. To test this hypothesis, the subject would be asked to fixate on a spot, after which the card containing the nine letters would be presented to the subject exactly as before, but on this occasion, however, one letter would be marked off from the rest *after* the exposure, so that the subject would not be aware of the marked letter while the card was exposed. If the subject were able to report with accuracy on each marked letter without knowing beforehand which letter it would be, this would indicate that every one of the letters must have entered the SIS during their brief exposure. The procedure is illustrated below; under these conditions subjects do show a very high degree of accuracy.

38. The stages of an experiment demonstrating the nature of sensory information storage

Step 1	Step 2	Step 3	Step 4
•	B E W N K C P S R		•
Subject fixates on the centre point	Stimulus card is presented to the subject for 50 ms	White card is shown to the subject	Marker card is shown to the subject to indicate the required letter

Short-term memory

Nearly a hundred years ago William James introduced the concepts of 'primary' and 'secondary' memory which are now commonly referred to today as 'short-term' and 'long-term' memory. The work of Ebbinghaus towards the end of the last century also pointed to a clear distinction between STM and LTM, proposing that STM had a capacity for about seven units. At about the same time Wundt demonstrated that the storage load of the STM is limited to approximately six or seven units, and this was substantiated over sixty years later by Miller, who referred to it as the 'magic number seven'. This is known as Miller's *'chunking' theory*, in which the emphasis is on storing 'chunks' of information rather than 'items'. While a restriction is placed on the *number* of chunks which can be held in STM, the *amount* of material contained in one chunk is unlimited.

Glanzer and Cunitz (1966) showed that it is possible to eliminate STM by introducing a simple task (like counting backwards) between the learning of material and its subsequent recall. The investigators divided their subjects into two groups and presented them with lists of words. One group recalled the material immediately after presentation, and the other group was delayed for thirty seconds before being asked to recall. A *recency effect* (STM) was noted for the first group but not for the second group, whose recall came from LTM.

Lloyd and Margaret Peterson (1959) asked subjects to memorize three letters and then to recall them after a space of eighteen seconds. In fact, the task was not quite as easy as this, because between the presentation of material and recall of the letters, the subjects were asked to count backwards in threes, for example 485, 482, 479, and so on. The rate at which the subjects forgot the material is shown in Figure 39. It can be seen that when subjects were tested at short intervals, the percentage number of times a letter could be recalled was greater than was the case when the subjects were tested at a longer interval. For example, there would be approximately 75% recall at a three-second interval compared with, say, a 20% recall after eighteen seconds.

Further evidence for the existence of a short-term memory is to be found in work undertaken with brain-damaged subjects. Milner (1967) cited a case of a brain-damaged patient who could cope normally when information was held in his STM, but was unable to transfer new material into LTM. The opposite may also be true, where a patient has a normal LTM but is incapable of retaining more than a couple of items in STM (Shallice and Warrington, 1970). This raises an interesting question as to whether new material must always enter STM before being transferred to LTM.

One reason which could account for why people forget items in STM may be found in the *decay hypothesis*, which receives some support from physiological evidence (Hebb, 1949). Another explanation comes from the *interference hypothesis*, which is associated with the limited capacity of the STM. It seems likely that new items entering the STM will interfere with those already present.

The interference theory assumes that there exists a limited number of short-term memory slots into which new material is inserted. This

39. Retention curve for short-term memory (rate of forgetting) (after Lloyd R. Peterson (1959), Journal of Experimental Psychology, 58(3), 193-8; copyright © 1959 by the American Psychological Association; reprinted by permission)

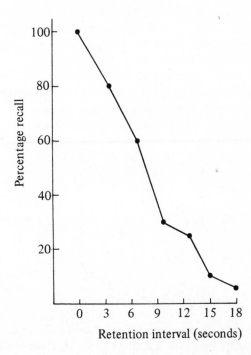

is in keeping with Miller's theory referred to above, where there are assumed to be seven of these slots. When a new piece of material is to be introduced, one of the existing seven slots would need to release its existing material to make way for the new item. One objection to this theory is that too much emphasis is placed on the idea that only a fixed number of items can be remembered. A second objection disapproves of the assumption that material is either permanently remembered or completely forgotten.

Both of these objections are valid, but they can easily be dismissed. For example, it is possible to conceive of memory as being partially existent: it need not be totally present or absent. The physiological change, as yet not fully understood, which occurs during memorization is known as the *memory trace*: new material will have a high-trace strength, while older items will have a low-trace strength. Thus it will be easier to recall high-strength items than those which have a weaker strength.

Perhaps there is not a fixed number of short-term memory slots as suggested earlier, but rather any number of items may be incorporated into the system. The addition of new items will, according to this theory, interfere with material already in the system. If this were true, the memory traces would become less powerful as new items were introduced. This is illustrated in Figure 40.

40. Demonstration of the capacity of short-term memory

Words	STM: strength of memory trace				
	5	4	3	2	1
1 Boat	Boat				
2 Cake	Cake	Boat			
3 Tree	Tree	Cake	Boat		
4 Book	Book	Tree	Cake	Boat	
5 Desk	Desk	Book	Tree	Cake	Boat

When item (1) is presented to the subject, the memory-trace strength will be high. It will be reduced a little when item (2) is introduced. By the time item (5) is presented, the trace strength of item (1) will have become much weaker.

As we said earlier, another way in which STM may be restricted is by time. This *time-decay theory* considers that the trace strength of an item will become weaker the longer the item remains in the memory system, irrespective of the number of other items in the system, and will ultimately disappear completely. The reader will observe the subtle difference between forgetting by interference and forgetting by time-decay, the former being item-dependent, and the latter time-dependent.

It has been suggested that encoding and storage in STM is largely dependent on acoustic characteristics, since errors appear to be more easily made in recalling items with similar sounds. To test the hypothesis that items with similar acoustic properties will be more difficult to retain in STM than items with dissimilar sounds, Wickel-gren (1965) invited his subjects to read four letters. The subjects then read a list of eight letters, to act as interference items, and were asked to recall the original four letters. It was noted that subjects experienced greater difficulty in recalling the four letters when the interference list had consisted of letters of similar sounds than when the interference list was acoustically dissimilar to the original letters.

Further evidence which supports these findings is contained in the researches of Conrad and Hull (1964) and Conrad (1964). These investigators demonstrated that subjects tended to retain more readily items which were acoustically dissimilar than items which had acoustically similar properties. Conrad held that there would be some confusion between items which were acoustically similar. To test this proposition, Conrad used the letters

B   C   P   T   V   F   M   N   S   X,

which he presented as auditory stimuli to approximately 300 subjects against a noisy background. His results showed a large number of listening confusion errors.

In order to test the recall of 387 subjects, he then presented visually a number of six-letter sequences which he selected from his ten consonants. Conrad discovered a correlation between errors in listening and errors in recall, from which he concluded that while the letters were presented to his subjects visually, they were transformed into an acoustic form, and any reported errors were of an acoustic nature.

A question which is often asked is, 'How selective is short-term memory?' Experimental studies have attempted to answer this question using perceptual defence stimuli, and this has presented a major problem at the outset. How is it possible for a person to prevent a perceptual stimulus from entering STM without his first recognizing the stimulus as one against which there should be some defence?

The question of perceptual defence is considered on pages 68–9. It is not possible to separate the processes of perception and memory at this level, because in order to report a word presented in a tachistoscope a subject must remember it. Perhaps the results of experiments such as that of Bruner and Postman (p. 68), who showed that subjects were able to report ordinary words but not taboo words when presented quickly on a tachistoscope, demonstrate a memory rather than a perceptual phenomenon; on the other hand, a subject may both perceive and remember a taboo word but be unwilling to report it.

In summary, it would seem that the STM has an extremely limited capacity capable of holding no more than about seven items at any one time. Forgotten material may be the result of either decay or interference, and similar sounding items are likely to be most easily forgotten. There is some evidence which points to the fact that STM is selective.

Long-term memory

Long-term memory is concerned with items which have been retained over a long period of time, ranging from several minutes to several years. At the outset, material may be encoded in LTM by means of either a *semantic code* or an *imagery code*. A semantic code deals with material in terms of its verbal meaning whereas an imagery code has a pictorial form. The former appears to be the more usual method, particularly when we have to deal with abstract material for which it is not easy to conjure up appropriate images. It would be difficult, for instance, to formulate an image for an abstract sentence such as, 'There seemed to be no justice in the punishment which was awarded.'

When the items are in the form of a sentence, it is usually the meaning of the sentence rather than the exact sequence of words which is encoded. There are, of course, occasions when it is necessary to commit a list of words to memory, or to attempt to memorize a series of words in sequence, as, for example, in the case of learning lines of poetry. Nevertheless, there seems to be sufficient evidence to indicate that when material is meaningful to the individual, it will be better remembered and more easily recalled. Craik (1977) showed that subjects remembered words far better when they were asked questions about them.

Some consideration has been given to the notion that items which are continually repeated or rehearsed will be more easily retained in STM. According to Rundus and Atkinson (1970) this also holds true when the subject wishes to store information in LTM. These researchers had their subjects rehearse aloud a number of word lists, and then reproduce them by means of free recall. They found that (1) rehearsal and recall from LTM were related; (2) the first words in the list received more rehearsal than did other words, thus contributing to a primacy effect in the recall situation; and (3) the last words in the lists would have entered STM and consequently were readily recalled.

The importance of organization cannot be overlooked in connection with memorizing verbal material. Verbal items will be more easily retained when some form of systematic organization has been employed at the encoding stage. Several investigations have been carried out into the importance of organization in learning verbal material. Some of these studies are outlined below. There is so much

41. *The minerals hierarchy* (after G.H. Bower, M.C. Clark, A.M. Lesgold and D. Winzenz (1969), *Journal of Verbal Learning and Verbal Behaviour,* 8, pp.323–43; copyright © 1969, Academic Press, Inc.)

Minerals				
Metals			Stones	
Rare	Common	Alloys	Precious	Masonry
Platinum	Alum	Bronze	Sapphire	Limestone
Silver	Copper	Steel	Emerald	Granite
Gold	Lead	Brass	Diamond	Marble
	Iron		Ruby	Slate

information entering the LTM that without some form of organization it would be almost impossible to retrieve it at a later stage when required. Organization helps in the encoding, storage and retrieval of information. This is well-illustrated in a classic study by Bower, Clark, Lesgold and Winzenz (1969). They organized lists of words into four hierarchies, one of which is outlined in Figure 41.

Subjects were divided into two groups – an 'organized' group and a 'randomized' group. The 'organized' group were shown the lists of words arranged in their hierarchical form, while the 'randomized' group saw words drawn at random from across the four hierarchies, but presented in what appeared to be a structured hierarchical form. Subjects were presented with each hierarchy in turn and tested by the method of free recall. The 'organized' group revealed a significantly higher pattern of item recall than the 'randomized' group, demonstrating the influence of organization on recall of material. This is more clearly seen in Figure 42.

42. Percentage words recalled by 'organized' and 'randomized' groups

	% recall
Organized group	65
Randomized group	19

Some confirmation of the view that organization aids recall is found in an experiment by Tulving and Pearlstone (1966). They prepared lists of words composed of 12, 24 and 48 words, and consisting of categories of 1, 2 or 4 words in each. The items of a category were placed together with the category name included. The lists were read aloud to a group of subjects who were asked to memorize the words (but not the category names). Half the subjects were asked to 'free recall' the words by writing them down on a blank sheet of paper: the other half were given sheets of paper on which appeared the category names as clues. Those who were given help in this way recalled more words than those who were offered no clues. When the free recall group were later presented with category names, their ability to recall words improved. The researchers concluded, therefore, that the words were stored in memory but that clues were required to aid recall. A similar study was conducted by Cohen (1966) using lists of 10, 15 and 20 words, with categories of 3 or 4 words. He found that if one word was recalled from a category, a number of other words would also be recalled. These findings tend to confirm those of Tulving and Pearlstone.

Much of the time, material is not pre-arranged in an organized fashion when it is presented to us, and we find ourselves attempting to impose our own subjective organization upon it. Tulving (1962) found that people recalled lists of words in the same order on several trials, indicating some attempt at organization.

The type of memory which helps us use our language has been termed *semantic memory*. Here again the importance of organization has been demonstrated by Quillian (1969), and reviewed by Collins

43. *The semantic memory model* (after Collins and Quillian, in
L.W. Gregg (ed.) (1972), *Cognition in Learning and Memory;* by
courtesy of John Wiley and Sons, Inc.)

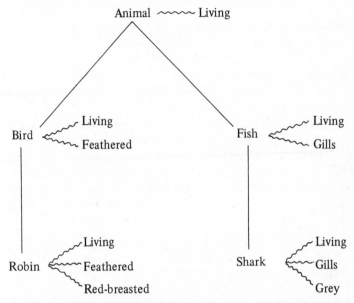

Semantic concepts have their properties alongside; straight lines indicate
relationships between concepts, and wavy lines connect concepts and
their properties.

and Quillian (1972). Part of their 'semantic network' is illustrated in
Figure 43, showing the interconnections of words in the three-level
hierarchy. Using this structure, it is possible to understand the truth
of a sentence if one can trace a route through the network which
connects each of the words in the sentence; for example, 'An ostrich
can move around.' The truth of this sentence can be ascertained by
relating it to the diagram – an ostrich is a bird, a bird is an animal,
and an animal is able to move around.

Collins and Quillian tested their theory by asking subjects to
evaluate the truth or falsity of a number of given sentences. There
were different kinds of true sentences, making use of the properties
associated with the three levels of the hierarchy. In the sentence 'An
ostrich has thin legs', the property 'thin legs' is at the same level as
the word concept 'ostrich'. Another sentence would employ a property one level away from the concept word, for example 'An ostrich

has feathers'. A third type of sentence might state 'An ostrich eats', using a description two levels removed from the concept word. Intermingled with these true sentences were false ones like 'A shark has feathers'.

Subjects were asked to look at a sentence and to indicate quickly whether it was true or false. The response time was recorded in respect of each sentence presented. The assumption was that a subject's response time would increase as he moved from one level to another in the hierarchy. Figure 44, taken from the Collins and Quillian studies, will help to clarify the point.

Turning now to mental imagery, most people claim they find little difficulty in forming mental pictures of stories they are reading, or of events being related to them by another person. However, people do show variations in the amount of detail they incorporate into those images or in the clarity with which they 'see' them. Some individuals find it reasonably easy to commit to memory unrelated words by

44. *Response time related to levels in the hierarchy* (after Collins and Quillian, in L.W. Gregg (ed.)(1972), *Cognition in Learning and Memory;* by courtesy of John Wiley and Sons, Inc.)

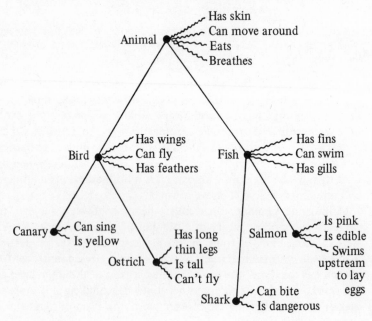

means of mental imagery, and this is well illustrated in a classic experiment by Bower (1972).

Subjects were given a set of one hundred cards, one at a time, each consisting of a pair of unrelated nouns, such as 'dog'–'hat'. The experimental group was asked to form a mental image in which there was an interaction between the two words on each card. The more unusual the details of the image, the better the image was considered to be. Without making any reference to imagery, the control group was instructed to memorize the pairs of words on each card. Both groups were allowed the same amount of time to learn the word-pairs. Later, each subject was shown the first word in each pair and instructed to recall the second word. The imagery group recalled 80% of the pairs, compared with only a 33% recall amongst the control group. Another experiment by Bower (1970) further demonstrated that it is not merely the ability to use images but the kind of images used which is important, a point supported by Morris and Stevens (1974).

There are individuals who can look at a picture and still see its image vividly in space for several minutes after the picture has been removed. They will also be able to offer a more accurate description than would be possible if they were relying solely on memory. The psychologist would refer to this sort of imagery as *eidetic imagery*, more commonly and erroneously referred to in popular speech as a 'photographic memory'. Eidetic imagery is not at all common: fewer than 7% of children experience it, and this percentage is further reduced in the late teens (Haber and Haber, 1964). Furthermore, it has been suggested that children will produce eidetic images only when the picture content is interesting to them.

The usual method for investigating eidetic imagery amongst children is for the experimenter to display a fairly detailed picture set against a grey background. Thirty seconds are given for the child to form an image before the picture is taken away, after which he is asked to give a description of what he is able to see on the screen. A study using this technique was undertaken in 1922 by Gordon Allport. Using sixty children in the experiment, he found that about half of them were able to offer detailed descriptions.

There is a particular kind of imagery known as the *method of loci*, or method of places, which requires an association to be made between the verbal material to be remembered and various imaged objects. In fact, this is a mnemonic device – a method which aids learning and the recall of previously learned material. The method of loci can be an extremely useful strategy for remembering a list of unrelated words. Here it is necessary to imagine a short walk through a series of locations – perhaps a journey through a street past well-known buildings, or a walk through certain rooms in your house or school. For example, as you enter your school or college, you find yourself in a large entrance hall to the right of which is a wall notice-board. From here, you mount a staircase which brings you to a corridor. Passing down the corridor, you enter a classroom on your left and sit down at a desk.

You would be able to commit your unrelated words to memory by taking each one in turn and associating it with each of your locations. The more 'unusual' the association, the more chance you will have of recalling the material at a later stage. Suppose the words you have to remember are items on a greengrocery list – a cabbage, haddock, celery, onions, tomatoes – you might visualize the entrance hall strewn with cabbage leaves to form a carpet, a haddock pinned to the notice-board, sticks of celery standing upright on each step of the staircase like courtiers, onions hanging in bunches round the lights in the corridor like chandeliers, and tomatoes forming a huge pyramid on your desk. In order to recall your words, all you would need to do would be to take your imaginery walk once again and recall each image in turn. In this way, the retrieval of the list of words should not prove too difficult.

A second kind of mnemonic device for learning lists of words, and similar to the method of loci, is that of *associations*. This entails finding relationships between each of the words so that they can be arranged into a sensible story. The story forms the background against which isolated items are to be remembered, and as the story is recounted, the words are recalled. For example, the following words are to be committed to memory: school, grocer's, bus, chemist, park, meal, TV. These items could be connected by means of the following story:

Jane came out of *school* and caught her usual *bus* home. When she alighted from the bus, she called at the *grocer's* with her mother's shopping list, and then paid a visit to the *chemist* with a doctor's prescription. After walking through the *park*, she arrived home, prepared herself a *meal*, and ate it while she watched TV.

Another mnemonic device takes the first letters of words to be remembered and forms them into another meaningful word; for example, helicopter, aeroplane, tank, lorry ('halt'). There are also mnemonics which make use of rhyme and rhythm:

Thirty days hath September,
April, June and November.

And everyone knows how to remember the colours of the rainbow from the fact that 'Richard Of York Gave Battle In Vain'.

A further interesting mnemonic device is the *method of key words*, which serves the purpose of associating two unrelated concepts by linking them to numbers. This is particularly effective if the words rhyme with the numbers (for example 'one'-'sun', 'two'-'shoe' and so on). A much more methodical system is the number–consonant alphabet, which dates from the seventeenth century. This is rather a

45. The number –consonant alphabet

0	1	2	3	4	5	6	7	8	9
s *or* z	t *or* d	n	m	r	l	ch *or* sh	k *or* ng	f *or* v	p *or* b

complicated system which is very difficult to apply in practice. Each number from 0 to 9 has its own special sound, the sound of a consonant, as shown in Figure 45. The principle is to convert numbers to their appropriate consonants and then to make words from the resulting sound. For example, 307 would be m: s: k ('mask'), though it will be readily seen that finding words to fit the sounds is not very easy.

If we accept for now that there are two sorts of memory – STM and LTM – it might be worthwhile to see how far they are related. One approach is the *two-process theory* of memory presented by Atkinson and Shiffrin (1971, 1977). Here it is assumed that material enters the STM, where it can either be retained by means of rehearsal or displaced. Material which is to enter LTM will do so directly from STM, and whereas STM has a very limited capacity, LTM can receive any amount of information (see Figure 46).

46. *The two-process theory of memory* (after Richard C. Atkinson and Richard M. Shiffrin, 'The control of short-term memory'; copyright © August 1971 by Scientific American, Inc. All rights reserved)

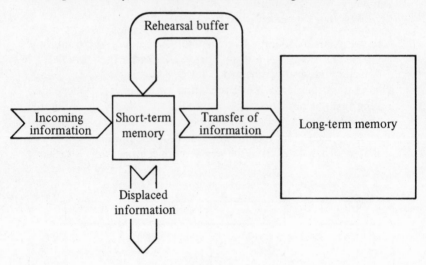

Some criticisms of the two-process theory

The two-process theory has been influential in studies of memory since the late 1960s, but in recent years some criticisms have arisen. Most discussion centres around the functions of STM, and doubts have been raised about whether STM even exists at all. The idea that STM codes information phonetically and LTM codes it semantically has been criticized, for example by Wickens (1972), on the basis that the LTM code is likely to be not a single semantic code, but a whole range of codes, including both semantic and phonetic ones. Ball, Wood and Smith (1975) found that subjects took just as long to identify the meaning or semantics of sentences as they did to recognize the acoustic or phonetic properties; in other words, in this experiment the sentences in LTM were coded semantically and phonetically.

Morris (1978) argues that the results of Conrad's work (see p. 125) show only that the phonetic code is used in STM and the semantic in LTM, but do not show that these are the only codes used by each system. Interference effects of any type are likely to affect recall from

STM more than from LTM, since STM is more vulnerable to any kind of interference than is LTM.

Craik (1971) asserted that STM must recognize the meaning of words, or must work directly with LTM, because the STM capacity is so small (only seven digits or a few words, as we have seen) that we would not be able to understand sentences using only STM, as proposed in the Atkinson–Shiffrin model.

Morton (1970) argues that STM is not a memory process as such, but a 'response buffer', which holds in store the next few words which we are about to utter. According to the Atkinson and Shiffrin model, STM allows the transfer of information to LTM through the use of the rehearsal buffer. Rehearsal should therefore improve retention, but Craik and Watkins (1973) found that if subjects were allowed to repeat the last few items in a free-recall list, recall of these words was not significantly improved.

Craik and Lockhart (1972) suggest that it is not rehearsal as such which is important, but what is done with the information during rehearsal. They believe that information can be processed to different depths, or in different stages. This 'depth of processing' approach suggests that there are three levels of processing: first, the structural level, which involves, for example, recognition of the types of letter (upper or lower case) in which a word is written, or the speech sounds which go to make up the sound of the word; next deepest, the 'phonetic' level of processing, which analyses similarities between the sound of a word and other words in store; and thirdly, deepest of all, the 'semantic' level, at which analysis is made of the meaning of a word and its relationship to previously stored word meanings. For example, Craik and Tulving (1975) found large differences in the later recognition of words which were presented tachistoscopically, when subjects were asked after being shown the word to process it at different levels. In one example, the word shown was 'table'. Subjects were asked to do one of three things, each corresponding to a different level of processing. At the structural level, they were asked: 'Is it in capitals?' At the phonetic level, they were asked: 'Does it rhyme with fable?' And at the semantic level, they were asked: 'Would it fit in the sentence "Put the vase on the ——"?' When semantic processing was used, 80% of the words were later recognized; for phonetic processing the recognition score was 50%; and for structural processing only 18%, suggesting that the deeper the processing the better the retention.

However, without some independent measurement of the depth of processing, it is difficult to be sure that the various levels are in the correct order. Nevertheless, it seems to be fairly well accepted that the level of processing may affect the strength of the memory trace. But levels of processing deal only with the encoding of information; Morris, Bransford and Franks (1977) suggest that problems of retrieval as well as encoding may affect performance on memory tasks. If, when an item is due to be retrieved, there is a *retrieval cue*, an aid to retrieval, present, retrieval is much better than if no such cue is provided. For example, subjects were given ten sentences such as 'The man tuned the piano', and later had to recall the objects mentioned in the sentences. Recall cues were given, some of which were appropriate, for example 'Something tuneful', and some of which were inappropriate, for example 'Something heavy'. The average recall score out of 10 with appropriate cues was 4.7, while with inappropriate cues the recall was only 1.6. These findings suggest that when some information is encoded, it is done so in a quite specific manner. In the case above, it is not just 'piano' which is stored, but more likely 'piano–tuneful'. When recall cues are given, the more closely they resemble the original situation or context of the information, the more likely the information is to be retrieved. In effect, this is what the police are doing when they reconstruct crimes at the same places and times as they originally occurred, in the hope that being at the original scene was encoded along with the actual events in the witnesses' memories.

The supporting evidence for the Atkinson–Shiffrin model which came from studies of brain-damaged subjects (see p. 122) has also come under close scrutiny. Milner's study (1966) of a man whose hippocampus had been destroyed (see p. 139) was taken by two-process theorists to mean that the *consolidation mechanism*, which recodes STM information for permanent storage in the long-term store, was destroyed. In effect, the link between STM and LTM no longer existed, and the man was unable to store any new information in LTM. Interestingly, there was at least one exception to this: he had apparently stored a little information about the assassination of President Kennedy. Since he could recall events from before the operation which damaged his hippocampus, his LTM and its retrieval system must have been intact. But a second case described by Shallice and Warrington (1970) (see p. 122) concerned a patient whose LTM was apparently intact, but whose STM capability had been seriously damaged to the extent that he could recall only two digits in a standard STM test. If information can no longer enter STM and its rehearsal buffer, how can it reach LTM? Critics of the two-process theory say that this suggests that information can enter LTM directly, but the two-process theorists themselves argue that what has been destroyed is not STM itself, but the retrieval pathway from STM, so that the STM-to-LTM system still works, but information cannot be retrieved whilst in STM.

Tulving (1972) proposes that the long-term store actually contains two sets of interrelated information. The first is 'semantic memory', which is akin to a dictionary, permitting us to understand language. 'Episodic memory', on the other hand, is the storage of personal experiences. Evidence of a kind comes from studies of amnesia and repression: no matter how much personal information an individual forgets, he never forgets how to speak the language he customarily speaks. Tulving argues that the two systems are necessary in order for us to understand language. If the two systems were not separated, every time we heard a word, all the information about where we heard it, what it means, what examples of it we have met, and so on would be retrieved too. This would cause a tremendous overload of information, so much so that we would probably miss what was said next. Despite being separated, the store of word meanings in semantic memory can be updated by transfer of new information from episodic memory.

Constructive and inferential memory

Because of the large amount of work on the organization of memory, and because of the feeling that a study ought to be made of 'real' information such as sentences or stories, rather than of lists of words, increasing interest has been taken in research which was conducted by Bartlett (1932) using the method of *serial reproduction*. He read an Eskimo folk-tale called 'The War of the Ghosts' to a subject, who then had to repeat as much of it as he could to a second subject, who then repeated it to a third, and so on. After six or seven reproductions the story had become much shorter, from its original 330 words to approximately 180 words. What was interesting, however, was the ways in which the story changed. The theme of the

Eskimo folk-tale was not easily understood by British subjects, and the first subjects in each experiment frequently constructed their own. This constructed theme tended to remain undistorted through all further repetitions of the story. In one unpublished experiment performed with students at a College of Further Education, the supernatural theme of the original story became transformed into a short tale of gang warfare, and a part of the original story, which ran ' "Arrows are in the canoe", they said', became distorted into 'We've got some guns in our car,' and 'Kalama', one of the place-names in the original study, was changed to 'Colombo'.

Bartlett believed that information which fitted into an individual's existing schemata was likely to be retained. Information which did not fit was liable to be either forgotten or distorted, so that it did fit. This distortion, Barlett believed, occurred as a result of the subjects' 'efforts after meaning', that is, the subjects' attempts to get the story to fit their schemata by changing the sentence structure from its original rather stilted form into a more flowing style, by interpreting the story so as to provide a more understandable theme or moral, and by rationalization, that is the introduction of subjects' own reasons for unexplained occurrences in the original story.

Parallel with *constructive memory* as an organizational process in memory is the drawing of inferences from the information to be retained. For example, in later reproductions of 'War of the Ghosts', if subjects are given the information that 'Indians' were involved, they might well infer that 'Indians' stood for 'Red Indians', and bias their story accordingly. However, when subjects leave out information about canoes and arrows, the subjects following them might well infer that 'Indians' stood for 'Indians from India' (which perhaps explains where 'Colombo' came from). It is therefore apparent that we do not passively receive information and store it just as a tape-recorder might: we process the information in an active attempt to understand it. If a nuclear physicist and a lawyer were given passages of material involving nuclear physics concepts to study, and were later given recall tests, it is a reasonable supposition that, other things being equal, the nuclear physicist's recall score would be higher than the lawyer's. In Bartlett's terms, more of the material would fit into the nuclear physicist's schemata than would into the lawyer's, who, if he were to attempt to obtain an equally high score, would have to show a great deal of 'effort after meaning'. This idea is, of course, not new: Ebbinghaus was aware of it in the nineteenth century, and used nonsense syllables specifically to control for differences in the meaningfulness of different words.

The physiological aspects of memory

One very interesting neurological model, the *cell assembly model*, was postulated by Professor Donald Hebb some thirty years ago. He proposed that the brain must have its own self-regulating processes which are independent of environmental stimulation, and these processes are known as cell assemblies. A cell assembly is an organized system of neurons in the brain and is, in fact, the neurological equivalent of a memory.

One might imagine the cell assembly as a complicated collection of interconnected pathways which allow nerve impulses to pass from cell to cell within the assembly. Sustained thinking is the result of nerve impulses moving around between cells within these assemblies. The formation of a cell assembly takes place when two or more cells which are continuously active become connected. More cells are then introduced into the assembly, with a consequent increase in new connections. Forming new connections is the neurological counterpart of learning, while the increase in the number of connections corresponds to an increase in knowledge and the need for a memory to retain it.

Bio-psychologists have discovered that patients who have undergone certain types of brain surgery are capable of acquiring and retaining new information for a time, but this disappears after a short while. Milner (1966) quotes the instance of a patient who was unable to remember where he lived, but could recall quite easily his address of twelve months previously. Information requires a certain amount of time before it becomes consolidated in LTM. This is known as a *neural consolidation model*, first proposed in 1900 by Müller and Pilzecker, and revised more recently by Hebb (1949, 1958).

The time factor here is important, because if the consolidation process is interrupted in its early stages, the individual will experience great difficulty recalling what he has learned. Interruptions to the process can be of various kinds - lack of oxygen to the brain (*anoxia*), concussion, extreme cold (*hypothermia*), extreme heat (*hyperthermia*) and *electroconvulsive shock* (ECS) - a controversial technique sometimes used in the treatment of severe depression in which the brain of the patient is subjected to a short electric shock.

Amnesia can be explained by means of the neural consolidation hypothesis. It is a well-known fact that brain-damaged patients often report loss of memory for events which have taken place immediately before their accident (*retrograde amnesia*). Such patients often find difficulty remembering anything which happened up to one hour prior to the injury.

Retrograde amnesia has been experimentally induced in human subjects by means of ECS, a treatment normally reserved for severely depressed patients. Cohen *et al.* (1968) administered ECS to left, right and both cerebral hemispheres of depressed patients, who had previously been given material to learn. The results showed that:

1 Less verbal material was recalled by those shocked in the left hemisphere than by those shocked in the right hemisphere.
2 Patients who received shocks in the right hemisphere recalled less non-verbal material than those shocked in the left hemisphere.
3 Least verbal and non-verbal material was retained by those shocked in both hemispheres.

There is a more positive side, however, for memory can be helped by electrical stimulation. Penfield and Roberts (1959) reported that conscious patients, whose cerebral cortex had been exposed, recalled events from the past when various areas of the cortex received electrostimulation. These researchers also found that the same memories were recalled each time the cortex was stimulated in exactly the same place. This evidence, therefore, seems to favour the concept of LTM, and to point to the fact that specific information is held in certain areas of brain tissue.

Chemical intervention has also been found to interfere with memory. Alpern and Crabbe (1972) injected large or small amounts of strychnine sulphate into rats after they had taken part in a maze-learning task. Presented with the same task again, the rats that had received the smaller dose of strychnine sulphate made fewer errors. In another experiment conducted by Irwin and Beunazizi (1966), the stimulant Metrazol was found to help retention in rats.

Investigations into the biochemistry of memory have shown that deoxyribonucleic acid (DNA) and ribonucleic acid (RNA) have important parts to play in storing, replicating and transferring molecular information in biological systems. Some of the research evidence remains controversial, and there are those who would argue that it is too unreliable for any safe conclusions to be drawn. Nevertheless, the criticisms seem to be levelled chiefly at the research methodology and techniques employed. Perhaps further development of both of these will help remove some of the scepticism which surrounds the studies.

In one of these studies, Braud and Braud (1972) trained rats to discriminate between a large and a small circle, offering a reward each time the larger circle was selected. The rats were then killed and extracts from their brains were injected into other rats. The latter also showed an ability to choose the larger circle. On the other hand, control-group rats which had received no such injection failed to demonstrate such preference.

McConnell *et al.* (1959) used electric shocks to condition planarians to contract to light. These creatures were then cut into two halves; the head portion grew a tail, and the tail portion a head. When placed in a light, contraction took place in each of the regenerated creatures, demonstrating that the memory of the conditioned response had passed over to each new creature.

McConnell's results have been treated with a certain amount of scepticism by Hebb. He accepts without reservation the notion that a chemical substance which is present in a trained animal can assist in the training of another animal. Nevertheless, his point of criticism is that what has been set up by RNA is not actually a memory but rather an aid to faster learning.

It should be evident from this chapter that studies of memory systems are of fundamental importance; but there are still many questions to answer. Research into memory has grown over the past few years, and many new ideas will be developed in the future which, it is hoped, will answer some of these questions and enlarge our knowledge of the area.

Further reading

Adams, J. (1967), *Human Memory*, McGraw-Hill

Hunter, I.M.L. (1964), *Memory*, Penguin

Norman, D.A. (1969), *Memory and Attention: An Introduction to Human Information Processing*, Wiley

Norman, D.A. (1970), *Models of Human Memory*, Academic Press

Whitty, C.W.M. and Zangwill, O.L. (eds.) (1966), *Amnesia*, Appleton-Century-Crofts

5 The biological bases of behaviour

It has been said, and with considerable justification, that psychology is not really a coherent, unified discipline at all, but rather a collection of specialisms united only by the logic of their method. Certainly the structuring of university courses into highly specialized and independent units tends to support and perhaps even exaggerate this state of affairs. This chapter examines one of the major sub-disciplines, physiological psychology. As we mentioned in the Preface this chapter is markedly longer than the others, largely because many students, and many teachers, find it the area which poses most difficulties in psychology courses.

The aim of the chapter is not only to give the reader a straightforward introduction to physiological psychology but also to 'service' certain other chapters by considering such areas as the physiology of visual perception, and genetics, an appreciation of which is important for a real understanding of the issues raised by the nature/nurture debate.

One major determining factor in man's ability to perceive, think, learn, remember and act is his underlying physiological makeup. The complex psychological capacities of humans are due to the interconnections of thousands of millions of nerve cells acting in conjunction with hormones on the rest of the body. It is the work of the physiological psychologists to answer such questions as, what happens in the nervous system when we learn? What parts of the nervous system cause us to feel hunger or thirst? How does our brain allow us to use language?

Discussion of the following story will help to focus attention on the relationship of physiological and psychological explanations.

Imagine a spaceship arriving from Alpha Centauri to study events on earth. Two officers decide to study a metallic object with a wheel at each end of its four corners; the natives call it a car. The first officer reports that cars can travel at great speeds along tarmac strips and do this in great numbers especially between eight o'clock and nine o'clock in the morning and five o'clock and six o'clock at night. They stop at junctions when the lights are red and go on green; in built-up areas they usually travel at around thirty miles per hour whereas on wide open roads seventy miles per hour is more usual. The second officer reports that cars can travel at great speeds along tarmac strips due to the burning of petrol in confined spaces known as cylinders. The petrol is mixed with air in a carburettor and the more of this mixture that is allowed into the cylinder the faster the car goes.

Both these officers give a valid, though limited, explanation of the behaviour of a motor car but they are using different levels of explanation. Sometimes one level may be more useful than another: it may be more useful when a car is stationary to note that it stands in front of a red light than to consider carburettor variables, but if it remains stationary when the lights change, other explanations may be sought.

The above two explanations of the behaviour of cars are analogous to two types of explanations of human behaviour. The highway-code type is akin to the psychological explanation, looking at stimuli and responses, perhaps theorizing about the decision-making processes between the two. The engineering explanation mirrors the physiological level of explanation which looks at the way that the nervous and endocrine systems affect and are affected by behaviour.

The relationship between physiological and psychological explanations of behaviour is similar to the relationship between the engineering and highway-code types: the levels are complementary rather than contradictory. Knowledge of the biological makeup and functioning of an organism may help an understanding of how and why it reacts to stimuli in certain ways. Sometimes physiological explanations are more appropriate than others, for example in explaining a patient's loss of speech after suffering a stroke. At other times a psychological explanation may be more appropriate; for example, although a signature on a cheque could be explained in terms of nerve action and muscle movement the real importance of a signature is its social (psychological) relevance, so that in fact the signature could be made with a completely different set of nerve and muscle actions by holding the pen in one's mouth but the resultant mark would have the same social meaning. In many other situations psychological and physiological explanations are both interesting and both add to our knowledge of behaviour.

A school of thought known as *reductionism* argues that the best way to explain anything is to break it down to its component parts. Behaviourists practise reductionism when they assert that we can explain complex human behaviour in terms of collections of reinforced responses. The logical conclusion of reductionism would be to explain behaviour in terms of physiology; it could be taken even further, since neurons can be seen in terms of collections of chemicals – and perhaps the ultimate would be to explain behaviour in terms of atoms and molecules.

Some reductionists argue that a thorough knowledge of physiology might replace the need for psychological explanations, but this is unlikely, for even with a full working knowledge there will be many instances, like the signature example, where a different level of explanation is more meaningful, simpler and more easily made relevant to normal social life. What makes one level of explanation appropriate at any one time depends not on the actual behaviour that is being explained but on why we want to know the answers. Much of the work in this chapter, especially that on perception, demonstrates the practical problem of explaining all behaviour in terms of physiology when we do not have sufficient knowledge and may never gain it. The other fundamental problem is logical: some realms of psychology such as the *experience* of emotions may be outside the realms of physiology, for although physiologists have studied emotion (see p. 152), many readers would agree that the human experience of feelings such as anger and ecstasy is lost in this approach. Gestalt psychologists argued that it was fruitless to attempt an explanation of complex processes by reductionist techniques because 'the whole is more than the sum of the parts'. They illustrated this by reference to melody: the component parts of a melody are tones, but the same melody can be played in different tones, by various instruments and in various styles, and still be recognizable. It is the overall organization of the parts rather than the parts themselves which is the characteristic of melody, as it is of many other experiences and behaviours.

One question that has dogged philosophers for centuries and is relevant to the extent to which physiology can explain behaviour is the mind/body problem. Some philosophers argue that man's behaviour is controlled, or at least affected by, a non-physical entity called the mind or soul; since this is non-physical, the physiologist cannot hope to fully explain behaviour on a physical level. Others take the view that mind and consciousness are simply by-products of the complex arrangement of neurons in the brain and are thus open to physiological levels of explanation. As a working hypothesis, most physiological psychologists take the view that if there is a non-physical mind, it works in such close proximity to the brain, as can be seen by the effects of damage to the nervous system, that we can learn a vast amount about organisms by studying at this level and are certainly nowhere near the point where the question raises practical difficulties.

Neurons

The nervous system consists of about twelve thousand million interconnected nerve cells known as *neurons*. Neurons vary in shape but have the same basic structure and can be classified into *sensory neurons*, which form chains to connect the sense organs and the brain, *connector neurons* within the brain itself and *motor neurons* connecting the brain and muscles. Any observable response to stimulation requires activity of all three of these types. Figures 47 and 48 show idealized versions of sensory and motor neurons. The cell body protrudes at one end to form the *dendrites* which receive information from other neurons; the message is passed along the *axon* as an electrical impulse to the many *synapses*, which produce chemicals that pass the message on to other neurons. Some neurons do not have an insulating *myelin sheath* surrounding the axon and in those cells the impulse travels more slowly from dendrites to synapses; in the case of motor neurons, to the *motor end plates* which stimulate muscle fibres. The *nodes of ranvier* are small gaps in the myelin sheath and the impulse seems to jump from node to node.

In the majority of cases, neurons can only receive signals through the dendrites or cell body, and can only transmit them via synapses, but G.M. Shepherd (1965) showed that some neurons are able to transmit and receive through the dendrites. The cell body may or may not be stimulated by synapses from other cells, but its main function is that of the absorption and use of chemical nutrients to ensure the growth and survival of the neuron. The vast number of neurons in the nervous system gives some idea of their size, which can be as little as a few thousandths of a millimetre in cross-section. Axons are usually a few centimetres in length, although some may be over a metre.

Nerves such as the *optic nerve*, which links the eye and brain, consist of many thousands of neurons whose axons run in parallel, bundled together in a protective sheath rather like the lead to an electric appliance but with many more individual 'wires'.

The speed of an impulse along a thick myelinated axon can be as great as 120 metres per second, meaning that messages from the

47. *A sensory neuron*

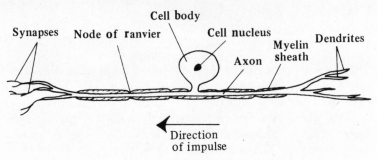

sense organs to the brain arrive very quickly despite the slowing due to passage across synapses. It is the processing of information within the brain, deciding what the stimulus is and what response should be made, that causes most delay in reactions. The passage of an impulse along an axon is electrochemical and depends upon changing permeability of the axon surface to sodium ions. In its resting state the axon membrane is impermeable to positively charged sodium ions, which are more concentrated on the outside than the inside of the axon. Due to this difference in the concentration of sodium ions the outside of the cell membrane is positively charged compared with the inside, which is negatively charged. When a dendrite is excited by the synapses of an adjacent cell, part of its membrane becomes permeable to sodium, which rushes in in such quantity that the inside temporarily becomes positively charged; this causes the next part of

48. *A motor neuron*

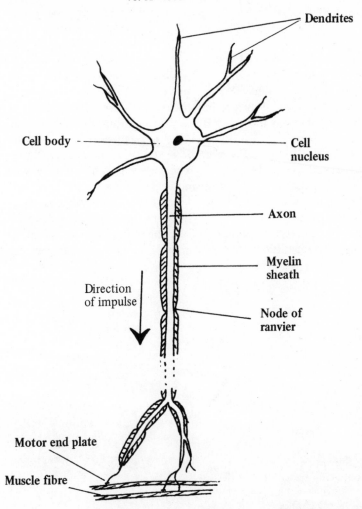

the dendrite surface to become permeable, thus repeating the effect and causing the impulse to travel further down the dendrite to the axon and along to the synapses. Once the impulse has passed to the next part of the membrane, the preceding part again becomes impermeable to sodium but permeable to positively charged potassium ions which are present inside the axon. The potassium flows out of the axon, being attracted by the negative charge, and does this in such quantity that the resting potential is again achieved. A process known as the *sodium pump*, which is not yet fully understood, pumps sodium out of the axon so that the process can be repeated.

Synapses and motor end plates

Neurons do not physically touch each other: messages have to pass across the small fluid-filled gap known as the synapse in order to reach the next cell. When an impulse reaches the end of the axon it is transmitted across the synapse by chemical means: *transmitter molecules* are released from the *pre-synaptic terminal* (see Fig. 49) and pass across the gap to the receptor site on the dendrites or cell body of the receiving neuron, which may then fire. In order to prevent continued excitation, the transmitter substance is removed from the receptor sites either by the action of an enzyme, such as acetyl-cholinesterase in the case of acetylcholine, or it may be re-absorbed into the pre-synaptic terminal. Only the pre-synaptic terminal can produce transmitter molecules and therefore messages can only pass in one direction across a synapse.

49. A synapse

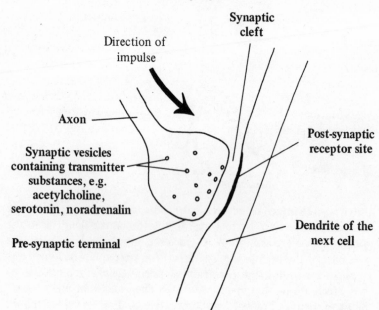

Excitatory synapses release a transmitter substance that produces an electrical charge at the post-synaptic receptor site, known as the *excitatory post-synaptic potential* (EPSP), which is proportional to the amount of transmitter substance received by the post-synaptic neuron. When the EPSP is high enough the neuron fires; it may require the action of many synapses firing at the same time onto one cell, or the same synapse firing in quick succession, to produce a sufficiently high EPSP to cause an impulse to pass down the axon of the neuron. The combination of excitation from several synapses or from a single synapse firing more than once in order to fire a neuron is known as *summation*. *Inhibitory synapses* have the same structure but produce an *inhibitory post-synaptic potential* (IPSP) proportional to the amount of transmitter substance passed, and this makes the receiving cell less likely to fire. The average neuron in the *cerebral cortex*, the top part of the brain responsible for complex processes such as thinking, receives about thirty thousand synapses from three thousand other neurons.

Individual neurons have both excitatory and inhibitory synapses acting upon them, and the probability of a cell firing depends upon the relative numbers of these synapses that are active at the time. If the EPSP is sufficiently greater than the IPSP, the impulse will pass down the axon to the cell's own pre-synaptic terminals. An individual neuron has many synapses at the end of its axon, each releasing the same transmitter substance, and yet some of these synapses are excitatory while others are inhibitory. It seems, therefore, that the excitatory or inhibitory nature of a synapse depends not upon the transmitter substance but upon the structure of the post-synaptic receptor site. Acetylcholine is found in both types of synapses, but gamma-aminobutyric acid (GABA), which is employed by up to a third of all brain synapses, may only be associated with inhibitory forms.

The need for inhibitory in addition to excitatory synapses should become clearer when processing of visual information is dealt with later in this chapter. But at this point it is obvious that since all neurons are directly or indirectly linked to all others, it is necessary to have some system that can prevent one strong stimulus from causing all neurons to start firing: inhibitory synapses can ensure that a chain of impulses passes along a particular set of neurons and does not 'flow over' into other networks. The role of inhibitory synapses can be experienced while playing sports which involve a great deal of physical contact: a kick on the shin during a rugby match is often not felt whereas the same strength of kick in other circumstances would be very painful. This is because during a rugby match it is not useful for the brain to process information about body knocks.

Neurons obey the *all-or-none-rule*, which states that once the EPSP is great enough, an impulse will pass all the way along the axon. This impulse is always of the same strength, whether the EPSP is the lowest that will cause the cell to fire (*threshold level*) or much larger. Neurons either fire or they do not: there are no in-between, half-hearted or graded impulses. The threshold level does vary, however: some cells have a high threshold and therefore need a much greater EPSP before firing than those with a low threshold. The threshold of individual cells varies depending upon when the neuron last fired. Immediately after firing there is a period of one or two milliseconds during which time no stimulus is strong enough to produce an impulse; following this *absolute refractory period* is a period known as the *relative refractory period*, when the threshold gradually reduces to normal.

The variety of threshold levels is important in coding information about the intensity of a stimulus. A nerve consists of a bundle of neurons each of which has a different threshold; an intense stimulus can fire more of these neurons than a weak one. For an individual neuron a strong stimulus will cause a repeat impulse immediately after the absolute refractory period, whereas a weak stimulus only exceeds threshold level towards the end of the relative refractory period, therefore producing an impulse less frequently than the strong sensation. The brain consequently has two ways of perceiving stimulus intensity: the number of neurons firing and the frequency of impulses.

Motor neurons terminate in motor end plates rather than synapses, and each of these is attached to a single muscle fibre which contracts when stimulated. Physical actions such as raising a cup to the mouth depend upon the co-ordinated firing of thousands of motor neurons, together with sensory and connector neurons which continually monitor activity and produce corrective measures via the motor end plates.

The nervous system

Most cell bodies are found within the brain and spinal cord, but their axons may extend beyond these regions, carrying information from the sense organs or to the muscles. Some of these axons are over a metre in length; they are grouped together in bundles known as nerves which are usually large enough to see with the naked eye in a dissected animal. The brain and spinal cord are known as the *central nervous system* (CNS); *cranial nerves* leave this system via holes in the skull, while *spinal nerves* depart from the gaps between the vertebrae of the backbone. Once outside the CNS, the nerves form part of the *peripheral nervous system*.

The peripheral nervous system
The peripheral nervous system has two subdivisions which have different structures and functions – the *somatic nervous system* and the *autonomic nervous sustem*.

The somatic nervous system
The somatic nervous system carries information from the sense organs to the CNS, and controls those muscles which are under voluntary control, such as those of the limbs and face. The axons of neurons in this system are myelinated and reach into the periphery from cell bodies within the CNS.

The autonomic nervous system
Autonomic neurons are only thinly myelinated, and extend from cell bodies that are in the periphery. The system controls the activity of the internal organs and glands of the body – those activities such as heart-beat, blood-pressure and release of sugar from the liver over which an individual has no voluntary control.

There are two main sections of the ANS, the *sympathetic* and *parasympathetic divisions*, both of which connect with most glands in the body, usually with opposing effects; for example, heart-rate is increased by sympathetic activity, but slowed by the action of the parasympathetic system.

The sympathetic system is particularly active in times of stress, producing what Walter Cannon described as the *fight-or-flight syndrome*, a condition in which the body is ideally prepared to expend energy in fighting or running away from a threatening stimulus.

When experiencing this syndrome, the blood flow to the limbs and brain is increased, the bronchioles of the lungs are dilated and sugar is released into the bloodstream from the liver. At the same time the sympathetic system inhibits bodily processes such as digestion which are not needed to prepare for action. The effects of the sympathetic system can be quite long-lasting because it also causes the release of adrenalin from the adrenal glands. Adrenalin is very similar to the transmitter substance in the sympathetic synapses: it induces increased firing of the sympathetic nervous system. For this reason you may feel your heart beating heavily for several moments after a dangerous situation, such as a near-accident in a car.

The parasympathetic section of the ANS controls the conservation and restoration of the body's energy resources. Because its effect is normally opposite to that of the sympathetic system, most of the organs and glands are controlled by a balance of the two sections. Consider someone suddenly confronted by an armed terrorist. His ANS becomes quickly active, particularly the sympathetic section: his heart beats faster; his blood-pressure rises; the blood vessels serving the voluntary muscles of his trunk and limbs enlarge; the blood vessels to his stomach and intestines become smaller; his mouth feels dry; the pupils of his eyes dilate; and contractions of the stomach and intestines cease or may even be reversed. In addition the *galvanic skin response* (GSR) – the electrical resistance of the skin – will decrease due to the greater production of sweat. (The GSR may be measured by a simple battery-operated device known as a GSR meter.) He experiences a strong emotion of fear. Imagine, on the other hand, someone whose friend has died. Again his ANS is active, but this time it will be predominantly the parasympathetic division; he experiences the emotion of sadness.

The role of the ANS in the perception of emotion The question of how we perceive our own emotions has been a subject of controversy for many years. The ANS produces changes in the body which occur at times of strong emotion, but do the changes cause the sensation of the emotion; are they caused as a result of the sensation; or are the two processes independent?

Towards the end of the last century W. James and C. Lange argued that it was the recognition of bodily changes that caused the feeling of emotion. They argued that different stimuli cause different patterns of physiological activity, resulting in different feelings: the sight of a charging bull causes bodily changes different from those produced by a seductive member of the opposite sex, and therefore the emotion experienced is different. This theory runs contrary to common sense but can sometimes be backed up by real-life experiences: as observed previously, in a near-accident your heart beats fast and you may then feel anxious, but this feeling occurs after the danger has passed. The James–Lange theory has not stood up to experimental investigation; physiological studies have demonstrated differences between fear and anger, but in many emotions the bodily states are similar. However, this lack of evidence for physical changes in emotion is not proof: it may well be that we do not yet have measuring instruments which are sensitive enough to measure tiny changes which may be important. Artificial induction of bodily changes by the injection of adrenalin does not result in a true feeling of emotion as predicted by James and Lange except under special circumstances (see Schachter and Singer's work, discussed below).

In the 1920s W. Cannon put forward the theory that the autonomically controlled physiological changes which occur during strong emotions have the role of preparing the body for action and play no part in the sensation of emotion. His theory states that emotion-provoking stimuli are processed by the thalamus, which then passes information to the cortex, where the perception of emotion occurs. The processes of preparing the body for action and perception of emotion were considered to occur at the same time, but independently. (Later investigations suggest that the hypothalamus rather than the thalamus is responsible for the integration of emotion.)

More recent theories have tended to assume a role for physiological changes in the perception of emotion but have stressed the importance of cognitive factors – the processes of thinking, association, interpretation and memory. The work of Schachter and Singer (1962) has been particularly influential. Schachter argues that both physiological changes and the perception of the stimulus evoking those changes are necessary to produce the sensation of emotion. He and Singer illustrated this in a now classic experiment. They injected subjects with either adrenalin, which produces the physiological changes in the body found in many emotional states, or a placebo which has no effect on body processes. Some subjects injected with adrenalin were told of the effects that it would have on their bodies while others were not. Each subject was then put into a room with another person who was actually a confederate of the experimenter and was scripted to act in either a happy or angry fashion: he was known as the *stooge subject*. Schacter and Singer found that those subjects who were not told of the effects of their injection interpreted their bodily changes as the emotion of happiness in the presence of the happy stooge, or anger when accompanied by the angry stooge. Neither the placebo group nor those informed of the side effects of the injection were affected by the behaviour of the stooges. Such results support the theory that the interpretation of the bodily changes that occur with emotion depend largely on the cognitive interpretation of the situation.

Schachter's work shows that cognitive events determine the perception of the type of emotion that is felt, but the research of G.W. Hohmann (1966) suggests that the degree of emotion felt is determined by the information available to the brain about the bodily changes governed by the ANS. Hohmann interviewed patients who had damage to the spine which severely limited the amount of information their brains received about changes occurring in their bodies: he found that although they still felt emotions, these were not felt to the same extent as before their accidents. Without information of bodily changes the subjects felt less intense emotion.

All the theories of emotion suggest a role for the central as well as the autonomic nervous system. The limbic system (see p. 157) appears to be involved, as does the right cerebral hemisphere (see p. 163). G. Gainotti studied patients who had damaged either the right or left sides of the brain – known as the right and left cerebral hemispheres. He found that those with an injury to the left hemisphere showed much greater emotional upset than those with right hemispherical damage. This might simply be due to the fact that damage to the left hemisphere has a greater effect on social life because it involves the loss of speech, but other findings suggest there may be a real emotional difference between the hemispheres. Gainotti (1972) found that patients with left hemispherical injuries could perceive the emotional tone of a statement even though they could not understand the words, while those with right hemispherical injuries showed no difficulties of comprehension but failed to recognize whether a sentence was spoken in an angry or relaxed fashion. This suggests that the right hemisphere is involved in the recognition of emotion in others. The right hemisphere seems far more sensitive to negative emotions than the left, since emotional reactions such as hysterical paralysis and psychosomatic pains (paralysis and pain without any recognizable physical cause) occur far more often on the left side of the body, whose sensory and motor functions are managed by this side of the brain.

The central nervous system

Figure 50 shows some of the major parts of the CNS, each of which has a slightly different function. The cerebrum controls complex voluntary behaviour and the interpretation of information from the sense organs; it is in this part of the brain that processes such as thinking and remembering occur. Detailed descriptions of the structure and function of the cerebrum are given in the section entitled 'Localization of functions on the cortex' (see p. 163). Lower sections of the brain deal with simple automatic behaviour such as reflexes, the control of breathing and digestion, and the passage of information to higher centres.

50. The central nervous system

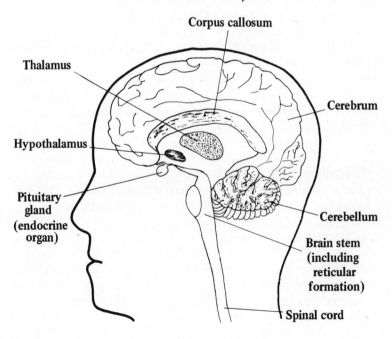

The spinal cord

The spinal cord connects the central and peripheral nervous systems, providing a pathway between the brain and the body. It passes from the brain stem down the whole length of the back, encased in the vertebrae of the backbone. Some of the very simplest reactions to stimuli, the reflexes – the reactions you give when you quickly remove your hand from a hot object or when your knee jerks in response to the doctor's hammer – are controlled by the spinal cord. Reflexes are extremely primitive items of behaviour because they are involuntary and always take the same form given the same stimulus; yet because they are so fast they can prevent the sort of damage we might do to ourselves if, for example, we did not let go of a hot object until nerve impulses had been transmitted to the brain, processed and then passed down again.

In the knee-jerk reflex a sensory neuron fires when the correct part of the knee is tapped; this message passes into the spine, where the synapse of the sensory neuron transmits the impulse to a motor neuron. The firing of this causes the knee muscle to contract and the legs to jerk forward. Most reflexes involve a connector neuron between the sensory and motor neurons; this simple system of connection is known as the *reflex arc*. The two or three neurons of the reflex arc do, however, have synapses with others which pass up and down the spine, and it is through these pathways that we actually become aware of the reflex.

If the whole central nervous system acted as a collection of reflex arcs, the number of responses to any situation would be extremely limited; the same response would always be elicited by the same stimulus. However, the connection between sensory and motor neurons is not usually as direct as in the case of a reflex; as we have seen, there are both excitatory and inhibitory synapses in the system, which act like switches, so that a particular stimulus may trigger one pathway in a particular situation, but if that pathway is being inhibited for some reason, it may trigger a different one.

The brain stem

The lower part of the brain, which is linked to the spinal cord, contains structures with a variety of functions. However, one of its main purposes is to control those kinds of internal behaviour over which we have little or no voluntary control, such as breathing, heart-beat and digestion.

The *reticular formation*, which is sometimes known as the *reticular activating system* or RAS, is a diffuse network of cells running through the brain stem up towards the thalamus. It receives inputs from all the sensory pathways and is closely connected with the spinal cord, thalamus and cortex. The RAS is thought to play an important role in the arousal of the cortex; indeed, many sleeping pills have their effect by inhibiting this region. It is also involved in selective attention, allowing some stimuli to reach conscious awareness while others of equal intensity fail to be perceived. Early studies showed that ablation of the RAS results in coma followed by death, but if the operation is done in stages partial recovery occurs after about a month. This suggests that, although normally involved in arousal and attention, it is not an indispensable structure. Electrical stimulation of the RAS can wake sleeping cats, increase the speed at which discrimination tasks are learnt and quicken reflexes.

The cerebellum

The *cerebellum* is involved in the maintenance of balance and the performance of skilled actions like walking or riding a bicycle. It allows us to perform complicated actions 'without thinking'; if it were damaged, such activities would require great concentration and might even become impossible. People with damage to the cerebellum display a noticeable loss of muscle control.

The thalamus

The *thalamus* is a relay station for nerve pathways leading to and from the cortex. The impulses passed to the cortex concern sensory information such as vision and hearing; those passing down are directed towards the cerebellum and concern complex limb movements. The lateral geniculate body discussed on page 190 with reference to visual processing is part of the thalamus. Another part has links with the reticular formation and influences sleep and wakefulness.

The limbic system

This lies just below the cerebrum and consists of a collection of individual structures involved in motivation, emotion and memory. Rosvold found that after removal of a part of this system known as the *amygdala*, monkeys behaved more aggressively towards the experimenter but in most cases dropped to the bottom of the dominance hierarchy. Damage to another part, the *hippocampus*, leaves patients with an inability to remember new information for anything more than a few minutes.

The endocrine system

Nerve impulses are not the only way in which bodily processes can be controlled; there exists a complementary system which relies on the secretion of complex chemicals, known as *hormones*, into the bloodstream from the endocrine glands. The effect of hormones is much slower than that of nerve impulses but is usually longer-lasting.

Some types of behaviour are affected by both nervous and endocrine systems; for example, the increased inclination for courtship during certain months of the year in birds and other animals has a hormonal basis, but the specific movements during mating are synchronized by the nervous system. Another example of the complementary activities of the two systems can be seen during the fight-or-flight syndrome (see p. 151) when the sympathetic nervous system mobilizes all the body's energy resources and causes the *adrenal medulla* (see Fig. 51) to secrete adrenalin and noradrenalin, hormones which maintain the activity of the sympathetic system. The

51. The endocrine system (by courtesy of M. Herbert)

Pituitary gland

Thyroid gland (regulates growth and metabolic rate)

Pancreas (regulates blood sugar level)

Adrenal glands (involved in fight-or-flight syndrome amongst many other functions)

Ovaries (in female)
Testes (in male)
} Influence sex drive and development of secondary sexual characteristics

52. Some pituitary hormones and their effects

Hormone	Stimulates	Effect
Growth hormone	Body tissues	Increases growth
Gonadotrophic hormone	Testes or ovaries	Stimulates production of sex hormones and sexual characteristics
Thyrotrophic hormone	Thyroid gland	Stimulates production of thyroxin which increases metabolic rate
Corticotrophic hormone	Adrenal gland	Stimulates production of adrenalin affecting emotional behaviour
Antidiuretic hormone	Kidneys	Causes the kidneys to excrete more concentrated urine

endocrine system consists of the glands shown in Figure 51. The *pituitary* is known as the *master gland* because it releases hormones which in turn stimulate the other glands to produce their own hormones.

There is evidence that some hormones secreted from the pituitary gland, such as *antidiuretic hormone*, which reduces the excretion of water, are in fact manufactured by the hypothalamus (Ebling and Highnam, 1969). The close links between the hypothalamus and pituitary can be seen in the regulation of sexual activity. Female cats that have not been neutered 'come on heat' about three times a year and then attract and accept willing males, yet at other times males that come too close encounter only hostility. The chain of reaction during the 'heat' periods starts with the production of *follicle-stimulating hormone* in the pituitary which stimulates the growth of eggs and the production of *oestrogen* by the ovaries. The presence of oestrogen in the bloodstream causes changes in the reproductive system, such as thickening of the uterus walls; it also stimulates the hypothalamus which, in connection with other parts of the nervous system, prompts the female to lift her rump, move her tail to one side and make treading movements with her rear legs when a male appears. The stimulus to the nervous system during copulation reaches the hypothalamus and is passed on to the cat's pituitary gland; this then releases *luteinizing hormone* which effects the release from the ovaries of eggs to be fertilized by the male's sperm.

The hypothalamus controls both the cyclic hormonal changes of females and the non-cyclic male pattern by its contact with the pituitary gland. Whether the hypothalamus of a rat gives the male or

53. The relationship between the nervous and endocrine systems

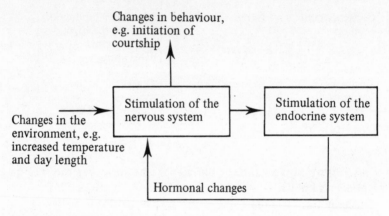

female instructions depends on the presence or absence of *testosterone* – the male sex hormone – in the blood during the first five days after birth (Tanner, 1978). Without testosterone during this critical period the hypothalamus will cause the female cyclic changes even if the rat used is genetically male. This critical period in rats corresponds to a period of twelve to fourteen weeks after conception of a human foetus, a time when testosterone levels are high in male offspring: the control of hormonal changes may, however, have a different mechanism in man.

Although the activity of the endocrine system may be changed by learning, this is mediated by the nervous system. Man has the most highly evolved nervous system, and so is not affected by the endocrine system as much as many other animals, but even so, this complementary system cannot be ignored in any analysis of the physiological bases of man's behaviour.

The research methods of physiological psychology and psychophysiology

The use of anatomical techniques reveals only the geography of the brain: other methods are necessary to determine the functions of the parts that these studies describe. It is possible, however, to make some educated guesses about the activity of a specific part if it can be shown to be physically connected to other areas of known function. Recent anatomical studies have explored the distribution of trans-mitter substances in different parts of the brain; this technique can show up pathways which are not visually distinct but are function-ally separate because they use different transmitters. The distribution of transmitter substances is found by chemically treating thin sec-tions of brain and illuminating them with ultraviolet light; each chemical then emits a different colour.

A lot of information has come from the study of brains that have been damaged in accidents or have suffered a stroke or the growth of a tumour. The speech areas of the brain were initially located by post-mortem studies of patients with linguistic problems resulting from such brain damage. It is difficult to draw conclusions from studies of accidental injury, however, because we may not know exactly where the damage is until the patient dies; nor can we set up an accident to damage only one part of the brain in order to deter-mine exactly what caused any change in behaviour that occurs. This problem can be overcome by the use of *ablation* or *lesion techniques* in which known parts of the brain are removed by operation. Abla-tion of areas on the surface of the brain can be performed with a surgical knife or by sucking the tissue away through a hollow tube attached to a suction pump; more inaccessible parts may be de-stroyed by burning out the neurons using micro-electrodes. If re-moval of a part of the brain results in a change in behaviour, the area removed is assumed to have some part to play in that behaviour, but there are many difficulties in such an interpretation, only one of which being that even ablation studies can result in the destruction of tissue other than the precise area intended, as demonstrated in the discussion of the roles of the hypothalamus in motivation (see p.

177). Other difficulties of the ablation technique are discussed on page 173.

Micro-electrode studies rely on the fact that neural transmission is electrical in nature and can, therefore, be initiated and recorded by electrical means. The work of Hubel and Wiesel (p. 190) illustrates the use of *micro-electrodes* to record the activity of single neurons in the visual cortex when stimuli are presented to the eye. The micro-electrodes used are fine, electrically conducting needles which can be inserted into parts of the brain and may be left there for some considerable time. Micro-electrodes may be used to stimulate, rather than record, activity of neurons by passing a small electric current down the implanted electrode; this may cause a change in behaviour as shown in the studies of the hypothalamus, but the interpretation of these results has some of the difficulties associated with ablation studies (see pp. 173 and 177).

More gross changes in the electrical activity of the brain can be gathered using the *electroencephalogram* or EEG. The EEG may be used to monitor the general activity occurring in a large area of the brain by the use of electrodes attached to the scalp; characteristic patterns of brain activity are found during different kinds of behaviour, for example when a subject is active, relaxed or dreaming.

Chemical stimulation and *interference techniques* rely on the fact that neural transmission is normally initiated by transmitter substances. Injection of transmitter substance to initiate nerve impulses has the advantage of *specificity*, that is, only neurons receptive to the particular chemical will become active, whereas electrical stimulation fires all nerve cells in the vicinity of the micro-electrode tip. In 1960 Grossman was able to show that eating and drinking are controlled by separate nerve pathways, by injecting small amounts of transmitter substance into the hypothalamus. Injection of acetylcholine resulted in drinking, whereas eating was elicited by the action of noradrenalin.

Drugs which interfere with the action of specific transmitters or hormones can be used to implicate those chemicals in the mediation of particular events. H. Fields (1979) has used this method to show that placebos have their effect by stimulating endorphin production (see p. 197).

Neurons use glucose to provide the energy necessary for their functioning; the more active a cell is, the more glucose it absorbs. L. Sokoloff has devised a technique in which a radio-active glucose derivative is injected into the brain where it is absorbed by the most active cells. The animal is then killed and its brain is sliced and placed on photographic plates. Development of the plates shows which cells were most active during the period following the injection. Using this technique, Sokoloff has demonstrated the columnar arrangement of cells in the visual cortex, backing up the work of Hubel and Weisel (see p. 192).

An increase or decrease in the activity of a part of the cortex is mirrored by a change in the blood flow to that area. N. Lassen, D. Ingvar and E. Skinhoj have devised a technique to monitor this change by injecting radio-active material into the blood and tracing its progress around the brain with a scanner producing a picture on a television screen. The most active areas of the cortex show up in red on the screen, while other less active areas are blue. Using this technique with subjects performing various tasks, Lassen *et al.* have explored the localization of function on the cortex (see below).

Each research method has its limitations, and these can only be overcome by the development of more and more techniques and the comparison of results so that interpretations do not rely on the idiosyncrasies of one type of study. It can be useful to compare the findings of what many writers (for example, J. Blundell, 1975) have argued to be two separate research traditions, *physiological psychology* and *psychophysiology*. The former, of which ablation, stimulation and interference techniques are examples, involves the manipulation of a physiological variable to find its effect on behaviour and experience, whereas electrical recording and radio-active tracing are examples of the latter, in which physiological changes are monitored while psychological variables are manipulated. The work of Penfield described on page 166 is a good example of research in the physiological psychology tradition: that of Hubel and Wiesel on page 190 exemplifies psychophysiological techniques.

Localization of functions on the cortex

The most notable feature of an intact brain is the *cerebrum*, consisting of a pair of large wrinkled lobes known as the *cerebral hemispheres*. These structures are separated by a gap from the front to the back of the head but are joined lower down by a mass of nervous tissue known as the *corpus callosum*. The most important part of the hemispheres is the *cortex* which, even though it is only about two millimetres thick, is responsible for such functions as learning, memory and perception, the activities which allow intelligent existence. The wrinkled appearance of the brain surface results from the packaging of about one-and-a-half square feet of cortex into the confined space of the skull. The cerebrum is divided into four lobes as shown in Figure 54.

In the early part of this century some physiologists thought that the cortex might consist of a number of sub-units, each of which was specialized to learn and remember a different type of task. If this was

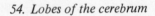

54. Lobes of the cerebrum

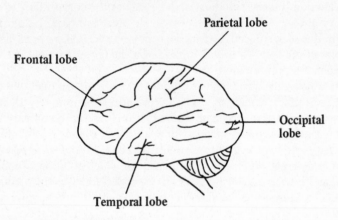

true, damage to different areas of the cortex would cause impairment of different learning and memory tasks, and once a memory had been lost due to destruction of its cortical storage area it could not be re-learned. Karl Lashley tested this hypothesis in the 1920s, studying the effect of cortical ablations on rats' ability to learn and remember mazes. He allowed rats to learn their way through mazes in order to get a food reward and re-tested them after removing equal-sized chunks of tissue from different positions on each rat's cortex. He found that the ablations had an equal effect on maze performance, showing that the position of the damage had no effect. The number of errors made by the rats after the operation depended solely upon the size of the chunk removed, larger areas of damage causing greater deficits in performance. Lashley concluded that rats' memories of mazes are not stored in one area of the brain but involve the whole cortex, performance depending upon the amount of functional tissue. This is known as the *principle of mass action*.

The rats' memories of complex mazes were partially disrupted by removal of 15% of the cortex, but in simple mazes no deficit was noticeable with up to 50% of tissue ablated. Lashley demonstrated that rats could re-learn mazes after ablation had caused errors, showing that other areas of the cortex were able to substitute for the damaged parts. His *principle of equipotentiality* states that all parts of the cortex have an equal potential for learning.

Despite the principles of mass action and equipotentiality, some areas of the cortex do affect learning in different ways from others; for example, removal of the visual cortex in the occipital lobe causes greater difficulties in visually based tasks than equal damage elsewhere. The study of people suffering from accidental brain damage suggests that mass action and equipotentiality of the cortex for complicated functions may be more applicable to the less complex cortex of non-human animals than to man. *Prosopagnosia* is an example of damage to a particular complex function which results from damage to a specific area of cortex in man. The disorder involves very little loss of vision but leads to an inability to recognize the faces of even the closest friends although they can be identified from their voices. The facial features can be perceived and even matched with photographs, but no association can be made between the face and the identity of a person. Patients suffering this disability have damage to the underside of both occipital lobes and the inner surface of the temporal lobes. The linking of an area such as this with a specific activity, in this case facial recognition, is known as localization of function. Figures 55 and 56 show areas of the human cortex associated with specific functions.

The somatosensory and motor strips
At the front of the parietal lobe is a strip of tissue which receives signals from the skin, bones, joints and muscles; it is concerned with body feeling and is known as the *somatosensory strip*.

The somatosensory strip has a functional rather than physical representation of the body, large sections receiving input from sensitive areas such as the hands and tongue but only small parts dealing with relatively insensitive but physically large areas such as the legs and back. The strip on the right hemisphere receives input from the left side of the body, that on the left hemisphere dealing with information from the right side. Patients with damage to one of these strips have no feeling in the opposing side of the body; they tend to reject the unfeeling side of the body, treating it as though it belongs to someone else.

Just in front of the somatosensory strip is another, similarly organized area, the *motor strip*. Again this has a functional, rather than physical, inverse representation of the body, but in this case the area deals with the control of muscle movement rather than body feeling.

55. Localized functions of the cortex

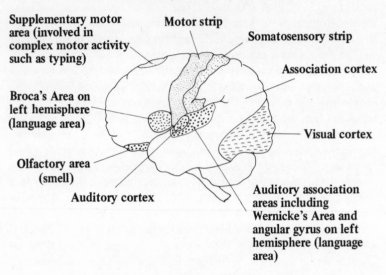

Supplementary motor area (involved in complex motor activity such as typing)

Motor strip

Somatosensory strip

Association cortex

Broca's Area on left hemisphere (language area)

Visual cortex

Olfactory area (smell)

Auditory cortex

Auditory association areas including Wernicke's Area and angular gyrus on left hemisphere (language area)

The somatosensory and motor strips were discovered by post-mortem studies of patients who had suffered damage to these areas resulting in observable changes in body perception and muscle control. Finer mapping of the areas was achieved by the method of electrical stimulation used by neurosurgeons, such as Wilder Penfield, who worked during the fifties and sixties with epileptic patients. In order to relieve epileptic fits Penfield ablated the part of the cortex where the increased random firing of neurons associated with these fits is initiated. Penfield's patients were given only local anaesthetic and were therefore fully conscious and could report experiences while the top of the skull was removed, revealing the cerebral hemispheres. Penfield then explored the surface of the cortex with fine electrodes until he found an area where stimulation caused the patient to experience an aura, the sensation of heightened perception that many epileptics feel just before a fit. When this small part of the brain was found it was ablated, most operations being successful in relieving further fits. This type of operation is of course performed only after other, less drastic, treatments have failed. It was when exploring the cortex to find the epileptic triggering point that Penfield was able to map areas where, for example, stimulation caused twitching of the big toe or a tingling sensation on the back of the hand. Stimulation of the association cortex often resulted in patients experiencing vivid memories of past events which varied with the position of the electrodes. The patients often remembered things that had not been recalled for many years, giving credence to the idea that forgetting involves a difficulty in retrieving memories rather than a total loss of particular information from brain storage (see Chapter 4).

Language areas
Up to the middle of the nineteenth century it was thought that the two hemispheres of the brain performed the same functions, and that each was fully capable of sustaining mental life. During the 1860s, however, P. Broca observed that patients with damage to part of the left hemisphere suffered language problems which were not found in those with right-hemisphere deficits; this was the first of many studies showing areas of the brain involved in the production and perception of speech and differences between the hemispheres. For the vast majority of individuals the left hemisphere controls language but some, mainly left-handed people, have right-hemisphere language areas instead.

A number of language areas have been demonstrated by studying the effects of damage to the cortex caused by strokes or accident. More recently these areas have been monitored during the production and perception of speech in fully conscious subjects using a technique of radio-active tracing. The language areas can be seen in Figure 56. Patients with damage to different areas show characteristically different speech problems. The speech of patients with *Broca's Area* damage is very slow and telegraphic: instead of producing full sentences they tend to miss out small words and the endings of nouns and verbs. When asked what he did the previous night a patient might reply, 'Went ... cinema.' Broca's Area appears necessary to prepare words for speaking, but not for understanding them: such patients have no difficulty in comprehending.

Behind Broca's Area, however, is a part of the cortex known as *Wernicke's Area*, damage to which does prevent a person from understanding language; nevertheless he may still be able to hear and enjoy music. While damage to Wernicke's Area does not prevent speech, the patient may forget some words and substitute others: he may ask for a pen by saying, 'Please pass the thing you

56. Language areas of the brain

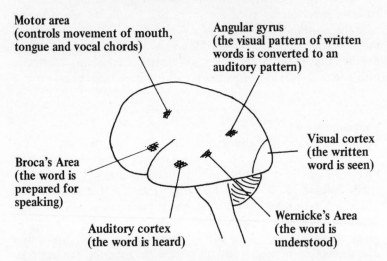

write with.' Damage to Wernicke's Area causes problems in the understanding of both written and spoken language; but damage to another area, the *angular gyrus*, causes the loss of reading ability while having no effect on comprehension of the spoken word. Patients with damage to the angular gyrus are able to see the written word but it has no meaning for them: it has been suggested that this part of the cortex converts the visual pattern of the written word into auditory patterns which are then passed along to Wernicke's Area for comprehension.

If you were to read this sentence aloud the presence of these marks on the paper which we call words would produce activity in your visual cortex; this would be passed on to the angular gyrus and then to Wernicke's Area, which would enable you to understand the words; the activity would then spread to Broca's Area, and finally to the motor area which would cause your speech muscles to produce the sounds that you would then utter. For the vast majority of readers most of this activity would be in the left hemisphere, but radio-active tracer techniques have demonstrated that a part of the right hemisphere equivalent in position to Broca's Area is also active during speech – although damage to this area has no effect on the ability to talk (Lassen, Ingvar and Skinhoj, 1978).

Psychologists sometimes study an individual's production and comprehension of language in order to help them locate specific areas of damage to the brain. It must be remembered, however, that an inability to use language may result from such things as the lack of an opportunity to learn, as well as specific brain damage. The most common cause of damage to areas of the cortex such as those involved in language is *cerebral thrombosis*, commonly known as a stroke. During a stroke, some arteries in the brain are blocked and the areas that they supply are irreparably damaged. This loss of function, however, is by no means always permanent, for it may be taken over by other brain areas. The best hope for recovery in the case of language is for left-handed patients or those with left-handedness in the family, since these people may have areas in the right hemisphere that have remained dormant while the dominant hemisphere was intact. Children below the age of eight usually make a good recovery, which demonstrates the great flexibility of young brains. P. Wall has demonstrated that there is a fringe of dormant neurons around the somatosensory strip (see p. 165) which can take over the function of this strip when damage occurs. It seems likely that these dormant fringes are present in other areas such as those for language, which shows that the brain is not as concretely functionally localized as the demonstration of speech, sensory and motor areas suggests.

'Split brains'

As we have mentioned, the two hemispheres of the brain are normally connected by a mass of nervous tissue known as the corpus callosum. The corpus callosum is sometimes cut in order to control epileptic fits, because these are the result of an increased, uncontrolled random firing of neurons which spreads across one cerebral hemisphere and into the other. The operation is successful in reducing the severity of fits and has so little effect on behaviour that in 1951 Lashley joked that the only function of the corpus callosum in a healthy brain was to stop it sagging. More recently researchers such as Sperry (1964) and Gazzaniga (1970) have used techniques which demonstrate differences between these *split-brain patients* and normal subjects, as well as giving information about the separate functions of each hemisphere. The corpus callosum allows the two hemispheres to communicate so that each has access to the information of the other. When it is cut, information can still reach both hemispheres because the *optic chiasma* ensures that each eye stimulates both sides of the brain; it is only under laboratory conditions that split-brain effects can be shown.

Sperry and Myers (1964) cut the corpus callosum and optic chiasma of cats so that information presented to the right eye reached only the right hemisphere and that to the left eye stimulated only the left hemisphere. The cats behaved in learning experiments as if they had two brains. After learning with the left eye covered, they showed no evidence of recognizing the same task when the right eye was covered leaving the left eye open; in fact, the cats could be trained to give opposite responses on a discrimination task, pressing a lever when a square rather than a circle was presented to the left eye, but pressing only when the circle was presented to the right eye.

Sperry and Gazzaniga have used two main methods to investigate the junction of the two hemispheres in split-brain human patients. These patients have an intact optic chiasma, and so each eye presents information to each hemisphere. The two methods are designed to overcome this problem. The first method involves placing objects in the subject's left or right hand behind the back and asking him for identification of these objects without seeing them: only the right hemisphere receives information from the left hand while the right hand connects only with the left hemisphere. The second method requires the subject to stare at a fixed point when a stimulus is presented to the right or left of this point: those presented to the right of the fixation point stimulate the left half of each retina and therefore reach only the left hemisphere, while those on the other side reach the right hemisphere (see Fig. 57).

Findings from these methods support the idea that the left hemisphere is more advanced in its language capacity, although patients show a varying degree of right-hemisphere language comprehension. When an object is placed in the right hand out of sight the patients have no difficulty in reporting its identity. If, however, the object is

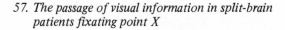

57. *The passage of visual information in split-brain patients fixating point X*

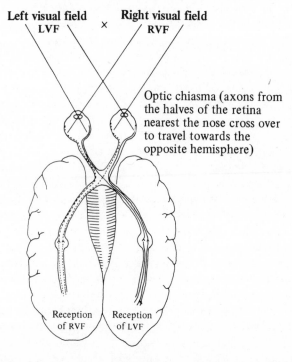

placed in the left hand and, therefore, is perceived by the right hemisphere, patients cannot verbally identify it. This does not mean that the right hemisphere does not know what the object is: the difficulty involves verbal reporting only, because when asked to pick out a similar object by feel alone from a range of items the subjects have no difficulty.

If the word 'comb' is flashed briefly onto a screen in a position so that it can only be received by the right hemisphere, the patient is able to pick a comb from a series of objects, thus showing that this hemisphere has some verbal comprehension; however, this seems limited to simple nouns, for subjects are unable to respond to commands such as 'Smile' presented in the same way.

The degree of right-hemisphere ability varies from patient to patient, one of whom could even spell words by manipulating letters with his left hand. This ability might be present in the normal brain or learnt after the operation. It has been suggested that hemispheric inequality develops throughout childhood, the right hemisphere giving up its language function as the left becomes more dominant. Sperry found a nine-year-old boy whose corpus callosum had never developed: this child showed equal linguistic abilities with both hemispheres.

The left has been called the dominant hemisphere due to its superiority in language and academic-type abilities and its control over the right (normally preferred) hand. The concept of left-hemisphere dominance is supported by observation of split-brain patients immediately after the operation: the left side of the body very rarely makes the first move in any action and appears to lag behind the right. The left hemisphere has been called the seat of consciousness because information in the right hemisphere of split-brain subjects does not appear to be available to thinking as we know it. The right hemisphere is not, however, merely an under-developed version of its partner: it has specialisms of its own related to non-verbal and spatial behaviour, such as dealing with melody and art. Damage to the left hemisphere can cause an inability to sing the words of a song, but humming is no problem. Split-brain subjects are far superior in their drawing ability. Gazzaniga (1970) reports that these patients have no difficulty in drawing a three-dimensional cube or arranging cubes to match a given pattern using their left hand; but with the right hand, performance is very poor. The spatial ability of the left hemisphere is similar to the language ability of the right, since although it has difficulty in producing drawings and patterns, the left hemisphere can match a test design to the correct one out of five options – it is capable of distinguishing some designs but not of producing them.

Gazzaniga (1970) suggested that both hemispheres were equally capable of generating an emotional response, but more recent work by G. Gainotti (1972) gives the right hemisphere a more important role, at least in the perception of emotion in the communications of others (see p. 154).

Although sensory and motor characteristics of each side of the body are controlled by the opposite side of the brain, there do seem to be some connections that do not cross over, for although a split-brain subject cannot identify an object in his left hand without looking at it, he can usually report whether there is an object in that hand or not. Each hemisphere can control fine finger movements of the hand on the opposite side of the body but can only produce the crudest of overall movement of the hand on its own side of the body; thus a verbal (left-hemisphere) instruction to move the fingers of the right hand can be successfully performed, but for the left hand only vague manipulation is possible.

The interdependence of areas of the brain

The previous sections may have given the impression that the brain consists of a series of comparatively unrelated parts; it is tempting to think that each section has its own particular function, and can perform this in isolation from other areas. This fixed view of localized function should not be taken too far. It is possible to recover from damage to areas of the brain that have been linked with specific functions, showing that at least a limited degree of equipotentiality is present, even for functions such as speech and body feelings, especially when the brain is young. Not all recoveries are due to equipotentiality: some, at least, may arise because a task comes to be performed in a different way, thus requiring no physiological adaptation.

Most of the localization studies have been performed by studying damaged brains, and the performance of such brains might not lead to a completely valid assessment of the functioning of complete structures. Different methods can lead to varying interpretations, for example Lassen (1978), using radio-active tracing techniques (see p. 163), showed that an area of the right hemisphere in the equivalent position to the Broca's Area appears to be very active during speech but that ablation of this area results in no noticeable language problems. Those researchers using ablation techniques must take care, in their design of experiments, to control for the effect of general shock to the nervous system, which may disrupt behaviour as much as the specific loss of function connected with the part of the brain that is removed. The method of double dissociation described by Teuber (1955) attempts to ensure that the interpretation of ablation studies in terms of localization of function is not confounded by the effects of general shock: when a portion of cortex is removed resulting in loss of an ability, the function lost is ascribed to the cortical area only if removal of similar-sized chunks in other areas of the cortex of control animals does not interfere with the same behaviour.

There is a logical problem in the interpretation of ablation studies.

If on removal of a part of the cortex a particular ability is lost, it is tempting to think of that area as the 'centre' for the lost function, but this is not necessarily the case. D. Ferrier, in the last century, made this point in the form of an analogy: he queried that if a watch stopped on the removal of a screw this would mean that the screw was the timekeeping centre. Obviously the answer was no. The area removed may simply be one, relatively unimportant, part of a circuit of interconnected parts.

Those who hold strictly to a theory of localization find it difficult to explain findings such as those of D.G. Stein (1974), who showed that ablations affecting visual discrimination and other tasks only produced this deficit when the cortical area from both hemispheres was removed in one operation; and that when the same areas were removed in two stages, the loss of visual discrimination was not found. Removal in two stages does result in some functional changes, and has only been shown to have different effects in some cortical areas. This may be because of differences in general shock to the nervous system, but whatever the reason, it suggests that other regions of the brain are involved.

Holistic theorists argue that no psychological function can be truly localized on the cortex, since no activity occurs in a vacuum. Luria (1973) argues that the brain has three sub-systems, each of which is necessary to perform any task. These are: (1) a unit for regulating levels of arousal, without which the brain would be unconscious; (2) a unit for receiving, analysing and storing information, without which the brain could not perceive or remember; and (3) a unit for the programming, regulation and verification of activity, without which no planning of behaviour or action upon feedback could be performed.

Motivation

If organisms always made the same responses to the same stimuli, psychologists would have a relatively simple task in describing and explaining behaviour, but this is not the case. The process of arousing, maintaining and regulating specific patterns of behaviour is known as *motivation*, and is a topic studied on many different levels in psychology. Many theories involve the concept of drive which energizes and directs behaviour toward specific goals as a result of bodily need. Physiological psychologists have been particularly interested in the neural mechanisms which are involved in such basic drives as hunger, thirst and sex.

In order to function, the body has to maintain a fairly constant internal environment. The blood should contain enough sugar, oxygen and water, but not too much, keep levels of carbon dioxide and other waste products as low as possible and, in the case of higher animals, be kept within certain temperature limits. The process by which this constant internal environment is maintained is called *homeostasis* and is one major factor in the motivation of behaviour. The maintenance of a constant internal environment requires that the animal performs some types of behaviour in order to obtain specific items from the external world; some of this behaviour, for example breathing, is relatively automatic, with little conscious control or choice, but some, such as feeding and drinking, is performed less continually, and in many animals involves some choice about when, what, where and how much to eat or drink.

For homeostasis to be successful the body needs some system that can sense changes in the internal environment and start behavioural or physiological events that have the effect of returning the equilibrium. This is the sort of function served by a thermostat in a central heating system: when the water cools, the thermostat sends a message to the boiler which ignites and heats up the water, and when the correct temperature is reached the thermostat then instructs the boiler to stop. In this system the thermostat functions as a sense organ for the internal environment which gives negative feedback to the boiler, that is, it stops the boiler when it has supplied enough heat. The effect of such sense organs in the body is not so automatic as that of the thermostat and may lead to many different forms of response. The flow of information may be shown as in Figure 58.

As in the visual system (p. 186), it is at the cortex that the perception of the motivation occurs, and this perception is affected by factors in addition to the information about homeostatic imbalance provided by the internal sense organs. These additional factors, which are not homeostatic in nature, may determine the degree of attention paid by the cortex to messages from the internal sense organs. When, for example, a person is busy, it is often the case that he doesn't feel hungry or thirsty until the task in hand is finished, whereas the worst thing for a dieter is to become bored, because it is

58. A possible sequence of events involved in homeostatic motivation

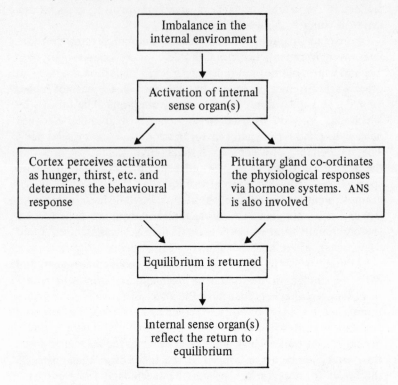

under these conditions that even small messages from the internal sense organs are attended to, producing the experience of hunger.

Taking loss of water from the blood as an example, there are two main types of response that can be made to restore equilibrium. The first is a behavioural response such as going to the tap, filling a cup and drinking. This type of response reduces the need by getting water from the external environment and can be directly observed. The second type of response is a physiological response which is more difficult to detect by casual observation. This type of response helps the water balance by action upon the internal environment – that is, within the body. In the case of a need for water, physiological responses would include increased uptake of water from the alimentary canal, decreased loss of water from the kidneys into the urine and decreased sweating. Normally both types of response occur, but in a situation where the cortex does not attend to the message, physiological responses may maintain the homeostatic balance for some time, but eventually will not be able to cope, causing increased firing of the internal sense organs, producing a stimulation of the cortex which is more likely to be attended to, thus leading to a behavioural response.

A great deal of research has centred around the problem of the control of activities such as eating and drinking, a lot of it concerned with finding the internal sense organs.

The role of the hypothalamus
In 1954 Stellar put forward the theory that motivated behaviour such as eating and drinking was performed in direct proportion to the amount of activity of the excitatory centres in the hypothalamus. The activity of these centres could, he argued, be affected not only by the internal environment as reflected in the constituents of the blood but also by inhibitory centres in the hypothalamus and non-homeostatic factors, such as learned and unlearned stimuli from the sense organs together with the inhibitory and excitatory influences of the cortex. The identification of the hypothalamus as the internal sense organ for homeostatic changes had been suggested by Hetherington and Ranson (1939), who demonstrated that damage to part of it resulted in excessive feeding in rats.

The hypothalamus is about a couple of centimetres in length in the brain of man and is situated below the cerebral hemispheres just above the optic chiasma. It has a rich blood supply and connections with the cortex, pituitary gland and reticular activating system, as well as the autonomic nervous system. It consists of a number of areas known as the *anterior, posterior, lateral* (LH) and *ventromedial* (VMH) *hypothalamus*, each of which has a slightly different role in motivation. Figure 59 is a diagrammatic representation of the hypothalamus, and summarizes some of the research findings associated with it.

Damage to the VMH caused rats to increase their body weight due to an increase in food intake during larger, rather than more frequent, meals. Miller *et al.* (1957) showed that although the animals would eat when food was easily available, they would not work for food. This suggests that damage to the VMH does not increase motivation to eat food but removes an area which normally controls the cessation of eating. Teitelbaum (1955) showed that these animals are more affected by taste than normal animals, refusing to eat bitter-

59. *Diagrammatic representation of the hypothalamus and associated research findings*

Hess, 1954: micro-electrode stimulation causes compulsive eating

Anderson, 1953: injection of salt water causes increased drinking

Teitelbaum *et al.*, 1954: ablation results in loss of eating and drinking

Hess, 1954: micro-electrode stimulation causes activation of the parasympathetic nervous system

Hess, 1954: micro-electrode stimulation causes activation of the sympathetic nervous system

Anterior   LH   VMH   Posterior

Satinoff, 1964: cooling causes shivering

Ranson and Hetherington, 1939: ablation causes compulsive eating

Olds, 1958: micro-electrode stimulation causes decreased food consumption

tasting food. Because animals with lesions in the VMH eat excessively when food is pleasant-tasting and easily available they are said to be *stimulus-bound*, that is, their eating is more affected by food as a stimulus than by internal needs. In a series of experiments during the 1960s S. Schachter showed that obese humans have eating habits similar to those of rats with VMH lesions.

Stimulation of the LH appears to have a direct effect on hunger drive, since the animal not only eats excessively, but will also perform tasks such as pressing a lever in order to receive food. From findings such as those in Figure 59 it was argued that eating and drinking were controlled by the combined activity of the LH and VMH.

The 'feeding centre' in the LH was thought to monitor the blood and become active when blood sugar or water-level dropped, initiating feelings of hunger or thirst by stimulation of the cortex and producing physiological changes in the body via its links with the pituitary gland and autonomic nervous system. The VMH was seen as a satiety centre, causing the cessation of eating or drinking

when stimulated by a rise in blood sugar or water-level or by indirect messages from the mouth, throat and stomach initiated by
consumption of food or drink. Arees and Mayer (1967) found
nerve connections between the LH and VMH to support suggestions that activity of the VMH produced satiety by inhibition of the
LH.

The hypothalamus was implicated in the motivation of other behaviour such as seeking warmth, by studies such as that of Satinoff
(see Fig. 59). A.E. Fisher (1964) initiated male sexual behaviour in
rats, even female rats, by the injection of testosterone, the male sex
hormone, into an area of the anterior hypothalamus. In a different
area Fisher found the same hormone released maternal behaviour,
causing the rats to build nests and carry young rats by the scruff of
the neck in the characteristic manner of female rats that have just
produced litters.

The sheer mass of evidence that was built up linking the hypothalamus with motivation caused many people to see it as *the* centre
for the initiation and termination of such behaviour as eating, drinking, seeking warmth or cold and sexual behaviour. This view has
fallen into disrepute. Teitelbaum and Stellar (1954) showed that the
effect of LH lesion on food intake can be reversed. They force-fed
rats for a period after the operation and found that their appetites
returned, although the animals would only drink while eating dry
food. The reversal was not total, since the rats showed excessive
aversion to bitter tastes and were unable to correct insulin-induced,
low blood-sugar level by compensatory eating (Teitelbaum and
Epstein, 1967). Teitelbaum argued that the recovery was due to
encephalization, by which he meant that the cortex took over control
of motivation. Powley and Keesey (1970) found that rats that were
starved to a low body weight before lesion of the LH did not refuse
food when it was presented: their results suggest that it is the reduction to a new lower body weight that causes the recovery of appetite
to be delayed, rather than the need for encephalization. It would
seem that the LH somehow controls long-term body weight rather
than day-to-day appetite.

Evidence from Zeigler and Karten (1974) questions whether
the LH has any role at all in hunger. They argued that hypothalamic lesions often damage nerves of the *trigeminal system* which
bring information from the head and neck region to the thalamus.
When they severed these nerves without damaging the LH, this

produced the pattern of eating and drinking loss followed by recovery normally associated with LH lesions.

It is possible that the LH plays no part in hunger motivation, although we cannot be sure of this; most of the evidence gained in the 1970s suggests that the liver, rather than the brain, is responsible for the control of hunger (see p. 181).

The concept of the VMH as a satiety centre has been largely over-turned by Gold (1973), who showed that lesions restricted to this area had no effect on eating: obesity was only found when the damage included the nearby *ventral noradrenergic bundle* (VNA). The VNA originates in the brain stem and may convey information from sensors in the body to higher areas of the brain. Friedman and Stricker (1976) suggest that VMH lesions (including damage to the VNA) have their effect by changing the activity of *adipose tissue* (layers of fat deposit) in the body. Adipose tissue normally absorbs nutrients and stores them as fats while the animal is digesting a meal; when digestion is complete the tissue releases nutrients to supply energy. VMH lesions may cause the tissue to absorb nutrients contin-ually, depriving the rest of the body's tissues and causing the animal to eat more in compensation. The VMH may also control the amount of adipose tissue, and hence have an effect on body weight. Liebelt *et al.* (1973) showed that although normal mice would reject trans-planted adipose tissue, those with VMH lesions accepted the trans-plant. One suggestion is that since extra weight is carried in adipose tissue, these tissues signal when some set point is exceeded, but that this signal is impaired by VMH lesion, or rather by damage to the VNA.

The mass of evidence that was collected in the 1950s and 1960s supporting the hypothalamic theory of motivation shows the danger of looking for evidence only in support of a dominant theory. Once the theory is questioned by contradictory data, much of the work that was supportive can be seen in a different light. For example, the fact that animals stop eating when the VMH is stimulated was seen as evidence for a satiation centre; but it may now be reassessed and simply regarded as an aversive stimulus which causes the animal to stop what it is doing. N.R. Carlson (1977) points out that an electric shock to the big toe during a meal might well cause a person to stop eating but would not implicate the toe as a satiety centre.

The role of the liver and other parts of the digestive system in the regulation of hunger

M. Russeck (1971) injected glucose into the blood of hungry dogs: he found that an injection into the blood vessels supplying the brain had no effect, whereas in the *hepatic portal vein* which connects the digestive tracts with the liver it caused an almost immediate halt in eating. This suggests that the receptors in the liver are responsible for signalling satiation to the brain, a suggestion which is supported by the fact that blocking the *vagus nerve* which connects the liver and the brain removes the effect of glucose injection. Friedman, Rowland, Saller and Stricker (1976) showed that the liver receptors are responsive to the availability of nutrients in general, rather than glucose in particular.

Russeck suggested that the liver is in an ideal position to signal hunger, since it is supplied with nutrients via the hepatic portal vein directly from the alimentary canal. He suggested that the completion of digestion of a meal causes a drop in the nutrient level of this vein, activating the receptors in the liver which then transmits the information to the brain via the vagus nerve, thus increasing the probability that the animal will eat. Damage to the vagus nerve causes prolonged loss of appetite.

When the animal starts eating, taste, smell and sight increase the amount of 'pleasant' food consumed; rats given food of four different flavours will eat nearly three times as much food as those with a single-flavour diet (Le Magnen, 1956).

The senses and stomach seem to have only a small effect on satiation, but the *duodenum*, the part of the intestine immediately following the stomach, seems to play a major role in this respect. Novin *et al.* (1974) showed that glucose injection into this area caused rats to stop eating unless they had been previously deprived of food. Carlson argues that this may be because satiety mechanisms in the stomach and duodenum have their effect through the sympathetic nervous system which causes the liver to release stores of glucose and hence to reduce the activity of the liver receptors; when deprived of food the liver would have no glucose to release, and therefore the hunger signals would be maintained.

The sympathetic control of glucose release from the liver is indirectly affected by the activity of brain receptor cells, which may be in the hypothalamus. Low nutrient levels activate these receptors, which cause the secretion of adrenalin from the adrenal glands, thus increasing the activity of the sympathetic nervous system. The evidence for the brain's control of adrenalin production comes from Friedman *et al.* (1976) who found that injections of keto acids, which can be absorbed by the brain but not by the liver, caused a reduction in adrenal secretion in hungry rats.

Obesity in humans

The work on motivation reported in the previous pages all relies on animal studies, and there may be differences in the way that the brains of different animals work. A.E. Fisher (1962) found that an injection of acetylcholine into a large number of sites in the limbic system caused rats to drink, but that the same chemical in the same parts of a cat's brain initiated anger, fear or a sleep-like trance. Studies on human brains must take a different form from those on other animals for moral and ethical reasons, but we do have some evidence that the control of eating is similar to that described in other animals. Reeves and Plum (1969) found a patient who over-ate and doubled her body weight in two years; a post mortem showed a tumour in the VMH. Quaade (1971) stimulated the LH of extremely obese patients before lesioning the area in an attempt to cure their obesity. They reported feelings of hunger when the current was turned on.

Schachter performed a series of experiments during the 1960s showing that obese humans are more affected by the availability and attractiveness of food than by tissue need, which has more effect on normal people. Obese people are less inclined to put effort into obtaining food, although they eat larger quantities during meals. These and other findings are very similar to the behaviour of rats with damage to the VMH and VNA, and led Schachter to postulate a deficiency in this part of the brain in obese people.

Le Magnen (1971) showed that the frequency of eating in rats is governed by tissue needs, but that the size of meal is determined by factors such as the palatability of the food. If the animal eats a large meal, a longer time will elapse before the next meal, which may be small or large independent of the time since it last ate. This fits in with the theory that the liver signals hunger when digestion of the previous meal is complete.

Carlson (1977) argues that early in his evolution man probably resembled the wolf in his eating habits, since he too was a hunter. Wolves hunt and kill when they are hungry, and if this results in a large meal they do not hunt again for a considerable time. The amount of food eaten by wolves is controlled by meal frequency rather than meal size and yet man's habit of eating at set times means that any control over intake must depend on the amount eaten at each sitting. Perhaps problems with weight control result from this change in habit, for which the body's control systems have not adapted. Like rats, man eats more when his meal has many flavours, since sensory factors then increase the appetite, making control of meal size even more difficult.

It is much easier to forget a meal when very busy than at times of relative inactivity. The cortex has a limited capacity for dealing with information at any one time and attends to only a small percentage of the stimulation available (see Chapter 2). Motivational arousal such as hunger and thirst may be ignored in favour of more pressing needs. Despite this, many people find that they eat and drink more when under conditions of stress. This may be due to childhood associations of food and comfort; however, recent work suggests a physiological cause.

Rowland and Antelman (1976) showed that rats more than doubled their calorie intake when pinched on the tail twice a day. Others have shown that tail pinching can reverse the effects of LH lesions and that this is due to the stimulation of a system known as the *nigro-striatal bundle* (NSB) (Fisher *et al.*, 1976). The NSB is a part of the *extra-pyramidal motor system*, which is a complex network composed of many areas of the brain involved in the control of muscle movement. The NSB passes close to the hypothalamus and, like the trigeminal system, is often damaged when the LH is ablated (see p. 179). It is not a feeding control system: stimulation can lead to other types of behaviour, such as aggression and copulation. Rather, it appears to have its effect by altering attention to stimuli and arousing relevant motor systems.

Stress in humans may cause stimulation of the NSB, as does tail pinching in the rat; eating is in this case due to increased attention to food as a stimulus, and arousal of the relevant motor responses, rather than actual feelings of hunger. In other individuals nail biting under stress might be triggered in a similar way. Carlson suggests that the social pressures associated with excess weight may cause enough stress to arouse the NSB, thus causing a vicious circle where excess weight leads to stress which leads to more eating and a consequent increase in weight.

Chemicals which block the action of *dopamine*, the transmitter substance in the NSB, cancel the effect of tail pinching in LH-lesioned rats (Antelman, Fisher *et al.*, 1975); but it is unlikely that this could be used as a treatment for obese patients because there are side effects on other behaviours affected by dopamine systems.

Our knowledge about the physiological controls of hunger suggests that there is not likely to be one treatment that will cure obesity for all. Some of the problems seem to be due to feeding habits such as mealtimes coupled with factors such as the variety of courses and the extent to which a person is confronted with attractive food. Other problems may be caused by deficiencies in the systems involved in the initiation or termination of feelings of hunger. Social factors have a great effect on eating behaviour; many satiated animals will continue feeding when others around them do the same. Many successful slimming organizations such as 'Weight Watchers' use social pressure in order to persuade members to reduce their weight, requiring public confessions when weight is not lost and giving rewards when the target weight is achieved. It may be necessary to maintain this social pressure after slimming, since it is an unfortunate fact that only about 5% of slimmers manage to avoid regaining lost pounds.

Pleasure centres

In 1954 Olds and Milner discovered that rats would perform a response in order to receive a short electrical shock in some regions of the brain; the stimulation appeared to be pleasurable and the areas involved became known as *pleasure centres*. Animals quickly learned to avoid any action which led to electrical stimulation of other brain areas known as *pain centres*.

Olds and Milner used a Skinner box to measure the reinforcement value of stimulation of different parts of the brain, and found that rats would press a lever more than a hundred times a minute if each depression was followed by an electric shock to the *medial forebrain bundle*, a group of fibres which stretch from the middle of the brain to the frontal lobes, passing close to the hypothalamus. Olds and Milner demonstrated that pleasure centres are present in many areas along the *mid-line* of the brain, particularly in the lateral hypothalamus, and are often only a short distance from pain centres. (The mid-line of the brain is an imaginary line passing from the centre of the forehead to the base of the neck.) A. Routtenberg (1978) has shown that the common factor in known pleasure centres is that they use dopamine as their transmitter substance.

Olds put forward the argument that the pleasure centres are the neural basis of reinforcement (see Chapter 3), and that reinforcers such as food and water have their effect by stimulating these areas. He showed that rats would press a lever for brain reward rather than for food, and that such lever pressing was increased when the animal was hungry. In many ways direct stimulation of the brain appears to be a 'super' reinforcer, for response rates are faster than those rewarded by food, and the animals often continue to respond until exhausted. Paradoxically, extinction occurs within a few seconds of switching the current off, and lever pressing can only be restored after a break by giving an initial 'free' reinforcement.

60. *A possible sequence of events if electrical stimulation fires both reinforcement and drive pathways*

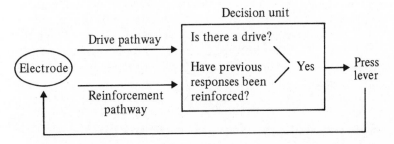

Deutsch (1960) attempted to explain the differences between direct brain stimulation and normal reinforcement by suggesting that brain reward activates a drive as well as a reinforcement pathway so that each lever press results in a reinforcement and an increase in the motivation to press the lever again (see Fig. 60). He argued that the activity of the drive pathway would decrease quickly unless further stimulation occurred, which would explain the rapidity of extinction and the need for the 'free' reinforcement after a break. Deutsch (1967) suggested that the drive pathway could also be activated by normal drives such as hunger, and showed that extinction was not as rapid with rats in this state – although this has not been found by other workers.

Gibson *et al.* (1965) showed that the extinction of brain-rewarded lever pressing was more like the situation with normal reinforcers when pressing one lever allowed the animal to press another lever which produced brain stimulation. The gap between the initial lever press and the brain reward was similar to that which occurs with normal reinforcers, showing that some of the differences between the two types of reinforcer can disappear when both are presented in the same way.

A. Routtenberg (1978) has shown that mood-changing drugs such as amphetamines increase rates of self-stimulation, and that neurons in the pleasure centres use dopamine, which is associated with emotional disorders such as schizophrenia, as their transmitter substance (see p. 198).

Pleasure centres have been found in the brains of many types of animal. Results from human patients are difficult to generalize from, since electrodes are only implanted in an attempt to alleviate some disorder and are therefore not placed in 'normal' brains. Campbell (1973) allowed his patients to press buttons to receive electrical stimulation of the brain; they reported pleasurable sensations and continued to press the buttons for the maximum permitted time of six hours. Other studies have shown that electrical stimulation has little effect. The full role of the pleasure centres in normal reinforcement has yet to be agreed, but they have certainly provided much raw material for science-fiction stories.

The physiology of visual perception

There is a great temptation to view the process of visual perception in a similar way to the production of a photograph. Indeed, some aspects of the structure of the eye are mirrored in the construction of a camera (although there are some great differences, such as the method by which light is focused on the retina). The analogy with the camera neglects the many psychological factors that can affect the interpretation of the images that fall on the retina. This section will consider the mechanics of the conversion of light images into patterns of nerve impulses and the transmission and reception of these impulses at the visual cortex. (Chapter 2 looks at the way that these nerve impulses may be perceived in a process which takes into account additional factors, such as previous experience, motivation and emotion.)

Visual perception is the process by which the sensation of light on the eyes is organized to produce the visual model of the environment which we take so much for granted that we often think of it as the real world, rather than an interpretation of it.

The eye

The purpose of the eye (see Fig. 61) is to collect the light in the form of a well-focused image, causing nerve impulses which describe that image. These impulses are passed out of the eye and up to the brain where they are received by structures such as the lateral geniculate body, the visual cortex and the *superior colliculus*.

61. Cross-sectional diagram of the human eye

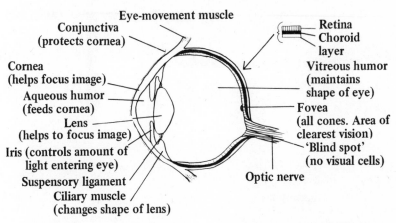

The process by which environmental energy such as light or heat is converted into nerve impulses in a sense organ is known as *transduction*. In the eye, transduction occurs at the *rods* and the *cones*, which are contained in the retina. The rods contain a substance called *rhodopsin* which, when exposed to light, is converted into *retinine* and *opsin* and a nerve impulse is initiated. Rhodopsin is later re-formed in the rods so that the process can be repeated. In bright light all the rhodopsin is converted into retinine and opsin so that the rods become of no further use under these conditions, because these substances take about thirty minutes to be re-converted. The rods are therefore of most use in twilight vision. The cones contain similar substances which can be used for transduction under normal daylight conditions. There are three different types of cones containing substances which are maximally affected by either red, green or

62. *A simplified diagram of the inverted retina showing the three main layers of cells*

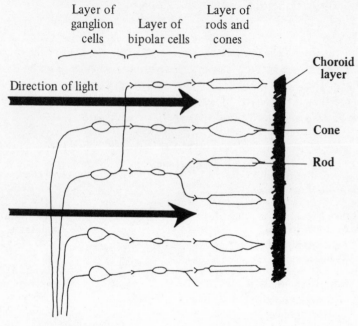

Axons of ganglion cells,
which converge on the
blind spot to form
the optic nerve

Horizontal cells which link the cells of the bipolar layer and amacrine cells which do the same in the ganglion layer have been omitted.

blue light, and it is the excitation of combinations of different cones which allows us to perceive many different colours during daylight. When the light gets dimmer it no longer affects the cones and colour vision is replaced with the monochrome vision of the rods.

If one actually designed an organ like the eye it would make sense to ensure that there were no obstacles in between the lens and the photosensitive layer, but as you can see from Figure 62 this is not in fact the case, since the light has to pass through two layers of cells before coming into contact with the rods and cones. When a nerve

63. The visual pathways

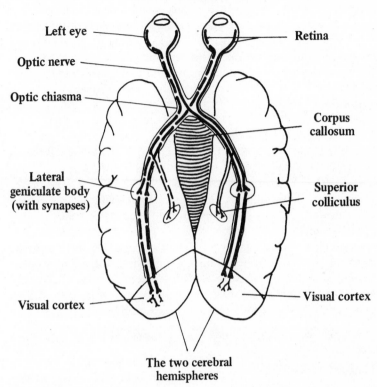

Feedback circuits from the visual cortex to the lateral geniculate body and superior colliculus are not shown.

impulse is formed at a rod or a cone it is passed to a *bipolar cell*, followed by a *ganglion cell* whose axon extends across the retina and out of the eye through the *blind spot*, joining with many others to form the optic nerve. The 'picture' passing up the optic nerve must be of very poor quality because of the structure of the retina, but it is improved by processing at the visual cortex, which appears to help the production of a clear image by exaggerating the edges of objects (see p. 192).

Large groups of rods may 'synapse onto' a single bipolar cell, whereas this is not the case for cones, which are therefore served with a proportionally larger number of bipolars. For this reason, vision with the cones (that is, daylight vision) has a greater degree of *acuity* (the ability to distinguish very small shapes). The reduced acuity of vision with the rods is demonstrated by the inability to read small print in poor lighting. Each eye contains about six million cones, predominantly situated in and around the *fovea*, which is therefore the area of clearest vision, and about one hundred and twenty million rods, which become increasingly sparse towards the periphery of the retina.

The lateral geniculate body
Over the last twenty years D.H. Hubel and T.N. Wiesel have been studying the activity of neurons in the visual pathways by using micro-electrodes to record the activity of individual cells in the brains of monkeys, while stimulating the retina with various shapes, in particular orientations and positions in the visual field.

They found that the LGB is divided into six layers of cells, three responding to input from the left eye alternating with three from the right eye. Each cell responds only to light on a specific part of the retina, known as its *receptive field*. The receptive fields of LGB cells are spread across the entire retina with much overlapping. Individual receptive fields are circular in shape and are divided into an

64. The effect of illumination of the receptive field of an LGB cell

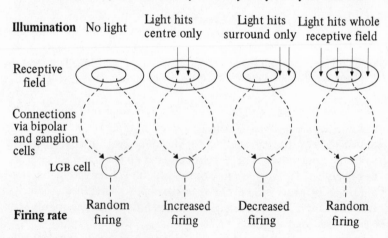

Illumination	No light	Light hits centre only	Light hits surround only	Light hits whole receptive field
Receptive field				
Connections via bipolar and ganglion cells				
LGB cell				
Firing rate	Random firing	Increased firing	Decreased firing	Random firing

\- - -► Excitatory connections

\- - -⊣ Inhibitory connections

65. *Possible connections between the photosensitive cells of the retina and a ganglion cell with an on-centre, off-surround circular receptive field*

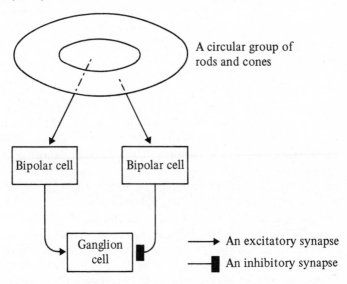

A circular group of rods and cones

Bipolar cell

Bipolar cell

Ganglion cell

→ An excitatory synapse

—■ An inhibitory synapse

excitatory centre and an inhibitory surround, an on-centre cell, or the opposite in the case of an off-centre cell. A spot of light shone onto the centre of the receptive field alone causes an on-centre LGB cell to increase its firing rate, but as the spot is made larger and stimulates the inhibitory surround, the firing rate decreases. This type of cell therefore gives the same response to the stimulation of its whole visual field as it does with a complete lack of stimulation; it is only when the receptive field is partially illuminated that its activity changes (see Fig. 64).

The same sort of receptive fields are found in retinal ganglion cells (S.W. Kuffler, 1953). Figure 65 shows the excitatory and inhibitory synaptic connections that may be present to give an on-centre, off-surround circular receptive field.

The function of the LGB is uncertain, since there seems to be no change in the receptive fields of cells compared with those on the retina, and although it receives input from both eyes, these are kept in separate layers of cells. Lindsay and Norman (1972) point out that it is unlikely to be simply a relay station, since nerve impulses do not decrease with the length of axons, and so the presence of a centre with so many synapses suggests that some function other than simply passing unaltered information is likely. They point out that the LGB receives input from the *reticular formation*, a structure known to affect arousal and attention, and suggest that processing at the LGB may serve to decide whether signals are sent on for higher processing. Feedback links from the cortex may also be involved in this activity.

Shape detectors in the cortex

Hubel and Wiesel have found a variety of cells in the visual cortex, each of which is characterized by its receptive field. Some cells, which receive input directly from the LGB, have circular receptive fields, but others are sensitive to lines. *Simple cortical cells* have receptive fields which cause them to fire when a line of a specific orientation illuminates a particular part of the retina; a slight change in the position or orientation of the line causes one cell to stop firing and another to start. *Complex cells* are also affected by the orientation of a line, but are not as particular about its position, and may continue to fire as the line is moved, provided the orientation remains constant. The line may be a light stripe on a dark background, or the opposite, depending upon the cell; it may be a single line or the edge of a more solid object. The activities of simple and complex cells can therefore code information about the shape of objects. The *temporal cortex* receives input from the visual cortex and is involved in higher levels of visual analysis. Gross, Rocha-Miranda and Bender (1972) found a cell in this area of the cortex which responded to a picture of a monkey's hand. Cells with these characteristics are called *hypercomplex cells* and presumably receive information from many complex cells.

The visual cortex is arranged in small columns about two millimetres deep and one millimetre square which are at right-angles to the surface. Each column receives a few thousand fibres from the LGB and dispatches about fifty thousand fibres, mostly to other parts of the cortex via the thalamus, but also to the superior colliculus and back to the LGB. A micro-electrode pushed vertically downward, measuring the activity of each layer of cells when a visual stimulus is presented to the eye, shows that each cell in a column is receptive to a line in the same orientation. If the micro-electrode is inserted slightly to one side of the original penetration the cells have a different orientation, but this new orientation is maintained as the electrode is pushed down through each cell layer. These vertical slabs of cells with the same orientation are known as *orientation columns*, and each orientation from 0° to 360° can be found in an area of cortex measuring about one millimetre square. This area of one millimetre square and two millimetres deep appears to be the elementary unit of the visual cortex, containing as it does information about all orientations on a given part of the retina of both eyes. The receptive fields of cells within this square millimetre overlap to cover an area of the retina which is minute if the unit is supplied from the fovea, but gets progressively larger for units dealing with more peripheral sections. The fovea, therefore, supplies many more elementary units than areas of similar size on other parts of the retina. In this way, the visual cortex matches the arrangements in the somatosensory strip, where more cortex is used to deal with the most sensitive parts of the body.

The superior colliculus

The superior colliculus has a role in the control of eye movement and the perception of the location of objects. The receptive fields of cells in this area are bigger than most of those in the cortex and they are more uniformly spread in the periphery of the retina, an area which is most sensitive to moving stimuli. Schiller and Stryker (1972) showed that stimulation of superior colliculus cells led to eye movement which meant that an object originally placed on the receptive field of the cell would be focused on the fovea.

Damage to the visual cortex in humans appears to cause total blindness, but if a patient with such damage is persuaded to attempt to point out the position of a spot of light he is often successful, and can even give correct guesses as to whether a line in front of him is horizontal or vertical. These patients argue that they are only guessing and that they cannot see the lights; this suggests that structures other than the visual cortex are important in determining the position of an object independently from its identification. Experiments on animals with damage to the superior colliculus show that *discrimination learning* (learning to give one response to one stimulus and a different response to another) is impaired, but this is because the animals have difficulty deciding where the stimuli are. Schneider (1969) reports an experiment which required thirsty hamsters to push open a striped door to gain a reward of water, when pushing an adjacent spotted door received no reinforcement. Animals with damage to the visual cortex never mastered this task, but those with impairments in the superior colliculus felt their way around the walls until reaching a door, when they stared at it 'as if inspecting the pattern'; if the door was spotted, the hamster continued around the wall, but if it was striped the door was pushed open and water drunk. Schneider argues that the animals with damage to the superior colliculus were able to discriminate the patterns on the doors but could not visually perceive where the doors were, and hence had to feel their way around the wall. One is tempted to compare this to the perception of a drunken man, although different brain structures may be involved.

Perception in three dimensions

The clues which enable the brain to perceive three dimensions from a two-dimensional retina are discussed on pages 49–57.

The physiological events which allow the perception of depth are not fully understood, but many researchers are investigating binocular cells in the visual cortex. These cells receive information from both eyes because of the crossing over of some, but not all, of the nerve fibres at the optic chiasma (about 50% in humans). Hubel and Wiesel have reported cells in the visual cortex of monkeys which respond only to stimuli presented to both eyes, and maximally to those at one particular depth. Researchers disagree about the position of these cells in the cortex and the range of depth and disparities to which they are sensitive. This is not surprising considering the conditions under which the research is done. The animals are immobilized and their eye muscles paralysed so that the gaze is in a fixed direction, then the pupils are dilated with atropine and contact lenses used to focus at particular distances. Micro-electrodes are inserted into the visual cortex to monitor the activity of individual cells when stimuli are presented at different distances.

B. Fischer and G. Poggio (1978) have developed a technique of monitoring the activity of binocular cells while their monkeys are fully conscious and have full control over their own eyes. They trained the animals to fix their gaze on a particular spot, known as the *fixation point*, and presented stimuli at different distances and positions. They found that most cells in the visual cortex receive information from both eyes, and could be grouped into four classes: the most common were those which increased firing when an object was presented very close to the fixation point and decreased as it was moved away. Another group acted in the opposite way, decreasing firing when objects were presented near the fixation point. Fischer and Poggio also found 'near' and 'far' cells which might be used to control eye movements: near cells were fired by objects in front of the fixation point and turned off by stimuli behind it and far cells reacted in the opposite way. These four types of cells each respond in different ways to a disparity of images on the two retinas, and are collectively known as *disparity detectors*.

Disparity detectors are only one part of the answer. Perception involves more than the determination of the depth of individual objects: these are somehow combined to produce a mental image that is totally three-dimensional. As with shape detectors, we cannot be sure whether the firing of these cells has any meaning for the animal. Their activity is related to the stimulation of the retina; but where does perception occur? The answers to these questions may not lie in the activity of single cells: Richard Gregory argues that the important aspects of perception are hypotheses rather than feature detectors. Analysis of the perception of movement shows that perception involves more than the stimulation of movement detectors. As Colin Blakemore puts it, 'Neurons present arguments to the brain based on the specific features that they detect, arguments on which the brain constructs its hypothesis of perception.'

Perception of movement
When the eye is stationary, the image of a moving object passes across the receptive fields of many cortical cells. Movement can then be coded by the passage of excitation from one cell to another and also by those cells in the cortex and superior colliculus which are responsive to movement in particular directions across their receptive fields. The detection of movement is, however, more complicated than that, since the images of stationary objects move across the retina whenever the eyes are moved, and yet the perceptual system is not fooled into thinking that the objects are in motion. The reason for this appears to be that as nerve impulses pass from the brain to the eye muscles they also act on the movement perception system, so that when the command is made to move the eyes, this also counteracts the effects of images passing across the receptive fields; these are perceived as stationary if they move in the opposite direction to the eye at a similar speed to that of the eye. An image that remains on the same spot of the retina as the eye moves is perceived

as moving; hence we can follow an object with our eyes and perceive it as moving in relation to its background.

The superior colliculus probably plays an important part in this process. In the analysis of images moving across the retina the brain can compensate for the fact that the whole body is moving, so that a driver perceives the road as still while he moves along. Confusion sometimes occurs when inadequate information is available; for example, when looking out of a carriage window at a station it can be difficult to decide whether it is your train or the one adjacent that has started to move. The brain uses more than the eye and image movement systems to perceive movement. K. Dunker (1938) showed that such factors as the relative size of objects can also have an effect. He shone a light onto a large screen and moved the screen to the right. Most observers reported that they saw the screen as stationary and the spot of light moving to the left: the perceptual system assumes that smaller objects are more likely to move. In this example the perception of movement contradicts the evidence of the eye and image movement systems and probably the movement detectors in the visual cortex.

Chemical factors in pain, anxiety and schizophrenia

It has been known for some time that opiate drugs such as morphine, which are used as pain killers, have their effect by becoming attached to specific sites on neurons in those areas of the nervous system associated with pain perception. Since morphine itself does not naturally occur in the body, researchers felt that the attachment areas must accept morphine-like chemicals present in the system under normal conditions. J. Hughes and H. Kosterlitz (1975) first identified these naturally occurring substances, which are known as *enkephalins*; and smaller related molecules, the *endorphins*, have since been found which also have opiate properties. The enkephalins and endorphins are known as *neuro-transmitter modulators* and may work by interfering with the release of transmitter substance from the synaptic terminals of neurons that are transmitting information about pain. Research into these opiates may reveal why some people feel pain more easily than others, and may result in the production of drugs with fewer side effects than morphine.

A drug known as *naloxone* reverses the effect of enkephalins and endorphins, and is therefore used to study the role of these modulators. Using this technique, H. Fields (1979) has shown that *placebos* may have their effect by stimulating endorphin activity. A placebo is a drug or therapy which has its effect simply because the patient believes in it, not because of any particular property of the treatment itself. Fields gave his patients an injection of weak salt solution after they had had wisdom teeth removed; 30% of them experienced pain relief, a placebo effect. He then injected naloxone, which had no effect on most patients but increased the pain felt by those benefiting from the placebo effect, thereby suggesting that the pain relief had been due to endorphin or enkephalin action. Other researchers have implicated enkephalins and endorphins in pain relief produced by acupuncture and hypnosis.

Benzodiazepine drugs, which include Valium and Librium, have anxiety-relieving properties and are widely used as tranquillizers. Like the opiates, these drugs have been shown to bind with specific receptor sites in the brain and this knowledge has led to the search for the body's own anxiety reliever. P. Skolnick (1979) discovered an endogenous chemical, *inosine*, which binds with the same sites as benzodiazepines. Recent research at the London School of Pharmacy suggests that the pituitary hormone adrenocorticotropin produces effects opposite to that of benzodiazepines on brain cells. Normal anxiety levels may be controlled by the transmitter modulation of both inosine and adrenocorticotropin; if this is the case, we encounter the question, what causes some people to develop an imbalance in this system?

In addition to adrenocorticotropin, other well-known hormones have recently been demonstrated to have effects on the brain; for example, N. Kasting and K. Cooper (1979) have provided evidence that antidiuretic hormone and vasopressin (see Fig. 52) have fever-reducing properties. These results stress the interrelationship between the endocrine and nervous systems.

The emphasis of brain research appears to have shifted in recent years from the study of physical and electrical properties to observing the activity of chemicals in the nervous system, tracing nerve networks using particular transmitters, discovering new substances such as endorphins and finding additional roles for well-known hormones. This interest in the chemistry of the brain has been followed keenly by those interested in finding organic bases for mental disorders, leading to new theories about the causes of conditions such as *schizophrenia*.

Schizophrenia is a collective term for a variety of conditions which involve major personality disturbances, featuring peculiar emotional responses, loss of interest in the world and the feeling that the individual has lost personal control of his thinking and behaviour. Many researchers have linked the transmitter substance dopamine with schizophrenia. Neurons using this transmitter can be found in the hypothalamus, limbic system and medial forebrain bundle. These areas have been associated with brain reward systems and are pleasure centres (see page 184).

The first indications of the link between schizophrenia and dopamine came with the realization that drugs which alleviate symptoms also block dopamine action. Recently T.J. Crow has shown that schizophrenics have unusually high concentrations of dopamine in the brain, especially in the limbic system (see p. 157). The endorphins have also been linked with schizophrenia, because animals injected with these chemicals show schizophrenic-like symptoms.

D. Harrobin (1980) argues that schizophrenia may be caused by a deficiency of a group of neurotransmitter modulators known as *prostoglandins*. He points out that this theory can account for the dopamine and endorphin evidence, since both of these substances inhibit prostoglandin formation; in the case of dopamine, this results from its inhibition of the pituitary hormone prolactin, which is necessary for prostaglandin production.

The links between various chemicals and conditions such as schizophrenia raise the question of causation: do the chemical changes cause the disorder (in which case what causes the chemical changes?), or does environmental stress cause the behavioural disorder which is accompanied by chemical change – in which case why do some people remain perfectly normal under conditions that disturb others? The answer to the question of causation is still being sought, and there will probably prove to be some sort of interaction between the chemical and environmental explanations. Horrobin feels that one of the two possible causes will prove to be most important, and that the outcome will have major implications for treatment, since treating a patient with a brain chemical problem by psychological means would be 'as valuable as it would be for a diabetic who needs insulin', whereas using drugs on a problem of psychological origin would be like 'the treating the pain of bereavement with a sticking plaster on the forehead'.

Genetics

In Chapters 2 and 6 you will read about the nature/nurture debate – the extent to which characteristics such as intelligence are affected by the inherited information in the sperm and egg that combine to produce an individual, and/or are affected by the environmental occurrences that mould him from conception onwards. This chapter gives some background to the debate by considering the way in which genetic information is stored and has its effect on physical and psychological characteristics.

Chromosomes and genes

When an egg is fertilized by a sperm it is called a *zygote*, and normally develops through millions of cell divisions to become a recognizable member of the species to which its parents belong. The zygote must contain information that will control its development to ensure that it becomes, say, a human being rather than a fish, that it will have two legs rather than four, and that cells in the region of the surface of the body will have the characteristics of skin whereas those in other positions will take the form of muscles, nerves and so on. This information is contained in the *chromosomes* in the nucleus of the zygote, which are reproduced each time the cell divides so that each cell of the body has the same inherited material contained within its nucleus.

Each species has a characteristic number of chromosomes, which are found in pairs in most animals: rhesus monkeys have twenty-four pairs, but the fruit fly Drosophila has only four. The number of chromosomes does not reflect the complexity of the organism and its behaviour, for goldfish have forty-seven pairs whereas man has twenty-three. One chromosome from each pair comes from the mother and one from the father.

Each pair of chromosomes contains information about thousands of different characteristics, which are each controlled by *genes*. The genes are the units of heredity; each is located at a particular spot on a chromosome and is predominantly involved in the control of a single characteristic, usually by its influence on the formation of a specific protein. Less than 20% of the body's genes are active at any one time. Genes that control the production of saliva are present in all human cells, but are only active in the salivary glands. Genes can be activated or deactivated by the action of controller genes in a way which is not fully understood. Although chromosomes can be seen through a microscope, visible as thread-like structures when the cell is stained, genes are much too small for this, and their presence and position can only be inferred from breeding experiments.

The genes are also arranged in pairs. If we consider a pair of chromosomes within a nucleus, the genes on one chromosome are responsible for the same attributes in the individual as those on its partner. The determination of a particular characteristic depends on the character of both genes: if both genes governing eye colour are blue-eye genes then the individual will have blue eyes, if both are for brown eyes he will have brown eyes. However, if the gene from one chromosome is for brown eyes and the other for blue eyes, the individual will have brown eyes because the brown-eye gene is *dominant*. This brown-eyed individual will still have a gene for blue eyes. Because the blue-eye gene is 'dominated' by the brown, it is given the name *'recessive'*. This means that we cannot tell simply by observation of an individual which genes are present in his makeup; there is an important distinction between *genotype* – the genetic makeup of an individual – and *phenotype* – the characteristics of the individual as they actually develop. The brown-eyed individual with a pair of brown-eye genes and the brown-eyed individual with one brown- and one blue-eye gene have similar phenotypes but different genotypes. Conversely, individuals with the same genotype may have different phenotypes, for example when one of a pair of individuals, each possessing the genotype to be tall, suffers from malnutrition, and therefore does not grow fully. The phenotype develops as a result of the interaction of the genotype with the environmental influences the individual encounters. The effect of a particular environmental force may be different on animals with a different genotype.

The nature/nurture debate on intelligence and perception (see Chapter 2) is complicated by the fact that we cannot directly observe the genotype, and also because many pairs of genes govern such complex characteristics of the individual.

Growth and reproduction

A type of cell division known as *mitosis* results in the growth of the body and the replacement of old cells. When mitosis occurs, the chromosomes reproduce themselves, ensuring that every cell in the body has a complete set. Sperms and eggs, however, are produced by a different type of division known as *meiosis*, which results in their containing only one of each pair of chromosomes, so that when fertilization occurs, the zygote has the normal number.

As we have said, the sperm of man contains twenty-three individual chromosomes, each drawn randomly from twenty-three pairs, making it possible for each individual to produce 8,388,608 different kinds of sperm which could fertilize any of the same number of variations of egg. So, theoretically, a single pair of humans could produce zygotes with a phenomenal number of different genotypes. Even more variation occurs because there are sometimes breakages during meiosis, and genes in the same position on chromosome pairs may be interchanged.

The chromosome pairs can be easily identified by their different sizes and shapes: each pair are identical in size and shape, apart from the twenty-third pair, which are known as the X and Y chromosomes. The X chromosome is longer and contains more genes than the Y. This pair determines sex: women have two X chromosomes whereas men have an X and a Y. Because an egg can only contain an X chromosome, but a sperm may have either an X or a Y, it is the sperm that determines the sex of the offspring.

Some of the genes on the X chromosome of males are unusual because they have no pair on the Y, and so affect the phenotype without the necessity for being dominant. This normally has no significant effect, but it does create some sex-linked disorders, such as *haemophilia*, which is suffered almost exclusively by males (see below). Most genes are present on both of a pair of chromosomes. They will be termed '*homozygous*' when the genes from each chromosome give the same instructions about a particular characteristic of the individual, as when a brown-eyed person has two brown-eye genes, and '*heterozygous*' when the genes give different instructions, one for brown eyes and the other for blue eyes.

Haemophilia

X chromosomes carry a gene which controls the clotting of blood; there are two forms of this gene, one of which is efficient in producing the enzymes that cause blood clotting while the other is not. The gene is not present on the Y chromosome, and so although females have the usual pair of genes controlling blood clotting, males have only one gene. Since the inefficient gene is recessive, it can only have its effect on the female phenotype if it is homozygous, but if present in the male who has only one X chromosome, the individual will suffer from haemophilia, a disorder which places him in continual danger of bleeding to death, since the smallest wound takes a long time to heal. A female who is heterozygous to blood clotting is known as a *'carrier'*, because she shows no outward sign of the disorder, but may pass the gene on to her offspring who, if they are male, will suffer from haemophilia. It is possible, though very rare, for a girl to have haemophilia if her mother is a carrier and her father a sufferer from the disorder; in this case the onset of menstruation would be fatal.

Figure 66 shows how this sex-linked disorder is inherited from the female parent, who shows no signs of the disorder herself. The chances of a normal male and a carrier female producing a son with the disorder are one in four. Queen Victoria was a carrier for haemo-

66. *The Inheritance of Haemophilia*

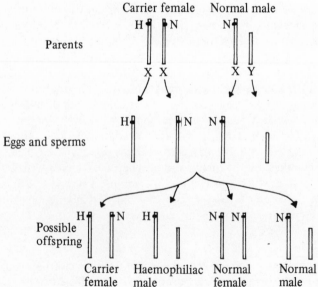

philia and through her daughters the gene was introduced into the royal families of Spain and Russia.

Genes and behaviour

Genes have their effect by controlling the production of enzymes which contribute to all the millions of reactions necessary to form and maintain the body. Since studies of brain damage and stimulation have shown that mental activities and behaviour are intimately linked with the physical structure and chemical processes of the nervous and endocrine systems, it is not surprising that genes have an effect on behaviour. The way in which they can have an effect is most obvious in examples such as the mental retardation of PKU (see p. 204) and the sexual behaviour of the fruit fly, Drosophila.

Drosophila has been extensively studied because it has a very short gestation period and has only four chromosomes, which are exceptionally large, especially in the salivary glands and alimentary canal. The genes on the four chromosomes have been named and their positions mapped as a result of many breeding experiments. A gene called Bar causes the male to have difficulty in its sexual behaviour, as does another called White. These genes have their behavioural effect by alterations in the physical makeup of the compound eye, which has a reduced number of facets in the case of Bar and less pigmentation in the case of White. The resulting restriction of vision makes the fly less successful in finding females and receiving visual stimulation during courtship.

Learning and instinct

It is generally acknowledged that the behaviour of lower animals is more affected by *genetic pre-programming* (or instinct) and less by learning than is that of those higher in the evolutionary scale. For many of these animals there is very little time for learning, since they are born in a relatively mature state and have a very short life-span. Man is born in a very immature state and has a lengthy childhood during which learning can take place. Both instinct and learning can cope with environmental change, but in very different ways. An animal whose behaviour is totally pre-determined can be very successful in the environment for which it is adapted, but if changes occur, the individual may not be able to cope. A learning animal is far more able to adapt to a changing environment. Animals whose behaviour is largely inherited adapt to changing circumstances on a species level: those individuals with the genetic makeup which fits them to the new environment survive and pass their genes onto the next generation, but the others die. A learning animal can adapt to changing circumstances on an individual level by varying its behaviour as a result of experience. The success of the insects in surviving until now testifies to the efficiency of genetic adaptation in a group of numerous, short-lived animals. Man has shown the way in which a learning animal can adapt on an individual level and can pass his experiences on to the next generation by social processes.

Students of the nature/nurture debate sometimes fall into the trap of assuming that some types of behaviour might be caused by heredity factors, and that others are caused by environmental influences. More sophisticated protagonists realize that both factors have an influence on behaviour, but many of these people make the mistake of trying to argue that one set has more effect than the other. Some of the following examples should show that the relationship between genetic and environmental influences on behaviour is far more complex than such arguments would suggest.

Phenylketonuria

The disorder *phenylketonuria* (PKU), which affects about one child in every ten thousand born in Britain, is known to be caused by the presence of a pair of recessive genes which control the breakdown of *phenylalanine*. The disorder causes sufferers to become mentally retarded under normal conditions. Phenylalanine, found in meat and other protein food, is normally broken down by the enzyme phenylalanine hydroxylase into *tyrosine*, which can be used in the repair and growth of cells or broken down further to aid in the production of adrenalin or skin pigment. The recessive gene causes a shortage of phenylalanine hydroxylase, and the digestion of phenylalanine results in a build-up of phenylpyruvic acid in the cerebro-spinal fluid which causes damage to the developing nervous system. Because the gene for phenylalanine hydroxylase production is dominant, only those individuals who are homozygous for the recessive gene suffer from the disorder, although heterozygous individuals may pass the recessive gene on to their offspring, who will be phenylketonuric if they also receive the recessive gene from their other parents.

Although the presence of a pair of recessive PKU genes causes mental retardation under normal conditions, the child can develop quite normally if the abnormality is discovered soon enough and he is reared on a diet low in phenylalanine with added tyrosine. This demonstrates that the effect of a genetic instruction depends upon the environment of the individual: change the environment and the effect of the genes may change. All children in the United Kingdom are now tested for PKU within the first fortnight after birth by analysis of a drop of blood.

Selective breeding
The genetic influence on many traits can be shown by studies of selective breeding, when animals showing high levels of the trait are interbred and compared with the offspring of animals showing low levels. W.R. Thompson (1954) studied learning capacity in rats using this method. He found differences in the speed at which rats solved the Hebb-Williams maze test, which involves finding the way round a maze containing many barriers in order to reach a goal box containing food. The barriers in the Hebb-Williams maze can be moved in order to discover how quickly the rats learn to adapt to a new route. Thompson bred the dull rats (those that made many errors) with other dull rats and bred bright rats (those making few errors) with other bright rats. There was very little difference in the maze-learning ability of the two strains, but when selective breeding continued to the third generation the differences were significant, and by the sixth generation the dull group produced about 80% more errors than the bright group.

The maze-learning differences for the Thompson rats were not reflected in the learning of other tasks, for an activity as complex as learning is many-faceted and influenced by the action of many genes: he had simply interbred to increase the presence of those genes affecting slow or quick learning of the Hebb-Williams maze task.

The dependence of genetic differences on the environment
Thompson's study stressed the genetic influences on learning ability because environment was kept constant, but research by R. Cooper and J. Zubek (1958) showed that whether rats demonstrate themselves to be dull or bright in learning mazes depends on environmental factors. In some environments there is a great difference in the number of errors made by maze-bright and maze-dull strains, but in others this difference disappears. Cooper and Zubek raised mixed groups of bright and dull rats in three different environments: the first was a normal laboratory cage; the second was an enriched

67. Mean error scores in maze performance for bright and dull strains of rats reared in enriched, normal or deprived environments

	Type of environment		
	Normal	**Enriched**	**Deprived**
Genetically 'bright'	117	111	170
Genetically 'dull'	164	120	170

environment with many toys such as marbles, swings and mirrors; and the third was a deprived environment containing only a food box and water container. The rats were raised in these environments from twenty-five days old, when they were weaned, to sixty-five days old. When rats raised under these conditions were tested in the Hebb–Williams maze, only those raised in the normal laboratory environment showed significant differences between the genetically bright and the dull subjects: when raised under enriched or deprived conditions the difference between the two strains disappeared.

The dependence of the effect of environment on genetic makeup
In Cooper and Zubek's study, both strains of rats benefited from the enriched environment, but N.D. Henderson (1970) showed that the effect of an enriched environment can differ depending on the geno-types involved. Henderson raised six different inbred strains of mice in standard laboratory conditions with no additional equipment in the cages. When they were six weeks old they were tested on a task which involved finding their way to food via a path containing a climbing frame, ramps and pipes. He found slight differences be-tween five of the strains, but one strain of mice consistently found the food much faster than the others, taking an average of thirty-five minutes compared to about fifty minutes for the other strains. He raised mice from the same six strains in an enriched environment to see whether their performances would be better than those reared under normal conditions. The enriched environment contained a small maze, a hollow log, tubes, ramps and rocks. When tested at six weeks, only three of the strains showed the expected improvement: for the other three strains enrichment had no significant effects. The effect of environment, therefore, depends upon the genotype: any

estimate of the performance of a particular mouse has to take into account both genetic and environmental factors.

The influence of both nature and nurture on behaviour
In practice, inherited and environmental influences are inseparable: no behaviour is totally independent of the individual's heredity or the environment within which the behaviour is displayed. D. Hebb points out that an argument about which factor is most important is as fruitless as one concerning the relative importance of the width and length of a rectangle in determining its area: both are necessary, since without either one, there would be no rectangle to discuss.

Further reading

Blundell, J. (1975), *Physiological Psychology*, Methuen

Carlson, N.R. (1977), *Physiology of Behaviour*, Allyn and Bacon Inc.

Rose, S. (1976), *The Conscious Brain*, Penguin

Scientific American, September 1979 (whole issue on the brain – to be issued in book form by W.H. Freeman and Co.)

6 Intelligence

Intelligence and its measurement have long been one of the controversial aspects of psychology. This may be because intelligence is one of the most visible areas of *applied* psychology: most people at some stage in their lives take IQ tests, whether they be the 11+ or similar school 'placement' examinations, intelligence tests incorporated into job selection procedures, or simply tests taken for interest from popular books or magazines. Another reason why the study and measurement of intelligence have been so vigorously debated is that many psychologists, fettered and restricted by the almost insurmountable problems of *defining* intelligence, have chosen to assume that we know what it is and to get on with the practical problem of its measurement. This has led to the questionable contention that 'intelligence is what the IQ test measures'. The third, and most current, reason for the controversy surrounding intelligence testing is its central role in the debate on racial differences – implicitly assumed to be innate – in achievement and potential. In this chapter we hope to present the reader with enough information to make up his own mind on these issues.

The nature of intelligence

In recent years, then, intelligence has become one of the most emotive topics in psychology. The first problem is, what is intelligence? It seems to mean all things to all people, and there appears to be little agreement on a suitable definition. Miles (1957) preferred the term 'intelligent behaviour' to the more usual 'intelligence', and Sir Cyril

Burt (1954) conceived of intelligence as 'innate, general, cognitive thinking'. Vernon (1960) believed there were three categories for defining intelligence: biological, psychological and operational. One definition of intelligence claims that it is 'the ability to learn quickly, to remember what has been learned, and to solve problems'. Alice Heim (1970) sees intelligence as 'the ability to grasp at essentials and to respond appropriately to them'. Another related approach, such as that exemplified by Gilbert Ryle (1967), includes application of what has been learned in adapting to new situations. There is also the empirical approach, to be dealt with later. Perhaps the most seemingly superficial definition of all, yet one with which all psychologists seem to be in agreement, is the one mentioned above which declares that 'intelligence is what intelligence tests measure'.

In 1904, Charles Spearman proposed that intelligence consists of both a single, general ability and a group of specific abilities. Having obtained a large number of scores from children on a variety of items, the scores were correlated and subjected to a complex statistical technique known as factor analysis. From this procedure emerged a *general intelligence factor* (**g**) and a *specific factor* (**s**) – the *two-factor theory of intelligence*. All mental tests would rely on the unique 'general' ability, while the performance of each mental task would require a 'specific' ability.

This was perhaps an over-simplification of the position, and was soon overtaken by Burt, who formulated his hierarchical system, later developed by Vernon. Burt considered that, in addition to general and specific factors, there were also *group factors*. This is brought out more clearly in diagrammatic form in Figure 68.

Dissatisfied with the somewhat global notion of 'general' ability, Thurstone (1938) sought to analyse it into a number of more clearly defined basic abilities. He assembled a large number of varied items (verbal, numerical and so on), incorporated them into several tests and gave them to groups of subjects. The scores obtained on these tests were factor analysed in order to obtain a number of primary factors or abilities. The items with the highest factor loadings or correlations within each of these primary factors were re-assembled to construct new tests. These were given to another group of subjects and the results were again factor analysed. The procedure was repeated several times until seven factors finally emerged – later to be known as Thurstone's *primary abilities*. These are outlined in Figure 69.

Thurstone proceeded to construct a battery of tests to represent

68. *Burt's hierarchical group-factory theory* (from P. Vernon, *The Structure of Human Abilities*; by permission of Methuen and Co. Ltd)

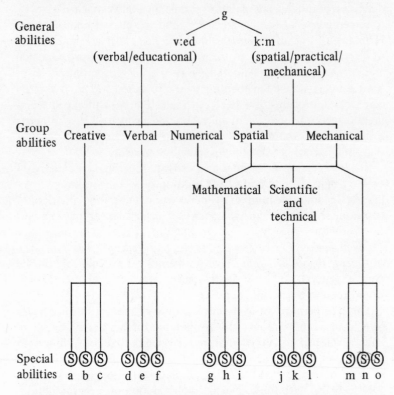

each of these seven abilities (*Test of Primary Mental Abilities*). Yet while its predictive efficiency was very good, it was no better than other tests of general intelligence. The criticism which was levelled at Thurstone's attempt to devise a test using factor analysis was one which has been levelled at other scholars who have employed this sophisticated procedure; namely, that the factors were bound to relate to the nature and content of the selected items. In this instance, as with so many other *psychometric tests* (tests which attempt to measure psychological factors such as intelligence and personality), there was certain to be some overlap or intercorrelations between items in the various factors. In other words, there was not sufficient evidence of item independence, and in the case of Thur-

69. *Thurstone's primary abilities*

Primary ability	What it represents
1 Verbal comprehension	The ability to understand what words mean — associated with tests of vocabulary
2 Numerical	The ability to handle numbers and carry out numerical calculations
3 Spatial	The ability to recognize relationships in space— form, such as an object at different angles
4 Perceptual	The ability to see things quickly and to observe similarities and differences in picture form
5 Memory	The ability to remember and retrieve verbal information
6 Reasoning	The ability to discover a basic rule for task completion given only one part of the task, e.g. 2 4 6 8 10 —
7 Word fluency	The ability to think of words quickly, e.g. word pairs and anagrams

stone's primary abilities, the intercorrelations between them offered clear support for a general intelligence factor such as Spearman had originally proposed.

This concept of general intelligence still remained quite inadequate for some scholars, notably J.P. Guilford (1967), who believed that it was necessary to be aware not only of the nature (that is, the content) of intelligence test items, but also of what one was expected to do with the content (that is, the operation) and the results (the product). He proposed 120 intellectual ability factors, produced by combining four types of content, five likely operations and six products. In addition to *convergent thinking*, which is the tendency to look for the conventional answer to a problem, Guilford also extended the concept of intelligence to include *divergent thinking*, the ability to produce new and creative solutions. Thus came into being the *structure of intellect model* (see Fig. 70).

Other approaches may be mentioned briefly, though the reader must be directed elsewhere for more extensive accounts. There is the theory of *fluid* (g_f) and *crystallized* (g_c) *intelligence*, which was put

70. Guilford's structure of intellect model

Contents	Operations	Products
Figural	Evaluation	Units
Symbolic	Convergence	Classes
Semantic	Divergence	Relations
Behavioural	Memory	Systems
	Cognition	Transformations
		Implications

forward by Raymond B. Cattell (1963). Here, the fluid factor (g_f) relates to the biological, innate contributions to intelligence, while the crystallized factor (g_c) is associated with the results of cultural influences such as home and school relationships. Both factors are capable of being measured.

Finally, a classic approach to the study of intelligence was provided by Donald Hebb (1949), with his emphasis on *Intelligence A* and *Intelligence B*. The former, he considered, was related to genetic and neurological factors, while the latter was a hypothetical stage of development, resulting from the interaction of Intelligence A with the environment. It would be very difficult for practical reasons to measure Intelligence A or Intelligence B directly, though Vernon (1955) introduced the notion of *Intelligence C* after sampling Intelligence B by means of standardized tests. This concept has important implications in the field of IQ testing.

Intelligence testing

A French doctor, Alfred Binet (1857–1911), working with retarded children, was one of the first people to use the type of intelligence test so familiar to us today. He assumed that intelligence would increase with age, and that older children would be capable of dealing with more items on a test. He concluded that the dull and retarded were those children who performed below the average for their age-group on a test. Thus their scores would be more like those of much younger children, and consequently the higher their actual age, the greater their retardation.

Binet proposed the concept of *mental age* to measure a child's intelligence. For instance, if an eight-year-old child's intelligence were average, he should be able to pass all the items on an intelligence test that a majority of others of his age passed. Fewer items successfully completed would suggest a lower mental age, while more items passed would point to a higher mental age.

His first intelligence scale appeared in 1905 with thirty tests. This was followed by revisions in 1908 and 1911. These revisions were constructed in levels, based on the stages at which the majority of children at certain ages could pass them. Thus the concept of mental age came into being. Unfortunately, it had one major drawback: it did not account for the child who was able to perform well on items at a level above or below his actual age-group; for example, there was no method of differentiating between a child of ten years who successfully completed test items at level ten, and a child of eight who passed at level twelve. In other words, the main drawback was that the test was too dependent on a child's *actual* (chronological) age.

This problem was overcome with the introduction of a new concept - *intelligence quotient* (IQ). This was a procedure instituted by Lewis M. Terman of Stanford University in 1916, which demonstrated the relationship between mental growth and chronological age. It was based on the idea of *mental ratio* expressed by Stern, whereby mental ratio was obtained as a result of dividing mental age by chronological age. Terman simply multiplied by 100 to give a much wider range of numbers. There is a simple formula for calculating IQ:

$$IQ = \frac{MA}{CA} \times 100$$

For example, what IQ has a child whose actual age is eight years and whose mental age is six years four months? Applying the formula:

$$IQ = \frac{6.4}{8.0} \times 100 = 80$$

$$IQ = 80$$

A score of 100 was considered 'average', 80–90 'dull' and 70–80 'feebleminded'. Anyone with an IQ below 70 was thought to be 'deficient', while at the other extreme, a person with an IQ of 170 or higher was regarded as a 'genius'. These categories, particularly those at the lower end of the scale, are interpreted with some reserve by psychologists today.

It will be noted that we have avoided talking about 'the' IQ, because quite simply there is no such thing. Before we can speak of 'the' IQ it is necessary to know which scale is being used, for the different tests have different distributions. Again, to speak of 'the' IQ erroneously assumes that intelligence remains constant in an individual, whereas, in fact, there is evidence that it will change over time (see the work of Escalona, 1954; Illingworth, 1961; and Bayley, 1970).

The construction of an IQ test

The intelligence test as we know it today has two main functions: (1) diagnosis, and (2) prediction. Items to be included in a test are chosen in accordance with their established reliability and validity under standardized conditions, and are given to a representative sample of adults or children. They must aim to test for reasoning ability, and not merely for knowledge. The items must also be carefully chosen in accordance with the cultural background of the candidates to be tested, and must not be biased or ambiguous. The test items will assume a variety of forms to reflect reasoning ability, including verbal and non-verbal content, analogies, ordering, classification, induction and so on.

An intelligence test is an *aptitude* test, not an *achievement* test, and items must be included for which no special training is required by the testees. This may be achieved by selecting either familiar or new items. In each case, the item must be familiar or new to all testees, in so far as they will have had the necessary experiences to tackle them. In this sense, the items must be fair and capable of being attempted by all the testees equally. For instance, there would be little point in expecting a non-English-speaking person to perform well on items requiring a grasp of the English language. Indeed, language may inhibit performance even amongst people within a particular country. Attempts have been made to avoid cultural bias by the construction of *culture-fair tests*. To ascertain whether an item is suitable for a given test, psychologists (1) find out how many individuals of the same age can respond to it (*validity*), and (2) correlate its scores with the scores on the test as a whole (*reliability*). More will be said about the concepts of reliability and validity below.

Having obtained a representative sample of subjects, a normal, or almost normal, distribution of scores has to be obtained for each group (see Fig. 71). These are scaled in such a way as to give an arbitrary mean – usually 100 – and a standard deviation of 10, 15 or 20 points. Thus, with some adjustment of the distribution, 68.26% of the scores would come within one standard deviation on either side of the mean, 95.44% would fall between two standard deviations on either side of the mean, and 99.72% within three standard deviations. Superficially at least, the test would now be ready for use, though in practice it must satisfy the two important criteria – reliability and validity.

71. The normal distribution curve

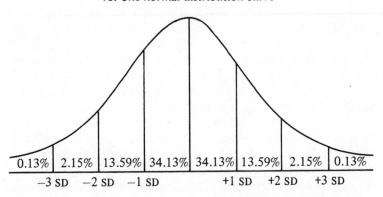

| 0.13% | 2.15% | 13.59% | 34.13% | 34.13% | 13.59% | 2.15% | 0.13% |

−3 SD   −2 SD   −1 SD   +1 SD   +2 SD   +3 SD

Reliability of a test means that it is dependable, reproducible, and consistently capable of producing the same results each time it is administered. Reliability may suffer if the test is too short. There are several methods of determining test reliability:

1 One method is referred to as *test/re-test reliability*, where the same test is given to the same people on two separate occasions, with an adequate time-interval between the two administrations. The two sets of scores are correlated to discover the extent of the test's reliability.
2 Another method is *alternate forms reliability*, where two versions of the same test are given and the two sets of scores are correlated. This method demonstrates internal consistency, or the degree to which the two sets of test items measure the same thing.
3 Internal consistency may also be obtained by using the *split-half method*, in which half the scores on a test are correlated with the other half. A high correlation would indicate that all parts of the test are internally consistent. Well-designed tests will have reliability coefficients in the region of $r = 0.90$.

As mentioned earlier, a test must also have validity, which means that it must measure what it is supposed to measure. Looking at the content of intelligence-test items can be deceptive. Does the test really measure intelligence, or is it largely a test of memory, English comprehension and so on? There are various kinds of validity (*face validity*, *content validity*, *construct validity* and others) and a number of techniques for obtaining it.

One way to find the validity of a test would be to administer it to a group of subjects along with another well-established measure of intelligence, referred to as the *criterion*. By correlating the two sets of scores, a coefficient would be obtained. This should be as high as possible, suggesting that the two tests are measuring the same kinds of abilities, for the new test to have any practical value. A test may be used to predict future success in a task. To discover whether the test had validity, it would be given to a number of individuals before they learned the task, and again after they had become proficient in the task. A validity coefficient would be obtained by correlating the two sets of scores. Again, this should be high if the test is to be any good at predicting success in the task.

Reference has been made above to Hebb's model of Intelligences A and B, and to Vernon's concept of Intelligence C, along with the implications for IQ testing. The tendency in the past has been for IQ tests to measure the nature component of intelligence (A) rather than the nature *plus* nurture aspect (C). It is hoped that this will be remedied in the new *British intelligence scale* which is at present being developed at Manchester.

The British intelligence scale is likely to contain 144 items designed to measure the intelligence of children between the ages of five and twelve. In terms of mental age (though this concept will not be applied), the range will extend from two to fifteen years. No reading material will be included in the items designed for the younger ages. It is anticipated that there will be twelve main scales and a number of sub-scales. The new test will be standardized on children from various geographical areas of Britain, and from different social groups. The conventional mean of 100 will be adopted, and an individual's test score will be given, not as a single figure, but as a score within a band or range of ten points. This new scale is an important venture and will take its place alongside the two American 'giants', the Wechsler and Stanford–Binet scales.

The nature/nurture debate

A much-debated question in psychology asks, 'How far is intelligence the result of inheritance, and how far is it the product of environmental influences?' The Austrian monk, Gregor Mendel, conducted basic research into the determinants of heredity during the nineteenth century. Using flowering pea plants, he discovered that certain traits are more dominant than others. He found that crossing red-flowering plants with white-flowering plants produced plants with red flowers. Yet when he crossed this second generation of red-flowering plants with white-flowering ones, 25% of the resulting flowers were white. Throughout the last century, geneticists confirmed and developed the laws of inheritance put forward by Mendel.

The mechanisms of hereditary transmission and the difficulties involved in assigning a genetic cause to any piece of behaviour were discussed in Chapter 5. While the science of genetics may be able to offer some solution to the question concerning the contribution which heredity makes to intelligence, it cannot ignore the environmental contributions. Nor are those scholars who accept the nativist standpoint obliged to dismiss out-of-hand environmental influences. For example, one ardent supporter of the genetic origins of intelligence was Sir Cyril Burt. He attributed 80% of intelligence to heredity and 20% to the environment, which is in accordance with the findings of others engaged in this field. Jensen, for example, showed that estimates of *heritability* may range from 0.45 to 0.87 according to the data and the type of calculations employed (a *heritability estimate* is the proportion of the differences in IQ within a population that is due to the action of genes). Burt's identification with the genetic school does not, however, imply that he ignored the contribution to intelligence made by environmental conditions. Indeed, his recognition of the importance of environmental factors led him to work in the slums of London, where he was able to gain useful insights into the environmental conditions which had such powerful influences on the development of mental abilities.

It may be useful at this point to remind ourselves what is meant by the term *'environment'*. This may be defined as anything which takes place from the moment of conception and which makes an impact on the life of the individual. It will be concerned with both the pre-natal and post-natal periods of the organism's life, and will include such factors as the cytoplasm of the cell, protein deficiency in the mother which may cause brain deficiency in her child, and types of emotional and social environments. Environmental factors may even cause mutations to take place in the genes themselves. All these factors have some implications for the development of human intelligence.

So, the question still remains as to how much variance in intelligence can be attributed to nature, and how much to nurture. It has been demonstrated that the relative contributions to intelligence made by heredity and environment may be empirically investigated in various ways. For instance, Anastasi (1958) proposed five methods:

1 Selective breeding. This is associated with Galton's *eugenics* (improving the quality of the race) and the more recent psychogenetics of Fuller and Thompson.

2 Developmental studies. Where behaviour occurs which requires no previous learning, it may be attributed to hereditary factors.

3 Structural factors. These relate to developments in the nervous system and the brain.

4 Development under certain conditions. This is a method by which young animals or human beings are allocated to special situations in order to determine whether or not any resulting change takes place in their development. This approach is best illustrated by the studies of Premack (1972) teaching language to a chimpanzee; the Gardners (1969) using American sign language (ASLAN), also to teach language to chimpanzees; and Zingg's studies (1940) with feral children (who are supposed to have been separated from their parents and been raised by animals).

5 Family resemblance. This approach is regarded as producing more substantial findings than the other four methods. It includes the 'human pedigrees' approach (Goddard, 1912), and the 'family resemblance' or '*concordance studies*' approach, which merits closer attention.

Concordance studies

It seems to be generally agreed that the closer the genetic relationship between two persons, the greater will be the correspondence between them of psychological characteristics. Thus the correlation procedure has become one of the main methods of investigating the contribution made to intelligence by genetic factors.

A number of studies have been conducted to assess the degree of association between individuals with regard to intelligence; for example, Erlenmeyer-Kimling and Jarvik (1963) summarized fifty-two studies of kinship data which included over thirty thousand pairs of correlations obtained over two generations. It must be said, though, that over fifteen thousand of these were concerned with unrelated individuals, where the correlation coefficients would be expected to be zero. One interesting study reported by Jensen (1973) revealed, as expected, a lack of correspondence on intelligence between people who were in no way related to each other (-0.01). Between foster-parents and children there was a correlation of 0.20. The correlation for uncles, aunts, nieces and nephews reached 0.34, while there was found to be a correlation of 0.50 on intelligence between actual parents and their children. Between siblings, this relationship increased to 0.55. A critical examination of these figures, and the kinship relationships with which they are associated, could point to an enviromentalist rather than a genetic explanation. Data available from twin studies, however, help to reduce the potency of the environmentalist argument.

The importance of twins for genetic studies was noted originally by Galton, who was aware that there are two kinds of twins – one kind which results from two separate female eggs (*dizygotic*), and another kind which is the product of the same egg (*monozygotic*). In the latter instance, the twins are always of the same sex. Galton sent out a questionnaire to the relatives of twins, as well as to twins themselves, in order to collect biographical information. He observed that same-sex twins tended to be alike in certain ways, while this was less noticeable in opposite-sex twins. Since Galton's day there have been a large number of twin studies, some of which will be mentioned below.

One scholar who spent a lifetime collecting data on IQ and heritability was Cyril Burt. His group intelligence test data on monozygotic twins (which have recently come under attack) demonstrated a correlation of 0.77 for twins reared apart, but this relationship increased to 0.94 for twins reared together, perhaps suggesting some environmental influence. When it came to his 'final assessments', the correlations were 0.87 and 0.93. Comparing sets of separated monozygotic twins with dizygotic twins reared together, the group test yielded correlations of 0.77 and 0.55 respectively, thus weakening the environmentalist point of view. It is rendered even weaker by the 'final assessment' category, where the correlation for separated monozygotic twins was increased to 0.87, and reduced to 0.45 for dizygotic twins reared together.

Another classic study is that of Shields (1962). He also considered that the influence of heredity and environment on intelligence could be separated by studying twins reared together and apart. With the help of the BBC, sets of identical twins were discovered who had been brought up away from their families during early childhood. Additionally, Shields found further sets of twins who had been brought up together in the same household. The two groups of twins were given a whole series of tests, including questionnaires, interviews, intelligence tests and medical examinations. A group of fraternal twins was also studied for comparative purposes. The results showed a correlation between heredity and intelligence.

For pairs of separated monozygotic twins, there was a correlation with intelligence scores of 0.77, and with pairs of non-separated monozygotic twins a correlation of 0.76. This separation produced virtually no effect on identical twins in respect of intelligence. By contrast, a correlation of only 0.57 was found for seven pairs of dizygotic twins, though these data are the result of the unsatisfactory method of 'pooling' four sets of twins reared apart and three sets reared together, where their respective correlations were 0.05 and 0.70. It should be noted that the researches of both Shields and Burt have been subjected to considerable methodological criticisms in recent years, and the reader is referred to Kamin's book, details of which are in the 'Further reading' for this chapter, for more detailed discussions of these criticisms.

There are two other studies which deserve a brief mention. First, an early American study conducted by Newman, Freeman and Holzinger (1937) produced correlations of 0.67 for separated monozygotic twins, and 0.91 for monozygotic twins reared together, while a sample of dizygotic twins produced a correlation of 0.64 with intelligence. Comparisons between groups are of little value, though, since the separated monozygotic group comprised mainly adults (with a median age of twenty-six), and the other two groups were children aged between eight and eighteen. Secondly, in Denmark Juel-Nielsen (1965) undertook a small-scale study into monozygotic twins reared apart. The sample consisted of nine sets of females and three sets of males. Juel-Nielsen found an overall correlation of 0.62 with intelligence, though because of the possible influence of age effects, a correlation of 0.59 would seem to be more realistic.

Despite the apparent uneasiness which some psychologists have expressed about certain aspects of these twin studies, there appears to be strong support from their findings for a genetic influence on intelligence. However, the hereditarians believe that, aside from twin studies, there are other kinds of evidence which subscribe to their point of view.

One such kind of evidence may be found in adoption studies. In child psychology, the home environment has clearly shown itself to exert considerable influence on a young child's social and intellectual development. In the case of adopted children, studies have been undertaken to attempt to determine the respective contributions made to intelligence by (1) the environment, as indicated by the adoptive parents' intelligence, and (2) genetic endowment, as assessed by the intelligence of natural parents.

As pointed out earlier, Jensen (1969) found the correlation between adopted children and their adoptive parents to be 0.20, whereas that between children and their natural parents was in the region of 0.50. Although one lesser-known study by Snygg (1938) reported a very low correlation of 0.13 between the IQs of adopted children and their biological parents (mothers), the celebrated study of Skodak and Skeels (1949) found a strong correlation between natural mothers and adopted children (0.44). Similar findings have been recorded by Burks (1928); Freeman, Holzinger and Mitchell (1928); Leahy (1935); and Honzik (1957). Nevertheless, in spite of the wealth of data, the results of these investigations must be interpreted with some caution and in their context.

Environmental enrichment and deprivation

The emphasis which some scholars have placed upon the genetic contribution to intelligence tends to obscure the part played by the environment. By some the environment is regarded as having at best only a meagre effect on intelligence, whereas it has been clearly demonstrated that it is capable of exercising a powerful influence on intellectual development. One of the best-known researches to illustrate this point is that of Skeels (1966), who studied a group of twenty-five nineteen-month-old orphans.

Thirteen of these children were found to be so badly retarded (some with IQs of only 60) that their adoption was impossible. They were moved from their overcrowded orphanage to a special institution where they were looked after for a considerable part of the time by older, slightly subnormal girls who acted as substitute mothers. These orphans were given a great deal of time and attention by their new 'mothers', and were provided with large rooms where there was a variety of toys and other stimulating material. The children were later able to attend nursery school, where they were provided with even more stimulation. Two years later, the average IQ for this experimental group was raised to 92.8 – an increase of 28.5 points since they left the orphanage. By contrast, the twelve children who had stayed back in the orphanage, the control group, lost as many as 26.2 points, reducing their average IQ to 60.5. Moreover, the superiority in intelligence of the experimental group was maintained over a twenty-year period. Clarke and Clarke (1954) also reported increases of 27 IQ points with subnormal adults when they were removed to hospital from 'adverse' environments.

There is ample evidence to show a marked relationship between social class and intelligence. There could be, for instance, a difference of 20 IQ points between the children of parents in the professional class and the children of unskilled manual workers. Poverty has revealed itself as one of the chief factors at the root of educational, social and cultural deprivation, and attempts have been made to compensate for this both in this country and abroad.

One of the best-known compensatory programmes in the USA was the Head Start Project, which began in 1965. This project aimed at providing 'deprived' pre-school children with a term or more of nursery education in advance of other children of their age, before actually starting school. It was hoped to improve both the children's IQ and academic performance, though the results of follow-up studies have failed to indicate any significant, permanent differences between those who had taken part in the project and other children of similar economic backgrounds who had not (Gordon, 1969). It could be argued that the failure of the Head Start Project was due mainly to the fact that it was inappropriate to the needs of the type of children for whom it was supposed to be catering. In other words, it tended to provide a middle-class programme for non-middle-class children, and was thus doomed to failure from the beginning. Indeed, Hunt (1969, 1972) questioned whether Head Start ever provided any kind of start for these non-middle-class children.

Other compensatory programmes proved to be more successful when they were related more specifically to the needs of poor children – and their families. Working with economically poor black children in the USA, Klaus and Gray (1968) not only succeeded in increasing the children's intelligence and academic performance

beyond those of their peers who had not participated in the programme, but their progress was maintained during their subsequent
school careers. Furthermore, these benefits were also extended to the
younger brothers and sisters of these children (Gray and Klaus,
1970). Maycer (1961) reported marked increases in IQ scores
amongst culturally deprived Negro and Puerto Rican students in
New York after they had undergone courses of remedial education.

Studies which have emphasized the development of language,
such as those of Bereiter and Engelmann (1966) and Blank and
Solomon (1968), have demonstrated marked improvement in intelligence amongst deprived children. One enrichment programme involving the interaction of mothers with their young children, using
toys to facilitate conversation, was undertaken by Karnes, Teska,
Hodgins and Badger (1970). Here the mothers had opportunities for
weekly discussions and training sessions with the investigators over
a period of two years. Their children's IQs had improved more than
those of children whose mothers had not taken part in the discussions and training sessions. (The relationship between linguistic
ability and the capacity to think is discussed on pp. 230–9).

Intelligence and race
The apparent failure of the Head Start Project prompted Jensen to
write an appraisal of it, to try to find out why it had failed. He
referred to the fact that 80% of the variance in intelligence was due
to heredity, and that there was a difference of 15 IQ points between
black and white Americans on the various IQ tests, suggesting an
inherited, unchangeable, racial difference in intelligence. This point
was also brought out by Shuey (1966) and more recently by Eysenck
(1971). 'Intelligence', however, is too wide a concept, and what
Jensen was referring to was the 'abstract reasoning' component of
intelligence which forms the basis of most IQ tests. He argued that
because black people were inferior to whites on abstract reasoning,
they should be persuaded to concentrate on learning specific skills,
that is, 'associative learning'.

Jensen made no attempt to explain this difference in abstract
reasoning between black and white people, and underestimated the
importance of environmental factors. He has been severely criticized
for misjudging the importance of the interaction of both heredity
and environment (Light and Smith, 1969). Tyler's studies (1965)
showed that on measured intelligence, Negroes in the North American

states were superior to Negroes in the South, and that Negroes who moved from South to North gained in IQ. Speaking of the equality of ethnic groups in the USA, Labov (1970) argued that environmental factors, such as poor schooling and bad housing, were largely responsible for creating some of the apparent inequalities between groups.

It has been carefully argued by Kaufmann (1973) that if it is accepted that black Americans are unable to perform as well as white Americans on abstract reasoning, this may be due to 'selective reproduction'. He suggested that probably the more intelligent black people (who also had little social or economic stability) are less likely to reproduce than the less intelligent blacks who follow more routine, repetitive occupations. Kaufmann opposed Jensen's implication that any child should be directed to a particular type of education simply on the basis of his race.

The controversial, emotive issue about the contribution of heredity and environment to IQ in the context of racial studies has created much interest amongst the public, and the amount of literature on the subject is beyond the scope of this short chapter. The ill-informed have attributed to *all* psychologists the notion that differences in intelligence between racial groups are the product of genetic factors alone. In fact, only a few psychologists would hold this extreme and precarious view, and few would seriously question whether scientifically adequate comparative studies could be undertaken into the question of intelligence amongst ethnic groups. As we have said, it remains for the reader to assess the evidence for himself, fairly and objectively, before making up his mind on this important issue. As Eysenck (1971) points out: 'We know very little, and if the reader expects any definite answer to the questions raised ... he will almost certainly be disappointed. Most people who write on this topic seem to know all the answers, and are firmly convinced that their point of view is correct; I know perfectly well that we do not know all the answers....'

Intelligence and age

What happens to our intelligence as we grow older? Thorndike (1948) demonstrated that measured intelligence is likely to wane after the age of fourteen once a child leaves school, but with extended education it may rise steadily until the age of twenty-one.

If the genetic approach to intelligence is accepted, it could be supposed that there will be a strong relationship between an individual's scores on intelligence tests at different age-levels. However, there is no evidence to support this supposition at the infant stage (Anderson, 1939; Lewis and McGurk, 1972). Long-term continuity studies with the same subjects which have extended beyond the period of infancy are interesting on this point. For instance, Honzik, MacFarlane and Allen (1948) found that the size of the relationship between test scores at various ages was low, (1) when the age of the child was low when first tested, and (2), when a larger period of time elapsed between testing.

Similar variations in IQ scores at different age-levels were noted by Sontag, Baker and Nielson (1958), who demonstrated that large changes in IQ scores amongst young children were often associated with motivation and emotion. Perhaps, too, the reason why infant scales of intelligence are unsuitable as future predictors is due to the fact that the scales tend, in the main, to measure visual–motor ability. There is, however, a new kind of intelligence scale for infants, which concentrates largely on the measurement of attention (Lewis, 1971). In a longitudinal investigation conducted by Bayley (1970), subjects were continually tested from birth to the age of thirty-six. It was found that, in some cases, there were changes in IQ of as many as 15 points, suggesting the possible influence of other variables.

It is not possible to say conclusively what happens to intelligence with advancing years. The tendency is for intelligence to decline, but this largely depends on the sort of mental abilities being considered, the personality of the individual and his general physical condition. Retaining and retrieving information and vocabulary are unchanged up to the age of sixty, but the ability to recognize numerical symbols declines quickly. This theory has received some support from David Wechsler (1958), who noticed an appreciable difference in the rate of decline between scores on the verbal and performance sections of his Adult Intelligence Scale amongst people aged between sixteen and seventy-five plus. Fifty people between the ages of twenty and seventy were tested on intelligence, and as many of these subjects who were available were re-tested seven years later. It appeared that mental abilities were at their peak at about the age of thirty-five, but declined after the age of fifty (Schaie and Strother, 1968).

Intellectual abilities that are dependent on speed or short-term memory are likely to decline over the age of forty. In connection with general and specific abilities, it appears that the former remain stable over time, while the specific abilities tend to decline at a greater rate unless they are in some way related to the person's occupation or habitual way of life. Could this perhaps be a reason why so many famous world figures are still in positions of leadership after they have reached the age of sixty-five?

In conclusion, it would seem that there is support for the belief that intelligence does not remain constant in an individual, but may alter over a period of time according to the number and kind of influences which bear upon it.

Further reading

Brody, E.B. and Brody, N. (1976), *Intelligence: Nature, Determinants and Consequences*, Academic Press

Eysenck, H.J. (1974), *Race, Intelligence and Education*, Temple Smith

Eysenck, H.J. (1976), *The Measurement of Intelligence*, Medical and Technical Press

Kamin, L.J. (1974), *The Science and Politics of IQ*, Potomac, Md, Lawrence Erlbaum Associates

Pyle, D.W. (1979), *Intelligence: An Introduction*, Routledge and Kegan Paul

7 Language and thought

It seems highly appropriate that the chapter on intelligence should be followed by one on language. In the first place, it has long been argued that a major justification for a *separatist* view of man and animals (that is, that man is 'up here' and animals are 'down there', and never the twain shall meet) is the existence of a qualitative difference in our intelligence – a difference which is attributed largely to our possession of a formal and complex system of language. This chapter will examine the accuracy of this long-held belief, along with a second, connected theme which also links Chapters 6 and 7 – the nature/nurture debate on cognitive abilities.

The process of thinking

'Thinking' is a term which is frequently used ambiguously, its meaning being dependent on the context in which it is used. It may be used as a synonym for remembering, as in 'I'm trying to think if I put the cat out', or for attention, as in 'Think what you're doing', or for opinion, as in 'What do you think?' It may be uncontrolled drifting and day-dreaming, sometimes called *autistic thought*, or it may be *imaginative thought*, which is more directed and coherent. McKellar (1957) describes autistic thought, or *A-thinking*, as a non-rational association of ideas, while *R-thinking*, or *reality-adjusted thought*, is logical and rational, and checked against external reality. R-thinking, or reasoning, is a cognitive process which is influenced by previous learning and experience and aimed towards a particular goal, and is a most complex form of human behaviour. It involves the use of symbols, standing for objects and situations which can be manipulated mentally rather than in reality. Thought thus goes beyond the perceptual here-and-now, acting as a highly flexible 'switch-board' process between a stimulus and the responses to it.

Symbols may be words, though they may also be other linguistic symbols – mathematical symbols, for example, are another kind of language. They need not be linguistic, but could be one of the many other symbols used in everyday life, such as money, traffic-lights or road signs. Symbolizing the world in order to think also involves forming classes of symbols to permit generalizations about the large numbers of stimuli available. Classification is achieved by the use of concepts, properties common to more than one object or event. 'Blue-ness' is a concept, a property which may be shared by many objects, as is 'roundness'. Concepts may be very specific and simple, relating to a single common feature; but they are more often complex, involving more than one common feature. Concepts which represent a class of stimuli which share one or more features in common are *conjunctive concepts*, while a *disjunctive concept* represents a class of stimuli which possess one of several possible features.

Bruner *et al.* (1956) describe the classifying of stimuli as

one of the most elementary and general forms of cognition which man uses to adjust to his complex environment. Concepts enable individuals to relate present experiences to past ones, and on the strength of the 'common-ness' between them, handle the present without continually learning anew. Concept formation and attainment is an essential feature of learning, and it has been demonstrated that laboratory animals can achieve concepts of form and colour. Thus language is not essential for the process of concept formation and attainment, though possession of it is intimately linked with human concept formation and attainment.

All symbols and concepts carry meaning, relating to the objects or events they represent, and it is meaning which is crucial for thought. Meaning may be *denotative* (it means the same thing to everyone encountering the symbol or concept, for example 'table', or 'no through road'); or it may be *connotative*, which implies some evaluation or emotional judgement of the object or event represented. The concept 'communist' has connotative meaning – it may not mean exactly the same to different people – and while denotative meaning is relatively easy to assess and measure, connotative meaning is much more difficult.

The difficulties of accurately assessing meaning cause considerable

72.

What does this symbol mean to you? Compare your interpretation with that of others.

problems for psychologists. Unless meaning can be measured, it is not possible to determine accurately how people differ in their interpretation of symbols and concepts. Subjects may simply be asked to say what a symbol or concept means to them, in a free-response situation. They may, less subjectively, be asked to discriminate between instances of particular concepts to demonstrate their understanding of meaning (for example, see Fig. 72). Osgood *et al.* (1957) devised a more complex method of assessing the meaning of concepts for different individuals, called the *semantic differential*, described in more detail in Chapter 12. More recently the meanings of particular concepts have been represented as *semantic networks* – diagrammatic and mathematical configurations of the links between one concept and other related concepts and symbols – particularly in devising computer simulation models of human cognition. An example of this is shown in Figure 43.

Concept attainment has been experimentally studied, generally by using various sorting problems in order to observe new subjects learning the concepts involved in the tasks. The sorting tasks may be learned by fairly simple discriminative learning, symbolizing objects and events and noticing which properties are shared. The context in which a symbol or concept is used can aid understanding of it. Try to derive the concept from the following context:

1 You can cut ziggle into many shapes.
2 Ziggle is hard but brittle.
3 Ziggle may be thick or thin.
4 You can drink from a ziggle.
5 Ziggle may be transparent or translucent.

(Ziggle = glass.)

Werner and Kaplan (1950) used materials similar to the example above in the study of the attainment of conjunctive concepts. The subject may also learn concepts as definitions by being told about them, rather than through personal experience of them. Prior experience of related problems aids the attainment of new concepts, providing as it does the opportunity both to learn the conceptual characteristics of objects and events, and to learn particular skills, for example, categorization, valuable to concept formation.

Bruner's work on concept attainment demonstrates that an important factor is the discrimination of particular readily identifiable attributes of the representations used, as the basis of classification, and his work has produced an extensive body of data. His experimental procedures frequently involve subjects in problem-solving tasks which require decisions about the attributes which define particular categories of objects or events, and require subjects to describe their thought-processes as they solve the problems. The order and pattern of decisions made during the problem solving reveal specific methods or strategies used by subjects in their observable behaviours. Problem-solving experiments devised with 'ideal' strategies in mind (that is, the most efficient ways of solving a problem) may be compared with subjects' actual strategies, in order to determine how, and how much, they deviate from the ideal.

The relationship between thought and language

Thompson (1972) believes that concept attainment is much more a matter of modifying and adapting one's existing concepts to new uses than forming completely original concepts, and that concept formation – the acquisition of new basic concepts – appears to take place in children up to the age of about fifteen years. Concept formation is an important aspect of Piaget's theory of cognitive development, which is discussed in detail in Chapter 11. It appears that object (or concrete) concepts are more easily formed than are abstract concepts such as number, and are therefore developed first by the young child, with more abstract concepts forming as the child gets older and has more complex language available to him. Observations of children's behaviours suggest that thought can exist before language, but not in the adult, or symbolic, form, and as language develops the child becomes able both to symbolize his thoughts and to communicate them to others. Clearly there is a close relationship between language and thought, because language is the medium we use to communicate our thoughts to others, and thoughts themselves are often couched in verbal form. Language may be *external* (communication with others via speech) or *internal* (communication with oneself via thought), and the two forms are closely linked. The nature of the links remains controversial, but the views of three leading researchers in the field will be considered here.

Whorf

Whorf's hypothesis, called the *'linguistic relativity hypothesis'*, or more briefly, the *'Whorfian hypothesis'*, states that the language one speaks leads one to perceive the world in ways different from those who speak different languages. Whorf, an expert in Red Indian languages, introduces many cross-cultural studies which seem to support his view. For example, Hopi Indians have one word which covers our words 'insect', 'aeroplane', 'pilot'; and Eskimos have many different words for 'snow', corresponding to snow in its different states (powdered, slushy, icy and so on). Whorf suggests that the verbal labels we give to things (or are forced by our culture to give to them) determine how we perceive the objects. This is known nowadays as the *'strong' version* of the hypothesis.

Carmichael, Hogan and Walter (1932) performed a now classic experiment to investigate this phenomenon. Two separate groups of subjects (I and II) were given identical stimulus figures to look at, but the two groups were given different labels for their figures. After a period of time both groups were asked to reproduce their figures, and the results are shown below (see Fig. 73). It can easily be seen that the reproductions of both groups were distorted away from the original stimulus, to become more like the verbal labels which were attached to them. But these results do not show that the two groups perceived the pictures differently. The difference may have been due to the effects of the labels on memory, rather than on perception.

Brown and Lenneberg (1954) carried out a series of experiments to check whether in fact labelling did alter perception. Different cultures, it was found, gave different 'codes' to colours (see Fig. 74). Does this mean that different cultures are unable to discriminate

73. *Figures used by Carmichael et al. in their experiment*

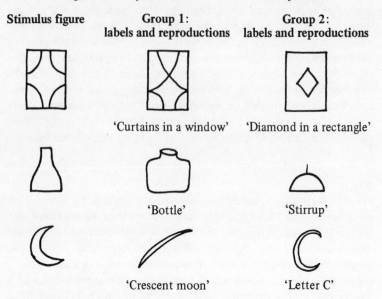

between different colours? Whorf would argue 'Yes' because of their different verbal labels, but Brown and Lenneberg's study suggests that this is not so. Colours for which there is no single name in a culture are not easily recognized by that culture, but this effect seems to be a result of the storage or coding of information (rather than of the direct influence of language on the perception of colours) – very much like the Carmichael experiment described above.

74. *The different colour codes of different cultures*

	Ultra-violet ← ———— Spectrum ———— → Infra-red					
English	Purple	Blue	Green	Yellow	Orange	Red
Shona (Rhodesia)	Cips^{w}uka		Citema	Cicena	Cips^{w}uka	
Bassa (Liberia)	Hui			Ziza		

Carroll and Casagrande (1958) investigated the effects of language, particularly on the development of form perception and recognition. They compared Navaho and American children on their development of form recognition. The Navaho language stresses the importance of form; for example, verbs of handling involve different roots, according to the type of object being handled. Long, flexible objects, such as pieces of string, have one verb form for 'to handle'; long, rigid objects, such as sticks, have another; and flat, flexible objects, such as cloth, have yet another verb form. It is known that American children of European descent develop object recognition in the following order: (1) size, (2) colour, and (3) form, or shape. If the Navaho language has had an effect on the Navaho children's cognitive development (as Whorf would argue), their developmental sequence for object recognition should differ from that of Amero-European children. Navaho-speaking children were compared with English-speaking American children and with English-speaking Navaho children. The results showed that the Navaho–Navaho children were best at form recognition, and showed it earliest. Next, however, came the English–American children ('middle-class'), while the English–Navaho children were last to develop form recognition. To an extent this supports Whorf's hypothesis, because Navaho–Navaho children did show an earlier development of form recognition. But English–American children came next, and Carroll suggests that this anomaly arose because the American children were atypical, as they had had much experience of shape classification at nursery school.

Whorf goes on to argue that it is not just the verbal symbols or the semantic content of words which causes us to perceive the world in different ways: the grammar of a language may have a similar effect. In English, for example, we think of words as denoting objects, and of verbs as denoting actions. Hopi Indian grammar, however, decrees that 'lightning', 'smoke' and 'flames', which in English are classed as nouns, act in the Hopi language as verbs. Thus, for example, the Hopi word '*rehpi*' means 'it lightened', and similar literal translations yield 'it smoked' and 'it flamed'. Followers of the Whorfian hypothesis argued that these grammatical differences led to differences in perception of the world. For example, Hopi Indians might see a burning house and say 'the house flamed', as if the house itself were the cause of the flames and the subject of the sentence. In English, the same situation is likely to be expressed more passively as 'the house was in flames', implying that 'the house' is the object of the sentence, and is not itself doing the burning.

Yet the experimental evidence cited so far does not support this view of the effects of language on thought. Judith Greene (1975) suggests that this discrepancy may be due to our reliance on literal translations: 'Imagine a Hopi linguist doing a Whorfian analysis on English. Would he think that we have "primitive" beliefs that ships are really female ... Or does the use of the same word for "drive a car", "a drive up to a house", "a drive in golf", and "to drive a hard bargain", mean that we "see" these things as being the same, as the Hopi is supposed to see insects and air pilots?' Certainly as far as the perception of everyday objects goes, there seems to be little evidence for cross-cultural differences, but it may be that our perception of social processes and events is modified by the language we use. Consider, for example, the complaint of a USAF colonel who complained to newsmen about their reporting of bombing raids over Cambodia, 'You always write about bombing, bombing, bombing. It's not bombing. It's air-support.' Ex-President Nixon, when ordering an intensification of the war in Vietnam, referred to it as 'pacification'.

Recently, Whorf's followers have modified his original hypothesis, and instead of the strong version, that language determines thought, they now advocate what they call the *'weak' version* – that different cultures' linguistic codes alter the ease of recognition of an object or situation, or the amount of attention paid to it. As a result, they have moved closer to the views of Brown and Carroll.

Basil Bernstein, an English sociologist, puts forward a similar hypothesis, suggesting that membership of a particular socio-economic class is associated with the type of language used, which can be termed either context-bound (*restricted code*) or context-independent (*elaborated code*). Bernstein proposes that the differing environments of middle- and working-class children have effects both on their language code itself, and on their cognitive development. Elaborated code users, according to Bernstein, are able to deal with more abstract concepts than the restricted code users, and this will particularly affect the range of thought processes possible, with a wider range being available to elaborated code users. There follows an example of each of the two codes (from D. Slobin (1971), *Psycholinguistics*). Children were given a series of four pictures, and asked to explain what was happening in them.

Elaborated code – context-independent (*middle-class*)

Three boys are playing football, and one boy kicks the ball and it goes through the window – the ball breaks the window and the boys are looking at it and a man comes out and shouts at them because they've broken the window – so they run off and then the lady looks out of her window and she tells the boys off.

Number of nouns: 13. Number of pronouns: 6.

Restricted code – context-bound (*working-class*)

They're playing football and he kicks it and it goes through here and it breaks the window and they're looking at it and he comes out and shouts at them because they've broken it so they run away and then she looks out and she tells them off.

Number of nouns: 2. Number of pronouns: 14.

The different language codes employed by the two groups affect the recall of the information. With the first story the reader does not have to have the four pictures which were used as the basis of the story, whereas in the case of the second story, the reader would require the initial pictures in order to make sense of the story. The first story is free of the context which generated it, whereas the second is much more closely tied to the context.

Criticisms have been made of the use made by Bernstein of language codes. Some of his followers appear to have overstated the case and to have suggested that all working-class children used restricted code and that all middle-class children used elaborated code. Much of Bernstein's work centres on grammar (syntax, the number of nouns and pronouns and so on), but does not concentrate so much on context. Although he talks about 'context-bound' and 'context-independent', he is wrong to use 'context' in this way, for whether or not an individual uses restricted or elaborated code depends on the context in which he speaks it, not only on the context in which he learns it. Thus, for example, if an individual is with others who share similar concepts, he is more likely to use restricted code. This seems to be true as much for 'middle-class' as for 'working-class' subjects (think of the stereotyped adult conversations at cocktail parties). In a situation where individuals do not share common concepts, they are more likely to use elaborated code. To the extent that members of the same 'social class' share common concepts about their environment, they will tend to use restricted code – irrespective of the particular 'social class' of which they are a member. If all 'working-class' individuals share common concepts which are different from those held by 'middle-class' individuals, then it is possible to uphold the idea that middle-class people use elaborated code and working-class use restricted code. But are the concepts held by, say, a Devon farm worker shared by a Liverpool docker? Are the concepts held by a marketing executive in London the same as those held by a country squire in Cumbria?

Piaget and Bruner

Piaget takes the view that language is not responsible for thought and that in fact thought comes first. As overt activity becomes internalized (memorized or learnt), language, says Piaget, may affect the range of symbolic thinking; but it is not necessary for its original development. He believes that children can be taught a language, but that they cannot understand the words until they have mastered the underlying concepts. In other words, Piaget's view is that language can exist without thought – but only in the sense that parrots can speak English. Thought is really a necessary forerunner to language, if language is to be used properly. However, some language does develop before the supporting conceptual thinking has appeared. The *egocentric speech* of young children, which can sound like a meaningless jumble of words, represented to Piaget an example of language without thought – language which was of little or no use for the communication of the child's ideas to others.

Sinclair-De-Zwart (1969) found that children who had *conservation of volume* (see p. 319) understood the meanings of words like 'bigger', 'more', 'as much as' and 'some', whereas children who had not got conservation of volume did not improve in their performance of the correct use of these words after having been given linguistic training. What these latter children needed was a grasp of the concept of conservation of volume. Until this had developed, the words, however well taught, were relatively meaningless to the child, and could not be used appropriately. This result supports Piaget's view that the use of language for communication (as opposed to its appearance as a meaningless self-directed babble, or egocentric speech) depends on the prior formation of the concepts which are to be communicated. This formation may occur as the result of maturational processes (see p. 318), in that concepts develop in a fixed sequence, which is not greatly modifiable by environmental factors.

Bruner's view of the development of the intellect broadly parallels that of Piaget, but without Piaget's insistence on the maturational nature of such development. Instead of relatively clear-cut stages of development, Bruner postulates three modes or ways of representing the environment. These modes can, in simple terms, be viewed as the ways in which an individual can retain and use information from the environment. Although all three are used, *symbolic representation* usually requires the use of language, and consequently is not used much by the pre-linguistic child. The second mode of representation is *enactive*; this could be compared with muscle memory, which is used to store and retrieve information and behaviours applicable to riding a bicycle, for example. The third kind is *iconic representation*, which is akin to 'picture memory', in which information is stored, retrieved and manipulated in picture form. These two modes do not require the use of language, but neither do they permit much flexible thought or problem solving, as they are limited in their ability to store information, which, in any case, must be in a relatively concrete form. All three modes, however, can be used to enable the individual to predict and therefore to control his environment, by storing information about what is going on in the environment, and then analysing this information in order to find predictable patterns (or as Bruner terms them, 'recurrent themes').

Therefore in early life (that is, when enactive and iconic representation are the most used), experience of the 'recurrent themes' in the environment is non-linguistic. Cross-cultural studies support this: children's early intellectual development is more affected by the amount of play, types of playthings and so on, than by the particular language spoken by their culture. With the development of symbolic representation, the child can store more information about the environment, and extract from this information the rules about how the environment works. However, in order to be able to do this, the child needs language to provide the symbols. It is at this point that the particular type of language becomes important (as shown in Carroll and Casagrande's study of Navaho children). Bruner regards language as acting like an amplifier for the child's intellectual development. Once language has developed, the child can store a larger quantity of more detailed information about its environment in symbolic form, and can manipulate these abstract symbols (that is, think) to solve problems.

Bruner believes that language and thought are separate things – non-linguistic thought (enactive and iconic) develops first, but does not really affect language development. Once language has developed, separately from thought, it acts as an amplifier or accelerator to thought. Different languages obviously can have an effect only when the child is old enough to use them. Before this time the amount of non-linguistic stimulation, for example play, is more important. This view of the relationship between language and thought is close to that of Vygotsky.

Vygotsky

Vygotsky sees language and thought as having separate roots, but coming together gradually between the ages of two and seven years. He was particularly interested in the phenomenon shown by all children of egocentric speech. Piaget views egocentric speech as being a kind of verbal diarrhoea, which gradually atrophies and has finally disappeared by the age of seven or eight, when the child has developed true social speech. Unlike Piaget, Vygotsky places much emphasis on egocentric speech. He sees it as being qualitatively different from social speech and as being the mid-point between fully fledged social speech (speaking out loud to others) and silent thought (inner speech):

> Our experimental results indicate that the function of egocentric speech is similar to that of inner speech. It does not merely accompany the child's activity; it serves mental orientation, conscious understanding; it helps in overcoming difficulties, it is speech for oneself, intimately and usefully connected with the child's thinking ... in the end, it becomes inner speech [Vygotsky, 1962].

Piaget himself now fully agrees with Vygotsky's work, and agrees that egocentric speech does have a function – that of helping to direct and plan the child's activities. It is noticeable that, as the child approaches seven, its egocentric speech becomes less intelligible to outsiders, more symbolic and briefer, finally disappearing from overt behaviour, to become inner speech (part, at least, of thought).

Conclusions

We can summarize the three approaches diagrammatically (see Fig. 75). The evidence reviewed in this chapter suggests that language

75. The three approaches to language and thought

Whorf's theory	Language ⟶ Thought
Piaget's theory	Language ⟵ Thought
Bruner and Vygotsky's theory	Social and egocentric speech ⟶ Social speech *Egocentric speech* Non-symbolic thought ⟶ Symbolic thought

neither controls thought (as Whorf thinks) nor is determined by it (as Piaget suggests). The most likely relationship seems to be an interaction of the two, some time between the ages of two and seven, when part of language becomes internalized in order to give guidance and planning to behaviour, becoming silent thought and providing a medium of '*symbolic internal communication*' (Vygotsky, 1962), or, as Bruner terms it, symbolic representation.

The nature/nurture debate on language

Whatever the relationship between language and thought turns out to be, the study of the development of language itself became an area of controversy. In the late 1950s and 1960s, an abrasive debate between B.F. Skinner and Noam Chomsky took place, the former believing that language was learnt by processes involving classical and operant conditioning, and the latter believing that humans have a biologically determined, or innate, competence to learn language, called the language acquisition device (LAD). The LAD allowed the child to extract from the sounds it heard the basic rules of the ways in which sentences are constructed, and to use this grammar to produce its own speech. Chomsky believed that the LAD also enabled humans to perform 'transformations' on simple sentences, to turn them into negatives, questions, passive tenses and so on. Chomsky's theory of language thus became known as 'transformational generative grammar', and became an important influence in the study of language development.

In the late 1960s criticism of transformational generative grammar grew. Most of this criticism was directed at its apparent failure to take into account semantic features of language, that is, at its near-total concentration on the structure, as opposed to the meaning, of sentences. Chomsky's theory could not, for example, explain single-word utterances, since there can be no sentence structure in such utterances. A theory developed by Fillmore (1968) put much more emphasis on semantics, and proposed that humans have some, probably innate, concepts of causality – who is the subject, who the object and so on. This *case grammar theory* enabled researchers to take into account single-word utterances in the development of speech, and they then began to look at language development in pre-linguistic children.

The question of whether nature or nurture is the more important in the development of language has largely been dropped; but it nevertheless produced very useful research ideas about language development. Greater emphasis is now placed on very early language development, and in particular on the transition from non-verbal to verbal communication in children.

Although the nature/nurture debate on language has subsided, conflict persists in one particular area – that of whether or not non-humans can acquire human language. Although this might appear to be an esoteric area of research, it does have quite profound consequences. As animal studies have progressed (see Chapter 12), the dividing line between human and animal abilities has become blurred: animals have been found to possess quite complex problem-solving abilities, and animal social-behaviour studies revealed a remarkably rich and diverse range of communicative behaviours. Consequently, the possession of language as the ultimate criterion for 'human-ness' became emphasized more. However, studies in the 1960s and 1970s began to suggest that some non-human primates may indeed possess the potential for the development of human language as well. If non-human primates could be shown to be able to learn a human language, the last dividing line between human and animal would become inoperable, giving rise to philosophical and legal issues about whether such 'animals' should have human rights and responsibilities. 'Is language restricted to humans?' has become a question, therefore, of far more than esoteric interest.

Is language restricted to humans?

The nativists believe that language is a species-specific ability, unique to humans. They think that it is not just quantitatively different from animal languages (that is, there is more of it), but that it is also qualitatively different – it is based on different principles and operates in a different way. The major method of testing this hypothesis has been to try to teach human language to non-human species. If they have the LAD, or language competence, they should be able to learn it. If they can learn it, this shows that they have a (presumably innate) competence, even though they may not use it in the wild.

We must first have some yardstick against which to measure the animals' language learning abilities: at which point can we agree that they have learnt a human language? The ability to speak it turns out to be not very useful. Dumb humans cannot speak the language, yet are assumed to have it. Similarly, parrots and mynah birds can speak but do not apparently understand language, largely because they cannot use it flexibly.

C.F. Hockett (1958) produced a list of criteria for human language, which he termed 'design features'. He believed that human language, and human language users, show all these features. It is these which have become widely accepted as the criteria by which non-human attempts at language development should be measured.

Criteria for human language

Note that features 1 to 4 are concerned with the ways in which speech carries information (there are ways of using language other than speaking).

1 *Vocal/auditory:* it is carried by sound, which is made vocally by one individual and received auditorily (through hearing) by another.

2 *Broadcast transmission/directional reception:* the sounds made are broadcast, and individuals receiving them should be able to tell from which direction the sound is coming.

3 *Rapid fading:* a vocal utterance fades rapidly (unlike written language, which can be read and re-read).

4 *Total feedback:* when you speak, you can hear what you are saying. (You could not see what you were saying if you were using semaphore, but you could hear what you were saying when using speech.)

5 *Interchangeability:* a speaker can send and receive information.

6 *Specialization:* the speech function is for communication only. It should not be a by-product of some other form of behaviour.

242 Understanding Psychology

7 *Semanticity:* language has meanings.
8 *Arbitrariness:* language does not need to look like or sound like the things it symbolizes.
9 *Traditional transmission:* language can be transmitted from one generation to the next.
10 *Learnability:* language can be learnt. (Humans can learn languages other than their native one.)
11 *Discreteness:* information is not coded by the length of the utterance, but by the position of the phonemes.
12 *Duality of patterning:* language has a double pattern:
(a) Phonemes are organized into words.
(b) Words are organized into sentences.
13 *Displacement:* language enables the user to refer to objects or situations which are displaced in time or space.
14 *Openness/productivity:* language is capable of generating an infinite number of new meanings (*novel utterances*).
15 *Prevarication:* language enables the individual to lie, or to talk about things which are impossible.
16 *Reflexiveness:* using language, an individual can talk about language.

Whether or not non-human primates possess language abilities can now be tested against these criteria.

Teaching human language to non-human primates
The earliest systematic attempt to teach human language to a non-human species was undertaken by Hayes and Hayes (1951). Using operant conditioning with their baby chimpanzee, Vicki, they managed to get her to speak four words ('mama', 'papa', 'cup' and 'up') by the age of three years. Kellogg and Kellogg (1933) reared a chimpanzee called Gua with their own child. Gua was able to understand seventy words or commands, but was unable to speak.

Allen and Beatrice Gardner (1969) thought that the failure of these early attempts meant either that chimpanzees could not develop language, or that they had language competence but were physiologically incapable of speaking. The various gestures which Vicki used in trying to speak gave them the idea of using a human sign language with a chimpanzee. The Gardners' chimpanzee, a female named Washoe, was born wild, and her language training began when she was about nine months old. The language used with Washoe was '*Ameslan*', short for *American sign language*, developed from Red Indian sign languages. Ameslan was the Gardners' sole means of communication with Washoe, and they were quickly impressed with her ability to imitate signs. If her signs were not accurate enough, the Gardners used behaviour-shaping techniques and their own development of these, *moulding*, which involved their actually manipulating Washoe's hands, in order to make the correct signs. Three years after training began, Washoe knew 85 signs, which increased to 160 by the time she left the Gardners two years later. Only ten months after the start of training, when she was approximately twenty months old, Washoe made her first combinations of signs ('Gimme sweet', and 'Come-open'). She showed an early ability to name objects (something which was previously thought to be unique to humans), and the Gardners used a double-blind technique (see p. 13) to avoid bias in their results, as follows. They presented a series of photographic slides of objects, in random order, to Washoe, who had to make the appropriate Ameslan sign for each of them. Washoe's signs were observed and noted by an experimenter who was unable to see the slides himself. Consequently, if Washoe's sign was clear enough for him to understand and interpret, and it was also correct, Washoe must have learned to name an object correctly. This technique controlled for the possibility that Washoe might simply be making sloppy or ambiguous signs which the Gardners wishfully interpreted as being correct.

After she left the Gardners Washoe went to Oklahoma, where she now lives with other Ameslan-using chimps under the care of Roger Fouts. He has compared the chimpanzees' performance with Hockett's design features, and believes that the chimps have demonstrated enough language ability to seriously damage the assertion that language is unique to humans. Of the other chimps in the colony, Ally is particularly interesting, since he is a very clear 'signer', learns very quickly, and can apparently translate spoken words into Ameslan signs.

Below is a summary of some of Fouts' findings and research techniques. Note that some of the design features are inapplicable to Ameslan-using chimpanzees: design features numbers (7), (8), (10) and (11) listed on p. 242 are properties of their language, not of the speaker, and numbers (1), (2) and (3) are inapplicable because Ameslan is not a spoken language. This means that the main design features for comparing animals and humans are interchangeability, displacement, openness/productivity, traditional transmission, prevarication and reflexiveness.

Interchangeability In the Oklahoma chimp colony the chimps use Ameslan among themselves even when no human is visible, both for sending and receiving messages.

Displacement Fouts has designed an investigation to see whether his chimps can show displacement. One chimp is taken out of sight of the others, who are caged. This chimp is shown two hidden 'presents'. One is food, and the other, something which chimps dislike (a stuffed snake, for example). The chimp is then put back into the cage with the others and left with them for a while. After this the other chimps are released and the original chimp kept in the cage. If the original chimp has managed to convey where the hidden 'presents' are, Fouts believes that this is evidence for displacement. (If only the whereabouts of the stuffed snake is conveyed, this might be evidence of prevarication!)

While with the Gardners, Washoe would sign 'time eat', which may suggest that she has some concept of time (the formation of which requires some displacement abilities). However, to date, displacement has not been conclusively demonstrated.

Openness/productivity Washoe invented her own sign for 'bib', since the Gardners did not know the proper sign – and Washoe's invented sign turned out to be close to the correct Ameslan. Lucy, one of Fouts' chimps, coined her own name for radishes – 'hurt-cry fruit' – and she also calls watermelons 'candy-drink' or 'fruit drink', even though she knows the correct Ameslan sign for watermelon.

Koko, a female gorilla taught by Francine Patterson, has devised her own form of swearing. Washoe shows displeasure with somebody by signing 'dirty' before their name. Koko goes one better: her favourite phrase is 'You big dirty toilet'.

Traditional transmission Washoe had a baby early in 1979, and its progress is at present being carefully observed. As yet there are no results available from these observations, but it has been noticed that when several Ameslan-using chimps are living together, they learn new signs from each other.

Prevarication Koko seems to have demonstrated this in her answer to the request 'Tell me something you think is funny'. She signed 'Nose there', pointing to a bird puppet's tongue; 'That red', and pointed to a green plastic frog. Francine Patterson also reports that when she puts a stethoscope to her ears, Koko smirks and puts fingers over her eyes.

Reflexiveness Michael, a male gorilla who lived with Koko, was trying to ask Francine Patterson to let him enter Koko's caravan. Patterson insisted that he make the correct signs, but he could not. Koko, watching through a window, demonstrated the correct signs which Michael copied, and he was then admitted. When she saw him enter, Koko signed 'Good sign Michael'.

Other researchers have used different techniques. Duane Rumbaugh at the Yerkes Primate Research Centre in Atlanta, Georgia, has investigated chimpanzees' abilities to deal with syntax. Lana, the chimp he used, lived with a computer, which would give her what she wanted only if she pressed the correct sign-buttons in the correct order. Thus, for example, she had to say 'Please machine give piece of apple' (full stop), but 'Please machine make music play' (full stop) or 'Please machine make window open' (full stop). Lana performs very accurately on these tests and can apparently tell the difference in meaning between 'Lana groom Tim' (one of her trainers), and 'Tim groom Lana' – a difference in meaning which is entirely due to syntax.

David Premack has devised a plastic sign language for use by his chimpanzee, Sarah. Using plastic symbols, she has been able to demonstrate her understanding of interrogatives, negatives, conditionals (if–then phrases) and full sentences, as well as object naming.

Such studies have not been without their critics. Despite the Gardners' use of double-blind techniques with Washoe, the decision as to whether or not a particular piece of behaviour satisfies one of Hockett's criteria is often a subjective one, and experimenters and critics differ on these judgements, and even on which criteria to use for judgement. Criticism of the experiments themselves has often been concerned with the degree to which the experimenters might have led the animal into signing what was required; for example, when Washoe signed 'Baby in my drink', H. Terrace, who himself attempted to teach Ameslan to a chimpanzee, claimed that he saw the Gardners 'cueing' Washoe. Other researchers, on looking at the film, disagree with him.

The feelings among the researchers themselves seem to be that interchangeability, productivity, reflexiveness and prevarication seem to have been demonstrated by the various primates, but that there does not seem to be enough evidence yet that displacement and traditional transmission have definitely been shown. However, it must be remembered that primate language studies are in their infancy, and the impressive results gained so far suggest that the possibility of primates acquiring a human language is not a remote one.

Further reading

Adams, P. (1972), *Language in Thinking*, Penguin

Greene, J. (1975), *Thinking and Language*, Methuen Essential Psychology Series

Trevarthen, C. (1974), 'Conversations with a two-month-old', *New Scientist*, 2 May

8 Personality

We have said that psychology is a collection of specialisms, and if this is true, then the study of *personality* may well be the biggest of the specialisms, for a 1970 survey showed that nearly half of American psychologists classify themselves as working in the fields of clinical psychology and personality (normal or abnormal). In addition, despite the domination of behaviourism and its allied philosophies in American psychology, American psychologists, when asked which psychologist has most influenced the development of the discipline, most frequently answered, Sigmund Freud. Freud devoted his life to studying the structure and development of the personality, and such has been his all-pervading influence that, while not wishing to mislead by oversimplifying psychology's study of personality, this chapter is divided into two main sections, which consider the Freudian and the non-Freudian theories.

Non-Freudian theories

Types and categories
There is a strong tendency to place people into categories according to the ways in which we have placed other people in the past. People appear to fall naturally into categories – pleasant, talkative, dominant and the like. Their physical appearance, the way they dress and their manner of speech also help to allocate them naturally to a 'group'. A closer association with these people will enable us to ascribe moral characteristics to them. The question then arises as to whether the personality which they present to others is their true self,

or merely a mask to conceal their real self. It is interesting to note that in the classical theatre an actor wore a mask (*persona*) to convey to the audience his role in the drama.

A single, adequate definition of personality is hard to find, though this has not deterred psychologists from offering them. For instance, Ernest Hilgard and his colleagues would see personality as the 'characteristic patterns of behaviour and modes of thinking that determine a person's adjustment to the environment'. Norman L. Munn suggests that personality may be defined as 'the most characteristic integration of an individual's structures, modes of behaviour, interests, attitudes, capacities, abilities and aptitudes....' Both definitions use the word 'characteristic' as an indication of the relative permanence of personality variables. To pursue a search for an adequate definition, however, would be non-productive, since there are so many and varied interpretations. Indeed, about fifty usages were discovered by Allport (1937).

One of the earliest attempts to examine personality differences was that of the Greek physician Hippocrates. He noted that there was some relationship between physique and personality, and he categorized people as *pyknic* (stocky) or *leptosomatic* (frail). Hippocrates also noticed how the emotional differences in people seemed to be affected by varying amounts of phlegm, blood, black bile and yellow bile. He further observed in his patients that certain diseases were specifically related to a person's physique.

In 1828, Rostan argued for an intermediate type and proposed the digestive, muscular and respiratory–cerebral types. Based on these types, Kretschmer (1948) introduced his leptosomatic (*asthenic*), pyknic and *athletic* types, to which he added a mixture of the other three – the *dysplastic*. Like Hippocrates, Kretschmer was able to relate illness (in this instance mental illness) to body types.

A number of unsuccessful attempts were made to associate personality characteristics with bodily types: the athletic type was supposed to be aggressive and energetic; extraversion was associated with the pyknic type; and the leptosomatic type of person would tend towards introversion. Unfortunately for the body-type theories, people do not in practice fit so neatly and conveniently into these categories. One study which examined a group of pyknics revealed that only 50% were categorized as extraverts, thus demonstrating the fallacy that personality characteristics can be accurately related to physique.

Using quantitative ratings, as opposed to subjective impressions, Sheldon carried out an ambitious investigation to demonstrate an association between personalty and physique. Thousands of men were photographed naked from three different angles to determine whether it was possible to identify specific types. In the event, no specific types were discernible, but it was found that all individuals possessed certain characteristics to a greater or lesser degree. Thus, three dimensions were evidenced:

1 *Endomorphy:* the digestive viscera originates in the endoderm of the embryo (pyknics).
2 *Mesomorphy:* muscle comes from the mesoderm of the embryo (athletics).
3 *Ectomorphy:* the skin and nervous system have an ectodermal origin (asthenics).

A person could be rated, or *somatotyped*, on a scale from 1 to 7 on each of these dimensions. For example, a somatotype of 4:4:4 would suggest that a person was about average on each dimension, while a somatotype of 7:1:1 would indicate a maximum amount of endomorphy with a minimum of mesomorphy and ectomorphy.

Sheldon attempted to attach temperamental ratings to each of his dimensions, and claimed a high correlation between a person's physique and his temperament. If this were so, it would be possible for us to predict someone's temperament from a cursory observation of his physique. However, the validity of Sheldon's conclusions has not been sufficiently established, and the findings of other researchers have disproved the existence of positive correlations between physique and temperament.

One of the earliest theories, which provides the basis for our modern theories, is that of the Greek physician Galen. In the second century AD he used Hippocrates' method of categorizing people according to the four temperaments – *sanguine* (associated with blood), *choleric* (associated with yellow bile), *melancholic* (associated with black bile) and *phlegmatic* (associated with phlegm). Unfortunately, Galen believed that a person could be fitted into only one of these four categories without any overlap at all. Two Germans, Immanuel Kant and Wilhelm Wundt, later adopted and developed Galen's categorical system, which also appears at a later stage in Eysenck's dimensional theory.

The factor analytic approach

Perhaps one of the greatest names in personality research in the United Kingdom is that of Hans Eysenck. He adopts a hierarchical view of personality, illustrated in Figure 76 below. The bottom part of the diagram shows the specific instances of a single response to a particular situation. At a slightly higher level come the *habitual responses* which refer to responses that are likely to be repeated. Sometimes there is a common factor between some of the habitual responses: they have a strong correlation. Taken together, these related habitual responses form a *trait*, and several traits may co-exist at the third level of the hierarchy. When intercorrelated traits are taken together, they form the personality type at the fourth level at the top of the diagram.

Using as a basis Jung's personality-type model (see p. 263), Eysenck proposes three major dimensions of personality which are considered to be sufficient to account for personality variance (see Fig. 77): E, extraversion/introversion; N neuroticism/stability; and P, psychoticism/normality. The *extravert* is outgoing, lively and sociable, while the *introvert* is shy and withdrawn. Unlike the *stable*

76. *Eysenck's hierarchical view of personality* (after H. J. Eysenck, *The Structure of Human Personality;* by permission of Methuen and Co. Ltd)

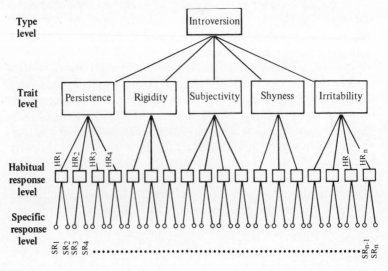

77. *Eysenck's dimensions of personality* (after H.J. Eysenck (1965),
   Fact and Fiction in Psychology, p.54, Pelican Books; copyright ©
   H.J. Eysenck, 1965; by permission of Penguin Books Ltd)

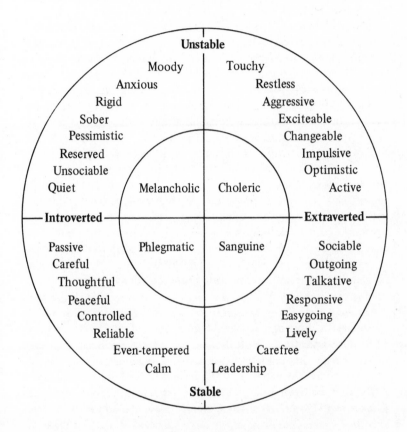

The inner circle of this diagram shows the famous doctrine of the four
temperaments; the outer circle shows the results of numerous modern
experiments involving ratings and self-ratings of behaviour patterns of
large groups of people. It will be seen that there is considerable
agreement and it will also be seen that a considerable part of personality
can be described in terms of two major dimensions, here labelled
introversion/extraversion and unstable/stable.

personality, the *neurotic* is anxious and moody. The *psychotic* exhibits behaviour associated with mental disorder – cruel, insensitive, inhumane. It is important to emphasize that the use of dimensions of personality indicates a continuum, and the majority of people would score around the mid-point on the extraversion, E, and neuroticism, N, scales, and very low on the psychoticism, P, scale.

The smaller circle in Figure 77 illustrates the four temperaments. The dimensions of extraversion–introversion and neuroticism–stability divide the larger circle into four quadrants, each with its associative trait names. These traits are the products of numerous experiments using personality inventories, such as the Eysenck Personality Inventory (EPI); the Eysenck Personality Questionnaire (EPQ); the Junior Eysenck Personality Inventory (JEPI); and the older Maudsley Personality Inventory (MPI).

Eysenck has attempted to examine the physiological as well as the psychological variables connected with the extraversion and neuroticism dimensions. He has discovered, for example, a negative relationship between extraversion and conditioning, contending that extraverts are not easily conditioned, and that their conditioned responses can be extinguished without difficulty (this difference in *conditionality* may have relevance to the socialization of these types of people: see p. 339). Similarly, he has found a notable relationship between neuroticism and the autonomic nervous system.

One might be tempted to ask whether two or three dimensions adequately describe personality, or whether more dimensions are necessary. As long ago as 1936, Allport and Odbert mentioned over four thousand trait descriptions and almost eighteen thousand words which differentiated one person's behaviour from that of another person. More recently, Raymond B. Cattell has made a fine distinction between traits which are basic to observed behaviour (*source traits*), and traits which emerge from the source traits (*surface traits*). Having collected a large number of words which described behaviour, Cattell reduced them to 171 and submitted them to a statistical technique known as *cluster analysis*. There emerged about forty clusters which he called surface traits, and these were factor analysed to produce twelve source traits or personality dimensions. To arrive at these source traits was Cattell's main concern.

Cattell intercorrelated his source traits and submitted them to factor analysis. A number of other factors, called *second-order factors*, appeared, of which two are considered to be particularly interesting, namely *anxiety* and *exvia*, corresponding to Eysenck's neuroticism and extraversion dimensions. Eysenck would argue, however, that Cattell's primary factors measure virtually nothing other than these two factors. 'Anxiety' in this context refers mainly to feelings of tenseness, guilt or worry; 'exvia' points to a sociable, outgoing, unreserved person, as opposed to the shy and withdrawn personality, who is described with the term '*invia*'.

A definition of personality put forward by Cattell states that 'Personality is that which permits a prediction of what a person will do in a given situation'. Since prediction of behaviour is fundamental to Cattell's theory, he considered it necessary to know how much of each particular trait a person possessed. This resulted in the creation and development of tests to measure each source trait.

78. *Some dimensions of the Sixteen Personality Factor Questionnaire*

Factor	Low-score description	High-score description
E	Humble	Assertive
H	Shy	Venturesome
O	Self-assured	Apprehensive
Q_4	Relaxed	Tense

Perhaps the best known of these tests is the Sixteen Personality Factor Questionnaire (16 PF), which can yield personality ratings on sixteen dimensions, each made up of opposing factors, some of which are illustrated in Figure 78.

Before leaving our discussion of the factor analytic approach it must be pointed out that its procedures are fraught with difficulties which have caused a large number of psychologists to be cautious when interpreting results obtained by this method. It is said that with factor analysis you obtain as an end-product no more than that which you introduce as raw material at the start of the procedure. This is perhaps evidenced in the findings of Guilford and Comrey, whose personality studies using factor analysis yielded factors which superficially seemed to be new, but in practice merely reproduced Cattell's main factors.

A number of personality theories tend to concentrate on 'units' or 'aspects' of an individual's personality, yet many psychologists would wish to understand the complete individual through his total units. Two psychologists who have emphasized the importance of studying the whole man – of *phenomenological studies* – are Allport and Murray, and to these we now turn.

Phenomenological theories
Gordon Allport defined personality briefly as 'what man really is'. He laid great emphasis on the uniqueness of the individual and argued for a study of *the* individual rather than the average individual. He attacked vehemently the tendency to make generalizations and apply them indiscriminately to all individuals. Allport recognized the need for psychology to differentiate between (1) personality which related to the individual case (*idiographic*), and (2) the general laws or dimensions of behaviour (*nomothetic*), while accepting for his purpose the idiographic approach.

Allport's trait theory is important, for he considered it to be the best method for understanding and explaining human behaviour. According to him, traits do not initiate behaviour but become dominant or otherwise in the context of a situation. He suggested that there are differences between types of traits; for example, some traits appear to be present to some degree in most kinds of behaviour, and these are called *cardinal traits*. There are, however, certain basic traits which one might use to describe an individual. It has been suggested that there are about seven of these essential traits in each individual, and these are referred to by Allport as *central traits*. Traits which are less typical of the individual, but which he possesses to a more general degree, are termed *secondary traits*.

Unfortunately, Allport was so concerned with the *whole man theory* that he was unable to introduce practical general laws of behaviour. Murray, on the other hand, was able to combine both approaches using small groups of subjects. His theory of personality had a motivational orientation based on *needs* and *presses*. According to Murray, needs are 'theoretical constructs' which help to explain human behaviour. He envisaged a need as the beginning of an event, with behaviour occurring in the middle of the event, followed by the satisfaction of the need, though this was not always possible in practice.

Having classified his needs into viscerogenic and psychogenic, he proposed twenty *manifest needs*, that is, needs expressed openly in behaviour, for example achievement, aggression, dominance and understanding. To his manifest needs Murray added eight *latent needs*, that is, needs which are inhibited or repressed. He further distinguished between *proactive needs*, resulting in spontaneous behaviour regardless of the environment, and *reactive needs*, which are very closely bound to the environment.

Needs, which occur within the individual, are paralleled by presses, which are concerned with an object or situation outside the person (*external determinants*) that brings about a particular kind of response. As with needs, Murray again differentiated between the various sorts of presses, of which the most important difference is that between *alpha press* and *beta press*. The former relates to a

79. *Maslow's hierarchy of needs* (after Abraham H. Maslow, 'Hierarchy of Needs', in 'A theory of motivation', in *Motivation and Personality*, 2nd ed.; copyright© 1970 by Abraham H. Maslow, by permission of Harper and Row, Publishers, Inc.)

situation which the individual is actually facing, while the latter relates to a situation which the individual thinks he is facing.

One of the best-known phenomenologists, Carl Rogers, incorporates into his theory two distinctive concepts – the *self-concept* and a need for *positive regard*. The self-concept depends on how an individual sees himself in the world, how weak or strong he is and the sort of person he is. It affects how the individual sees the world and his own behaviour. Positive regard is an ideal state. When it is expected that a person will be a certain kind of individual, or behave in a certain way, a state of anxiety will be created whenever the individual falls short of these expectations. The anxiety will be removed when the *self-concept* is altered to portray the individual as he really is (see p. 388).

Self-actualization (the individual's need for self-development, and for reaching his or her full potential) has been carefully investigated by Maslow, using characteristics representative of eminent persons. He held the view that a person has five essential needs, ranging in a hierarchy from lower to higher (see Fig. 79). The lower needs relate to biological requirements (for example, food and drink) and they progress through safety, love and esteem to self-actualization. The highest level of self-actualization can only be attained when each of the other levels has been satisfied (see p. 389).

Learning theories

Miller and Dollard believed, like Freud, that childhood experiences play a large part in the development of personality. Their theory is centred on the infant's initial need for food, water and warmth. In the early stages, the infant is able to satisfy these needs in an elementary way, but eventually other, more complex, behaviour has to be learned. Dollard and Miller proposed four main constructs in the learning process – *drive*, *cue*, *response* and *reinforcement*. For instance, a man who feels thirsty (the drive) sees a public house (the cue). He goes inside and orders a drink (the response) which reduces his thirst drive (the reinforcement). An example given by Dollard and Miller is that of a hungry rat (the drive) running round a box; it sees a lever (the cue) and touches it (the response), releasing food (the reinforcement) which reduces the hunger drive. The main criticism of Dollard and Miller's theory is that it is 'non-social', concentrating solely on experiments with animals. Some scholars question whether they are correct in generalizing the results they have obtained from animals to human behaviour. (The impact of learning theory on personality development is discussed in Chapter 11.)

The research of Skinner has had a tremendous impact on personality theory, but as his work has received a more detailed treatment in Chapter 3 it will be necessary here only to refer to the emphasis which he places on positive or negative reinforcement in changing behaviour. In Skinner's work the individual behaves normally, though the experimenter knows beforehand whether he will reward or punish that behaviour. It is possible, therefore, using the reinforcement principle, to modify or even completely change the behaviour of delinquents, psychotics, smokers, gamblers and others.

As we have seen, the principle of reinforcement is a common factor in the work of Skinner, and Dollard and Miller. It plays no major part, however, in the work of two other learning theorists, Bandura and Walters: they adopt the *social learning approach* which lays emphasis on *identification* and *modelling* (imitation). This approach supposes that man's behaviour is the product of constant interaction between himself and his environment. A person's situation will dictate what type of behaviour he will adopt. Behaviour which would be perfectly acceptable on a sports field, for example, might be quite inappropriate in church. Social learning theory demonstrates that behaviours are specific to a given situation.

A cognitive approach

The work of George A. Kelly contrasts with that of the other theorists studied so far, and his theory merits some detailed discussion. He believed that *cognition* (the processes involved in thinking, problem solving, and predicting events in one's environment) has the most important part to play in personality development, and he considered that just as a scientist attempts to predict and control the behaviour of others, so we try to predict and control the events which take place in our everyday environment. According to Kelly, the individual views his world through transparent patterns of *constructs* (or hypotheses about the world: see p. 70) which he creates. He then endeavours to place these constructs over the realities of the world.

Since these constructs represent the events of an individual's personal environment, Kelly refers to them as *personal constructs*. (When we 'construe' or use a set of constructs, we do so from a personal point of view. Thus each individual has his own special repertoire of personal constructs.)

Not only do people possess a set of constructs, but they put them to the test in a systematic manner. For example, a student hypothesizes that a new tutor at his college is fairly easygoing and therefore likely to accept written work of low quality and quantity from his students. The student makes a prediction from this construct (that is, that he can get away with very little work, of poor quality) and proceeds to test it. If the prediction is maintained, the construct will be supported. If the prediction fails to produce the expected response, the construct could be eliminated, or at least revised.

As we said earlier, Kelly's theory contrasts with the work of many other personality psychologists in that he is more interested in the person who makes the construct than he is in the person who is the object of the construct. The tendency in personality studies has been to observe how person A evaluated person B on a particular dimension, and then to examine whether this evaluation was supported by other 'judges' of person B. For example, if person A labelled person B as 'honest' on the 'honest'–'dishonest' continuum, would this be borne out by other observers of person B? However, Kelly was more interested in person A in order to see how far his tendency to categorize people as 'honest'–'dishonest' was important for his life. He organized his theory on the basis of one fundamental postulate and eleven corollaries, but these require a fuller explanation than this chapter will permit.

How does one evaluate the personal constructs which an individual employs? For this purpose, Kelly devised the *Role Construct Repertory Test* (*Rep Test*), whose principal function is to determine the constructs a person uses in describing roles. For example, a subject is given a list of role descriptions, such as 'a neighbour you find it hard to get along with' or 'a teacher who influenced you most'. The subject is asked to write alongside each role description the name of a person known to him who best fits that description. He is then given a group of three 'role people', selected from the list of about twenty-five, and asked to state in what important way two of them are alike and different from the third. Finally, the subject is asked to state in what way the third person differs from the other two. This method produces a construct which tells the investigator how a person sees his world.

A variation of the Rep Test is the *Repertory Grid*. Here, each 'role person' is indicated across the top of the page (policeman, priest, nurse, shopkeeper and so on), and a set of constructs is listed down the left-hand side of the page (polite, religious, grumpy and others). In this version, the objective is to determine how far each construct and its contrast can be applied to each 'role person'.

One weakness in Kelly's theory is that it does not give any indication as to how personal constructs are created and developed, or how they relate to an individual's behaviour. Nevertheless, Kelly has advanced beyond the trait, type, and *deterministic* (*Freudian*) *psychologists* who have long maintained the viewpoint that an individual's personality, at least in its later stages, is difficult to change, since he does believe that our behaviour changes according to our role.

Freudian and neo-Freudian theories

Sigmund Freud (1856–1939) was first and foremost a neurologist until his middle years, and took a keen interest in the treatment of patients suffering from mental illnesses. His own particular theory of personality gradually developed over a period of about fifty years as a result of self-analysis and case histories. He employed the *free association approach* to elicit information about his patients, and he later extended this to dreams.

Free association enables one to speak freely about anything at all without feeling in any way inhibited. Freud observed carefully not only what his patients said, but where they faltered or stopped talking altogether. In this way, Freud assumed a connection between these aspects of behaviour and repressed material. His interpretation of dreams is also based on associations. The persons or objects in dreams were not necessarily important in themselves: Freud encouraged his patients to freely associate in order to arrive at the crucial material. This was the basis of psychoanalysis.

Freud placed a great deal of emphasis on those aspects of behaviour or mental activity which are undertaken *unconsciously*, that is, without our being aware of them. Indeed, he argued that it was only through psychoanalysis that it was possible to penetrate the bounds of the unconscious. This is not to be confused with the *preconscious*, where concepts lie in the unconscious possibly because they have been repressed, but can be recalled when required. *Conscious* mental processes, of course, are concerned with those aspects of our lives of which we are totally aware.

Freud gave us the three underlying structures of personality – the *id*, the *ego* and the *super-ego*. The id consists of unconscious processes which we inherit. It strives after immediate gratification and thus relates to the pleasure principle. The ego keeps a steady watch over the wishes of the id. It can be conscious, preconscious or unconscious, and is governed by the *reality principle* – the need to behave in ways which will be acceptable to those in the outside world. The super-ego is concerned with 'must' and 'ought', and from it the conscience develops (see pp. 330–1).

The ego controls behaviour by means of unconscious defence mechanisms, some of which we will examine. One such mechanism is *sublimation*, where outlets are provided for forms of behaviour which would otherwise be forbidden. Not all defence mechanisms are successful, however. For example, *repression* will not allow an instinct to break through into consciousness. It thus remains within the organism and shows itself as anxiety. *Denial* prevents us from admitting to reality: when someone really upsets us, we pretend before our friends that we hardly noticed (the experimental investigation of perceptual defence is discussed on pp. 68–9).

It will have become apparent that Freud placed a great deal of emphasis on the term 'unconscious'. For him, and in the development of his theory, this became a key concept. He proposed that some of our major personality characteristics originated unconsciously in our childhood, and psychoanalytic theory stresses that the *psychosexual stages* (see p. 261) are very relevant to the development of personality, because they emphasize the importance of the first five years of life.

There is, according to Freud, a conflict at each of these stages which must be overcome before the individual can proceed to the next stage. A certain amount of energy (*libido*, or sexual energy) has to be used in order to overcome these conflicts. Furthermore, the greater the amount of energy used at a particular stage, the more likely it is that the individual will carry through into later life some of the major characteristics of that stage.

When *fixation*, or a halting of development, has taken place at a psychosexual stage in childhood, behaviour associated with that stage tends to be noticeable in adulthood. It has been suggested that the degree to which childhood behaviour patterns are transferred into adult life depends on the amount of libido which was expended in trying to overcome the conflict associated with a particular stage. It is as one proceeds through the various psychosexual stages that the id, ego and super-ego appear. It would now be appropriate to take a closer look at each of these stages.

The oral stage

Here the id is dominant. The baby seeks to reduce tension by satisfying the basic needs of hunger and thirst. He also obtains a great deal of pleasure from body stimulation. The mouth plays an important part at this stage in helping to reduce tension (for example by eating) and to give pleasure (for example by sucking). The conflicts to be resolved by the child at this stage are *incorporation* (absorbing his environment) and *independence* (being cared for by others). Failure by the baby to overcome these conflicts can lead to fixation: success in overcoming them, and recognizing a world external to himself, will bring about the development of the ego.

The anal stage

At about the age of two years, the child tends to concentrate on the anus, which becomes the immediate source of pleasure, known as an *erotogenic zone*. This pleasure is gained by expelling faeces (anal-expulsive behaviour) and by withholding them (anal-retentive behaviour). This is the time when parents make their first real demands upon the child. The conflict at this stage is between obtaining pleasure and reducing tension on the one hand, and coming to terms with the attempts of society to control the child's behaviour on the other hand.

The phallic stage

The most important erotogenic zones at about the age of four are the genitalia. The assumption Freud made was that the child had a desire to possess the parent of the opposite sex and to destroy the parent of the same sex. Thus come into existence the *Oedipus* (or *Electra*) and *castration complexes*. An early Greek myth describes how Oedipus unwittingly killed Laius, his father, and married Jocasta, his mother. He blinded himself when he realized what he had done. Another legend tells how Agamemnon was murdered by his wife's lover, and how his daughter Electra bitterly despised her mother for her behaviour.

The mother is the first object of a boy's love and, according to Freud, his rival is his father. The Oedipus complex is repressed for fear of castration by the father, and the boy begins to identify with his father. In the same way, the girl's first love object is her mother, but she experiences feelings of inferiority about the clitoris, believing she has been castrated by her mother. Her father then becomes the object of her love, giving rise to the Electra complex. Eventually, through fear of losing her mother's love, she begins to identify with her. As the Oedipus and Electra complexes are overcome, the super-ego begins to develop.

The latency period

This follows at about the age of five when the Oedipus and Electra complexes have been resolved. Since attention is not centred on the libido, and no major conflict appears, the latency period is not a psychosexual stage.

The genital stage

This is the final stage of psychosexual development, which occurs at puberty. While attention is still focused on the genitalia, the libido is directed towards pleasure of a heterosexual kind.

Freud's theory has received severe criticisms over the years, some of which are listed below:

1 Many psychologists would agree that Freud's concepts are metaphoric and imprecise, and are therefore not easily testable.
2 Freud used middle-class, wealthy Jewish women from Vienna, and from these restricted samples made sweeping generalizations.
3 Much of Freudian theory is based on the clinical evidence of emotionally disturbed people.
4 For any theory to be claimed as scientific, it must be capable of being proved wrong. This is generally not possible with Freudian theory.
5 It has been questioned whether the two fundamental instincts of aggression and sex remain unchanged throughout life.
6 One important criticism questions whether Freud's psychosexual stages are, in fact, culturally determined.

In spite of these and similar criticisms, one must not undermine the tremendous contributions which Freud has made to the study of personality – the importance of the unconscious; the scientific study of sexuality; and the developmental aspects of personality. Some of the later psychologists who followed Freud's fundamental approach (the neo-Freudians) modified Freud's theory by concentrating more on the cultural and social aspects of personality development, thus removing some of the emphasis which had been placed on the importance of instincts. To some of these neo-Freudians we now turn briefly.

Carl Gustav Jung put forward the view that there are two types of unconscious material – the *personal unconscious*, and the *collective unconscious*, which is derived from our ancestors. The contents of the collective unconscious he termed '*universal archetypes*'. There is no emphasis in Jung's theory of personality on the Freudian concepts of childhood influences or the sex drive.

For Alfred Adler, the social environment was of paramount importance in helping to develop the personality. He proposed that an individual strives for superiority, trying to perfect himself by means of *compensation* – that is, compensating for recognizable weaknesses within himself.

The importance of the social environment was also stressed by Karen Horney. She was particularly concerned about the effect of anxiety on a person, especially in conflicts between a child and its parents and in conflicts between the parents themselves. Horney's belief was that if such anxiety were severe or prolonged in childhood, this would possibly produce neurotic tendencies within the individual in his adult life.

An individual seeks security; the opportunity to express his creativity; the chance to realize his personal identify; and the ability to make social relations in late adolescence after breaking away from the familial home. These elements are the basis of Erich Fromm's theory of personality. He would contend that personality is the end-product of the interaction between these elements, and that society has a tremendous responsibility to provide adequate opportunities for such interaction to take place. Thus an individual's personality is largely the product of society. It is interesting to note that his theory, based on the late adolescent period, is in opposition to Freud's proposition that the first five years of life are crucial to personality development.

It would perhaps be appropriate to end this chapter with some reference to Erik Erikson, who related Freud's concepts of stages and instincts to the social and environmental approaches of the

80. Erikson's psychosocial stages

Stage number	Psychosocial stage	Conflict
1	Oral—sensory (1st year)	Trust *v.* mistrust
2	Muscular—anal (2nd year)	Autonomy *v.* doubt
3	Locomotor—genital (3rd—4th year)	Initiative *v.* guilt
4	Latency (6th year— puberty)	Industry *v.* inferiority
5	Puberty and adolescence	Identity *v.* role confusion
6	Young adulthood	Intimacy *v.* isolation
7	Adulthood	Generativity *v.* stagnation
8	Maturity	Ego integrity *v.* despair

psychologists discussed above. Thus, for him, the individual passes through eight *psychosocial stages* which cover the period from infancy to maturity. According to Erikson, each stage presents a social conflict for the individual in his interactions with other people. His eventual psychological functioning will be dependent on how successful he is in resolving each of these conflicts. A person's readiness to interact with increasing numbers of people plays a significant part in the development of his personality. Figure 80 illustrates the eight stages of psychosocial development and their respective conflicts.

These, then, are some of the more well-known personality theories. Another important part of personality theory is concerned with the roles people play in social interactions, the qualities we find in other people, and their impressions of us. Some of these topics are dealt with elsewhere in this book (see Chapter 14).

Further reading

Allport, G.W. (1961), *Pattern and Growth in Personality*, Holt, Rinehart and Winston

Cattell, R.B. (1965), *The Scientific Analysis of Personality*, Penguin

Cattell, R.B. and Dreger, R.M. (eds.) (1977), *Handbook of Modern Personality Theory*, Hemisphere

Eysenck, H.J. (1970), *The Structure of Human Personality* (3rd ed.), Methuen

9 Animal behaviour

One of the many problems that has confronted psychology is that of achieving the right balance, and of resolving the conflict, between its two aspects – its subject-matter (behaviour and experience) and its generally preferred methodology (the experimental and observational methods of science). The subject-matter of Chapter 8 is pursued by psychologists despite the near-impossibility of finding and   e-menting the 'approved' method: this chapter considers a field   e the method may be applied relatively easily and extremely p   ably, but where, some psychologists claim, the subject-matter been lost – the field of animal psychology.

Why study animals?

All psychology is concerned with animal behaviour since man himself is an animal, but some psychologists spend a great deal of time studying non-human animals. In this section we shall use the word 'animal' to describe any non-human living organisms other than plants. Part of the definition of science is 'the pursuit of knowledge for its own sake', and for some people this is sufficient reason for this type of research; but, apart from pure academic interest, these studies may help to control animals for commercial and domestic purposes and give some clues about the behaviour of man himself. Animals have provided food, comfort and protection for man over thousands of years. Studies of selective breeding have increased the efficiency of farm animals in terms of food production, and behavioural studies have helped choose and train dogs for guard duty and sheep gathering, as well as for entertainment in circus acts and advertisements.

The most controversial reason for studying animals is that it may lead to an understanding of human behaviour; this immediately raises the question, 'Why not study humans directly?' The short answer to this is that it is not always possible to study humans directly, because there are greater moral and ethical restrictions on the type of research that can be performed using humans as subjects; and that animals are less complex and therefore easier to understand (it is a basic principle of science to start with the simple and progress to the complex). In particular, animal studies have the following advantages. First, it is possible to administer greater rewards and punishments with animals and to use experimental techniques such as rearing in isolation which are not possible with humans. However, it is worth noting that a growing number of people argue that animals suffer too much in the cause of the search for knowledge. Secondly, with animals it is possible to study instinctive behaviour, little or none of which remains in humans. Similarly, it is possible to study the evolution of behaviour since animals can be cross-bred in tightly controlled environments and usually have shorter gestation and maturation periods than humans, allowing research into many generations in a short time.

Still, we cannot be sure that research into the causes of animal behaviour are applicable to humans. If we study part of the brain of an animal we cannot be sure that it has the same function as in man – although experimenters try to take into account differences between animals and man by using an animal whose brain is similar in structure to man's. Then again, even if the structures are similar their functions may be different. In addition, although there may be similarities between a species and man, there may be differences we have not yet found. Some of these problems can be reduced by careful choice of experimental animals; for example, the frog's eye works in a similar way to the human eye, so it is used in visual experiments. It is known, however, that the frog's brain attends to different classes of stimulus than man's does, and so although some of the findings of visual experiments on frogs may be generalized to man, those in the field of perception may not.

Some people argue that even if the structures of an animal and humans are identical, it is still not valid to generalize the results to humans because of man's unique possession of consciousness and his power of thought. However, psychologists generally agree that all mental processes are ultimately dependent on physical structures and chemical changes within those structures (see p. 144). Animals have nerves and brains; the messages passing along those nerves do so in the same way as in man; and the similarities in the structure and function of nerves and brains are more noticeable than the differences. It is possible to argue that man's uniqueness is not a qualitative difference from animals, but a quantitative one; in other words (and with the possible exception of speech), the elements of behaviour displayed by humans are also displayed by animals, although in a simpler form. Hebb argues that animal findings are not, by themselves, directly applicable to humans, but they may be used as hints – to give clues and to generate hypotheses which can then be tested directly on humans.

When studying humans we can ask subjects to give verbal reports of their experiences in experiments. Since animals do not talk, we have to get an animal to report its experiences by its behaviour. Thus, in order to find out whether a rat can discriminate between two colours we would condition it to press one lever when a red light comes on and a different one when a blue light comes on: if the rat can do this, it must be able to distinguish between the two lights. Bower used similar procedures with human babies to test their perceptual capacities.

One of the biggest 'sins' that an animal researcher can commit is that of *anthropomorphism*, the tendency to see human-like qualities or motives in non-human organisms or objects. It can be seen in statements such as 'The rat is pleased' and 'The cat thinks she will get a reward'. We may be right when we think the animal is happy, but we can never know this with certainty.

The case of 'Clever Hans' is a classic example of the mistaken application of anthropomorphism. Hans was a circus horse which could apparently compute arithmetic equations. If asked to solve the problem 'two plus two' the animal would answer by striking the ground four times with its hoof. The number of problems that Hans could answer suggested that the horse was doing more than recalling the responses to a few standard questions, and many scientist took the view that it actually worked out the calculations just as humans do. It was only after exhaustive research by Pfungst (1911) that it was discovered that Hans was simply responding to clues given by the questioner. Pfungst showed that if the questioner hid from

Hans's view the horse would go on striking the ground even after it had reached the correct answer. The horse had learnt to stop 'counting' when its questioner made the slight change in posture that we all make when we have received the desired answer and believe that a communication has ended.

The common brown rat shows apparently 'intelligent' behaviour when it avoids a favourite path when a farmer puts poison on it. If, however, a harmless paper parcel is placed on the path rather than poison, the rat will still avoid the path: rats simply avoid new objects.

Although animal behaviour has interested people for a long time, it is only in recent years that systematic studies have been carried out on it. A two-pronged investigation has taken place, using rather different research techniques. These two sets of techniques, ethology and experimental psychology, will be discussed next.

Ethology

The group of researchers who now call themselves ethologists was founded in the 1930s and 1940s by Konrad Lorenz and Niko Tinbergen. The group was made up of Europeans, mainly zoologists, who had in common a wish to study a wide range of animals, preferably in their natural habitat.

In the 1950s and 1960s, a spirited debate took place between the ethologists and the (largely behaviourist) experimental psychologists, on the relative merits of their approaches to the study of animal behaviour. The ethologists were often concerned with investigations into the function of the animals' behaviour – how and why certain kinds of behaviour furthered the survival of the individual or species. To this end, they examined a wide range of animal behaviour during such times as the establishment of territories, courtship and parenthood.

The ethogram
It is very difficult to observe and manipulate variables in the natural habitat of an animal, so ethologists have developed a research tool, the *ethogram*, which is a detailed catalogue of the behaviour of an animal. This catalogue of behaviour is made up two kinds of description. The first is the *description of motor patterns*, literally, the

description of the physical movements made by the animal. This has the advantage that it is relatively objective, since it avoids the possibility of anthropomorphism and is accurate, but has the disadvantages that it does not relate the animal's movements to its environment, and that it can also be cumbersome to use – often all individual limb movements have to be described. Secondly, *description by consequence* is used. In this method the description is of consequences of the animal's behaviour in relation to its environment. As an example, consider the description 'The rat approached the lever'. Were this activity being described by motor pattern alone, it would have been concerned with the limb movements, and how the animal moved. Description by consequence is more concerned with why the animal moved – what the consequences were of the movement. Description of behaviour by consequence is a more economical form of description; it relates the animal to its surroundings, but it has the disadvantage that it is not appropriate to the study of detailed differences in behaviour, or of motor patterns, between different animals. In order to obtain a full description of animal behaviour, ethologists usually use both forms of description.

The example below is taken from Niko Tinbergen's work on territorial and courtship behaviour in the stickleback ('The curious behaviour of the stickleback', *Scientific American*, December 1952, vol. 187, no. 6, pp. 22-6). Description by motor pattern is enclosed in square parentheses, whilst description by consequence is enclosed in round parentheses.

... (The threat display of male sticklebacks is of two types. When two males meet at the border of their territories, they begin a series of attacks and retreats. Each takes the offensive on his own territory, and the duel seesaws back and forth across the border. Neither fish touches the other, the two dart back and forth) as though attached by an invisible thread.

When the fight grows in vigour, however, the seesaw manoeuvre may suddenly change into something quite different. [Each fish adopts an almost vertical head-down posture, turns its side to its opponent, raises its ventral spines and makes jerky movements with the whole body.]

Experimental psychology

The experimental psychologists, unlike the ethologists, studied a limited range of animals, usually using the experimental method, in laboratory settings. They were more concerned with animal learning; so much so that one unkind wit compared behaviourists with magicians – one pulls rabbits out of hats, while the other pulls habits out of rats!

Probably as a result of their choices of methods of study, the ethologists and experimental psychologists quickly came into conflict. The ethologists were interested in the functions of animal behaviour and how such behaviour had evolved in a particular species – a process known as *phylogenesis*. In the early days, they were not much concerned with the investigation of how behaviour develops within the individual – such development being known as *ontogenesis*. On the other hand, ontogenesis was a primary concern of the experimental psychologists. Consequently the main arena for debate took place over ontogenesis, with the experimental psychologists stressing the role of learning and of the environment, and the ethologists, having seen so much stereotyped behaviour among individual species, reintroducing the term 'instinct' as a means of explanation for these stereotyped acts of behaviour.

The instinct debate

In order to survive, an animal must be able to cope successfully with its environment in order to find food and a mate, and to rear its young. Such adaptive behaviour was often thought by the ethologists to be instinctive; that is, it was thought the behaviour was due to the genetically determined structure of the animal, usually of its nervous system. The experimental psychologists criticized the use of 'instinctive' as an explanatory term, preferring instead to stress the importance of the animal's learning and experience. Out of the instinct debate came the attitude which now prevails in studies of animal behaviour – the attitude that behaviour develops, with both hereditary and environmental factors being necessary; and that the task of research should be to investigate how these two factors together contribute to development. It is worthwhile, therefore, to examine in more detail how this change of attitude came about.

The Stoic philosophers in the first century AD held that men and gods were one community, but animals were excluded because they were not creatures of reason, as it was considered that all their behaviour took place 'without reflection' (Seneca). Aristotle, who, unlike the Stoics, actually observed animal behaviour, accredited humans with superior intellectual powers; but this was a quantitative, not a qualitative, difference from animals.

But the major use of the term 'instinct' was made by religious philosophers, from St Thomas Aquinas, through Descartes and Bishop Berkeley, to modern times. The ideas run as follows. Man has a soul, and because he possesses a soul, he will have eternal life. But he cannot be given this eternal life 'free of charge': he must earn it by being good and by avoiding evil. Therefore he has to have free will and reasoning ability. Eternal life belongs to humans only; therefore animals cannot have it. Because they cannot have souls, or eternal life, animals do not need, or have, free will and reason. How, then, can complex animal behaviour be explained, if not by reason? By God-given 'instinct'.

Monsignor Fulton J. Sheen in his book *Peace of Soul* says:

> In animals, there are only instincts, but not in man. As St Thomas points out, there cannot be any deliberation in a subrational being (even though we may get the impression that there is). Instincts in animals seem to operate according to the pattern of physical forces, where the stronger always prevails; for animals are utterly devoid of the freedom which characterizes man.... That is why when one studies human behaviour one must rise above the purely animal pattern and concentrate upon those two faculties, intellect and will, which separate man from animal.

The rise of 'human instincts' seems to have begun with Darwin. His theory of evolution postulates that there has been a continuity of development of man from the animals. However, Darwin was faced with the prevalence of the view that humans were qualitatively different from animals, particularly in the existence of human reasoning ability. To try to merge these opposing views he argued that humans had instincts like animals and that animals had primitive reasoning ability like humans. William James, who was influenced by the evolutionary movement, insisted that humans have more instincts than any other animal. McDougall in his famous book *Social Psychology* listed many human instincts (for example flight, repression, repulsion, parental feeling, reproduction, self-abasement and others). Even Thorndike, originator of the Law of Effect, thought that human behaviour was an expression of instinctive drives or needs. There was, however, little agreement about the number of instincts.

Freud and Lorenz held broadly similar views about the instinctive nature of human aggression. Freud believed that aggression, for example, will eventually find its way out, and that attempting to repress or inhibit it will only cause it to appear in a distorted form. Lorenz, too, believes that aggression is driven by instinct, and that socially acceptable ways of allowing it to be expressed should be found (see p. 296).

The constant use of 'instinct' as an explanatory term, when it really is only a descriptive term, led to a revolt against its use. In the 1920s and 1930s, Z.Y. Kuo fought against the use of the concept, but still admitted the existence of unlearned *'units of reaction'* (reflexes). By doing this, he admitted the learning-versus-instinct dichotomy, and had to try to find learning explanations for everything except a few reflexes. The real question, as will become apparent, is not 'Innate or learnt?' but 'How does behaviour develop?'

Criteria for instinctive behaviour

Lorenz and Tinbergen postulate that much behaviour is instinctive, and it is important here to specify exactly what they mean by instinctive behaviour. It is, they say, hereditarily determined, part of the original constitution of the animal; arises independently of the animal's experience and environment; and is distinct from acquired or learnt behaviour.

In order to provide some means of investigating such behaviour Lorenz and Tinbergen produced a list of criteria, by which behaviour can be determined as innate or instinctive.

1 The behaviour must be stereotyped and constant in form.
2 It must be characteristic of the species (that is, *species-specific*).
3 It must appear in animals which have been reared in isolation from others.
4 It must appear fully developed in animals which have been prevented from practising it.

That some animal behaviour conforms to these criteria is clear, but a lot more which is claimed to conform is, when studied more closely, found not to do so.

First, an example of behaviour which does fulfil the criteria – swimming in the frog tadpole. Carmichael (1927) kept the eggs in an anaesthetic solution which prevented any movement by the developing larvae. When the tadpoles had long passed the stage at which they would normally have begun to swim, they were placed in fresh water. When the effects of the anaesthetic had worn off, they were able to swim as well as any non-anaesthetized tadpoles in about half an hour and apparently without practice.

To control for the possibility that the anaesthetized tadpoles might have had some practice while the anaesthetic was wearing off, Carmichael anaesthetized the group that could already swim, and then removed the anaesthetic. It took this group approximately half an hour to begin swimming again, suggesting that the originally anaesthetized group were not practising.

The second example of 'innate' behaviour, however, is by no means as clear-cut as that example. It was a study by Reiss (1951) of maternal behaviour in the rat. Rats were reared in isolation from other rats, and Reiss found that they developed the normal 'maternal instinctive' behaviour – nest building, and retrieval and licking of the young. This, at first glance, seems to be another example of behaviour satisfying the criteria for innateness. But because a rat has been kept isolated from other rats does not mean that it has been kept in isolation from its species' normal environment. Is it a valid assumption that the only way in which behaviour can occur without being innate is by learning from others? Experimental work on maternal behaviour in the rat suggests not.

Kinder (1927) found that nest-building activity is linked to temperature – the higher the temperature, the less nest building. Reiss (1951) reared rats which were prevented from carrying anything in their paws (faeces fell through the floor-grid and food was powdered, not pelletized). When such rats had litters they did not build nests, nor did they retrieve their young. If female rats are prevented from licking their own genital organs (which they apparently do to obtain salt), they do not lick or retrieve their young, and in fact eat a high percentage of them (Birch, 1948). If rats are kept in transparent cages they do not develop a tendency to build nests in corners (Patrick, 1934). Environment may thus drastically affect behaviour.

Tinbergen argued that the pecking response of the laughing gull was innate, and also demonstrated how specific the appropriate sign stimulus had to be. The chick would peck only at the red spot on the parent's beak, who would then regurgitate food for it: it would not peck at the red spot if it was moved from the beak to the forehead. However, Hailman (1967) showed that this specificity only occurred when the chicks were a few days old. Newly hatched chicks would peck at the forehead. He showed that although the laughing gull chicks had an innate tendency to peck at the red spot on the parent's beak, this was at first a very crude piece of behaviour, which improved with experience and food reinforcement.

Hailman suggests that the development of the pecking response and other 'instincts' involves a component of learning. It is necessary only that the learning process be very much alike for all members of a species for a stereotyped, species-specific behaviour to occur. Given that the structure of an animal (hereditarily determined) is relatively standard between individuals of a species, and given also that the type of environment which the individuals share is also relatively similar, it is perhaps no surprise that stereotyped behaviour patterns emerge.

It should be seen from this that several environmental factors play a part in the development of 'instincts'; but once the ontogenesis of the behaviour is studied more closely, it no longer appears to be quite so innate. In addition, some doubt is cast on Lorenz and Tinbergen's criteria. It is as well to remember that if behaviour is to be classed as innate, it must occur even though the animal is held in entire isolation from the normal environment of the species.

A quotation from Lehrman (1953) sums up the argument:

... nest-building in the rat probably does not mature autonomously, and it is not learned. It is not 'nest-building' which is learned. Nest-building develops in certain situations through a developmental process in which at each stage there is an identifiable interaction between the environment and organic processes, and within the organism, this development is based on the preceding stage of development and gives rise to the succeeding stage.

What then is 'genetically determined'? Is the behaviour pattern present in the fertilized egg? Or do the genes set out certain possible patterns of development, during which the organism, right from conception, affects, and is affected by, its environment? Lehrman says: 'The interaction out of which the organism develops is not one, as is so often said, between hereditary and environment. It is between organism and environment. And the organism is different at each stage of its development.' (These questions receive additional consideration on pp. 199–207.)

In view of the disagreements about whether or not 'instinct' is a valid term with which to explain behaviour, the term 'species-specific' is now preferred, since it does not pre-judge the issue of whether the behaviour is innate or not. The sections which follow, on *fixed action patterns* and *behaviour sequences*, deal with forms of behaviour which earlier would have been called instinctive but which are now known as species-specific behaviours. Ethologists assume both to be innate, and believe that they differ largely in their level of complexity.

Fixed action patterns

This term was coined by Lorenz, to describe those forms of behaviour, often taking the form of courtship or aggressive displays, which are extremely stereotyped. This means that different individuals of the same species will perform the same actions in the same way in the same circumstances.

FAPS are more complex than reflexes, as the three following examples illustrate. The first instance is that of egg retrieval by the greylag goose. If one of its eggs is moved out of the nest, the female stretches her neck out, so that her beak goes beyond the egg. She then uses the underside of her beak to roll the egg back to the nest. All greylag females perform these same movements in the same situations. So stereotyped is this behaviour that if the egg is removed by the observer, the female continues to make the retrieval movements.

The second example is from one of the classical ethological investigations by Tinbergen (1937) mentioned earlier. Ethologists are interested in determining what stimuli trigger (or, as they put it, '*release*') certain forms of behaviour, and Tinbergen's studies provided some of the earliest clarification of the nature of these 'sign stimuli', as they are called. He found that the male sticklebacks he was studying, even those reared in isolation, would attack other males in spring. They would also attack their own image in a mirror, showing that the sign stimulus for attack did not involve smell. He built a series of models, ranging from those roughly shaped like a male stickleback to some which were almost circular in shape. Some of these models were painted to imitate the red underbelly of the male stickleback. Tinbergen found that the major sign stimulus was not the shape of the model, but the red underbelly: models with the red underbelly were attacked much more frequently than those without. There was also a second sign stimulus: the models were more likely to be attacked if they were near the centre of the male stickleback's territory.

Thirdly, as we have seen, the red spot near the tip of the beak of the adult laughing gull releases pecking behaviour from the chick, which then eats the food regurgitated by the adult. Tinbergen showed that the chicks would also peck at a pencil with a red dot on it; but when the pencil had three red bands on it, it released even more pecking than did the natural stimulus. Such extra-powerful releasers are known as *super-releasers*.

Egg retrieval by the greylag female, the attacking of a male intruder by the male stickleback, and pecking at the red spot on an adult's bill by the laughing gull chick, are thus all examples of FAPS. FAPS are released by sign stimuli, in these cases respectively the sight of the egg outside the nest, the sign of the intruding male's red underbelly and the sight of the red spot.

Behaviour sequences

Although FAPS are fairly simple pieces of behaviour, they can be chained together to form more complex sequences, such as the courtship behaviour of the three-spined stickleback studied by Tinbergen. The function of the sign stimulus or releaser, he believed, was to release the appropriate innately determined behaviour via the *innate releasing mechanism* (IRM) (see p. 277). This, however, would only happen if the animal was in a state of 'readiness'. In the case of the male stickleback this was thought to be some kind of hormonal change, associated with the onset of spring. This idea of 'readiness' masked a problem in explaining and predicting animal behaviour.

The hydraulic model of motivation

The ethologists produced a *hydraulic model of motivation* in order to explain the variations in behaviour which they had observed in animals. They noticed that at some times a particular form of behaviour was easily released and was performed intensely (at some times, a sign stimulus was not even necessary, the behaviour appearing apparently spontaneously and being known as *vacuum activity*). At other times, however, even the appearance of the appropriate sign stimulus would not release the behaviour, or would do so only in a weakened form.

In addition, *displacement activity* was often observed in conflict situations. This takes the form of the release of a type of behaviour which seems to be irrelevant to the activity in progress. For example, two gulls engaged in threat displays may suddenly break off and begin to preen their feathers.

The hydraulic model of motivation (sometimes called the *psycho-hydraulic model*) was an attempt to explain these variations in response strengths, vacuum and displacement activities. It is important at this point to note that, although the model is a hydraulic one, this does not imply that animals have taps and valves inside their heads;

81. *The hydraulic model of motivation*

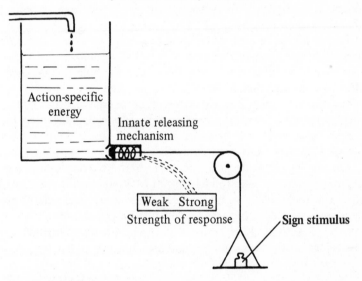

rather, the model is an analogue of the processes which may occur within the animal.

Each different FAP or behaviour sequence was assumed to have its own releasing mechanism, of which the valve in Figure 81, termed the innate releasing mechanism or IRM, mentioned on page 276, was an analogy. The IRM was opened by the appropriate sign stimulus (represented by the weight), to release the fluid (*action-specific energy* or ASE), which then 'powered' the behaviour. The container permitted the build-up of ASE, or 'readiness'. This model explained how response strengths and response thresholds could vary. Response strength depended on the level of fluid in the container (the more fluid, the more strongly the behaviour was performed); and on the strength of the sign stimulus, or the amount of weight pulling the valve open. The stronger the stimulus, the more the valve would open, thus the stronger the behaviour. If the amount of fluid in the container was large enough, the pressure of the fluid alone might be enough to force open the valve, so vacuum activity, activity without a sign stimulus to release it, would occur. As the behaviour occurred, it used up ASE, so that there was less pressure against the valve and a stronger sign stimulus was required to release the same behaviour again, until the ASE had had time to build up. If all the ASE had been used up, no sign stimulus, however strong, would release the behaviour; this explains the variations in thresholds.

Displacement activity was thought to occur when two mutually incompatible hydraulic systems were released simultaneously, as they would be in a conflict situation where tendencies both to fight and to flee were present. Since the two systems were incompatible, they inhibited each other, and the ASE in each overflowed (or '*sparked over*') into another hydraulic system or form of behaviour (preening, for example) which then occurred, more or less as a vacuum activity, with no relevance to the current situation.

Despite its explanatory powers there have been substantial criticisms of the hydraulic model, the most fundamental ones being aimed at the model's emphasis on the ASE being accumulated and used up, and on the predictions which the model makes about displacement activity. First, if ASE is used up only by performance of the particular behaviour, how could the hydraulic model explain the results of the following 'classic' experiment by Adolph (1939)?

Water was placed directly into the stomach of a thirsty dog via a tube, so that the dog did not need to perform any drinking activity. It was left for ten to fifteen minutes, and it was then offered water to drink in the normal way. (The ten- to fifteen-minute waiting period was necessary for the water to be assimilated.) The hydraulic model would predict that the dog would still be thirsty, since it had not performed any drinking behaviour and so had not used any 'drinking ASE'. In fact the dog in Adolph's experiment did not drink, so a prediction based on the hydraulic model was incorrect. Also, since, according to the hydraulic model, displacement activity is performed without relevance to the situation at hand, the strength or absence of a sign stimulus for the displacement behaviour should not affect how much it is performed. This prediction is not borne out in practice; for example, Manning reports work by Van Iersel and Bol, in which nesting terns who were in a conflict situation (between staying on the nest and fleeing) performed displacement preening more when their feathers were wet than when they were dry. Rowell found the same effect in chaffinches.

The disinhibition hypothesis

A more recent attempt to explain displacement activity has been the *disinhibition hypothesis* (Van Iersel and Bol). It explains why behaviour which occurs as displacement activity is affected by the stimuli which affect that behaviour under normal circumstances. They postulate that at any given time the animal has a hierarchy of possible responses available, and that the response at the top of the hierarchy will be performed and will inhibit those below them in the hierarchy. If, as can happen in a conflict situation, the top two responses are incompatible, they will mutually inhibit each other, and also remove their inhibitions on the next-highest response. For example, Van Iersel and Bol's terns could have had 'remaining on the nest' and 'escape' responses at the top of their hierarchy. Since these two responses inhibit each other, they would also release each others' inhibition of the next-highest response, preening. The stimuli for preening would probably have been present all the time, and wetting the feathers would increase the strength of the stimuli. If, however, the next-highest response had been feeding, instead of preening, feeding would have taken place as a displacement activity, but still in response to external or internal stimuli, not as a piece of behaviour irrelevant to the situation.

Social behaviour

At some time in their life-cycle most animals interact with others of their species, even if only for the purpose of mating. Species vary in the extent to which they mix in groups, from the highly social animals such as humans, and the social insects (bees, ants and so on), which spend most of their time in the presence of others and have evolved complex methods of communication which allow individuals to perform different roles within their society, to animals such as the digger wasp, whose only contact with others occurs in order to mate. Between these extremes is a wide variety of levels of social behaviour.

Some writers have suggested that animals form groups purely for the sake of the pleasure of being with other individuals, but there are in fact sound biological reasons for grouping. Social groups make it easier to find a mate, and larger groups have a greater range of genetic makeup, making genetic adaptations to environmental conditions more likely. There is more safety from predators because there are more 'lookouts', and some hunters seem to be confused by large groups. Vegetarian animals spend most of their time eating, and groups may be more efficient in finding food; for example, sparrows tend to land where they can see other birds feeding, so that large flocks form around good food sources. Barnard (1979) showed that individual scanning for predators decreased as the size of the sparrow flock increased, thus giving each bird more time for feeding; the random scanning of each bird in a large flock ensures that there are always a few lookouts to warn of approaching danger. Carnivorous animals such as the lion are far more successful when hunting in groups than they would be individually, since a group may approach the prey from different directions; and smaller animals increase their physical advantage over their victims by sheer numbers.

V.C. Wynne-Edwards argues that the major reason for the development of social grouping in animals is the control of population level, for grouping ensures that this level is in equilibrium with the available food supply. Many forms of social behaviour have evolved to meet this end. The study of voles by Krebs and Boonstra (1979) is an example of how population control can be achieved by animals. They found that when the numbers of a particular type of vole, *Microtus pennsylvanicus*, caused a high population density, only the larger animals were successful in their mating attempts. The larger animals were more successful because of their greater aggressiveness, which forced smaller animals to migrate. The remaining voles did not, however, reproduce fast enough to maintain the population numbers, and as the number of animals decreased, so the smaller ones were again allowed to mate. In this way the vole population fluctuated but never became too overcrowded for the available food.

Chapman (1928) demonstrated the way in which flour beetles are able to keep their population in a very precise ratio to the food available. He put an equal number of beetles into closed containers with different amounts of food. The food in each container was continually renewed so that it was never exhausted. Chapman found that after six months each environment contained a different number of beetles but that the ratio of beetles to food was constant: there were forty-four beetles for every gram of flour in the container. Those in the containers with a lot of food bred rapidly, but those with limited resources kept their populations low by laying fewer eggs and by cannibalizing the eggs and larvae. This experiment has been repeated with other animals such as mice, rats and guppies, with similar results.

Wynne-Edwards suggests that many forms of social behaviour have evolved to allow population control. He suggests, for example, that starlings flock at night in order to monitor their numbers and compare this figure with the available food supply: if the numbers in the flock are too high, some members leave and migrate to other areas. The synchronized 'morning chorus' of birds may fulfil a similar purpose. Phenomena such as *dominance hierarchies* (see p. 291) ensure that at least some members of a group will survive at a time of food shortage: rather than all members receiving a small, insufficient amount of food, those high in the hierarchy eat reasonably well at the expense of lower individuals. Since animals with dominance hierarchies know their position they do not waste energy fighting over scarce resources, which could result in survivors too weak to benefit from their winnings, and which could thus cause the whole group, and perhaps the whole species, to become extinct.

Many writers (most recently the group known as sociobiologists) attempt to explain social behaviour with reference to its hereditary basis. They argue that some forms of social behaviour make it more likely that an animal will successfully reproduce and pass on its genes. This is easy to see if the behaviour is something like co-operating with others in the hunt for food, but it is more difficult to credit in the case of *altruistic behaviour*, which is discussed on page 294.

The sociobiologists point to man's evolutionary connections with apes and monkeys and the similarities in responses that result from this. They also argue that behaviour today is influenced by the fact that man has evolved through a million years and was formerly engaged in hunting and gathering; that although this was largely abandoned ten thousand years ago it still affects social behaviour today. This evolutionary history has its effects in two ways: first, genetically, because those genes that favour hunting and gathering are likely to have been maintained in the population; and secondly, culturally, in the form of the socialization of successive generations (see Chapter 11 for a full discussion of the socialization process).

The sociobiologists argue amongst themselves about the degree to which cultural rather than genetic evolution determines man's behaviour today. Those who stress the biological origins of man's behaviour have been heavily criticized on political grounds: it is argued that their approach is an attempt to justify inequalities by saying that they are a result of 'human nature' which has evolved over centuries, and by saying that deviations from this nature are abnormal. Edward Wilson, whose book *Sociobiology* sparked off much of this heated debate, replies that his critics are falling into the naturalistic fallacy of ethics which uncritically concludes that what is, should be. He points out that it may be human nature to rear as many children as possible, or to indulge in warfare under certain conditions, but that in our present environment these behaviours are likely to lead to ultimate destruction; he argues that evolutionary explanations should be an addition to, rather than a replacement for, other viewpoints on human and animal behaviour.

Whatever the reasons for the formation of groups and societies, it is obvious that forms of behaviour must develop to regulate activity in these collections. The next few sections consider some of these forms of social behaviour, looking at courtship and parental and aggressive behaviour.

Courtship behaviour

Especially in those species of animals which do not form permanent male–female relationships, the particular displays or FAPS which act as a prelude to mating are vital for the reproduction of the species. In such solitary species the male and female may meet only to mate, and at all other times act aggressively towards one another. In some species hormonal factors, perhaps influenced by temperature or day length, provide a means of general synchronization of the onset of the reproductive period. However, a more precise synchronization is usually required if the pair is to mate successfully, and this process of synchronization must also inhibit both sexes' aggressive behaviours. Courtship displays therefore seem to have evolved to both synchronize reproductive behaviour and inhibit aggression, thus enabling mating to occur.

Observational studies had suggested that courtship displays take place when an animal is in a state of *approach–avoidance conflict*; for example, the male chaffinch, several weeks after he and the female have formed a pair-bond, loses his dominant status over her, and becomes her subordinate. When he approaches her, two sets of drives appear to be present: one drive is to mount her, and to copulate, while the other is to flee from her. These drives are obviously in conflict. Hence when he approaches her, he does so hesitantly, with small steps and in a zig-zag route, instead of directly.

Experimental studies have demonstrated that courtship behaviour can indeed arise from conflicting drives, for example the study by Blurton-Jones (1968) using the experimental manipulation of drives in the great tit. By trial and error, he developed artificial stimuli which would elicit various forms of behaviour in the hand-reared birds. A pencil poked into the cage elicited attack, a small lamp bulb elicited fleeing, and food held in forceps elicited feeding behaviour. By combining these artificial stimuli, Blurton-Jones was able to create artificial conflict situations, and to observe their effects on the incidence of displays. For example, by eliciting intense attack behaviour strongly and then introducing the fleeing stimulus, he showed that the amount of attack decreased and the amount of threat display increased. With a lower level of attack, introduction of the fleeing stimulus led to the 'head-up' display, one which observational studies had shown to be associated with conflict behaviour in which the tendency to flee was stronger than the tendency to attack.

Similarly, as we have seen, Tinbergen's work on mating in the stickleback showed that the zig-zag display dance of the male had attack components in it (when it swan towards the female; occasionally it might even nip her), and also escape components (when it swims away from her).

Since conflicts between attack and escape tendencies are often present in courtship, it might be expected that displacement activities would occur too, for their occurrence also depends on this same situation. In fact, displacement activities of a sort do occur; for example, the male mallard reaches back with its bill, behind its slightly raised wing. Instead of performing normal preening, it wipes the tip of its bill across the stems of the feathers, producing a loud rattling noise. It can also dip its bill briefly in the water and raise its head suddenly, producing a spray of water. But these displacement activities are not normal ones – the 'preening' display is not normal preening in its displacement form, but a highly stereotyped and simplified version of it. Neither is the 'drinking' display real drinking – the male does not actually take in any water. These displacement activities have become ritualized by natural selection: they have become common to a particular species and are stereotyped, that is, always performed in the same way. In addition, they have become emancipated from the original stimuli which in the past elicited them. They are now elicited by the escape and avoidance stimuli emitted by the female, instead of by wet feathers or thirst. The displays are performed with what is known as *'typical intensity'*; that is, no matter how strong or weak the stimuli from the female, the male will perform the courtship display with full intensity. A weak stimulus will release a short-lived display, and a strong stimulus a longer display, but whether long or short, the display will be performed just as intensely.

Most ritualized courtship displays have the effect of making the animal (usually the male) more conspicuous, for the obvious reason that the male is then much more likely to be recognized by the female.

Maternal behaviour

In some species, the male may share or take major responsibility for the young, but in mammals the female is more likely to care for them. The young of relatively advanced species are born at an immature stage in development, cannot fend for themselves, and consequently depend for survival on parents. Parental behaviour is of evolutionary significance because animals which look after their young ensure their survival and that of the species; animals who do not, or who display inadequate maternal behaviour, are not likely to have young which survive. When the young of inadequate parents do survive to maturity they are frequently incapable of attracting a mate, mating or rearing young of their own. Parents provide defence, protection from exposure, food and water, and sometimes some form of behaviour shaping.

Several researchers have noted quite clear phases in the feeding and nursing behaviour of mammals towards their young. The length of each phase varies from species to species. Rosenblatt and Lehrman (1963), for example, describe three phases. The first is a phase where the mother takes an active part in presenting the nipple to her young. Secondly, the infant is the more active in initiating feeding, actively seeking the female's attention; the female readily assists feeding by remaining fairly still in the nursing position and making the nipples available. In the third phase, the female becomes increasingly reluctant to assist the young with feeding and eventually takes active steps to prevent it (weaning).

Harlow (1963), in studies of maternal behaviour in rhesus monkeys, found three stages analogous to those above. The earliest stage is that of attachment, where the infant clings to its mother's underside, spending much time at the breast even though it is not necessarily actually feeding. The mother increasingly grooms the infant. (Grooming is at first performed only by the mother, but later other animals do it. As well as preventing parasites and cleaning, grooming has social significance since it helps to maintain pair bonds and patterns of friendship.) The second phase involves the young becoming more active, spending less time clinging to her, and being groomed by her less. The mother at first restricts the infant's activities, preventing it from straying too far, but later allows more independence. At this stage the young approach the mother more than she does them, often leaving her to explore new situations but always returing to her. The final stage is that of separation, where the mother punishes and rejects the young more often. Most male young, for example, are separated by the end of the second year. Male adult rhesus monkeys may approach and touch the young while in their mother's arms, and may carry the young during long treks. They are highly sensitive to the distress calls of the young and would, for example, attack a human observer who came between the young and the rest of the group.

Hinde (1966) showed that disturbance of these processes, by forced separation of mother and infant, could have drastic effects on the infant's development. Harlow (see p. 290) had shown that separation of an infant from its mother only twelve hours after birth had a profoundly damaging effect on the infant's social and sexual responses, even when mature. Hinde suggests that separation may occur much later, and be much briefer, yet still have damaging consequences. Six-month-old rhesus monkeys can fend for themselves. If the mother is removed from the group, even though a young monkey may be 'fostered' by other adults, it still shows signs of gross distress (much distress calling, reduced exploration, and occasional bouts of sitting hunch-backed in corners). When the mother returns, there is a very swift reunion, and the baby monkey spends more time than usual clinging to its mother. This pattern may last for several weeks, following a separation of only a few hours. Hinde believes that such effects are still observable years later, for 'separated' young appear to show more fear in new situations than normally reared young.

In sub-primate species, much research has been concerned with the development of maternal behaviour, mainly in rats and mice. Although this research is probably not directly applicable to humans, it does give a useful impression of how physiological and behavioural factors interact. Female mice, when pregnant, build nests. Weisner and Sheard (1933) showed that injections of *prolactin* (a hormone produced by the pituitary gland during late pregnancy which stimulates milk production) stimulated maternal behaviour such as nest building and the retrieval of young, even in virgin females, and to a lesser extent in males. During late pregnancy, the mother becomes less active and therefore produces less body heat. To test whether or not it was the reduced body heat which elicited nest-building behaviour, rather than some expectation that birth was imminent, Kinder (1927) raised pregnant rats in higher-than-normal temperatures, and found a strong negative correlation between temperature and nest building – the higher the temperature, the less nest building.

However, it would be wrong to think that all maternal behaviour is hormonally controlled. Rosenblatt and Lehrman (1963) found that the young, once born, acted as stimuli to release maternal behaviour in rats. Normally, female rats continue nest building for two weeks after the birth of the young; if the young are removed from the mother at birth, however, nest building declines immediately. It seems that hormonal changes are necessary to initiate nest building, but that once this has occured the presence of the young is necessary to maintain it. The gradual decline of maternal care seems to be associated with two factors: first, the increasing size of the young; and secondly, perhaps the reduction in prolactin production. However, Noirot (1964) has shown, with mice, that the same gradual diminution of care occurs even if given by virgins who do not produce prolactin. The young themselves may therfore be more important as stimuli in the cessation of maternal behaviour. Hinde suggests, for example, that young rhesus monkeys gradually become rejected because, as they get older and larger, their nipple biting and hair holding become painful to the mother.

Previous experience of motherhood, or certain forms of environmental stimulation, may have an effect on maternal behaviour; with the possibility that this is more so in the higher mammals than the lower. Rats and rabbits show very little change in maternal behaviour between the first and subsequent litters, when 'maternal behaviour' is defined as interest shown in the young, the level of aggression response and the length of time devoted to nest building. The rate of survival of the first litter does not differ significantly from that of later litters, although Calhoun (1962) has demonstrated that, in rat colonies, environmental variables such as overcrowding can lead to breakdowns in maternal behaviour and infant mortality rates close to 100%. Primates also rear young adequately on the first litter, but do show greater improvements in infant care with subsequent litters. Mitchell *et al.* (1966) showed that first-born infants play less with their parents and show less emotion, but appear to be more disturbed by strange environments than later infants.

Maternal behaviour, then, has obvious survival value for the individual and the species. However, in species whose young are mobile shortly after birth there is the danger that the young will wander off, or fail to form attachments with their parents. The next section, on *imprinting*, looks at the means by which the young may be kept close to their parents.

Imprinting

Imprinting is a three-stage process. First, a young animal which is mobile shortly after birth follows its mother (usually). Secondly, and as a result of the first action, it learns to discriminate her from all other stimuli, and forms an attachment to her. Thirdly, the sexual preference of the animal is determined by the former two processes, although this is obviously not noticeable until the animal is sexually mature.

Lorenz was one of the first to study systematically the processes of imprinting, in the greylag goose; but imprinting has since been demonstrated in many breeds of ducks, fish, insects and some mammals which are mobile shortly after birth, such as sheep, deer and buffalo. In these animals, imprinting relies on an inbuilt tendency to follow moving stimuli, with which the young form an attachment. Lorenz found that *imprintability* occurred for only a short period early in the animal's life (the *critical period*). It took place very rapidly, often needing only a few minutes' exposure to the object; and it was apparently unreinforced: no external reinforcers such as food or water were required for imprinting to occur. Once established, Lorenz believed, imprinting was irreversible, and this applied too to sexual preferences later in life. Finally, it was a species-specific behaviour, in that it was shown by *all* members of those species which display imprinting. '*Sensitive period*' is the term now preferred to 'critical period', since further research has shown that imprinting is not so time-dependent as Lorenz had supposed.

It would be wrong to think that imprinting is an innate tendency to follow and form an attachment with the mother as such, since animals will follow and attach to a wide variety of stimuli. Hess (1958) showed that mallards would imprint on models of the adult, Jaynes showed that animals would imprint on moving cubes and cylinders, and Bateson showed that imprinting would even take place on flickering lights.

Although Lorenz stated that imprinting could take place only within the critical period, later research has shown that Lorenz's description of the critical period (that its length was genetically predetermined and could not be affected by environmental stimuli) was perhaps overstated. True, Ramsey and Hess (1958) had shown that the optimum period for imprinting in mallards was between one and twenty-four hours after hatching, with the peak time at between nine and seventeen hours. (Typically, imprinting experiments involved raising the young in social isolation, for different periods of time, then allowing them ten minutes in the presence of a moving model. They were then removed from the model, and after a time were offered the choice of following either the model they had originally seen, or a new one.) But other researchers have shown that the end of the critical period is not as clearly defined as was previously thought: Moltz and Stettner (1961) imprinted twenty-day-old chicks which had been deprived of patterned visual stimulation by wearing transluscent goggles, which permitted only diffused, non-imaged light to enter the eye. Hence the term 'sensitive period' is to be preferred to 'critical period'. Little evidence exists, however, that the sensitive period can be extended beyond this time.

Lorenz's assertion that once imprinting took place it was irreversible has also come under criticism. Salzen (1967), for example, imprinted ducklings on a coloured ball, and later re-imprinted them on a ball of a different colour, or on a different shape.

No extrinsic reinforcers appear to be necessary for imprinting to take place, although one testable suggestion was that imprinting is reinforcing, because it reduces the chick's anxiety. In experiments where chicks have been given tranquillizers, which should theoretically have reduced imprintability, the results have not been clear-cut enough to say whether or not fear reduction is the motivator.

The fact that the sensitive period can be extended means that its end does not occur simply because of maturation. Perhaps the animal has to learn to distinguish between familiar and unfamiliar objects, and when it can do this it avoids the latter. If no appropriate model is available, the animal will imprint on its immediate environment. Bateson (1964) showed that this could happen with striped cage walls. Chicks kept in this environment for three days preferred a moving model with the same pattern to one with a different pattern.

D.O. Hebb (1949) hypothesized that early learning often had more profound effects on behaviour than later learning. The imprinting studies seem to demonstrate the truth of this, especially in the investigation of the determination of sexual preferences. *Crossfostering* experiments, where the young of one species are reared with the foster parents of a different species, demonstrate that the youngsters' sexual preferences lie most often with the foster parents' species. Immelmann (1969) showed that male zebra finches reared with Bengalese finch foster parents and then isolated until they were mature, demonstrated a very clear sexual preference for Bengalese finch females; even forced pairing with members of their own species would not reverse this preference. The time needed for sexual imprinting to take place appeared to be thirty-three days, at which point the young birds became independent and could look after themselves. Keeping them with the foster family beyond this time did not strengthen the imprinting, for by thirty-three days the young birds' sexual preferences seemed to be completely determined. Thus a relatively short period in early life has profound effects on the rest of an animal's life.

In mammals, the processes of imprinting do not seem to be as clear as they are in birds. The problems of identifying sensitive periods are more difficult, usually because mammals develop more slowly than birds, and consequently there is more time for learning and environmental factors to affect development. However, some mammals do show some aspects of development which are like sensitive periods. For example, Scott and Fuller (1962) showed that the formation of social contacts in dogs seems to have a sensitive period, between three to ten weeks after birth. If a puppy is socially isolated until after this period has passed, it seems to be unable to form normal social bonds either with other dogs or with humans.

Harlow (1959), experimenting with rhesus monkeys, showed that there was a kind of sensitive period between birth and eight months for the development of an affection bond between the infant and its mother. Separation from the mother could lead to the development of abnormal social and sexual behaviours in later life. Harlow (1962) also demonstrated that 'group therapy' might alleviate some of the problems caused by disruption of the affection bond: maternally deprived monkeys who were allowed to live together showed less abnormal behaviour, although they were still by no means 'normal'. Hinde claims that brief separation of infant and mother for only a matter of hours may have damaging effects which persist later in life.

Largely on the basis of Harlow's work, Bowlby argued that there was a corresponding sensitive period for the formation of attachments in humans, which extends from the age of eighteen months to three years. Opinions are somewhat divided on how clear the sensitive period is, what actually constitutes 'deprivation', and whether behavioural disturbances which are correlated with maternal deprivation are actually caused by it or by some other factor. For example, Rutter (1972) has argued that it is not deprivation which leads to the failure to form affectionate relationships in later life (labelled '*affectionless psychopathy*' by Bowlby): a child who has been allowed to form an affection bond with somebody and then had it broken has at least learned to form such bonds, and presumably could learn to form bonds with other people. Children who were never permitted to form affection bonds, who suffered from *maternal privation* rather than *deprivation* (that is, the subsequent breaking of affection bonds which *have* been allowed to form), would be unable to form such bonds with others, since they had never learnt how to. It should be remembered however, that the human childhood period is longer than the equivalent in any other species, so there is a much greater chance for remedial measures or situations to have an effect on the child's behaviour.

Agonistic behaviour

The responses that animals make when involved in social conflict are known as *agnostic behaviour*. These responses include attack, threat, fight, flight and submission. Lorenz points out that it is useful to distinguish between aggression that takes place between members of the same species and that between animals of different species. Different rules apply to the two situations, and the motivation for aggression is usually different: in the former case agonistic behaviour is often motivated by rivalry, and rarely results in fatal injury, whereas aggression shown between species often involves hunting, which may well result in the death of the prey.

Agonistic behaviour is often prompted by competition for such things as food, water, sex and status; it is also a common reaction to frustration and pain, but is most regularly seen in the establishment and protection of territories. The males of the majority of birds and mammals establish an area at the beginning of the breeding season which they defend against males of the same species. A piece of land may contain the overlapping territories of many different species, for it is rare that animals will need to defend them against other types of animal unless they share the same food requirements. The possession of a territory is an advantage, because the possessor will not then have far to search for food and will not encounter competition for scarce resources. Not all animals use their territories for feeding; for example, the herring gull has a territory of only a couple of square yards, which it uses only as a nesting site. Territories are usually breeding areas, and since there is usually not enough space to go round, some animals miss out and may not breed. In times of food shortage animals which feed within territories need larger areas for food gathering; consequently fewer but larger territories are developed, so fewer birds can breed.

Observers have noted for many years that an animal in its own territory seems to have an advantage in a conflict with an intruder which outweighs any physical differences between the two. Yasukawa (1979) demonstrated this phenomenon experimentally with dark-eyed junco birds which were matched for sex, size, colour and age. He put groups of birds into different aviaries for a week, during which time each group established a dominance hierarchy. Dominance hierarchies (mentioned earlier) are found in many species which live as a group within territories; those animals at the bottom of a hierarchy are subservient, and allow higher-ranking animals their pick of desirable commodities, such as food and sex. After a week, some of the birds were moved to other cages. When a group of birds was introduced to an aviary containing residents that had lived there for a week and formed a dominance hierarchy, they took their position at the bottom of the hierarchy with relatively little fighting. When birds from two different groups were introduced to a neutral cage, however, there was much more fighting, and the resulting dominance hierarchy was a mix of the hierarchies of the original groups. Individuals maintained their position relative to members of their original group: if the original ranks had been A, B, C and 1, 2, 3, the resultant dominance hierarchy might be A, 1, B, 2, 3, C. Yasukawa argued that introduction to a neutral cage had resulted in more physical fighting because there was no obvious advantage for any of the birds on account of their having been matched for physical characteristics and having no home territory advantage. When one of the groups was on home ground this had been enough to determine the outcome without escalation of the conflict.

Two competing drives are usually present when performing agonistic behaviour. The first is the *attack* or *fight*, *drive* fuelled by the need to defeat an opponent; the second is the *submission*, or *flight*, *drive* which is a result of the fear of personal injury. The response elicited in a particular confrontation depends on the strength of these two drives. An animal is most likely to fight when it is inside its own territory, the drive being strongest at the centre and decreasing towards the boundary. As the tendency to fight decreases, the flight motive increases; on the edge of a territory the two drives may be equal, resulting in the production of displacement activity. Some fish and birds display *pendulum fighting*, which is when an animal on its own territory swims or flies at an intruder which flees, followed by its attacker, across the border into its own territory, where the relative strengths of the fight and flight drives in each combatant reverse, so that the original attacker is chased back into its own area, and the sequence may start again.

Animals rarely kill other members of their own species because they use elaborate rituals rather than actual fighting to determine which animal should win the dispute. Factors such as relative size, territory and the possible rewards or losses determined by the outcome affect the extent to which each individual is willing to escalate the conflict. Within established groups the dominance hierarchies limit the extent of intra-group aggression because low-ranking individuals quickly submit to those higher in the scale.

A dispute usually starts by one or both animals demonstrating a *threat display*. These differ between species; for example, dogs bare their teeth, snarl, raise the ears and stiffen the tail, standing with a characteristic posture that is recognizable even to humans. Threat postures are most often seen in territorial animals at the border between adjacent territories; since neither animal is likely to advance into the other's territory, the result may be nothing more than a demonstration of displacement activity. If there are no obvious deciding factors such as territory to determine which animal should win, the episode may escalate into actual physical contact, although rules still apply.

Bernstein and Gordon describe the behaviour of thirty-six rhesus monkeys which first met as adults introduced into a single enclosure: the fighting appeared to be bloody and unrestrained, but an inspection of the wounds showed that they were limited to areas of the body such as the shoulders, face and tail rather than those parts where injury might be fatal, such as the throat and abdomen. Monkeys withdrew from fighting by adopting an *appeasement display*, which involves crouching and turning away from the attacker. This type of display is common to most animals and inhibits further attack; it is usually obviously different from any threat posture, and often involves the exposure of vulnerable parts of the body. Natural selection favours animal species which can terminate their aggression in this way rather than those which continue until the death.

Some appeasement displays seem to work by eliciting behaviour from the attacker that is incompatible with aggression: baboons adopt the female sexual presentation posture, and may be briefly mounted by the dominant animal, but they are usually allowed to slink away. Bernstein noticed that submissive monkeys allowed small bites by an aggressor, but would immediately resume fighting if these bites involved the use of the potentially lethal canine teeth. It is therefore advantageous to a winning animal to discontinue its attack on sight of an appeasement display: he can then enjoy the rewards of his victory, which may be territory, food, a mate or long-lasting establishment in a dominant position.

The introduction of new animals to an existing group, or the first formation of a group, are the surest ways of producing violent fighting. Once the group is established and the newcomer has been ejected or assimilated, most disputes are quickly resolved by reference to the existing dominance hierarchy. Throwing a piece of food between two monkeys may result in agonistic behaviour, but usually this is one-sided, with the dominant animal chasing off its subordinate. Bernstein argues that in the case of monkeys, fighting occurs more often between animals of roughly equal status than between those with a great difference in rank: this means that adult male monkeys rarely attack juveniles because they are not perceived as a threat, whereas another adult male may be chased away if it approaches too close when a dominant male is eating. Shortage of food may increase aggression briefly, but as we mentioned earlier the dominance hierarchy ensures that high-ranking animals survive to maintain the species without suffering the weaknesses produced by starvation, or the sorts of injury that might result from unrestrained fighting, while the lower-ranking animals seem to starve and even die so that the group can survive.

This seemingly altruistic behaviour on the part of some members of the group has presented problems for evolutionary theorists, because an animal that dies in this way cannot pass on its genes to the next generation whereas a selfish animal might live to produce offspring, so that surely any genes that favour altruism would disappear after a few generations. John Maynard Smith points out that members of groups are usually related, sharing common genes, and that any behaviour which allows a group to survive ensures the maintenance of those genes; so in this way natural selection favours altruism toward relatives. He argues that it is the survival of genes rather than individuals that is evolutionarily important. The evolutionary advantage of some forms of altruism can be seen most easily in the case of parents risking their lives for their offspring. A bird which flies noisily away from its nest to draw an intruder away from its young is more likely to be caught than one which slips away quietly, but its young are more likely to survive. The genes associated with this form of protection of the young may be present in the offspring and therefore be passed down to more and more individuals of succeeding generations. This is known as *kin selection*.

Bernstein's work shows how dominance hierarchies are built in groups when individuals are introduced as adults, but most individuals are born into existing groups. Manning argues that the emergence of dominance within a group is largely dependent upon maturation. The animal which matures earliest will for a time be bigger and stronger than the others and will therefore be able to dominate them; this dominance is maintained even when all the others have matured. Brown notes that lion trainers put themselves at the head of the dominance hierarchy by intimidating a harnessed young lion until it indicates submission by appeasement gestures; then the lion will still respect the trainer's rank when it is adult. Bernstein describes the assimilation of young monkeys into a dominance hierarchy as a socialization process, which differs from species to species. For most monkeys, rank position is maintained by alliances with other individuals, so that an old animal may maintain a high position because it is supported by its offspring and peers. Since a young monkey is seldom attacked because it is not perceived as a threat, its socialization will consist of learning its mother's position in the hierarchy, which monkeys support her and which responses it can get away with without provoking older animals.

Most species show a sex difference in the type and frequency of aggressive responses, though males are usually more aggressive. This fact has been linked with the male sex hormone, testosterone, mentioned on page 160. Castrated rats usually show a decrease in aggression towards other rats – although they still attack mice, reinforcing the argument that there is a difference between inter- and intraspecies aggression. Bernstein points out that adult male monkeys are more often involved in the less restrained fighting that occurs when two groups meet, but that at other times they show very little aggression, though females and juveniles may involve themselves in threats and chases. He argues that natural selection probably favours this difference, for if the lethal fighting abilities of females and juveniles were used within a society this would make group survival less likely.

Agonistic behaviour is influenced by an animal's habitat. Southwick showed that aggression was more frequent in captive groups of rhesus monkeys than in those living around rural villages, and that it occurred least in forest-dwelling groups. He noted that food shortages did not lead to increased aggression; the changes seemed to be caused by crowding, though social changes such as the introduction of a stranger into a group had the greatest effect. Calhoun (1962) studied the effect of crowding on the behaviour of rats. He placed thirty-two rats into a ten-by-fourteen-foot room in which they were given adequate food and opportunity for play. The animals reproduced, but the amount of space was not increased. Once the number increased to about eighty rats the social patterns changed, there was an increase in aggression and homosexual behaviour, and the young were neglected and sometimes eaten by the males.

Comparisons between animals and men

Some writers see man as an innately aggressive animal who has lost the ability to control his agonistic behaviour in the way that is common amongst lower species. Ethologists have tried to explain why man appears to be an exception to the rule as far as killing members of his own species is concerned. Tinbergen and others point out that man's behaviour is heavily influenced by cultural factors which affect the expression of any genetic relationship with the lower animals; for example, man's cultural heritage may have upset the balance between fight and flight drives, because combatants are taught that it is 'cowardly' to run away and in many armies the punishments for desertion are greater than those for staying in battle. Also, modern warfare often involves killing at a distance: the bomb-aimer cannot see his victims and any appeasement displays they might produce. Lorenz (1966), using his hydraulic model to explain the motivational basis of aggression, argues that man has an inborn tendency towards agonistic behaviour, which inevitably finds an expression, no matter what the physical environment. As the action-specific energy builds up, the strength of stimulus needed to release it in the form of aggressive responses becomes less and less, and unless it is diverted into some socially acceptable behaviour such as sport or political argument aggression will spontaneously erupt as a form of vacuum activity.

Lorenz backs up his assertion that aggression is inevitable by referring to examples such as the cichlid fish, which can only mate successfully when other males are present because in the absence of another fish to attack, the male will fight with its female partner. When another male is present as the target of aggression, little agonistic behaviour is found between the courting pair, and they successfully mate. Lorenz argues that the cichlid fish attacks its partner in the absence of another fish because the action-specific energy has to find an outlet. However, Hinde argues that other explanations are possible which do not stress the inevitability of aggression: he points out that all courtship behaviour involves a conflict between the agonistic and sexual drives elicited by the mate. When another cichlid fish is present, the agonistic arousal can be redirected away from the mate, but this is not possible when they are alone. Hinde points out that cichlid fish are exceptionally aggressive compared with most other animals, whose sexual arousal during courtship usually outweighs any aggression. Heiligenberg found that even in cichlid fish the aggressive drive decreases after a few days when presented with no arousing stimuli; this is the exact opposite of Lorenz's expectations.

Wilson (1976) argues that human and animal aggression is more affected by factors such as crowding, food shortage and frustration than any innate inevitability. He points out that it is common to find closely related species of birds or mammals who differ greatly in their levels of aggression, and so it is unwise to assume that it is a deeply rooted instinct in animals as diverse as cichlid fish and man. Man has a capacity for aggression which may have been an evolutionary advantage, but that behaviour is finely adjusted to circumstances, and capable of remaining dormant for long periods in the correct environment. Man's cultural heritage and his experiences of socialization are the most important factors in determining his aggressive behaviour.

Many of the animal aggression studies have suggested human parallels which have been further studied. For example, Calhoun's work on the effect of crowding on rats prompted Ehrlich and Freedman (1971) to study the effect of room size on human groups playing games which could be performed in either a co-operative or a competitive manner; they found that in small rooms males were more likely to be competitive, dislike each other and give more severe sentences in a mock trial. In a large room, male behaviour was less competitive, the subjects liked each other more and gave less severe sentences.

Hinde criticizes the way in which Lorenz and others draw parallels between the behaviour of man and other animals. He points out that the ethologists are careful to describe animal behaviour fully, determining the functions and causes of responses by close observation and experimentation; but by comparison their analysis of human behaviour is very crude, grouping together such diverse activities as playing games and contributing to political argument under the general heading of aggression. The use of the ethologist's techniques in the study of man himself is likely to be more useful than these crude comparisons between human and animal behaviour.

Further reading

Birney, R.C. and Teevan, R.C. (1961), *Instinct*, Van Nostrand

Eibl-Eibesfeldt, I. (1975), *Ethology: The Biology of Behaviour* (2nd ed.), Holt, Rinehart and Winston

Hinde, R.A. (1970), *Animal Behaviour: a Synthesis of Ethology and Comparative Psychology* (2nd ed.), McGraw-Hill

Manning, A. (1979), *An Introduction to Animal Behaviour* (3rd ed.), Arnold

10 Conformity and obedience

In Chapters 10 to 14 inclusive, we turn our attention to social and developmental psychology. This chapter looks at *conformity* and *obedience*, the ways in which our behaviour is modified as a result of being in the presence of other people.

Conformity

Conformity is usually seen as adherence to the demands of a group, whatever its ideological or practical convictions. The punk rocker is conforming to his group's expectations just as much as the City businessman is to his. The former is a non-conformist to society, but a slavish conformist to the rules, or *norms*, of his own reference group, and it is important to note that the social psychologist's use of the term 'conformity' is not the equivalent of everyday use. He does not mean conformity to the attitudes and behaviour prescribed for the maintenance of an orderly society and the status quo, but conformity to those attitudes and behaviour which an individual feels his *significant others* require of him (the term 'significant other' refers to a person who is important to an individual such as a parent, teacher or friend). This may include a requirement to behave in particular ways, to subscribe (at least publicly) to certain views, and to dress in a particular style so that he can be readily identified by others as a certain type of person. Mann (1969) writes: 'The essence of conformity is yielding to group pressures, but it may take different forms and be based on motives other than group pressure.' He distinguishes between three main types of conformity, summarized below.

Normative conformity

Normative conformity occurs when group pressure forces the individual to yield under the threat of rejection or the promise of reward. It is called normative conformity because the individual feels that he should not break the norms of his group. There are two levels at which normative conformity may operate, illustrated by the following example. Imagine that a group of friends have all seen a particular new film, and that on comparing views afterwards all except one found it exceptionally funny or meaningful. The odd-one-out is fairly unlikely to make his views strongly known, and if required to do so by direct questioning is likely to appease his companions somewhat by making suitably similar comments. This type of normative conformity is called *compliance*: an individual verbally agrees with the views of a group, but privately maintains his own views. Compliance can be contrasted with *true conformity*, exhibited by all the other members of our film-going group – the ones who really do believe the film was good and say so. There is no conflict between what they believe and what they say, and their accordance with the views of the other group members is genuine. To identify compliance or true conformity, it is necessary to observe an individual's behaviour and views both within a group and when he is away from the group; there have been many classic studies of compliance.

Informational conformity

Informational conformity occurs when an individual is in a novel or ambiguous situation and is uncertain how to respond. He usually looks to the behaviour and statements of others for guidance. This type of conformity is prompted by his not wishing to appear foolish or ignorant, or inexperienced and naïve. Gahagan (1975) writes that

Many highly-educated, intelligent and mature people, when confronted with the performance of an odd new stage piece or musical composition, wait anxiously for the morning papers for cues from the select body of opinion, the critics, to find out how they should be reacting.

Ingratiational conformity

Ingratiational conformity is when a person agrees with someone else in order to impress them or to gain their acceptance. A low-status employee, when talking with his boss, may avidly agree with all the views and arguments the latter expounds, even though they may be outrageous or contradictory, and both males and females may display ingratiating speech and behaviour in advances to the opposite sex.

Non-conformity
Just as conformity may be confused with the idea of status quo, or Establishment behaviour, so may two quite distinct types of *non-conforming* be confused. If an individual goes against his colleagues, his behaviour may be interpreted in two ways. He may be quite uninfluenced by the other group members, or he may stand firm despite pressure from them, possibly risking ridicule or being ostracized in order to be true to his beliefs. This may require considerable courage and self-discipline to avoid capitulation, and demonstrates *independent behaviour*. Alternatively, he may disagree with the group out of perversity, or because he sees himself as someone who won't 'toe the line' or fall in with a group. Such a person is not really independent at all, but just as dependent as the conformer he might condemn, because his behaviour is determined by the group just as much as the conformer's is. The only difference is that the conformer feels obliged to follow the group, while the 'rebel' goes against it, but in both cases it is the group which is determining the individual's behaviour. This type of non-conforming is called *anti-conformity*, to distinguish it from genuine independence.

Clearly, then, two people may behave in the same way by non-conforming, but reflect two very different sets of motives. Schein (1957), in a study of why some American prisoners of war did not collaborate with the Chinese during the Korean war, found that there were two types of resisters, that is, soldiers who did not 'give in'. Some resisted because they knew that admitting guilt for the war, or broadcasting peace appeals, was wrong, and these constituted the independent non-conformers. Others had a long history of unwillingness to accept any kind of authority, and did not conform to commands in either the American army or later to commands by the Chinese army, and these could be classified as the anti-conformists.

Studies of conformity
One of the first ways of measuring conformity was introduced by M. Sherif (1935), in a study of an optical illusion known as the *auto-kinetic effect*, in which a small stationary light seen in a totally darkened room will appear to move. This is easy to demonstrate to

yourself: place a lighted cigarette on the edge of an ash-tray and black out the room (draw the curtains and switch out the light). Fixate on the glowing end of the cigarette and observe the effect. It will appear to wander about in front of your eyes, and even knowing that it is in fact stationary will not help.

Sherif tested subjects individually and asked them to estimate the 'movement' of the light which they observed. He found that after considerable initial variation, the judgements of each subject became quite consistent, though there were marked differences between subjects. At this point, Sherif began testing subjects in groups, with each individual hearing other people's estimates (although there was no other contact between them). He found that in time the subjects' estimates began to converge towards some 'compromise' estimate, until at the end of the experiment most subjects responded with this middle, group-produced estimate. Sherif also ran a group of subjects who worked in each other's presence from the outset, and found that they also rapidly converged to produce consistent estimates which characterized their group, though the different groups produced different and group-unique consistent responses. Sherif's subjects were acting in a way that we should expect if we do indeed believe that perception is a process of hypothesis testing, as suggested on page 70. Their brains were using additional information from their particular groups when interpreting the apparent movement, because the stimulus itself did not provide sufficient clues.

These experiments have been criticized in works which claim that it is obvious that the individuals would conform and modify their views in accordance with group views, since no other information was available to them and the light was not actually moving anyway. However, the study did stimulate research in the area of conformity, and influenced the work of Asch, described below.

The classic experiments by S. Asch (1952) extended the original method and application of Sherif's work, and stimulated further research. He tested individuals in groups of between six and nine members for compliance, but unknown to the one genuine subject in each group, all the other members were confederates in the experiment. At the outset participants were seated in a straight line, or round a table, so that the real subject would respond last on each trial. Subjects were given two cards, one displaying a single straight line or standard, and one with three comparison lines, one of which was identical with the standard (see Fig. 82).

82. An Asch-type Figure

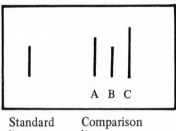

Standard   Comparison
line   lines

Subjects were required to state which of the three comparison lines was matched with the standard, and replied individually and sequentially, the genuine subject answering last. It was always clear which was the correct answer, but on certain predetermined 'critical' trials, the confederates unanimously gave the same *wrong* answer. Figure 83 shows in table form the number of subjects who made conforming responses, and the number of such responses.

83. Asch's results

Number of real subjects who made conforming responses	Number of conforming responses they made
13	0
4	1
5	2
6	3
3	4
4	5
1	6
2	7
5	8
3	9
3	10
1	11
0	12

The mean average for the fifty real subjects studied is 3.84 conforming responses, or 32%. This tells us that, using the mean as the measure of central tendency, the 'average' subject conformed on 32% of the critical trials. Asch also ran a control group of individually tested subjects, and none of them made errors. Naïve subjects interviewed after they had worked in the group situation all said that they had been influenced to some extent by the opposition of the rest of the group, with many of them distorting their private judgement to avoid ridicule.

The Asch design lends itself to a whole series of experiments studying the effects of minor modifications to the basic operation, and the results of the more important ones are summarized below.

1 Task difficulty. If the experimental task was made more difficult by making the comparison lines more equal in length, conformity on the critical trials increased.

2 Majority size. Asch systematically varied the number of confederates used, to produce different-sized majorities to oppose the genuine subject. He found that there was greater conformity if two people opposed the lone subject than if only one opposed him, and even greater conformity if three opposed him. However, the number of opposers beyond three did not alter the likelihood of conformity.

3 Unanimity of subjects. Apart from varying the size of the majority, it is possible to vary the degree of its unanimity. Asch found that it needed only one confederate to support the genuine subject for conformity to disappear.

4 Losing the 'partner'. Asch arranged one situation where the fourth subject in response order answered correctly on the first half of the critical trials (as a partner for the real subject), but then switched to the incorrect majority view for the remainder of the critical trials. The effect of having a partner and then losing him restored the level of conformity to almost the usual level (28.5%).

5 Status of subjects. The perceived status of group members affects the real subjects' level of conformity. If the real subject regards the other group members as high-status in some respects (such as task ability), he is even more likely to agree with their incorrect judgements. It has also been found that real subjects who are members of ethnic minority groups conformed highly when working in groups in which they were the only minority-group member.

6 Conditions of response. Subjects in Asch-type experiments may conform because they are reluctant or too embarrassed to expose their private views in face-to-face situations. If so, the level of conformity should decrease if subjects respond in individual cubicles unseen by other subjects, or where there is no personal contact *and* subjects believe that their responses are quite private. Crutchfield (1954) showed that this is the case.

An evaluation of the Asch study provides a revealing aspect of statistical analysis. The *mean* conforming response quoted in most textbooks (32%) hides the fact that the raw data, presented in Figure 83, shows a *skewed distribution* of responses – that is, one which is asymmetrical if displayed graphically. It is a statistical convention that if a distribution is skewed, a mean average should not be used. Instead the *median score* provides a more appropriate measure. This has the effect of reducing the level of conforming to 25%, instead of 32%, and so, though this is less dramatic, it is a more realistic percentage.

There is also the question of whether the results of the Asch study can be extrapolated to real life, and a number of points may be made here. In the experiment, subjects were unable to reserve judgement but were obliged to voice an opinion. In real life most people tend to withhold comment and say nothing if they are unsure of, or unwilling to express, their view. They are also quite likely to ask for guidance or advice if in any difficulty about a decision, but in the experiments a subject was allowed no communication except a bald statement about his decision. The actual experimental task of judging the length of lines is a relatively unimportant one compared with many real-life issues involving personal feelings and commitments, and it is questionable whether conforming on a trivial issue can accurately reflect conformity on more important issues. Also, in real life we are rarely in a minority of one, as the genuine subject was in most of the experimental conditions. All these factors tend to exaggerate the level of conformity demonstrated by Asch.

However, the simple, unambiguous task, with an obvious correct answer, should have made resistance to opposition easier, and since issues in real life are not likely to be so clear-cut, it might be argued that conformity would probably be greater rather than less. Similarly, because the experimental group was an artificial one, whose members the subject would not meet again, their influence on him would probably be less than that of real friends, and he might conform more in real-life groups than in the experimental group.

Instead of using university students as subjects, as both Sherif and Asch did, Crutchfield (1954) used business or military men attending a three-day assessment programme. On the final day the men were grouped in fives and seated in front of apparatus consisting of five adjacent electrical panels. Each panel formed an open cubicle, preventing each subject from seeing his fellow subjects' panels, and each had to respond to a series of questions projected onto the wall in front of him. The questions were in multiple-choice form, and subjects indicated responses in order, using one of five lights on the panel from A to E. If a subject was A, he responded first; B, second, and so on. Each subject found that he responded first for a while, then third, then fourth, then second and finally last. Each subject also received feedback about the other subjects' responses via lights on his own panel, though in fact these were not connected to the other panels but to an experimenter-controlled panel, and it was he who supplied 'feedback' to the subjects. Moreover, each subject at any one time received the same information sent to the other four subjects, so that on any given trial all five might be responding first, for example, or later, all might be responding last.

Wrightsmann argues that Crutchfield's procedure is more efficient than Asch's, because it needs no use of confederates and permits the testing of five subjects at once; and certainly he obtained high levels of conformity. On a trial in which a star and a circle were juxtaposed, with the circle being about one-third larger than the star, 46% of subjects succumbed to the false consensus that the star was larger. On a question asking for the completion of a number series (like those found in IQ tests), 30% conformed to the false majority, and on the Asch problem there was 30% conformity. Conformity was also found on a highly personal attitude expressed as the statement, 'I doubt whether I would make a good leader.' No subject in a control group agreed with the statement, but when told that the other four subjects agreed, 37% of the experimental group agreed with it. Of twenty-one critical items, only two did not produce significant conformity, and both these asked for very personal, subjective judgements about preferences between two drawings. Only one subject out of fifty conformed with the false group consensus.

It should be noted again that the figures given for Crutchfield's work are means, producing the result that the 'average' subject conformed about 38% of the time.

A major advantage of Crutchfield's work was that since his subjects were taking part in a three-day assessment programme, his conformity data could be compared with other data collected about them from other tests. He found that, compared with the highly conforming subjects, non-conformers showed 'more intellectual effectiveness, ego strength, leadership ability and maturity of social relations, together with a conspicuous absence of inferiority feelings, rigid and excessive self-control and authoritarian attitudes'. One of the strongest correlations was between subjects' estimated intelligence and conformity, with a coefficient of −0.63 (indicating high intelligence associated with low conformity, and vice versa).

Many people might be tempted to believe that there is a 'generally conforming personality', a type of person who consistently displays conforming behaviour. However, some writers believe that too much has been made of the observed differences such as those noted above, and too little attention paid to the discrepancies. If conformity *is* proposed as a consistent characteristic, such as intelligence or introversion/extraversion, it follows that a conformist in one situation (say, when on jury service) would also be a conformist in other fairly similar situations such as those of the classic studies here described. However, McGuire (1968) found that such consistency is not high, and it may be that a search for a 'conforming personality' is misguided. Gahagan contends that situational factors are just as important as psychological ones in predicting conformity and argues that

No researchers have really investigated the effect of subjects' interest in, or investment in, the task at hand ... When we think of examples of people who have stood firm on some issue, against pressure, or have introduced a radically new idea into a unreceptive environment, their outstanding characteristic has been tremendous obsession or investment in the issue itself – which has made them immune to social considerations.

Hollander and Willis (1967) list the following failings of the Sherif/Asch/Crutchfield studies.

1 The studies fail to distinguish the motivation or cause of the conformity, whether it is normative, informational, ingratiational, or a combination.
2 They fail to differentiate between compliance and true conformity in subjects' responses – whether they merely ostensibly agree with the consensus opinion or whether they really come to agree with it.
3 No distinction is possible between independence and anti-conformity.
4 An implicit assumption underlying the work is that independence is 'good' and conforming is 'bad', and indeed Asch (1952) makes this explicit. However, conformity can be highly functional, facilitating the satisfaction of social and non-social needs and 'interactive synchronization' – though it might be easily manipulated in some circumstances.

Obedience

The conformity studies were concerned with subjects' willingness to behave like others in a shared situation because of group pressure, uncertainty as to what behaviour was appropriate, or the desire to gain acceptance in the eyes of another. Obedience, however, is acquiescence to the direct demands of another – not imitation or conformity, but literally obeying instructions.

Studies of obedience

A famous experiment was carried out at Yale University by S. Milgram (1963), who sought to measure the level of subjects' obedience to an experimenter's instructions when the result of acquiescence would be to inflict severe pain on another person, even to the point of endangering his life. The experiment has aroused considerable controversy and outrage, and people have queried the ethics of such work.

Milgram used forty male subjects, who volunteered by replying to newspaper advertisements or to a postal circular and were offered $4.50 for taking part in a psychology experiment on 'learning'. The non-representative nature of the sample has been much criticized – though it should be remembered that most psychology experiments use volunteer subjects, that the psychological bias of such individuals has been well documented, and that his sample was in fact quite heterogeneous, reflecting age ranges of between twenty and fifty, and occupations including teachers, salesmen, clerks, engineers and manual labourers.

On arrival at the laboratory, subjects (who were tested individually) were greeted by the experimenter, dressed in a laboratory coat, and then introduced to the 'other subject' with whom they were to work, who was actually an actor working with Milgram. The purpose of the experiment was explained to be to evaluate the effect of punishment in a paired-associate learning task; one subject was to be the 'teacher' and the other the 'learner'. The teacher was to read out a series of word-pairs, and then to read the stimulus word followed by five words of which one was the original paired response. The learner was to remember the pairings in the series, and choose the correct response to the stimulus word. If he made an incorrect response, the teacher was to administer an electric shock, beginning at fifteen volts, with further mistakes to be shocked on a schedule increasing by fifteen-volt stages.

Lots were drawn at the outset in such a way that the genuine subject was always the teacher and the actor the learner. Milgram took them both into an adjoining room, where the learner was strapped into a chair 'in order to restrict him and prevent him from escaping'. An electrode was fixed to his wrist, and just to demonstrate its functioning, the real subject (the teacher) was given a sample shock of forty-five volts. The teacher was then returned to the original room accompanied by the experimenter, who seated him before a console for generating electric shocks. A series of lights indicated the learner's replies, and a series of thirty flick-down switches administered the shocks, each switch labelled with the voltage and a verbal description such as 'Slight shock', through to 'Danger: severe shock', and to 'XXX'. To ensure that the teacher increased the shock progressively with each error, the switches stayed down after being pressed. Milgram further ensured that the teacher knew exactly what strength of shock he was administering by having him announce the voltage to the learner before pressing the switch. The whole generator was in fact an elaborate but convincing fake, which fooled all the subjects.

When the experimental task began, Milgram took up a supervisory position fairly close to the teacher at the console, carefully scrutinizing the administration of the shocks. After seventy-five volts, the 'learner' began to cry out in pain, and as the severity increased, asked, and then demanded, to be released, saying that he suffered from a heart condition. At the 'Severe shock' level he simply twitched and screamed with pain. The teacher's usual response at this stage was to look for guidance from Milgram, who ordered him to continue. Suddenly, at 315 volts, there was complete silence from the learner's room, in dramatic contrast to the earlier screams, but teachers were then told to treat no response as an incorrect response, and to continue. Most expressed concern that 'something bad had happened' and wanted to stop the experiment and go and see. Milgram said it was imperative that the experiment should not be stopped, and that they should continue.

As part of the original study, Milgram asked a group of Yale staff and students, and forty psychiatrists, to estimate how many subjects they believed would carry out the experiment completely and not refuse to continue. The psychiatrists estimated that only 0.1% would not withdraw at some stage, while the former group predicted that only 1% would not withdraw. Milgram's results showed that 65% of subjects in fact did not withdraw. Figure 84 shows that no subject withdrew before 300 volts (at which point the learner began kicking the wall in 'agony'), and here five subjects refused to continue. At

84. Milgram's results

Verbal description and voltage		Number of subjects for whom this was the maximum shock
Slight shock	15 30 45 60	0
Moderate shock	75 90 105 120	0
Strong shock	135 150 165 180	0
Very strong shock	195 210 225 240	0
Intense shock	255 270 285 300	0 0 0 5
Extreme-intensity shock	315 330 345 360	4 2 1 1
Danger: severe shock	375 390 405 420	1 0 0 0
X X X	435 450	0 26

some later point a further fourteen of the remaining forty subjects refused to obey the experimenter's orders, but the other twenty-six did not: 'A substantial proportion of people do what they are told to do, irrespective of the content of the act and without limitations of conscience, so long as they perceive that the command comes from a legitimate authority.'

The structure of Milgram's basic experiment lends itself well to the systematic variation of certain conditions, to study their effects on obedience.

1 Proximity of the 'learner'. Milgram observed three different teacher–learner proximities. One had them in separate rooms (and the results of this are given above). One had them in the same room and only eighteen inches apart so that the 'teacher' could see and hear the effects of his actions – and still 40% completed the experiment. The third had them in touch proximity, with the 'teacher' actually having to force the 'learner's' hand down onto an electric plate to receive the shock – and still 30% obeyed completely.

2 Proximity of the experimenter. Again Milgram observed three conditions. In one the experimenter was only a few feet away from the teacher; in the second condition he was present at the beginning, but then left the room and gave subsequent instructions by telephone; and in the third he was never actually present, but instructions were given by tape-recorder. Obedience was almost three times higher in the first condition than in the last, and also in the last condition subjects frequently administered lower shocks than they were supposed to. This was perhaps an attempt to appease their consciences by making the compromise of continuing to give shocks as they were supposed to do, but at a weaker level than they should, and more in line with what they felt they ought to do.

3 Having a partner. Milgram ran one condition in which the subject had two 'partners', who were also expected to shock the learner and who both withdrew half-way through the series. In this condition 90% of subjects followed their example and refused to obey the experimenter, in a clear demonstration that social support enables people to disobey orders which they might otherwise feel they had to obey.

Milgram (1974) published *Obedience to Authority*, explaining why people obey and claiming that it is because of the essentially hierarchical organization of human society. He argues that such organization has developed in many animal societies because it is an efficient system, and that when an individual operates in such a system he learns that he must subordinate his own feelings to what he is required to do, often without explanation. He says that we are consequently familiar with the need to accept and obey orders given from different parts of the system, thus enabling it to function: 'The person entering into an authority system no longer views himself as acting out of his own purposes but rather comes to see himself as an agent for executing the wishes of another person.'

As mentioned, there have been criticisms of Milgram's obedience experiments, and Baumrind (1964) wrote in the immediate after-math of Milgram's first publication criticizing the studies on two grounds – the ethics involved, and the questionable generality of the work. Milgram himself says that subjects in his experiments were observed to 'sweat, stutter, tremble, groan, bite their lips and dig their nails into their flesh. Full-blown uncontrollable seizures were observed for three subjects.' One of the subjects had such a violently convulsive seizure that his experiment had to be stopped, and in the face of such reactions it is reasonable to ask why the whole series was not stopped. Apart from the trauma felt by many subjects while actually participating, it is likely that subjects' self-images suffered when reflecting on the implications of their actions when the experiment was finished.

Milgram offers two justifications. First, he claims that his debriefing session after the experiment revealed all, and 'ensured that the subject would leave the laboratory in a state of well-being'. Secondly, he claims that the end justified the means, and that the insights into human nature which the studies gave justify any disturbances in subjects which may have arisen. This problem is not unknown in psychology, though the consternation is usually expressed on behalf of animals of a lower order than human participants. You will probably have your own views on this emotive issue.

Baumrind also called into doubt whether the high rate of obedience found by Milgram would extend to real-life situations. He drew attention to the non-representative nature of Milgram's sample of subjects, and questioned the validity of generalizing his findings to a wider population. It would be possible to claim that they would be true of 'all volunteers', but the argument becomes much shakier if it is extended to say that they are true of 'most people', or 'American men', or some other general, undefined population. The only certain conclusion to be drawn is that we do not know if Milgram's results are generally applicable. His sampling does not enable us to say that they are, but neither can it be assumed that they are not.

A further argument against the real-life applicability of Milgram's findings is that many subjects may have continued against their better judgement because they felt constrained to obey in such situations as experiments, where they are required to perform an accepting, co-operating role. In addition, they may have felt unable to oppose a figure of authority while on his territory and in his province of work. Milgram foresaw this criticism. Because the prestigious reputation and imposing nature of Yale University might have intimidated subjects into obeying the white-coated scientist, while they might not have obeyed in a more equal-status situation, he repeated the experiment outside the University in a 'run-down office building in a deteriorating area of Bridgeport, Connecticut', only to find that nearly 50% of the men still obeyed, and continued to the end of the series of shocks.

In Milgram's experiment, if a subject was showing signs of wanting to stop, he was given the following 'prods', in this order: 'Please continue' or 'Please go on'; 'The experiment requires that you continue'; 'It is absolutely essential that you continue'; and 'You have no choice, you *must* go on'. We have no way of knowing how different the incidence of total obedience would have been if these had not been used, though it is likely that it would have been considerably less dramatic. Baumrind seems to argue that it was the presence of these prods which caused the obedience, but the criticism seems somewhat obtuse: in a study of obedience, subjects surely must be required to obey some order or command. Even though the orders in the final prods were strongly phrased, the important fact is that few people refused to obey them. A frequent analogy is drawn between the Milgram studies and military atrocities such as those of the Nazi concentration camps: the experiments demonstrate that it could well have been any ordinary people taking all those lives in Nazi Germany. Obviously the soldiers were under strong coercive pressure from their commanding officers to obey; but the point is not that the orders were strongly phrased, but that they were obeyed.

Perhaps it would be reasonable to say that obedience is not an all-or-nothing phenomenon, but probably changes as a function of a variety of factors – the status of the person giving the orders, the recipient's relationship to him, the context and environment of the situation, personality characteristics, and the manner of ordering and the strength of phrasing used. Whatever one thinks about the ethics of Milgram's studies one cannot ignore their importance. Mann (1969) says:

> Milgram's findings are much more disturbing than Asch's. Not only is the number of yielders more numerous but the act of conformity itself involved graver implications. With great regularity, decent and responsible people gave in to the proddings and trappings of authority (personified by the white-coated experimenter), and performed, albeit under protest, an act which they knew was harsh and callous.

Further reading

Gahagan, J. (1975), *Interpersonal and Group Behaviour,* Methuen

Mann, L. (1969), *Social Psychology,* Wiley

Milgram, S. (1974), *Obedience to Authority,* Tavistock

Wrightsman, L.S. (1972), *Social Psychology in the Seventies,* Brooks/Cole

11 Socialization

Socialization focuses on the way in which the individual relates to his society, and on how the organism that is a new-born child becomes an adult member of his society. Bandura (1972) speaks of socialization as 'concerned with the characteristics that individuals acquire and the psychological mechanisms through which the desired changes are brought about'. The previous chapter provided evidence for some of the characteristics which people acquire through socialization – conformity, and obedience to authority – and this chapter examines some of the theories which purport to explain how such socialization is achieved. Piaget's structural model, Freud's psychoanalytical model and Skinner's S–R model will each be considered.

However, it should be borne in mind that socialization processes do not act on a passive, blank slate but with an interactive, social being. There is now considerable evidence that the neonate or newborn subject is capable of significant perceptual activity, as well as possessing several innate reflex behaviours, and that he interacts with his environment from the earliest days of life. Fantz (1961) found that young infants have clear visual preferences for complex patterns rather than simple ones, while Gibson and Walk (1960) showed that depth perception is present at least by the time the human infant is ready to crawl (see Chapter 2). During the long and complex process of socialization, the personal and social characteristics of the individual have a part to play, as well as the pressures acting upon him.

The structural model

Most attempts to trace the process of socialization acknowledge the existence of discontinuities in child development. There seem to be fairly distinct 'levels' at which different types of interaction are observed and which follow sequentially. Piaget's account of the stages of cognitive development has stimulated a wealth of research and 'has done the most to make the stage concept of development plausible' (Hilgard *et al.*, 1975). It is important to understand these stages of cognitive development, since the interactive social demands made by individuals on each other change as cognition develops. His account also draws attention to the active relationship between organism and environment.

Cognitive development

For Piaget, human intelligent behaviour is the external display of a general, internal, biological tendency towards *adaptation* and *organization*. If an organism adapts to its environment this presupposes that some internal organization or structure exists, and that the behavioural adaptation is an external manifestation of this. An infant who can suck at an object, and can grasp it, but not both at the same time, is at a lower level of internal organization than one who can do both together, and the differences in internal organization are reflected in overt behaviours. Once the adaptation to the environment is regularly observable, an internal reorganization must have occurred. Piaget sees intelligence as an adaptation, contributing to the survival of the species, and, like biological adaptation, involving external and internal factors.

Piaget uses the term *'functional invariants'* for organization and adaptation, viewing them as parallel and interacting processes which characterize the relationship between an organism and its environment for the whole of its life. The interaction of the two is essential to cognitive development. The internal organization comprises a number of *schemata* – internal representations of particular actions – which are demonstrated in behaviour as characteristic ways of responding to the environment. The earliest schemata are the *innate reflexes* (grasping, sucking, rooting and so on), and an individual's environment and experiences can only be interpreted in terms of the schemata he has available to him. These gradually elaborate and form a more complex classificatory structure, permitting more complex analyses of the environment and of experiences as development progresses.

Piaget describes two processes which describe the formation of new schemata, and the development of exisiting ones. *Assimilation* occurs when an individual reacts to his environment by applying his already existing schemata, organizing input by 'assimilating' it into his current internal organization. *Accommodation* is a process of modification of existing schemata to take account of particular properties of input stimuli; for example, the grasping schema must 'accommodate' to take account of the weight, size and shape of objects grasped. With repetition, a schema assimilates a variety of inputs, and by having to accommodate to this variety it becomes more complex and more able to differentiate between variations in the input it receives. Piaget further proposes a process of *equilibration*, a relationship between assimilation and accommodation, which tends to maintain a balance between them. Assimilation alone would produce only rigid, fixed behaviours in terms of existing schemata, while accommodation alone (constant modification of schemata in line with small differences in input) would not permit sense to be made of the 'buzzing confusion' of the environment. Equilibration acts to ensure that accommodation is consolidated via assimilation – that is, it maintains an equilibrium between the two. Once such consolidation has been made, the individual is ready for further disequilibrium, or new learning.

This point is important, for Piaget sees the very existence of a structure as stimulating the need to use it: the existence of schemata motivates the individual to use them, thus impelling the individual to those behaviours which make demands in the accommodation of schemata. As long as the input makes reasonable demands on the accommodation process – too little is not motivating, but boring; too much is not motivating, but off-putting, because the amount of accommodation needed is too much at once – then every schema is self-motivating. Just as cells do not need to be psychologically motivated to divide, organize and differentiate, neither do schemata. This reveals Piaget as a *genetic epistemologist* – a biologist interested in the adaptive development of knowledge.

One of the most important human characteristics is the capacity for learning, and Piaget's view of motivation offers an insight into this. If a deprived or disadvantaged child does not perform well in school, and appears poorly motivated, it may be because his already existing schemata cannot all at once accommodate the very different demands and inputs of the classroom. If a gifted child has problems and is poorly motivated it may be because input to his schemata is only producing assimilation, without demanding accommodation. Equilibration is thus necessary for optimum cognitive development.

The gradual elaboration and creation of schemata, the growing complexity of internal organization, is reflected in behaviour, and Piaget has distinguished certain behavioural characteristics which he believes typify certain stages of development. These invariably occur in the same order in all children, though they may be manifested at different ages in different children. Piaget does not claim that an individual functions exclusively at one stage once he has reached it – he may function intellectually and behaviourally at one level for one task or set of demands, but at a higher or lower level for another. The main stages of cognitive development are outlined below.

The sensorimotor stage
This runs approximately from birth to eighteen months and is described as a stage of motor activity, without thought as adults know it, when the child understands his world through the actions he performs on it and when he discovers the relationships between his sensations and his actions. An important concept developed by the child during this stage is that of *object permanence* – a realization that an object continues to exist even if it is not immediately available to the senses. At about eight months old, an infant will not look for a previously visible object which is covered with a cloth while he watches. The object seems to have ceased to exist for him. Just a little later, at about ten months, he will change his behaviour and search for the object where he sees it hidden. He has therefore acquired the internal organization for this concept. However, after retrieving the object from one hiding-place, he will continue to look for it there even after watching it being hidden elsewhere, until about twelve months old. It is the development of object permanence, and most importantly the beginnings of language, which enable the child to represent events to himself, and to free himself from relying exclusively on 'here-and-now' inputs.

The pre-operational stage
This period, from approximately two years to seven years, sees the consolidation of language acquisition, which for Piaget is the

external manifestation of a process of internal representation of the world (see pp. 236–8). Once language has developed, cognitive development can occur through instruction and interaction, instead of only through sensorimotor learning – though Piaget argues that most intellectual development still occurs via actions and operations which the individual makes on his environment. Piaget uses the term '*operation*' in a specialized way here, defining it as an internally represented action which is systematically linked with a broader set of schemata to form a '*structure*'. Unlinked schemata are termed *intuitions*. Imagine a child who is asked to take a bunch of flowers and group together all the pink, white and orange flowers respectively. To be able to do this he must possess the operation of class formation, which links together a class called 'all flowers' with some other classes ('pink ones', 'white ones' and so on), which can be added to or subtracted from 'all flowers'. He cannot behave as requested unless there is an overall organization, an operation, to direct his complex behaviour. Piaget describes all the mathematical functions ('less than', 'greater than', 'equal to', adding, subtracting, multiplying, dividing) as operations.

The pre-operational stage may be seen as one in which schemata become linked via operations to form gradually a permanent mental framework, and this gradual linking may give rise to some interesting behaviours. Self-contradiction is characteristic of this age-group: a child may confidently assert that he is going to draw a railway, then proceed to label it as anything from a ladder to a road. His attention is easily distracted and he is markedly egocentric – that is, he finds it difficult to view situations from another's point of view (he may definitely agree that he has a brother, but will equally definitely assert that his *brother* does not have a brother). Considerable evidence is available to demonstrate a pre-operational child's apparent inability to *conserve* matter. Shown two identical beakers containing equal quantities of water, a child will agree that they are the same. After watching the water from one beaker being poured into a taller, thinner beaker, the child will probably now claim that there is 'more, because it's taller'. Similarly, having agreed that two balls of clay are equal in quantity, if one is then rolled to a sausage-shape the child is likely to decide that there are now different quantities in each. Restoring the water, or the clay, to the original state restores the first judgement that they are the same again. Such contradictions are termed *syncretic reasoning* – not reasoning as an adult would understand the word, but an indication of the existence of mental processes used to direct behaviour, and a reflection of the linkages (as yet partial) between mental processes. The pre-operational framework requires a long, slow period of development before it becomes fully integrated. At this stage, the child's thinking is dominated by his immediate perception of the various objects, such as the different-sized glasses which make up the problems, rather than by a conceptual grasp of them.

The concrete operational stage

The period from approximately seven to twelve years old sees the further co-ordination of operations, and the acquisition of the concepts of conservation, of *seriation* (serial ordering of items) and of classification. When faced with contradictions between perceptual and logical interpretations, he is increasingly able to draw on internal logical structures to help him to reason. He develops the ability to understand the *reversibility* of operations – that if an operation is reversed, the result is as if the operation had never been carried out. Thus pre-operational child presented with two rows of counters (see Fig. 85) will claim that one row has more counters after watching them being spaced out (see Fig. 86), while a concrete operational child will understand that the counters could be spaced closer together again to return to the original position, and that the numbers therefore remain the same. This two-way characteristic of concrete operational reasoning is a real progress from the pre-operational stage. However, such reasoning is restricted to the manipulation of actual objects and the concrete operational child cannot reason hypotheti-

85.

○ ○ ○ ○ ○ ○ ○

● ● ● ● ● ● ●

The child indicates there are the same number in each row.

86.

○ ○ ○ ○ ○ ○ ○

● ● ● ● ● ● ●

The child now indicates there are more black units.

cally – that is, in purely symbolic terms. He could cope with concrete problems of seriation, such as arranging three dolls in serial order of hair colour, but not with the following, if only verbal representations were available to him: 'Edith is fairer than Susan; Edith is darker than Lily; who is the darkest of the three?'

The formal operational stage

Starting at about twelve years old the child becomes increasingly capable of reasoning in an abstract way and of forming and testing hypotheses. His thinking becomes more systematic and does not rely on the presence of actual objects. He can determine that Susan is the darkest of the three girls (see above) without even picturing them in his head. The divorce of the child's thinking from concrete objects increases his ability to generalize and apply principles to new situations.

The change from one stage to the next is not a sudden transition and may be marked by what Piaget has called *décalages* – a slow, step-by-step acquisition of new operations – and by the developments of sets of operations, with both processes perhaps being slightly out of step with each other. *Horizontal décalage* may be observed when a child can use an operation for one problem but not for others; for example, he may be able to conserve number, but not yet mass. *Vertical décalage* occurs when a child has fully developed one operation, say, conservation, but not yet another, such as classification.

The implications for socialization and moral development

During the early sensorimotor period, when the child knows the world through his own actions upon it, thinking and doing are one and the same. He does not differentiate 'his action' and 'the world': rather all is one – himself. Only gradually does he distinguish between himself and other things, and more importantly between himself and other people, until he finally understands that people and objects continue to exist even when out of his sight, even his most significant other (usually his mother). Communication develops from being an enjoyable social act to being also a means of attaining ends through the help of others; when during the pre-operational stage he becomes capable of internal representation, then symbolic play becomes possible too – for example, treating toys as real people.

Together with the development of early vocalizations into increasingly clear speech, and then into internal or 'silent' speech, this developing understanding of the separateness of others is important for socialization, indicating a lessening of egocentricity.

During the concrete operational stage, the ability to reverse operations has its social parallels in *reciprocity* – that is, in being able to take into account the views of others. The child can to some extent co-ordinate his view with those of others, and perhaps modify his own behaviour in the light of the perceived intentions of others towards him. This 'social thinking' is sometimes reflected in a child's talking to himself in monologues when he takes two roles in turn, though it may also take the form of an internal 'discussion', where he represents to himself the views of another. Piaget argues that the development of such social reciprocity is very dependent on interaction with other children; concrete operational children generally do show a marked propensity for social activity with other children. On reaching the stage of formal operations, coinciding as it does with a stage of 'physiological metamorphosis', the adolescent typically displays a kind of social egocentricity, believing others to be as sensitive to his appearance and behaviour as he is himself. Elkind (1971) speaks of how an adolescent anticipates the reactions of others, 'based on the premise that others are as admiring or as critical of him as he is of himself ... the adolescent is continually constructing, or reacting to, an imaginary audience'. He goes on to suggest that this imaginary audience perhaps has a role in the self-consciousness which characterizes early adolescence.

Socialization involves many emotional factors as well as cognitive ones, and Piaget has been criticized for over-emphasis on cognitive development without linking it to emotional development (quite the opposite of Freud, who is thought to emphasize emotional development at the expense of intellectual development). The dynamic relationship between cognitive and emotional development is under-researched. Piaget's main contribution to social development relates to moral judgement (1932) and the development of (1) children's attitudes to rules, (2) their judgements about stealing and lying, and (3) their ideas of justice, which we shall now consider in turn.

Piaget used the game of marbles to study attitudes towards rules, since the game is rarely taught by adults but is developed by children themselves. He asked children of various stages of development to teach him the rules and play with him, then carefully observed their explanations and their reactions to Piaget's rule transgressions, and their own obedience to the rules. He also elicited their opinions on whether the rules have always been the same, whether new ones could be invented, and where the rules came from originally.

Very young children aged two or three appeared to have no rules, but rather devised and ritualized their own private version of the game. These little rituals might be thought of as pre-rules, since they displayed some order and structure but had no social reference, and the child apparently did not really feel obliged to abide by them. Somewhat older pre-operational children continued to play as individuals in an egocentric manner, but displayed some imitation of each other's play and enjoyed the participation of another – that is, they liked playing as individuals, but in a social situation. Piaget (1926) draws attention to the similarity between this type of play and the '*collective monologue*', in which a child carries on an individual commentary in the presence of another, without really listening and responding to what the other is saying. At this age rules are seen as absolute, unchangeable, having always existed and invented by some awesome authority, such as God or older children. Despite such respect for rules, however, they are not yet internalized by the child, but merely imposed upon him.

It is during the concrete operational stage that rules become internalized, and scrupulously kept, though they lose their aura of being God-given, absolute and unchanging and become clearly social. They are devised for players, and can be changed by them as long as fairness to all is maintained. This view of rules cannot be available to the child until he has '*decentred*' enough to see the point of view of another in reciprocity, and indeed children at this stage may take a delight in inventing rules to govern all kinds of social activities.

To take Piaget's second area of study, Piaget looked at children's judgements about right and wrong. He presented pairs of stories, some concerned with stealing and some with lying, then questioned the children and noted comments. One of the pair relating to stealing would describe the act done for a 'creditable' motive; for example, a little boy stealing buns from a shop to give to a poor, starving friend. The other of the pair would describe stealing for selfish gain of some kind. Two pairs of stories related to lying. The first pair dealt with a lie which was so obvious an exaggeration that no one would be deceived by it, and an intentional and convincing lie that did deceive an adult. The second pair dealt with a lie to an adult that was really an honest mistake on the part of the child, but whose consequences unfavourably affected the adult, and a deliberate lie which, by chance, did not cause any real inconvenience to the adult.

Piaget found that pre-operational children, though they could differentiate between intended and unintended behaviours, showed little or no regard for intention when judging right or wrong, but assessed the level of 'naughtiness' by the consequences, or by the size of the departure from the truth. A child claiming to have seen a dog as large as a cow was more wicked than one who told a more 'possible' lie. A child's innocently misleading an adult and causing him some trouble was worse than a deliberate lie which had no serious consequence. Lies were seen as 'naughty words', wrong because 'you get punished for them' - hence it was more wrong to lie to an adult than to another child!

Older children were much readier to take intention into account when judging right and wrong, so that stealing for selfish motives was worse than stealing for altruistic motives, and an intentional lie was worse than the innocent misleading of an adult, whatever the consequences. There was less differentiation between lying to adults and to peers: lying was viewed as intrinsically wrong and damaging to social interaction, rather than as wrong because it attracted adult wrath.

Piaget also studied children's ideas about justice, by eliciting their opinions on the merits of different punishments for wrong-doings, on the justice of collective punishment, and on immanent justice (that is, the belief that chance events after wrong-doing are punishments for the wrong). He presented children with stories about a child damaging a toy belonging to another, and asked which of several punishments was fairest - for example, replacing it with one of his own toys, or paying to have it repaired, or being forbidden to play with his own toys for a week. He also asked about the justice of several children's being punished for the misdemeanour of one, again by using a story in order to elicit opinions. He illustrated the concept of immanent justice in a story of two children raiding an orchard. One was caught by a policeman but one escaped, only to have an accident on the way home.

Pre-operational children seemed very dogmatic about justice - punishment should expiate for the crime, and the more severe the punishment, the better - and showed little evidence of relating the form of the wrong-doing to the nature of the punishment. They thought it fair to punish all for the crime of one of the group, and considered that any accidental unpleasantness following a misdeed was a punishment for it. Piaget describes this level of moral development as 'the morality of adult restraint', since adults tended to be seen as the arbiters of justice, and the children's opinions reflected the influence of authoritarian, imposed discipline.

Older children tend to relate the nature of the crime to the nature of the punishment, and this 'reciprocal justice' contrasts with the pre-optional child's notion of expiatory punishments. Piaget discerned several types of reciprocity of punishment. One was exclusion from the group for crimes which trangressed social rules; another was making the punishment fit the crime closely, like making a child do without something he had refused to help to make. 'An eye for an eye, a tooth for a tooth' was another form of reciprocal punishment, or restitution or compensation for the victim in some way. Such children also showed great sensitivity to the justice or otherwise of adults' punishments, rejecting collective punishment as unjust, and believing less in immanent justice.

In moral development, then, a gradual shift seems to occur from an early moral realism to a morality of co-operation or reciprocity, or moral insight. As in cognitive development, not all individuals develop morally at the same rate, and an individual in a later stage may occasionally revert to a type of behaviour or attitude shown at an earlier stage. The egocentricity of the young child is reflected in his early cognitive development *and* in his early social development, before egocentricity diminishes and reciprocity in intellectual operations and in social relationships emerges.

Alternatives to Piaget

Other psychologists have proposed stage theories of cognitive development which differ somewhat from Piagetian theory. J. Bruner proposes a theory of cognitive stages which, like Piagets, assumes that 'knowing' is a form of cognitive construction, with the individual taking an active role rather than being a passive receiver of stimuli. He views cognitive growth as dependent on the development of competence – competence in the ability to represent cognitively the 'recurrent regularities' of the environment, and competence in the ability to link past, present and future. He calls these two processes *representation* and *integration*. Though he proposes stages of cognitive development, he does not see them as representing different, separate *modes* of thought at different points of development, but as a gradual development of early cognitive skills and techniques into more integrated, 'adult' cognitive techniques. This developmental, skill-integration model of cognitive development involves three main stages, which describe the individual's changing forms of representation of the world.

The earliest stage is one of *enactive representation*, in which a child 'represents past events through appropriate motor responses' (this is roughly analogous to Piaget's early sensorimotor period). This stage covers the period before the child can conceptually separate his actions from the objects he acts upon. Secondly, *iconic representation* is a further development of representational ability, when the child becomes able to replace his action or an object with an image, a representation in the way that a map or a picture 'represents' something else. Finally, an even greater development of representational ability comes at the stage of *symbolic representation*, when the child becomes able to order his multitude of experiences through symbols, rather than merely through his own actions or through images. Symbols (words, for example) can be used much more flexibly and adaptably so that categorizing and ordering can become much more complex and more integrated.

Since Bruner views the symbolic level of representation as crucial for cognitive development, and since language is our primary means of symbolizing the world, he inevitably attaches great importance to language in determining cognitive development – in contrast to Piaget, who sees it as the external manifestation of internal cognition rather than as a determinant of it. Bruner argues that language can *code* for stimuli, and can free an individual from the constraints of dealing only with appearances, to provide a more complex yet flexible cognition. The use of words can aid the development of the concepts they represent, and can remove the constraints of the 'here-and-now' context. Efficient inner representations of problems and situations enable easier mental management of them, and hence the formation of cognitive concepts.

Such a brief outline of Bruner's theory of cognitive development cannot do justice to the wealth of experimental evidence he has amassed relating to cognition. His work has also included careful investigations of the attributes of problems and situations which individuals use to develop problem-solving strategies, as well as studies of concept development and attainment.

Lawrence Kohlberg's work also uses the cognitive devlopment approach to social development, but while drawing upon Piagetian theory he has considerably extended and modified it. He argues that cognitive structures shape action and feeling as much as they do thinking, and he emphasizes the importance of role taking and an awareness of others for early moral development, and the importance of actual experience of moral decision making at a later stage. While much research on moral development has examined individuals' behaviour in resistance to cheating and stealing, guilt and altruism, less research effort has been directed to studying the development of their moral philosophy. Kohlberg's approach involves presenting individuals with about ten examples of moral dilemmas in which there appears a conflict between obeying a moral rule and concern for another person. One example is that of a man desperate to obtain an expensive medical drug for his dying wife, who, unable to afford the extortionate price demanded by its sole producer, is finally driven to stealing the drug. Kohlberg's interest lies not in the actual judgement made – whether the man was right or wrong – but in the arguments used to justify their judgements, and the hidden assumptions these reveal. He has differentiated thirty or more aspects of moral decision making, and uses them to assess the stage of moral development evident in each, from subject's responses. Though he agrees with Piaget that there are sequential stages of moral development, he defines these rather differently, distinguishing three levels, each of which has two stages.

First, at the *pre-moral level* these stages are, originally, one in which moral behaviour is exhibited to avoid punishment, and then, one in which it is hedonistic – exhibited in order to obtain reward or favour. The second level is that of *conventional role conformity*, which displays a first stage of 'good-boy' morality, or of conforming to maintain acceptance by others, and then a stage of authority-maintaining morality, a respect for authority and a desire to avoid its disapproval. Clearly at this level the child must have a concept of the views of others. The third level of morality is that of *self-accepted moral principles*, at which one phase demonstrates a morality based on a sense of contract, of democratically accepted law, and the final stage shows maturation to a morality of individual conscience.

Both Piaget and Kohlberg demonstrate links between cognitive and moral development – though they regard cognitive development as necessary but not sufficient for the development of moral judgement.

An evaluation of Piaget

Piagetian theory has been a major stimulus to psychological research, and influential in education in the western world. It offers insights into appropriate teaching procedures and into the age placing of topics within the curriculum, and remains a rich source of both theory and data on intellectual development. However, his work is not without its critics, though many of these fail to offer alternative explanations of how cognitive functions originate at whatever age, or of how experience influences cognitive behaviour.

Dulit (1972) used certain Piagetian problems to assess what proportions of adults and older children actually reach the stage of formal operational thought, to find that only about a third of average adolescents and adults do exhibit it. There were also differences between the level reached across several tasks, though the tasks all purported to test the same cognitive level. He concluded that such formal operational tasks are not mastered more or less simultaneously, as Piagetian theory suggests, nor are they ever mastered by a substantial number of individuals.

Niemark (1975), in a replication study, also found little evidence of the concurrent development of formal operational cognitive skills. Other work suggests that some cognitive functions are available earlier in life than as proposed by Piaget, adding to doubts about the tasks he used as criteria to define his stages. Bryant (1972) argues that pre-operational children do understand the principles of conservation, and that it is certain properties of the Piagetian tasks which tend to produce the results commonly found, not the lack of conservation. He found that using alternative types of displays produced different results.

Flavell (1963) writes of what he calls 'undergraduate critcisms' of Piagetian theory which focus on the limitations of the subject sample used and the contingent limitations of generalizing results to humanity as a whole; on the over-complex task instructions used, and the sometimes arbitrary scoring of results; and on the clinical methods of collecting data which are not easily amenable to experimental testing. Even though very many replication studies have now been made, including cross-cultural studies, to reduce the influence of such methodological deficiencies, Flavell argues that Piaget frequently goes beyond the evidence obtained when interpreting his data.

Wohlwill (1968) criticizes the presentation of data as consonant with the theory (that is, as illustrative data rather than as confirmatory proof); while Bryant (1974) has concluded that the development of memory, along with the development of other cognitive skills, plays its part in the results obtained by Piaget, so that they do not derive solely from the structural model of cognitive development which Piaget proposes.

In the light of an increasing number of studies critical of Piagetian theory, especially of his concept of stages and the formal operational stage in particular, the validity of parts of his theory, and indeed of parts of his procedures, seems doubtful. The general thrust of related new research suggests a more continuous development than Piaget's theory proposes. Evidence from across all age-ranges indicates that Piagetian criterion tasks have low discriminating power in diagnosing cognitive behaviours, thus casting doubt on the tasks as tools for diagnosing the stage of moral development. However, in evaluating Piaget's work, it is important to note that far from dogmatically asserting the all-embracing nature of his theory, he remained open-minded enough to be willing to modify it in the light of further work by himself or others, as Lovell (1978) point out. It is significant, too, that many of the critical studies begin or end with a tribute to the man whose immense volume of work and great intellectual scope have stimulated related research on such a scale.

The psychoanalytic model.

The Freudian theory of psychosexual stages of emotional development has already been outlined and evaluated, along with a discussion of other analysts, in Chapter 8. Of the three underlying structures of personality proposed by the theory – the id, the ego and the super-ego – it is the development of the latter which, as 'the repository of social norms' (Miller, 1962), is most important in socialization.

As we have seen, during the phallic stage the child develops the Oedipus–Electra complexes, superseded by the castration–penis-envy complexes. These two are crucial for the development of the super-ego, and if not satisfactorily resolved may lead to difficulties in socialization. Without the development of the castration–penis-envy complexes, children may come to identify less strongly with the same-sex parent, and fixate their psychosexual development at the phallic stage. Identification with the same-sex parent underlies the development of the conscience (the super-ego is the child's internalized version of the parents), and failure at this stage prevents the transfer of discipline from an external source to an internal one, from the parent forbidding anti-social behaviours to the child forbidding himself. Failure to lessen ties to the opposite-sex parent may also lead to neurosis, and affect attitudes to sex and marriage. Men may come to seek out women who are very like their mothers, or may use the defence mechanism of reaction formation and be attracted to women who are totally unlike their mothers. Unresolved father rivalry may be sublimated as anti-authoritarian attitudes in later life. Firm indentification with the same-sex parent also provides the basis of *sex typing* which is so characteristic of young schoolchildren: they often have firm views about behaviours appropriate to their sex. However, the castration complex may produce such psychosexual fear that the defence mechanism of denial may be used, denying to the self the possibility that beings without penises do exist, and leading to homosexual tendencies. Similarly, lesbianism may be regarded as a denial of penis envy.

Freud (1940) says of the super-ego that it 'observes the ego, gives it orders, judges it and threatens it with punishments, exactly like the parents whose place it has taken'. Without the adequate development of the super-ego, psychosexual development remains dominated by the id and the ego, by the self-gratifying pleasure principle checked only by the reality principle of the ego. For socialization to be successful the dynamic equilibrium between id, ego and super-ego must be maintained by the use of defence mechanisms. Successful defence mechanisms allow expression of the id's instinctual drives in a way that is acceptable to the ego (that is, in a way which can in reality be permitted). An example of this might be that while it is not socially acceptable to express the id's instinctual desire to handle and smear faeces, such a drive may be sublimated as expression in some artistic activities, or even in children's mud-pie making. Sublimation is not only important because it permits the expression of socially forbidden drives, but also because many of these sublimations form essential parts of what we regard as civilized life, such as the arts.

However, if expression of the id's drives as sublimations is prevented, they will continue to seek an outlet, so that the defence mechanisms acting to contain them will need to be used almost continuously; that is, they will not be successful defences. As mentioned in Chapter 8, repression and denial are unsuccessful defence mechanisms, and there are others. Fear that the ego will not be powerful enough to restrain the impulsive id may cause neurotic anxiety, perhaps expressed as *phobic anxiety* (fear fixed on a particular object or situation) or as *free-floating anxiety* (where no specific object or situation is linked with the fear).

The super-ego develops as not only the conscience – the individual's concept of what his parents would condemn – but also as the ego ideal, the view of what his parents would actively approve. Both depend on the internalization of parental norms: the ego ideal develops through receiving rewards and the conscience develops through being punished. Moral anxiety may result from the awareness of transgressing these internalized rules, which will lead to 'conscience-stricken' feelings about past or intended behaviours. An imbalance in the id-ego-super-ego equilibrium which places too much stress on the super-ego may produce excessive feelings of guilt, shame and *moral anxiety*. Moral anxiety may sometimes be expressed in the defence mechanism of 'undoing', of performing an action to 'undo' another real or imagined action, or in obsessional behaviours such as obsessive hand-washing, or cleaning. Such unconscious guilt, producing disproportionate reactions to even mild 'transgressions', may have a destructive psychological influence on the individual, and provides an extreme illustration of Freud's belief that some of the psychological privileges of human social life are gained at some cost to the individual's psychological well-being. His conception of society suggests that it has been developed and is maintained only by the individual's suppression of his selfish id's pleasure principle.

One of the major criticisms of Freudian theory centres on its clinical, case-study methodology, and this method certainly has many scientific disadvantages. However, as Danziger argues (1971), 'It is sometimes forgotten that the development of a sound theory requires the *generation* of good hypotheses as well as their testing,' and the clinical methods of Freud have proved fruitful sources of hypotheses about processes of socialization, however difficult their rigorous testing has been.

The social learning model

This approach to the study of socialization regards socialization as conformity to social norms, and assumes that a child's behaviour is shaped by external reinforcements acting on the child. Social behaviour is determined by the individual's conditioning, and the reinforcements and models of behaviour to which he is exposed; and because there is an enormously varied range of possible experiences operating throughout life, development is continuous, rather than progressing by stages.

Developments from learning theory

Learning theory is concerned with stimulus and response, input and output – that is, observable data. The theoretical base of Skinner's learning theory is detailed in Chapter 3, and is an essential preliminary to what follows. The theorists who have extended this approach to social learning theory have not done so without difficulty. It is one thing to study relatively simple learning in isolated subjects in controlled laboratory conditions, and quite another to describe and account for complex human social behaviours learned in interpersonal situations and mediated by the actions of others. It is because of such difficulties that some modifications of the basic concepts of learning theory have been made by social learning theorists. One of these is to acknowledge the limitations which would be imposed on a behavioural repertoire if it derived only from the reinforcement of the spontaneously emitted behaviours of a young child. Another concept, that of *observational learning*, has therefore been introduced, emphasizing the role of observation and imitation in learning. Chapter 12, too, deals with the role of observational learning in the formation of attitudes.

The prolific work of Bandura and his colleagues has shown that observational learning is efficient and adaptive, and therefore well-suited to the learning of complex, interactive behaviours. The basic technique of their studies is to show child subjects a 'model' who behaves in a particular manner, and then to measure the extent to which they imitate the model. Such work has shown that children are more likely to imitate models who have some prestige because of their strength, power, or possessions, than non-prestigious ones and models similar to themselves more than dissimilar models, with all that that implies for the influence of interaction with peers. They are also more likely to imitate the behaviour of models who are seen to be rewarded for their actions than those who are seen to be punished, or not rewarded. Other factors also play a part. Increasing the motivational set, by emphasizing instructions to attend to the model's behaviour or by promising reward for accuracy of imitation, increased the subjects' willingness to imitate. Previous experience also influenced their readiness to notice particular aspects of the model's behaviour; for example, those used to violence were more attentive to violent aspects of modelled behaviours than were subjects without that experience. Mussen and Rutherford (1963) were able to show that warm and supportive adults are more likely to be imitated than those who are not; the perceived power of the model also influences the level of imitation and identification (Hetherington and Frankie, 1967).

Bandura was also able to demonstrate that observational learning may occur without necessarily being demonstrated in overt behaviour. He showed three groups of children a film of a model behaving aggressively, using three experimental conditions: first, a model severely punished for behaviours; secondly, a model generously rewarded for behaviours; and thirdly, a model neither punished nor rewarded for the behaviours shown. When tested, the children in the model-rewarded condition imitated more than the other two. However, when Bandura then went on to offer the children attractive rewards for imitation, he found that all three groups were equally capable of imitating the behaviours they had seen modelled. He concluded that for the *acquisition* of behaviours, mere observation of a model is sufficient, but that for the *manifestation* of that learning in behaviour, other contextual factors operate. (Further studies of imitation learning and its effect on socialization are discussed on pp. 355-6.)

Interestingly, these findings demonstrate that it is necessary to modify basic learning theory to account for social learning. Learning theorists normally accept only directly observable behaviour as evidence; but here a learning theorist himself shows that social learning may occur without any observable change in behaviour being apparent at the time. The need to resort to 'other contextual factors' and to 'cognitive mediators' in the explanation of how social behaviour is learned tends to weaken the claim that learning theory is a sufficient explanation of all human learning. Learning can be seen to require not only stimulus and response, but also a proliferation of cognitive mediators such as memory, thought and other non-overt concepts.

Limitations to the social application of learning theory have also been shown in its account of the emotional bond between mother and child. This bond is essential to the concept of socialization, since it makes the child responsive to the influence of socializing agents as reinforcers. Social learning theorists reject the notion that bond is innate, claiming that it is learnt, initially as a result of the mother's satisfaction of the infant's physical needs, until eventually she herself becomes a secondary reinforcer (Dollard and Miller, 1950). An initial set of biological drives to satisfy physical needs thus becomes conditioned until it eventually provides social motives. A weakness of this account is that very young animals demonstrate needs that are not merely physical. Fantz (1961) showed that very young human infants have an innate tendency to react more to face-like patterns than to non-face-like (but equally complex) patterns, suggesting a 'programmed' response to some particular social stimuli rather than a learned one. Harlow (1958) demonstrated that infant rhesus monkeys preferred a soft, terry-towelling surrogate 'mother', who did not provide milk, to a wire-mesh 'mother' who did, and though extrapolation to human infants is difficult, such evidence suggests that very young infants may have some non-physical needs which the mother satisfies, and which help to account for the mother–child bond more adequately than the social learning theory explanation of 'cupboard love'.

Child-rearing techniques

The proposal that individuals learn only through specific reinforcements for particular behaviours is increasingly untenable, as evidence accumulates to show that complex behaviours are learned through cognitive processes, rather than by parental schedules of reinforcement. However, this does not mean that the reward and punishment of particular behaviours have no effect on socialization. Learning theory predicts that by virtue of the parents' satisfying his early, physical needs, the child comes to need the social presence, the affection and the approval of adults – at first of his immediate caretakers, and later of other adults in general. The secondary reward value which adults, especially parents, possess in the eyes of a young child gives them considerable power to gratify psychological needs, in addition to their power to meet his physical needs. The

manner in which adults wield this power has implications for socialization, and some important aspects of child-rearing practices are
summarized below.

Dependency
This concept is crucial to social learning theory, because it is the
dependency of the young child which makes it possible to socialize
him into the norms of his society, by making him vulnerable to the behaviour towards him of his significant adults. Rewards of approval
reinforce him for socially desirable behaviours – such as feeding from a
spoon, or not wetting his nappy – while non-reinforcement, or
anxiety-arousing maternal disapproval, extinguishes unacceptable
behaviours. This early dependency, developed at about six to eighteen months, later generalizes to other adults, and if not successfully
established at this early stage may lead to later difficulties in socialization. Bowlby (1965) argues that early maternal deprivation can
lead to delinquency and psychopathy in later life, and many studies
have considered the effects of separation on young infants. Temporary separation does produce reactions of protest from young infants,
followed by responses indicating at first despair and then detachment if separation is prolonged; but more recent work suggests that
such effects may not be permanent, and that only in relatively rare
circumstances is psychological damage long-lasting. Maternal responsiveness to an infant's needs produces *secure attachment* in the
child, while inconsistent maternal behaviour leads to *anxious attachment* (Ainsworth, 1973), and these qualitatively different dependen-
cies influence the social development of the child during the later
handling of dependency behaviour.

The development of dependency as the precursor of socialization
has to be reversed as the child grows older, to be replaced by more
self-reliant and independent behaviour. Having learnt to be psychologically dependent (that is, to be vulnerable), he must now learn
that complete dependency is unacceptable. The techniques which
parents use to achieve this vary, and were studied by Sears *et al.*
(1957) in an American investigation of child-rearing techniques. According to learning theory, a schedule of non-reinforcement (ignoring a child when he clings), coupled with reinforcement by admiration and attention when he is not being too demanding, should
quickly establish self-reliance. In reality, however, parents do tend to
react occasionally to the undesired dependent behaviours, hence

changing the schedule to intermittent reinforcement – a VI schedule – which produces a steady persistence of behaviour, highly resistant to extinction (see Chapter 3). Even if the parent manages to ignore the great majority of the undesired behaviours and only reacts to the most extreme ones such as violence or self-damage, the child learns via this VI schedule to be violent, or to hurt himself, to achieve the required parental attention. Alternatively, parents may actively punish the undesired behaviours, but punishment is less effective in conditioning than either positive or negative reinforcement, though it will inhibit behaviours. A child who became *securely* attached to his 'caretaker' during infancy is likely to handle this period of lessening of dependency better than an *anxiously* attached child. A child's extreme anxiety about dependency may blunt the parents' main tool of socialization – the child's need for affection and approval – so that the socialization process in general becomes difficult. Sears *et al.* were able to show in their study that working-class mothers tended to rely more on stricter and more punitive methods of lessening dependency than middle-class mothers.

Toilet training
Sears *et al.* also found social class differences in toilet-training techniques, again with working-class mothers using punishment more than middle-class mothers. Operant conditioning techniques were commonly used, building on the child's natural routine of excretion and using maternal approval and affection as reinforcement for appropriate toilet behaviours. The use of punishment for 'accidents' was less frequent for younger children than for older ones, and when it was used, middle-class mothers tended to use withdrawal of maternal approval as the punishment, while working-class mothers used more direct physical punishments.

The timing of toilet training varied with social class, too: working-class mothers trained their children more rapidly than middle-class mothers. Emotional upsets later in life correlated with either the very early or the very late beginning of training (less than five months and later than nineteen months respectively), and very severe training correlated with bed-wetting problems later. Such training was often accompanied by the use of tangible punishments and rewards as reinforcements in general, while less severe training was linked with less direct reinforcements.

The study also noted that sex-related behaviours, as well as toilet-related behaviours, were more strictly controlled and more often physically punished by working-class mothers than by middle-class mothers. However, while dependency, toilet training and feeding behaviours were, in social learning terms, responses to stimuli which were then controlled and modified by the mother's schedules of reinforcement, evidence of sexuality in children was controlled by avoiding stimulation in the first place. Verbal labels for toilet functions were common, but sexual behaviours were rarely given a name, and were severely dealt with, expecially by poorly educated working-class mothers. Middle-class mothers showed less anxiety and emotional reaction to child sexuality, and Sears argued that intense maternal anxiety might lead to the child's becoming anxious about sex-related behaviours, with possible adolescent and adult anxieties developing in later life.

Aggression
While the reinforcement of certain behaviours may help a child to learn to fit into his social world - that is, may be functionally adaptive - this description is less easy to apply to aggression, which is apparently a dysfunctional behaviour. Destructive and hostile behaviour is superficially a failure of social learning, but social learning theory can actually help to account for it. For example, an angry and irritated 'caretaker' may establish an association for the child between her behavioural signs of anger, and the satisfaction of his physical needs. As suggested in the earlier section on dependency, this association may be further reinforced in situations where a tantrum or violence produces maternal reactions but more socially acceptable behaviour does not. Most adults concerned with young children are guilty of this at some time, almost to the point of quite overlooking the child when he is 'good' and being extremely attentive to him when he is 'bad'. A young child who finds that anger and aggression are more effective in gaining satisfaction of needs and drives than less annoying behaviours is having his aggression reinforced. However, such reinforcement is likely to be accompanied by punishment of some kind, so that the behaviour is being both reinforced and inhibited at the same time. This may produce anxiety, and a conflict between the urge to express aggression and fear of the consequences, and hence a potential for the development of anti-social aggression.

Miller (1948) suggests that such conflict may lead to the displacement of aggression, so that it is expressed against somebody other than the parent, and generalized to other adults, or inanimate objects, or possibly other children. Sears, in a study of aggression in young children, found that subjects with non-punitive mothers displayed little aggression themselves in school and in doll-play situations, while children of moderately punitive mothers showed more aggression in both types of situation. However, children of severely punitive mothers were very aggressive in doll play, but lowest of all in school situations, possibly because strict maternal punishments led to the generalization of inhibition of aggression to other adults, but not to other situations.

The reinforcement learning theory of the development of aggression contrasts with the observational learning theory of Bandura and his colleagues, who point out that reinforcement theory does not account for some aggression which may be noted in non-frustrating situations. A father playing at fighting with his child is reinforcing him for aggressive behaviours, though the situation is not frustrating for the child. Observational learning theory would argue that responses imitating aggression, followed by the reinforcement of these responses, leads to the rapid learning of aggressive behaviours, making them available for use in later situations, which may be frustrating.

Aggressive parents act as models for their children and are likely to encourage aggression in their children towards other people, though not towards themselves. Bandura and Walters (1959) compared highly aggressive boys in probationary care with a control group of 'normal' boys (neither very aggressive nor very withdrawn), and both groups were matched for age, intelligence and socio-economic background. Each boy was interviewed, and tested for reactions to socially deviant behaviours, and both parents were interviewed too. The aggressive group showed much more direct aggression than indirect and verbal aggression, against peers and against adults except their parents – though they reported hostile feelings for their fathers. The control group showed more indirect and verbal aggression than direct aggression, though this was still less than the indirect and verbal aggression of the experimental group. Parents of the aggressive boys tended to encourage their sons' aggression, to use more physical punishment and to be less accepting of dependency behaviour, while parents of the control boys were more accepting of this and used reasoning more frequently as a discipline technique. It seemed to be the case that the generally aggressive parent provided a model for aggression and for a lack of inhibition, rather than that aggression was learned by reinforcement and conditioning.

Conscience and self-control

Theories of observational learning and of reinforcement learning are also used to try to explain the development of conscience and self-control. Observational learning theorists propose that *identification* with 'care-taking' adults – the adoption and internalization of behaviours and attitudes exhibited by a significant other – gradually enables the child to become his own 'caretaker', exhibiting the acquired attitudes and behaviours himself. This process underlies the adoption of gender-appropriate roles and behaviour patterns, and the development of conscience. Internalizing the morality of a significant adult (whose own standards are culturally determined, as are those of the child) provides a means by which the child acquires socially acceptable morals.

Some learning theorists propose that conscience may be developed by direct reinforcement and conditioning, beginning by learning to *inhibit* a socially deviant response through parental punishment. Though the punishment initially provokes the inhibition, gradually just the presence of the parents, and associated anxiety about potential punishment, serve to inhibit it. Later still, just the anxiety serves to inhibit potential misbehaviour, perhaps through the child's construction of a 'rule' for himself.

Hans Eysenck argues that because introverts are more susceptible to conditioning (see p. 252), they are more likely to have highly developed consciences than extraverts. He points out that prison populations are more extraverted than other groups, and that individuals suffering from excessive guilt feelings for no apparent reason are more likely to be introverted. This is not to say that all extraverts will become criminals or that all introverts will have overdeveloped consciences, because all individuals have different learning experiences during childhood.

Parental characteristics

It should be noted that though social learning theories have brought a more objective, empirical approach to the study of socialization than the clinical methodologies of Piaget and Freud, there remain doubts about the role of child-rearing practices as antecedents for later social behaviours. The work of Sears, involving 379 mothers of young children, was a major study in this area and influenced subsequent research. However, replication attempts (for example, Yarrow *et al.* 1968) have produced inconsistent results, and it has proved difficult to show reliably that particular child-rearing practices lead directly to particular characteristics such as dependency and aggression. Despite the difficulties of isolating practices and effects, however, all studies suggest that the *manner* in which they are practised is important. Maternal responsiveness and attachment have been discussed, and maternal warmth or coldness has an effect too. Some mothers openly demonstrate affection, and warmly accept and cope with behaviours such as dependency, while others are undemonstrative and even cold and impatient of child care. The dimension of permissiveness–restrictiveness can be applied as a criterion for maternal tolerance of displays of aggressive or sexual behaviours, or of disobedience and so on. Approaches may vary from the relaxed control of such behaviours to a rigid insistence on prescribed behaviours. A further dimension, that of maternal emotional involvement or calm detachment, also emerges as important.

Parents tend to display different techniques of child discipline, related to the parental characteristics discussed above. Physical punishment inhibits the undesired behaviour in the presence of the punisher but has little effect on behaviour elsewhere, and only shows the child what he should not do, without teaching him what is acceptable. It may be more successful as a socialization technique if combined with reasoning, and if the parent–child relationship is warm; but there is still a correlation between physical punishment, and aggression outside the home.

Psychological punishment by withdrawing love and approval, perhaps by isolating the child or by not talking to him, is also more effective if the general relationship between parent and child is warm and dependent. It is associated with the formation of the conscience and the ego ideal, and with feelings of guilt about breaking the rules. If both physical and emotional punishments are outweighed by the proportion of rewards and praise given to the child, he is more likely to identify with the parents, and internalize their norms.

Discipline which involves reasoning with the child, explaining the need to change his behaviour, is most effective in the development of self-control and in producing real learning about social behaviours, as is firmness and consistency in discipline. Over-strict, authoritarian disciplinary techniques may lead to an anxious, guilt-ridden child, likely in his turn to develop authoritarian patterns of behaviour. Less strict discipline may produce less respectful children, but the cost to their psychological well-being will also probably be less.

Further reading

Danziger, K. (1971), *Socialization*, Penguin

Donaldson, M. (1978), *Children's Minds* (Appendix), Fontana

Eysenck, H.J. (1965), *Fact and Fiction in Psychology* (Chapter 7), Pelican

Miller, G.A. (1966), *Psychology: The Science of Mental Life* (Chapter 15), Pelican

Wright, D. (1971), *The Psychology of Moral Behaviour*, Pelican

12 Attitude structure and formation

A subject which is one of the corner-stones of the field of social and developmental psychology is that of attitudes. Such is the topic's importance, and the volume of research it has generated, that two chapters are given over to its exposition – this chapter being devoted to the nature of attitudes, and Chapter 13 to the variables influencing attitude change.

It is significant that such an important concept as *attitudes* should have given rise to the plethora of definitions which exist in the literature: it is an ambiguous concept. This ambiguity is also reflected in the different types of studies of attitudes, which can be considered as sometimes sociological, sometimes psychological, or sometimes both: 'for attitudes have social references in their origins and development and in their objects, while at the same time they have psychological reference in that they inhere in the individual and are intimately enmeshed in his behaviour and his psychological make-up' (Warren and Jahoda, 1973).

Though a few writers suggest a possible hereditary basis for some attitudes (Allport, 1950, and McGuire, 1969), all agree that attitudes develop primarily through learning. A famous definition of an attitude is Allport's (1935), in which he says: 'An attitude is a mental and neural state of readiness, organized through experience, exerting a directive or dynamic influence upon the individual's response to all objects and situations with which it is related.' Similarly, Rokeach (1968a) defines an attitude as 'a learned orientation or disposition, toward an object or situation which provides a tendency to respond favourably or unfavourably to the object or situation'. Most definitions of attitude share this important characteristic, that an attitude is learnt, though not necessarily from personal experience: we may also learn from and internalize the attitudes of those among whom we live, and from other social sources and institutions such as education and the media.

Most definitions of an attitude also encompass what Secord and Backman (1964) have termed the *affective, cognitive* and *behavioural components* of an attitude. The affective component consists of feelings about an attitude object, reflecting its place in the individual's scale of values; the cognitive component equates more with what an individual believes is so; and the behavioural component represents the overt expression of attitudes in actual behaviour – though this component is not wholly reliable as an indicator of attitude, because social and situational demands may constrain it. Attempts have been made to measure attitudes by using one or more of these three components as the basis of measurement, and attitude measurement will be considered in more detail later in the chapter.

Beliefs, values and opinions

The ambiguity of the concept of attitude, then, stems in part from the complex interaction of its related components such as beliefs, values, and opinions or actual behaviours. Morgan and King (1971) succinctly describe a belief as 'the acceptance of some proposition'. Some beliefs do not necessarily involve attitudes; for example, you may believe that Edinburgh is in Scotland without having any particular attitude about this belief. However, many beliefs do involve attitudes, and can change them and hence change behaviours: a belief in God is just one example. The interaction of beliefs with attitudes can also operate in the other direction, with attitudes shaping beliefs. For example, a negative attitude towards coloured people may lead to a belief in unfavourable reports about them, even in the light of evidence to the contrary.

It should be clear, therefore, that while belief and attitude may be involved in a dynamic interaction, they are constructs which can be differentiated. But if a belief is only the acceptance of some proposition, what is it that produces a favourable or unfavourable attitude, a positive or a negative attitude? Some other construct appears to be involved, which gives a *value* to an attitude. The term 'value' has been variously defined at different periods in the social sciences, but it is widely accepted today as an individual's conception of what is desirable; his abstract ideals about behaviours and goals. While a belief reveals what an individual thinks is true, his values reveal what he would like to be true. Campbell (1963) proposes that attitude and value are indistinguishable, but Rokeach (1968b) argues that a value is a special kind of belief which goes beyond the mere acceptance of some proposition to include a notion of *worth*. He suggests that 'A grown person probably has tens of thousands of beliefs, hundreds of attitudes, but only dozens of values', with the latter ranked in a hierarchical value system, with some values being more important than others. A well-known technique of assessing categories of values is the Allport–Vernon–Lindzey Study of Values (1960), which ranks an individual's level of concern with each of six value categories – theoretical, social, political, religious, aesthetic and economic values. Rokeach (1973) developed a Value Survey which differentiates between *terminal values* (desirable end-states or goals such as wisdom, an exciting life, equality and so on) and *instrumental values* or desirable attributes such as capability, helpfulness, intellectualism and others. Subjects were asked to rank the eighteen terminal values and the eighteen instrumental values, and Rokeach compared the responses of different groups of individuals such as American, Australian, Israeli and Canadian students.

Elms (1976) writes:

> In addition to an individual's criteria for judging the worth of things (values) and his assumptions about the state of things (beliefs) he will also have positive and negative feelings about many (though not all) of the things in whose existence he believes.... An attitude thus may be seen as a blend of belief and value.

Beliefs, values and attitudes certainly overlap and interact in intricate ways. They may be usefully differentiated for some purposes of psychological investigation, but they do have some key characteristics in common. First, none of them can be directly observed or measured, but must be inferred from observations of behaviour, whether verbal self-report or other ways of behaving. Secondly, they are learned through relationships with the external world.

A technique used widely in market research and other studies is familiar to most people as the *public opinion poll*, in which the opinions of very many individuals are elicited in order to assess general attitudes. 'Opinion' is a term generally accepted as meaning a verbal expression of an attitude, but it is in fact only roughly equivalent to attitude. Hildum and Brown (1956) demonstrated experimentally that it is possible to control the expression of opinions using reinforcement techniques. They elicited the opinions of subjects on a particular topic, reinforcing the responses of one group of subjects by saying 'good' whenever a 'favourable' opinion was expressed, but reinforcing the responses of a second group of subjects by the same method whenever an 'unfavourable' opinion was expressed. The first group expressed a significantly greater number of 'favourable' opinions than the second group.

A careful experimental study by Singer (1961) also used reinforcement techniques to influence expression of opinions, with subjects being asked to answer questions while the experimenter reinforced certain responses by saying 'Good', or 'Right'. Sixty questions were used from the *F-scale*, or *fascism scale*, originally constructed by Adorno *et al.* (1953) to identify subjects with authoritarian and antidemocratic tendencies. Thirty questions were selected from an *E-scale*, or *ethnocentric scale*, also constructed by Adorno *et al.*, designed to measure ethnocentric tendencies, which correlate highly with authoritarian tendencies (*ethnocentricity* is the belief that one's own cultural or social group is superior to, or different from, all others). All Singer's subjects were matched initially for their F- and E-scale ratings, then re-tested under experimental conditions some months later. Subjects in the experimental groups were reinforced each time they expressed an anti-authoritarian opinion, or disagreed with an authoritarian statement, while no reinforcement was given to subjects in the control group. The experimental group showed a 30% gain in pro-democratic opinions compared with the control group, in response to such minor social reinforcements as saying 'Good'.

Quite apart from demonstrating the significant effects of simple reinforcement techniques on opinions, such studies also indicate how influential interviewer bias might be, unless great care is taken at the interview stage of opinion polling. Katz (1942) found that working-class interviewers obtained more favourable opinions on questions related to work than did white-collar interviewers, while Cantril (1944) found that in an American pre-election public opinion poll, pro-Democratic interviewers elicited more pro-Democratic opinions than did pro-Republican interviewers, and vice versa. Since public opinion polls are today used not only to record public opinion, but in some cases to provide data on which policy makers may act, it is essential that such data are reliable and valid – that is, that sampling, data collection and analysis are precise and accurate. Public opinion polls necessarily use only a sample of the total population to obtain data, and the representativeness of the sample is therefore crucial. This demands an initial definition of those characteristics, or *parameters*, of a population which are believed to be related to the topic the poll is studying, and the sample selected for polling must include these parameters in the same proportions as they occur in the total population – that is, the sample is stratified as is the initial population. The parameters chosen may include socio-economic groups, groups differentiated by sex, age, geographic region, and many others, depending on their relevance to the topic of the poll. Interviewers are told how many respondents to use from each stratum in order to achieve a representative sample, but if interviewers then operate on an 'opportunity sampling' basis, perhaps just stopping people in the street or knocking on doors till they have filled their quota, considerable bias may be introduced. Street sampling may yield respondents who are all housewives shopping, and day-time door knocking effectively eliminates a large proportion of the working population from the sample. The size of the sample and its representativeness largely determine the accuracy of the poll, and the smaller the sample the less accurate the poll tends to be, though size without representativeness is always unacceptable. A notorious example of this occurred in a poll carried out in America in 1936 by the *Literary Digest* on voting intentions. Ten million people were used in the sample, but they were all chosen from telephone directories and therefore represented only the telephone-owning middle class. On the basis of this large, but unrepresentative, sample a Republican victory was wrongly forecast.

When public opinion polls, or survey interviews in general, address topics which involve moral issues rather than more factual topics such as voting intentions, the wording of the questions demands very careful attention. 'Have you stopped beating your wife?' is a cliché for poor presentation of a question, since it forces a particular inference about the respondent's behaviour. The structure of the questions may be varied too, the two main types of question being the *fixed-alternative* or *multiple-choice question*, and the *open-ended question*. The former provides the respondent with a choice between a number of already specified answers, of which he must choose the one which most nearly represents his own views. This can be a rapid and efficient interview technique when unambiguous factual information is being sought, and responses can be easily coded and scored. However, it is less appropriate as a method of eliciting more subjective information, since the response categories used may not adequately reflect the respondent's own views, thus forcing him into the 'Don't know' category. In such a case the open-ended type of question provides more opportunity for the respondent to describe his views, encouraged, but not directed, by the interviewer. Coding and scoring of responses to such questions are obviously less easy than for responses to fixed-alternative questions, but responses must be grouped into a smaller number of categories as a means of classifying types of responses. Both types of question may fruitfully be used in a study, with open-ended questions delineating the problem to be studied and its associated context, and specific multiple-choice questions providing a quantitative measure of particular aspects of the general topic being investigated.

In all interview surveys or opinion polls the reliability and validity of the data obtained depend upon three main factors: the quality of the sampling techniques, the amount of interviewer bias and the construction of the questions used. All must be carefully considered in the design of a survey, and *test-re-test*, or *split-half*, *methods* of checking reliability (see below and p. 215) must be used to legitimate its structure.

Attitude scales

Assuming the Rokeach (1968a) definition of an attitude as a disposition or tendency to respond favourably or unfavourably to an object or a situation, it is possible to measure this tendency to some extent. Considerable efforts have been made to develop techniques of attitude measurement, including self-reporting techniques of attitude scales and interviews as the basis of inferring attitudes.

Attitude scales consist of a set of statements or items to which subjects are asked to respond, and from the pattern of these responses inferences can be made about the subject's attitudes underlying the responses. Attitudes scales vary in kind and in construction, but most aim to assign the respondent to a position on a unidimensional continuum which represents positive–negative 'strength' of attitude towards an object or situation. Anastasi (1961) describes attitude scales as being designed 'to provide a quantitative measure of the individual's relative position along a unidimensional attitude continuum'.

The criteria used in evaluating any measuring instrument are related to its purpose, and attitude scales must therefore systematically discriminate between people holding different attitudes, and as sharply as possible between different degrees of the same attitude. The number of items in an attitude scale is one clue to its discriminatory power: a large number will tend to increase reliability, since errors of measurement will then tend to cancel out. Any ambiguous items are less likely to introduce a systematic bias among numerous items, while they may cause significant distortion among few items. There are practical limits to the number of items which can be used, however, and the reliability of an attitude scale can be checked in other ways. The methods of assessing the reliability of attitude scales are the same as those employed in the evaluation of intelligence and personality tests. These methods (test–re-test, alternate forms and split-half) are described on page 215.

If the coefficient of correlation suggests a high degree of consistency between sets of results obtained by using an attitude scale, it is generally accepted as an indicator of the reliability of the scale. However, if the coefficient of correlation is low, that may not necessarily mean that the scale is unreliable. Other factors must be checked before reaching that conclusion; for example, wide differences between sets of results may be due to differences in the physical or the psychological conditions in which the scale was administered. Subjects may respond quite differently to items about their attitude towards their immediate colleagues, or their superiors, depending on whether responses are being made anonymously or whether they can be identified. Wide differences between sets of results may also occur if the subject's experiences between testings have actually led to a change in his attitudes. Both apparent variations in attitude, arising from differences in conditions of test administration, and true variations, arising from real changes in attitude, must be accounted for when assessing the degree of reliability of an attitude scale.

It is possible for an attitude scale to be reliable (to consistently reproduce an individual's score on repeated trials) and yet not be valid, where validity is the degree to which the instrument measures that which it is supposed to be measuring. For example, a scale for measuring attitudes to immigrants would have dubious validity if typical members of the National Front failed to score towards the negative extreme. Methods of checking on the validity of a scale include testing it on 'known' groups or individuals, in other words subjects who are known in advance to hold different attitudes, and then measuring the degree to which the scale differentiates them. Alternatively, the opinions of experts may be sought on the *content validity* of the items – whether they are indeed relevant to the measurement of particular attitudes. Finally, if the results obtained from an attitude scale permit the accurate prediction of the respondents' behaviour in some future situation, the scale can be said to have predictive validity.

A common technique of attitude measurement is the *Thurstone method* – not itself a particular attitude scale, but rather a method for devising such scales. A large number of statements about the topic of the attitude scale are collected, each implying a certain evaluation of the topic, that is, reflecting a particular attitude towards it. This initial selection of items must cover a wide range of views about the attitude in question, and be worded as unambiguously as possible. This array of items is then given to a number of 'judges', who each estimate the degree to which each item implies a positive–negative attitude, on an eleven-point scale. Any items which produce considerable disagreement about their position on this eleven-point scale are discarded, as are any irrelevant or ambiguous items, until thirty or forty final items remain, each having a numerical rating assigned by a consensus of judges and ranging from extremely favourable' to 'extremely unfavourable' as the opposite ends of the scale. This attitude questionnaire is then piloted on subjects, who indicate which items they agree with. Since each item has a numerical score associated with it which places it in a certain position on the 'favourable'–'unfavourable' attitude continuum, subjects' responses can be scored and a mean attitude score assigned to each subject as a measure of their attitude towards the topic of the scale.

Since Thurstone developed this method in 1930, many other attitude questionnaires have been produced and new techniques developed. One which appeared soon after Thurstone's was the *Likert technique*, which presents a set of attitude statements, towards each of which subjects are asked to express agreement or disagreement on a five-point scale, whose range is 'strongly agree', 'agree', 'undecided', 'disagree' and 'strongly disagree'. Each degree of attitude towards an item is given a numerical value from one to five, so that a total numerical value can be calculated from the responses to all the items. At its simplest, the Likert-type scale is quicker and easier to construct than a Thurstone-type scale and involves no judges, and since attitude measurements made using both techniques tend to correlate well, the Likert scale tends to be used quite frequently.

A more recent attitude measurement technique developed by Osgood *et al.* (1957) is the *semantic differential technique*. Osgood and his colleagues researched the attributes which people use to evaluate objects and concepts, and found three major factors or dimensions of judgement. These were an *evaluative factor* ('good–bad' types of judgements), a *potency factor* ('strong–weak' types of judgements) and an *activity factor* ('active–passive' types of judgements). The evaluative factor proved most important for most people, and is the factor underlying Thurstone and Likert attitude measurement scales, but Osgood believed that attitude measurement should tap the other factors involved too. A semantic differential questionnaire, therefore, usually includes at least three seven-point scales linked to each of the three factors, and an average of these then provides a numerical attitude score for each major dimension of judgement. An example is given below.

Ratings of Richard Nixon

1	Pleasant _____	Unpleasant
2	Strong _____	Weak
3	Cruel _____	Kind
4	Active _____	Passive
5	Hard _____	Soft
6	Good _____	Bad
7	Beautiful _____	Ugly
8	Aggressive _____	Defensive
9	Tense _____	Calm
10	Favourable _____	Unfavourable

Scales 1, 3 and 6 tap the evaluative dimension of judgement, scales 2, 5 and 7 the potency factor, and scales 4, 8 and 9 the activity factor. The semantic differential questionnaire can therefore differentiate between components of attitudes in a way which other techniques do not, and this can enhance an understanding of the links between attitude and behaviour. Osgood *et al.* provide an example of two subjects' ratings of the concept 'Negro', one of which rated the concept as unfavourable: strong: active, while the other rated it as unfavourable: weak: passive. Though both rate Negroes as unfavourable, the first subject may behave towards them quite differently from the second subject – perhaps in a placatory manner as opposed to an exploitative manner – and it is the measurement of more than just the evaluative factor which makes such behavioural–attitudinal interaction clearer.

The links between behaviour and attitude are not easy to trace unequivocally. LaPiere (1934) found considerable discrepancy between the relatively high level of prejudice expressed towards Chinese nationals in a questionnaire survey and the actual behaviour of Americans towards Chinese people. Since his study, others have consistently indicated a low correlation between stated attitudes and overt behaviours, and Wicker (1969) concludes that 'it is considerably more likely that attitudes will be unrelated or only slightly related to overt behaviours than that attitudes will be closely related to actions'. Some social psychologists such as Cook and Selltiz (1964) suggest that attitudes should be conceived as underlying, latent predispositions which, *along with other influences*, help to determine behaviours towards attitude objects, including such behaviours as self-reported statements of beliefs about attitude objects, as well as actions towards them. Attitudes may be expressed in overt behaviours, unless such expression is constrained or modified by other influences on behaviour, such as social norms or other personal and individual characteristics. The self-report techniques of attitude measurement described earlier are vulnerable to such constraints and modifications, whether attitudes are described in subject's own words or in responses to standardized items on a scale. It is well known that subjects tend to express socially desirable responses, which perhaps mask real attitudes, and that the problem of *response set* (the tendency to consistently agree or consistently disagree with presented items, or to make consistently moderate responses) may reduce the reliability of attitude scale data.

Techniques to reduce the effects of such tendencies are devised and built into most attitude scales. One example is that of varying the wording of test items so that agreement with some items and disagreement with others is required to indicate a particular attitude; another is to stress the anonymity of the responses and the importance of honest answers; while yet another is to include items not relevant to the attitude in question as 'red herrings', to make the real aim of the test less obvious and so less susceptible to distorted responses.

Because of the vulnerability to distorted responses of self-report techniques of attitude measurement, attempts have been made to evaluate attitudes by other methods, though the development of such alternatives has been much less extensive than that of questionnaires and surveys. One group of alternative measures derives inferences about attitudes from observations of overt behaviours, assuming that such behaviours are indicative of underlying attitudes. DeFleur and Westie (1958) developed an adaptable attitude measure based on presenting subjects with a test situation which they believed was real rather than merely experimental, and in which they expected their behaviours to have real consequences for themselves. Subjects were presented with photographs of a young Negro male with a white female, or a white male with a Negro female, taken in social settings, and were questioned about the pictures. They were then asked to agree to model for similar photographs and to sign their agreement to the use of these photographs for a range of purposes, from laboratory experiments with other subjects through to publicity campaigns for racial integration. The authors suggest that the use of test situations which subjects believe are real, and the requests for behaviours which will apparently have real consequences for subjects, permit more reliable inferences about the subjects' attitudes than do conventional self-report techniques of attitude measurement.

Another attitude measure based on observation of overt behaviours is that of role playing in a deliberately staged test situation. Stanton and Litwak (1955) found that evaluations of the attitudes of potential foster parents made through role-playing methods were significantly better predictors of future behaviours as foster parents than were intensive interview techniques. Yet another behavioural technique of attitude measurement is the study of sociometric choices made within a group that includes some members who are themselves 'attitude objects'. This technique derives initially from Moreno (1953), the founder of *sociometry* or social measurement, and is a method of obtaining information about the social relationships within a group. Usually expressed as a diagram or sociogram, it indirectly elicits information about attitudes towards individual group members. Patterns of friendship choices made by subjects can reveal, for example, racial or sexual attitudes which might be concealed or modified through self-report techniques of attitude measurement.

However, though behavioural approaches to attitude measurement may reduce the possibility of such concealment, the fact remains that the link between attitude and behaviour may be mediated by social and personal factors not elicited by either self-report or behavioural approaches to attitude measurement. Actual behaviour is not only a function of attitudes, but also of the constraints of specific situations and contexts, whose demands may significantly limit the behavioural expression of personal attitudes.

Attitude formation

It has already been noted that attitudes are learned, and not necessarily from first-hand personal experiences but often from others. From birth onwards individuals in all societies are involved in interactions which are a product of their own personal characteristics and those of the social environment in which they find themselves. Living as part of a complex pattern of social relationships, individuals learn to accept norms indicated during interactions with others. Clearly then, there are multiple factors involved in attitude formation, each complex in its own right and becoming more so in combination. Attempts to differentiate between these interacting factors inevitably lead to over-simplification, but, bearing this in mind, one can consider the major influences on attitude formation.

Whatever theoretical framework one adopts as a view of personality development, it is generally accepted that personality characteristics influence an individual's receptiveness to socializing influences and hence the development of specific attitudes. Eysenck (1972) assumes that conditioning underlies the learning of social values and attitudes, and that introverts, with a lower threshold for external stimulation, are more susceptible to such conditioning and to the internalization of social values and attitudes than are extraverts, who are less easy to condition because of their higher threshold for external stimulation. Freud (1940), emphasizing the importance of early childhood experiences for personality development through the resolution of innate psychological conflicts, assumes that it is the development of the super-ego, by identification with the parents and the internalization of their values and attitudes, which paves the way for later identification with peer groups and internalization of *their* values and attitudes. One important study of personality and attitudes and their relationships (Adorno *et al.*, 1950) found that certain personality characteristics correlated highly with particular attitudes and values measured on the scale developed specially for this study (mentioned earlier) – the *F-scale* or *fascism scale*. Their results supported the view that personality characteristics do mediate the reception and transmission of values and attitudes, but the scale is not without its critics. Rokeach (1960) suggests that it is not the relationship between personality and particular attitudes which is important, but that between personality and the *structure* of attitudes held. For example, an individual may profess liberal, even left-wing, attitudes and values, but do so in a very closed or dogmatic manner, and it is this manner of holding an attitude, rather than the specific attitude itself, which Rokeach claims links with personality, and which he measures on a *dogmatism scale* developed as an instrument for his investigation. He proposes that the way in which attitudinal responses are made depends on an individual's positing on a continuum between open and closed belief systems – that is, on the degree to which an individual can receive, evaluate and act upon given information without being influenced by other internal or external factors, such as anxiety reduction needs or social desirability needs, among others.

Personality is therefore one factor to be considered in attitude formation and development, but such basic personality traits do not totally determine attitudinal responses. Another factor which plays an important part in attitude formation is the process of socialization. Bandura (1972) defines this as 'the process whereby individuals develop the qualities essential to function effectively in the society in which they live' – and such qualities include the development of appropriate attitudes for effective social functioning. Several psychological processes are involved in both socialization and the formation of attitudes. Learning theory provides a useful explanation of how many attitudes may be learned, with both classical and instrumental conditioning involved in the establishment and reinforcement of particular attitudes. Initially, parents dominate the shaping of a child's behaviour and attitudes, reinforcing the expression of particular actions and attitudes at the expense of others until the child learns and internalizes those deemed appropriate. From this early learning of the values given to certain actions and expressions of cognition, other behaviours and attitudes acquire value through the process of association.

However, while learning theorists view behaviour largely as a function of influences imposed upon the child, with behaviour and attitudes explained in terms of contingencies of reinforcement, other psychologists point out that this approach fails to take into account the child's own active role in his own socialization (Schaffer, 1974). It is a truism that no two children behave identically, and an infant's responses can reinforce and shape parental behaviour in significant ways. Some learning also occurs through processes other than those of S-R learning, and a behavioural repertoire based only on the reinforcement and shaping of spontaneous responses randomly emitted by a young child would be very limited. Imitation is one of these alternative learning processes. Children frequently imitate parents, siblings and others in their social groups, and the phenomenon is so common that until some thirty years ago the innate nature of imitation was unquestioned, and still remains controversial. However, Miller and Dollard (1941) found no evidence of an innate tendency to imitate in an elaborate series of experiments studying imitative responses. They found it equally easy to train rats and children to imitate *or* to counter-imitate (to consistently make responses opposite to those of a model), and they argued that if imitation was an innate tendency it should have been more difficult to train to counter-imitate.

Imitation depends on the availability of an actual or a symbolic model, and the relationship with the model is important for the learning which takes place. Bandura *et al.* (1961) showed that children's perception of the appropriateness or otherwise of the role demonstrated by the model significantly affected their level of imitation of the model, with a male aggressive model being more readily imitated than a female aggressive model – in itself a significant demonstration of the presence of already-acquired attitudes! Experiments have also shown that adult models who exhibit warm, supportive characteristics are more closely imitated than non-supportive adults (Bandura and Huston, 1961), and that boys achieving high-masculinity test scores and girls rated as highly feminine each have closer and more affectionate relationships with their fathers and mothers respectively than do low-scoring boys and girls (Mussen and Rutherford, 1963). These and other similar findings have considerable significance for the process of attitude formation through imitative learning.

Imitative behaviour may be observed when the model is actually present or at a later time when the model is removed. *Empathic imitation* (imitating while watching a model) has been little studied, though the phenomenon of empathic emotional response is well known. Vicarious emotional involvement in a modelled situation is common, as in watching a tense and stressful film. Alfert (1966) showed that the pattern of autonomic reactions during vicarious stress is very similar to reactions to real stress, and Bandura *et al.* (1965) have shown that dog phobia in subjects can be reduced by watching others behaving towards dogs in a non-anxious manner. Bandura (1965) suggests that such vicarious emotional conditioning can also be mediated symbolically through language, and that this mechanism can help to account for the transmission of attitudes from parents to children. Imitative behaviour may also occur when the model is no longer present, and though imitation may be a product of curiosity, it is more likely to occur if a child sees that the model is reinforced in some way for his behaviour or expression of attitude.

Like imitation, the process of identification is based on the availability of a model or models, but usually involves a relatively long-lasting relationship between individuals as opposed to that involved in imitative processes studied under experimental conditions. More important for a discussion of attitude formation, the modelling which occurs is qualitatively different from that observed as imitation, with the modeller behaving *as if he was* the model, matching not only observed overt behaviours but values, beliefs and attitudes too. The concept of identification derives from Freudian psycho-analytical theory, as an unconscious process by which an individual acquires these psychological characteristics of another. The identification of a young child with the same-sex parent leads to the adoption of specific sex roles, and is seen in Freudian terms as a defence mechanism by which the child resolves the Oedipal conflict. A male child supposedly feels threatened by the strength and power of the father as a potential punisher of the child's sexual attachment to his mother. By identifying with the father, adopting many of his characteristics, the child reduces the threat of paternal aggression against himself. Identification with the aggressor was reported by Bettelheim (1943) in a study of prisoners in concentration camps, but other studies have argued for identification as a result of love of a significant model, and a desire for the experience of the states of the powerful model such as his mastery of the environment (Kagan 1958), while Whiting (1960) suggests that status envy can lead to identification with another.

Whether or not one accepts distinctions between different forms of identification, most studies of the concept confront the problem of measurement. Many such studies avoid direct measurement and use correlational links between *parental nurturance*, or parental dominance, and behavioural similarities in the offspring (for example, Hetherington and Frankie, 1967). Others use as a measure the degree of similarity between the subject's self-concept ratings and his ratings of his significant model, though the validity of this technique is questionable. Difficulties in the measurement and the definition of the concept of identification have led to doubts about its explanatory power, yet for many psychologists it remains one of the basic processes by which attitudes are apparently acquired.

The helplessness and dependence upon others for survival which characterize human infants and young children are closely linked with the psychological need for the love and approval of significant others in a child's life, and to achieve this he must learn to be acceptable to these others. By the mechanisms of reinforcement, association, imitation and identification he learns the values and attitudes which contribute to his social acceptance. Later in life, parental influence on the formation of attitudes diminishes as peer-group influence increases in importance in modifying established attitudes and initiating new ones, though there is evidence that parental influence has long-term effects on some attitudes (Hyman, 1959). Jennings and Niemi (1968) found significant correlations between the religious and political attitudes of adolescents and their parents. However, an important aspect of the process of attitude formation is that individuals tend to be exposed to generally very similar attitudes and values in their parents and in their friends and reference groups (see below), and a relatively homogeneous environment in terms of attitudes and values produces exposure to a biased sample of available information. Such selective exposure is reflected in the attitudes developed and in their maintenance, because a child continues to be exposed primarily to information which supports them. Socio-economic factors such as class, colour, level of income, education, occupation and so on operate to present information consistent with attitudes already developed. Sears (1969) suggests that a 'critical period' in attitude formation exists between the ages of twelve and thirty, during which most of an individual's attitudes achieve a long-lasting form, and certainly during adolescence the influence of peer groups becomes very important. It has long been recognized that an individual's *membership group* strongly affects his attitudes, and more recently that his *reference groups* – groups of which he would like to be or remain a member – are also important. Membership and reference groups may or may not be one and the same, and both affect attitudes held (Sherif and Sherif, 1953).

Every social group has certain norms or expectations shared by group members which act to define behaviours, values and attitudes appropriate to the group. There is considerable social pressure on group members to conform to such norms, and both implicit and explicit sanctions may exist to ensure conformity. Secord and Backman (1974) describe how groups' norms are communicated to members, either by clearly defining attitudinal and behavioural requirements, or by monitoring the level of conformity of members and applying group sanctions as necessary, thus indirectly defining group requirements. A voluntary member of a group is likely to identify strongly with its attitudes and values anyway, minimizing the need for attitudinal or behavioural change, but involuntary membership can cause problems, requiring either attitude change or ostracism; for example, the membership of an atheist to a devout community. The power of group influence is illustrated in a classic study by Newcomb (1943), in which he traced the attitude changes exhibited by female students attending the politically liberal Bennington College in Vermont. Initially conservative students with affluent and conservative home backgrounds showed considerable and progressively liberal attitude changes as they progressed through college. There were individual differences in the degree of peer-group influence, with some socially insecure students, or others with rigid family ties, participating little in peer groups, but in general the effect of peer-group influence was very marked. Newcomb (1963) made a follow-up study of his subjects and found that college-formed attitudes had persisted, with final-year attitudes being better predictors of adult attitudes than first-year attitudes. The Bennington study shares with many others the finding that education correlates very highly with attitudes, with a higher level of education positively related to more tolerant, liberal attitudes, and a lower level of education positively related to dogmatic, conservative attitudes. (Experimental studies of conformity are discussed in Chapter 10.)

The principles of attitude formation and maintenance discussed above apply equally to the learning of those attitudes we call prejudices. Prejudice can clearly be the result of an uncritical conformity to group norms, whether of family groups, peer groups, social class groups, or of society itself. Horowitz (1936) showed that prejudice, like other attitudes and values, can be the result of adopting and conforming to the attitudes of significant others, and concluded that 'attitudes towards negroes were chiefly determined not by contact with negroes but by contact with the prevalent attitude towards negroes'. Pettigrew (1958) argues that conformity to dominant group norms is a crucial factor in prejudice, and that racial prejudice in the USA and South Africa correlates more significantly with measures of conformity to group norms than with measures of individual personality.

Though prejudices are usually thought of as being negative attitudes towards some attitude object, it is quite possible to be prejudiced in favour of an attitude object, holding a positive attitude towards it. What really differentiates prejudices from the many other attitudes that individuals hold is that prejudices derive from a prejudgement of the attitude object which leads to the formation of an unjustified attitude. Krech *et al.* (1962) state that 'Prejudiced attitudes lead to what has been called a stereotype. This is any widespread, oversimplified, and hence erroneous belief.' However, it is arguable that stereotypes are the result not of prejudiced attitudes, but of a psychological categorizing process used as part of our need to classify and predict about our physical and social environments. Assigning particular characteristics to certain groups can aid the prediction of the 'expected' attributes of individual members of that group, and hence can be important to our own sense of classification and control of features of everyday life. Categorization in terms of stereotypes does, however, provide a ready basis for prejudice, though the extent of this may be largely determined by other factors such as the personality characteristics of the prejudiced individual. An important feature of prejudice is its resistance to change, which perhaps indicates that it functions as an extreme attitude meeting a psychological need.

Thus, despite many studies pointing to the development of prejudice as a result of group influences, there is evidence that its development may also be linked with personality factors. Adorno *et al.* (1953) found that for some individuals, prejudice served an important psychological function in their own self-concept, and was indeed highly resistant to change. Feelings of insecurity or a need to feel superior may lead to a dogmatic perception of the social world in terms of good or bad, right or wrong, and to a strong conformity to 'in' groups and aggression to 'out' groups as a defence against psychological insecurity. Prejudice may also provide an opportunity to express hostility and aggression, which often originate in the frustration of needs. When direct aggression against the frustrator is not possible, displaced aggression against an alternative target both releases tension and diverts possible self-blame for the failure to achieve the goal set by the original need. Prejudiced individuals who encounter frustration can often most conveniently displace their aggression against the object of their already existing prejudice in a process called *scapegoating*. Several studies have demonstrated the links between frustration and scapegoating, measuring racial attitudes before and after experimentally manipulating levels of frustration: Miller and Bugelski (1948), for example, showed that subjects expressed significantly more prejudice after being frustrated than before. The evidence suggests that, once learned, prejudices are frequently maintained by the personal needs they serve, and that by creating social handicaps for some objects of prejudice (such as providing poor housing, education and job opportunities for non-whites) the results of these are then used as apparently justifying the prejudices, and they continue.

Prejudice may also arise out of personal experience of an attitude object, though this seems to be relatively rare. Indeed, opportunities for interaction and contact have been shown to reduce prejudice. Deutsch and Collins (1951) report that the racial prejudice of white housewives towards Negroes significantly diminished after living in a bi-racial housing project, while Bagley (1970) found that racial prejudice in five English boroughs with a proportion of coloured immigrants higher than the national average was no higher than that in a national sample. However, Secord and Backman (1974), in a review of relevant literature, conclude that although increased contact reduces prejudice by providing opportunities for the object of prejudice to disprove pre-judged expectations and beliefs, generalization of this reduction in prejudice to other situations is very limited. Stouffer (1949) found that racial prejudice diminished when white and Negro American soldiers served in integrated companies, especially when combat was shared too, but that relations back in camp were less friendly. Harding and Hagrefe (1952) found that white department store assistants accepted Negroes as assistants too, but did not generalize this acceptance to personal friendships. The reduction of prejudice is apparently restricted to the contact situation. In the housing project it was reduced at a personal level because contact was enforced at that level, while work contact reduced prejudice in *that* situation but not at a personal level. It is thus important to remember that an attitude is not a single entity but the product of the interaction of several related components, and it is insufficient to impose physical integration in order to reduce prejudice. Both the affective and the cognitive components of attitudes require modification as well as the behavioural component, if attitudes are to be changed.

Further reading

See the reading list for Chapter 13.

13 Attitude change

Attitude change is dependent on many interrelating factors – differentiated and simplified for purposes of study, but in reality very difficult to separate. Hovland and Janis (1959) proposed a model of attitude change which includes as the main factors the source of the message and the message itself, the situation in which it is presented and the recipient of the message. Each of these may vary in such a way that it influences the degree of attitude change. Figure 87 illustrates some of the main factors involved in attitude change.

Characteristics of the recipient

It should be clear from the previous chapter that the formation and maintenance of attitudes derives from several sources. Some attitudes appear to be the result of conforming or complying with the norms of the group or groups of which an individual is a member. Others seem to develop to meet individual psychological needs, to act as ego-defensive attitudes. Some psychologists have developed attitude theories based on the study of the functions of attitudes, categorizing them in terms of the psychological functions they apparently serve. Smith *et al.* (1956) propose that some attitudes help in dealing with material reality and serve an object-appraisal function, others serve a social adjustment function and help in dealing with social relationships, and a third category of attitudes help in dealing with an individual's psychological reality and serve an externalization function by reflecting inner needs and problems. Katz (1960) also proposes functional categories of attitudes, along some-

87. *Characteristics of communications and recipients which influence attitude change*

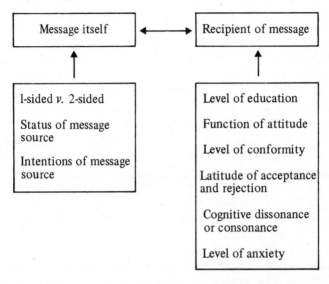

what similar lines to those of Smith *et al.*, but while the latter's categories are used mainly to describe and understand an individual's attitudes relative to his personality, Katz's functional categories have led to work in devising more effective ways of producing changes in attitudes.

Kelman (1961) argues that conformity to the views of others may differ in degree. He suggests three distinct processes, of compliance, identification and internalization, each occurring in different conditions and leading to different degrees of attitude change. As we have seen, compliance is a relatively superficial process in which an individual conforms to attitudes expressed by others in order to gain approval or avoid disapproval, regardless of what his private values might be. Kelman's concept of identification, not entirely equivalent to the Freudian term, describes the acceptance of the attitudes of others whose relationship with the individual is valued; such acceptance persists as long as the relationship with the significant other lasts. Internalization is the process in which an individual totally accepts the attitude of others because it closely fits his own existing values or needs, and, once accepted at this level, its maintenance is not dependent on a continuing relationship with others.

If attitudes do serve a variety of psychological functions, it follows that they will be more or less difficult to change, depending on the function they serve. Attitudes serving an object-appraisal function, or attitudes held at a level of compliance, are likely to be more amenable to change if circumstances and the climate of opinion change. This is less likely to be true of attitudes serving an externalization function, reflecting a deep, ego-defensive need; the resistance to attitude change shown by some prejudiced individuals and groups is one example of this.

There are other characteristics of the recipients of information intended to produce attitude change, which influence the degree of attitude change. Hovland *et al.* (1949), in a classic study of the effects of different types of communications on attitude change, gave one-sided arguments about the American war with Japan to one group of subjects, and two-sided arguments to a second group. Significantly more attitude change was produced in better educated subjects by the two-sided argument than by the one-sided argument, while among less well educated subjects, the one-sided argument produced greater attitude change. It may be that the educated soldiers had a self- image of not being swayed by one-sided information. However, Kelvin (1969) suggests that the less well educated were unused to handling conflicting arguments, and therefore merely continued to use their usual approach to the ordering of their environment, thus showing less attitude change in response to the two-sided information. The better educated, on the other hand, were not only more intellectually able to deal with conflicting views but were in fact accustomed to doing so. The lack of a two-sided argument created uncertainty for them, and the one-sided presentation of information therefore produced less attitude change in them. The Hovland study is frequently discussed as evidence of the effect of message characteristics on attitude change, but it also demonstrates that recipient characteristics play an important part in attitudes change too.

Sherif and Hovland (1961) proposed a concept of an individual's *latitude of acceptance* and *latitude of rejection* as another characteristic influencing attitude change. Their study produced evidence that any statement lying far outside an individual's range of feelings about an attitude object tends to be perceived by him as even more hostile or favourable than the statement really is. However, statements which are fairly close to his latitude of acceptance may gradually be accepted into his range of feelings about the attitude object, thus slightly shifting his latitude of acceptance. These slight modifications are reflected in a gradual change of attitudes. The selective interpretation of information in line with existing attitudes is a factor influencing the degree of attitude change possible for an individual.

Other individual differences in persuasibility have been found. Cohen (1959) found that subjects with a high degree of self-esteem tended to try to influence others more than did subjects with a low level of self-esteem, and were less easily persuaded by others, and it has been shown that inducing social anxiety in subjects by threatening criticism of their views made them more easily persuaded by others. Low-self-esteem subjects or socially anxious subjects appear to value their own opinions so little that they are less reluctant to change them when persuasion is applied than are high-self-esteem subjects (the development of self-esteem is discussed in Chapter 14). There is also some evidence of sex differences in persuasibility, and Janis and Field (1959) suggest that women change their attitudes more, and conform more to the opinions of others, than men do. This may reflect society's sex-role expectations rather than true individual differences, and this is supported by Abelson and Lesser's findings (1959) that sex differences in persuasibility exist in adolescent subjects, but not in children in their first year at school, when sex-role expectancies are less developed.

A group of theories of attitude change which have stimulated a major research effort in social psychology are those relating to the consistency or balance which apparently exists between an individual's values, beliefs and attitudes. Such theories are not new, though they have been variously labelled at different times. Despite some differences of emphasis, all share the assumption that an individual's system of attitudes is a balanced system, and that changes in one or more attitudes may produce an inconsistency or imbalance in the system which has to be minimized. For example, Heider (1946) argued for a balance theory, Osgood and Tannenbaum (1955) proposed a congruity theory, Festinger (1957) used the concept of consonance, and more recently, psychologists have preferred the idea of consistency as the basis of such theories.

Perhaps the most widely known of these consistency theories is Festinger's *theory of cognitive dissonance*, proposing that individuals will try to maintain internal psychological consistency or consonance between their particular cognitions, such as items of information, beliefs, values and attitudes. If one or more of these are in conflict, then cognitive dissonance results, and there ensues a psychological state of tension which motivates the individual to re-establish consonance, or balance, between all the things he knows about himself, his behaviour and his environment.

The degree of dissonance experienced depends in part on the importance to the individual of the conflicting cognitions, in part on the number of dissonant cognitions relative to the number of consonant cognitions, and in part on the degree of overlap between the dissonant cognitions. Someone 'torn between' joining in a week-end excursion and being at home for a special occasion will experience greater dissonance caused by the two contrasting cognitions than he would if the decision was between two more similar choices. The greater the dissonance, the more intense will be the motivation to reduce or avoid it.

Festinger also suggested that not only would the individual seek to reduce such dissonance, but that he would actively avoid any situation or information which might increase it, and also actively seek information consonant with his attitudes and cognitions. A number of studies have concluded that most people tend only to read or attend to what they already agree with: how many times have you literally or metaphorically 'switched off' when presented with views not consonant with your own cognitions? However, Ehrlich *et al.* (1957), in a study of purchasers of new cars, found that although they read 65% of advertisements about their own cars compared with only 40% of advertisements for other cars, the results seemed to stem from a tendency to prefer consonant information, rather than from a tendency to actively avoid dissonant information. Later studies have led to similar conclusions (Freedman and Sears, 1965; Sears, 1968): that people attend to consonant information rather than that they actively seek to avoid dissonant information, and that attitudes are more usually expressed in appropriate behaviours than in avoidance behaviours.

Festinger's theory has implications for various decision-making situations. Having to decide between equally attractive alternatives creates dissonance and in turn pressure to reduce it. Brehm (1966) investigated whether, given a free choice between alternatives, subjects reduced dissonance by decreasing the apparent attractiveness of the rejected alternative. Half his female subjects were tested in a high-dissonance experimental condition, having to choose between two almost identically desirable household items after being told that they could keep the chosen item. The other subjects were in a low-dissonance condition, choosing between items separated by three points on a 'desirability' scale. Post-testing on subjects' ratings of the desirability of items showed that subjects did appear to reduce dissonance by increasing the attractiveness of the chosen item and decreasing the attractiveness of the rejected item.

A free choice between alternatives does not always exist, and some situations may be ones of forced compliance to a particular type of behaviour which is dissonant with an individual's private values, where he is pressured by threats of punishments of various kinds, or by the possibility of reward. The proportion of dissonant to consonant cognitions partly determines the degree of dissonance experienced, and the prospect of a valued reward may act to reduce dissonance by increasing the proportion of consonant cognitions. Kelman (1953) pre-tested schoolchildren to determine their preferred comic-book heroes and then asked them to write essays favouring other heroes. Half wrote believing that free film tickets for the whole class were available as a reward for compliance, while the others expected a reward of only five tickets for the whole class. Both groups complied and changed their earlier preferential attitudes somewhat, but the five-ticket reward group changed most. Festinger's dissonance theory would interpret this by suggesting that for the first experimental group the generous reward increased the proportion of consonant cognitions relative to dissonant cognitions, and 'justified' the group's action of writing essays they did not really believe in. This achieved a reasonable balance between consonant and dissonant cognitions, and hence minimal cognitive dissonance. For the second group, however, the smaller reward was insufficient to achieve such a balance, and some real attitude change towards the attitude objects was also needed in order to balance the consonant–dissonant cognitions and reduce dissonance.

A careful consideration of the implications of such results, and of those obtained by Ehrlich *et al.* and discussed above, illustrates the dynamic relationship between attitudes and behaviour. The Ehrlich study suggests that attitudes lead to behaviours which are consistent with them – that is, appropriate behaviours, or perhaps avoidance behaviours – while the Kelman work indicates that in some circumstances behaviours may induce attitude change. However, most of the research on counter-attitudinal role playing, such as that of

Festinger and Carlsmith (1959) up to more recent work by Fishbein and Ajzen (1975), tends to demonstrate the great complexity of behaviour–attitude relationships. (For a more complete review of such research, see Elms, in Warren and Jahoda (1973), Chapter 11.) The nature of the rewards offered, the timing of their presentation, the social situations in which they are offered, are all factors which influence the degree of dissonance arousal and reduction.

Though dissonance theory has generated a large body of research, it has also generated some controversy and some modifications. Brehm and Cohen (1962) argue that an individual's *commitment* to a particular cognition or attitude will influence dissonance arousal and reduction, and that it forms an essential construct in dissonance theory. Limited commitment enables an easy dismissal or modification of a cognition in a dissonance-arousing or dissonance-reducing situation, while greater commitment will make such flexibility more difficult. Aronson (1968) points to the importance of the relationship between self-concept and cognitions about a particular behaviour, and argues that dissonance is less about inconsistencies between cognitions than about inconsistencies between an individual's self-concept and his behaviour. It is certainly true that succeeding stages of dissonance theory have moved from Festinger's initial broad definition of dissonance through several attempts to identify increasingly specific situations in which dissonance is likely to occur. Festinger himself does not claim that dissonance theory is a complete explanation of attitude change, and acknowledges the importance of other processes such as learning, while Chapanis and Chapanis (1964) provide a critical review of dissonance theory and its experimental techniques. Kelvin (1969) suggests that a consistency theory of attitude change is 'somewhat metaphysical and potentially beyond disproof', and argues that since there are alternative ways of achieving attitudinal consistency, experimental testing of consistency theory and the interpretation and replication of data are frequently difficult. The fact that there are many ways of achieving attitudinal consistency diminishes the explanatory power of consistency theory, providing description rather than explanation. However, consistency can be viewed as a basic characteristic of attitude systems, and attitude systems themselves as an individual's method of ordering his environment and his actions upon it.

Characteristics of the message

Hovland's experiment (1949), discussed earlier, is only one of many which have considered how different types of communications relate to attitude change. In order to have any real effect on attitude, the message must of course be credible, and this relates to two important factors – the content of the message, and the credibility of its source.

Janis and Feshback (1963) presented three groups of subjects with information on dental hygiene designed to arouse three different levels of fear and emotional reaction to the prospect of tooth decay. Post-test checks on attitude change showed that only 8% of the maximum-fear group had adopted the practices urged in the message, while 25% and 32% had changed in the moderate- and minimal-fear groups respectively. One explanation of these results is that the more extreme messages lay so far outside the recipients' latitude of acceptance that they seemed more impossible than they really were, provoking a reaction of 'It couldn't happen to me' and hence undermining the credibility of the message to the recipients. Leventhal *et al.* (1965), however, found a positive relationship between the level of fear and attitude change, in an experiment using messages about tetanus: greater levels of fear led to greater changes in beliefs about the importance of preventative immunization. What did emerge was that in order to translate changed attitude into actual behaviours, specific details of *how* to behave were required, such as precisely where and when immunization was available. A further factor which may have influenced the experimental group given this additional information was that they were told that the medical authorities were expecting some response from the subjects. The combination of this expectancy plus specific information about possible behaviour helps to explain the differences between these results and those of Janis and Feshback, though McGuire (1968) suggests that attitude change follows an inverted U-shaped pattern, with increased fear producing attitude change up to a certain optimum, but thereafter provoking defensive avoidance reactions.

The style in which the message is presented has implications for attitude change, as the work on one- and two-sided communications showed. Some messages use clear and explicit arguments for a particular point of view, while others transmit an implicit message, apparently leaving the recipient to reach what seem to him to be his own conclusions. Sargent (1939) made a careful study of journalists' use of 'loaded' words to create the attitudes favoured by their particular newspapers, and since then many analyses have been made of media messages. Whether implicit or explicit attempts are more effective in promoting attitude change is, again, related to recipient characteristics. McGuire (1968) argues that implicit messages may be more effective if one can be certain that the recipients can and will reach their own conclusions. Some experimental studies seem to favour explicit messages as more effective for attitude change (Hovland and Mandell, 1952), though these may reflect characteristics of the recipients, such as low intelligence or motivation, rather than the effectiveness of the explicit message itself. Clearly, attitude change is a product of the interaction between message characteristics and recipient characteristics.

A further important influence on the credibility of a communication is the source of the message and the recipient's perception of the value of that source; again, the interaction of the two should be noted. A prestigious or expert source of information is more likely to effect a change of attitude than an unknown or unreliable source. However, the similarity between the source of the message and its recipient is important too, and friendship and liking for the communicator influences his effectiveness in attitude change. McGuire (1968) proposes that in laboratory situations, conflict between the credibility of powerful and prestigious figures and that of peers usually produces a tendency to believe communications from the superior source – though in real life, peers are more important instigators of attitude change, perhaps because contact with them is much more frequent than with power figures.

Hovland and Weiss (1951) investigated types of sources and their effects on attitude change, pre-testing for subjects' views on a variety of topics, some of which were critical for the experiment. Subjects were later given articles to read, some apparently emanating from a high-credibility source such as a medical journal, others from low-credibility sources such as a popular newspaper. Post-tests showed 22.5% and 8.4% attitude change in the direction suggested in the message for the high- and low-credibility sources respectively. Kelman and Hovland (1953) demonstrated like findings in a similarly designed experiment, with pre-testing for attitudes towards juvenile delinquency followed by exposure to tape-recordings of talks by a high-credibility source ('a juvenile court judge'), a low-credibility source ('a dope peddler'), and a neutral source ('a randomly chosen

member of a studio audience'). Post-tests showed the greatest attitude change towards leniency for the high-credibility source and the
least for the low-credibility source, even though the actual message
was the same for each of the three experimental groups.

Walster and Festinger (1962) found that the perceived intention of
a communicator also influenced attitude change, with information
obtained in an 'overheard' manner being more effective in changing
attitude than information given direct to subjects, as long as the
information related to issues in which subjects were personally involved. An overheard source seems to acquire greater credibility
because the communicator is not, apparently, giving the information
to suit his own purposes, while a direct presentation of information may imply that the communicator has a particular interest in
pressing his own view.

The recipient's perception of the source of a communication is not
only important as a factor influencing attitude change, but also as a
determinant of the meaning attributed to the message. Asch (1952)
presented some subjects with a quotation supposedly originating
from Lenin, and others with the same one attributed to Jefferson.
Although in fact the quotation was by Jefferson and the same for all
subjects, arguing the merits of rebellion, the subjects who were told
that Lenin was the source interpreted the word 'rebellion' as revolution, while those believing Jefferson was the source interpreted it as
agitation.

A careful consideration of the evidence presented in this section
makes it clear that the characteristics of messages are inseparable
from the characteristics of recipients of messages. The relationship
between contributory factors in attitude change is not simple.

Attitude change in everyday life

Experimental evidence about attitude change is important for an
understanding of the process, but persuasion is a part of everyday
life too. Hovland (1959) noted that although attitude change can be
relatively easily manipulated in laboratory studies, the effectiveness
of attempts to change attitudes in real life is generally much less
successful.

Persuading others to adopt particular beliefs, values and attitudes
may involve a variety of techniques, some of which are informal and

not deliberately intent on attitude change, while others do involve some measure of intent. An example of informal techniques of attitude change is group discussion, in which individuals may be exposed to views different from their own and in which they may argue for their own personal values and beliefs. Hammond *et al.* (1959) found that attitude change about social aspects of care in a group of medical students was most effective when practical experience of their patients' home backgrounds was supplemented by discussions during group sessions with minimal tutor direction. A similar technique is also used, though rather more deliberately, in changing attitudes towards others in a group; this is a well-established therapeutic technique for helping mentally disturbed individuals and has more recently been used as an experience for mentally healthy individuals. *Encounter groups* (Rogers, 1967) provide an opportunity for people to experience an atmosphere in which feelings and emotions are emphasized and can be expressed without the usual social inhibitions. Negative attitudes, aggression and interpersonal conflicts are typical of the early group interactions, but as these are worked through, supported by group feedback and discussions, individuals can achieve more favourable attitudes towards themselves and others. The total process is not easy or comfortable, but if it is handled adroitly by the group leader the positive outcomes can be considerable. A third example of the use of group discussion to change attitudes is that of *T-groups*, or *training groups* (Smith, 1969), in which trainees discuss at length their interrelationships as group members. The behaviours of individuals are discussed and the consequences for others evaluated, reactions to each other are expressed, and T-group members tend to improve both the relevance and flexibility of their responses within groups and their sensitivity to interpersonal reactions between themselves and others.

Another informal technique with implications for attitude change is that of role playing. Role relationships constitute an important aspect of social life, and role occupants tend to have a particular set of behavioural and attitudinal expectations which they and others associate with their role. Individuals find themselves occupying particular roles and combinations of roles at different times during their lives – sibling, parent, occupational roles such as teacher, plumber or shopkeeper, teenager or old-age pensioner, and many others. An analysis of roles and the expectations associated with them helps clarify the relationship between society and individuals; and, for example, Milgram's obedience experiments (see Chapter 10) demonstrate the power of the expectations associated with the experimenter and subject roles. Lieberman (1956), in a study of workers who were promoted to foremen, concluded that individuals acquiring new patterns of behaviour as a result of changing roles also changed their attitudes in a pro-management direction. Several experimental studies suggest that attitudes change can be achieved if subjects are induced to role play – that is, actually to behave in a way that implies acceptance of a particular set of attitudes and beliefs. The Kelman experiment (1953) discussed in the previous section is one such study, and Elms (1969) discusses many others.

Culturally defined roles, or formal roles, can be differentiated from the more informal roles and sets of expectations which develop within specific relationships and enable individuals to understand, and respond to, the behaviours of others in these relationships. In interactions, people tend to take particular role identities and behave accordingly, and if the behaviour is successful and elicits a satisfactory response, then the initial self-concept underlying the role identity is reinforced. However, if a person's social and expressive abilities are inadequate he may be unable to elicit the response he would like, and may thus be unable to obtain any reinforcement or legitimation of his own self-concept. This can be psychologically damaging for some individuals, and role playing is sometimes used as a therapeutic technique to help in establishing and developing self-confidence and self-esteem. In other words, there is a considerable weight of evidence that occupying a role, or even just 'acting' a role, helps to change attitudes in the direction of the expectations associated with the role.

More formal attempts to change attitudes include the techniques of propaganda and advertising. Both propaganda and advertising are familiar overt attempts to change attitudes, and though propaganda is commonly assumed to have rather sinister overtones, this is not necessarily so. Health improvement propaganda and road safety propaganda are just two examples of deliberate campaigns to change attitudes and beliefs in the direction of particular values and attitudes. While propaganda tends to relate to attitudes towards social issues, however, advertising is intended to change attitudes and beliefs about commercial products and their producers. Advertising today is an elaborate, sophisticated, multi-media process, and the level of commercial investment in advertising reflects the advertisers' perceptions of its value to them. The subtle messages expressed in many TV commercials are frequently as important in the advertising process as the product information itself. Viewers are not simply shown a toilet roll, for instance, and told about its properties, but are also exposed to carefully chosen images of affluent country living, and appealing young animals and children, reinforcing the ideas of gentleness and softness with which the advertisers are trying to persuade us to buy their product. The techniques of propaganda and advertising are very similar; the differences lie largely in the content of the messages being communicated.

Education is another technique by which attitudes and beliefs are both formed and changed, and schooling is a formal expression of this. Education is usually differentiated from the process of propaganda by its aim of imparting knowledge. In practice it plays an important covert role in the formation and modification of attitudes and beliefs because teachers interpret knowledge as well as imparting it, and their interpretation is related to their own attitudes and beliefs. Impartiality in disseminating knowledge is difficult, and the selection of a curriculum and its content will reflect educators', and ultimately society's, attitudes and values. However, education is a process which occurs in many other settings apart from schools, each of which can contribute to attitude modification.

The role of the mass media in today's society would suggest that it too is an important and effective agent of attitude change, yet in practice it seems that, with some exceptions, it is difficult to produce mass changes in attitudes and beliefs associated with issues that people really care about. The health education and road safety campaigns mentioned earlier seem to stimulate slight changes of attitudes immediately after each intensive campaign, but these effects tend to be short-lived. For all the very expensive, multi-media election campaigns mounted during American presidential election years, only about 8% of voters change their voting attitudes and opinions during the year. Important, deeply held attitudes with which people have a personal involvement display high resistance to change, and require intensive and long-term exposure to persuasive techniques to modify them.

Resistance to attitude change is the result of the activity of many variables, some of which have been discussed earlier. The level of committment to an attitude, especially if commitment is made publicly, has a strong influence on whether it is easy or difficult to change. Personal factors such as the function of the attitude for the individual, his personality, motivation and ideology, all make their contribution to resistance to change, as does the status of the source of the message. McGuire (1964) investigated methods of increasing resistance to attitude change, drawing an analogy with the medical process of immunization. He argues that one way of increasing resistance to persuasion is to provide support and reinforcement for existing attitudes, in the same way that diet and exercise contribute to a healthy body. A second method is to improve defences against attitude change, rather than to strengthen the attitudes held, by subjecting the individual to a mild attack on his attitudes, insufficient to change them, but sufficient to stimulate a defence of them. Help may also be needed to show the subject how to argue against the attack, or by denigrating the source of the attack, but once a persuasive message has been successfully resisted, further persuasion is less likely to succeed. McGuire proposes that some commonly held attitudes and beliefs or 'cultural truisms' are very vulnerable to persuasion, partly through lack of practice in defending them and partly through lack of motivation to defend them, as widely held attitudes should by definition not need defending. McGuire and Papageorgis (1961) studied the effect of support and inoculation methods in resisting attitude change using three experimental groups: one merely received support for their existing attitudes, the second received weak attacks and support in refuting them and the third acted as a control group. A strong attack on the attitudes of all three groups clearly indicated that while the support-only method improved resistance, it was the weak attack-and-support (inoculation) method which was most successful in helping resistance to attitude change.

Further reading

Fishbein, M. (ed.) (1967), *Readings in Attitude Theory and Measurement*, Wiley

Insko, C.A. (1967), *Theories of Attitude Change*, Appleton-Century-Crofts

Kelvin, P. (1969), *The Bases of Social Behaviour* (Chapters 1–3), Holt, Rinehart and Winston

Reich, B. and Adcock, C. (1976), *Values, Attitudes and Behaviour Change*, Methuen Essential Psychology Series

Warren, N. and Jahoda, M. (eds.) (1966), *Attitudes*, Penguin

14 Social perception

Social perception, the process of recognizing the attitudes, motives and abilities of ourselves and others, is governed by many of the factors that influence object perception, discussed in Chapter 2. However, perception affects our responses to people and objects. The difference here lies in the fact that people will alter their own behaviour in response to the way that they are treated. If a teacher perceives his student as intelligent he may teach in a different way and get a different response than he might if he were to perceive the same student as dim-witted. Paradoxically, in this way a perceptual hypothesis (see p. 70) may alter the real world.

Self-perception

Many of us feel that we alone really know ourselves, that only we are privy to our own inner thoughts and 'real nature'. And yet many people are fascinated by the attitude tests and personality profiles that proliferate in the popular press, and take great interest in their results. During adolescence there is a particularly acute demand for information and evaluation from other people about ourselves – 'What kind of person do you think I am?', 'How do you find me?' If we choose to ignore other people's evaluations, how confident can we be in the accuracy of our own self-judgement? It may be thought that because of internal perceptions and thoughts we have special knowledge about ourselves. But we do not see how others perceive us. Brown (1967) gives the example of the individual who 'forces a smile' in a social situation: 'The organism that thinks it is the only one that knows its smile is forced should see the face the rest of us see.'

The field of self-perception has greatly increased in influence and impact in recent psychology. This is largely due to the counselling and therapeutic work associated with Carl Rogers, and various trends in society which have led individuals in the direction of exploration and liberation of the self. So what do we mean by the term '*self*'? As we shall see, there is no real agreement amongst the leading theorists, but a working definition will serve the purpose of beginning our discussion. Murphy (1947) says, 'The self is the individual as known to the individual.' This emphasizes existence in consciousness, but would, consequently, be unacceptable to Freudians, who argue that the contributory sources and construction of the self are unconscious.

Secord and Backman (1964) propose three aspects to the self: the cognitive, the affective and the behavioural. The cognitive component represents such judgements as 'I am tall, blue-eyed, blond-haired, male', and so on; these are essentially descriptive; an affective component represents one's feelings towards oneself, and may not often be expressed in words. It would include a general self-evaluation as well as specific judgements, such as someone seeing himself or herself as being honest. The behavioural component is the tendency to act towards ourself in various ways: a person may behave in a self-deprecating or a self-indulgent manner, or may show over-sensitivity to some of his characteristics.

It has been said by Argyle (1967), 'The more integrated the self-image, the more consistent a person's behaviour will be: one effect of the self-image on behaviour is the supression of behaviour that is out of line.' We can thus see the interrelationship of the different components of the self.

The term 'self' is one of the current century. Previously writers talked of the 'soul', 'nature', 'will' and so on. Its importance has, however, been long recognized. In more recent years Bidney (1953) suggested that it is the possession of a self-concept rather than language that differentiates man from the lower animals. He says that only man has the ability to see himself objectively; to stand apart from himself, and consider what he is and what he would like to do and become. The first psychological, as opposed to philosophical, contribution of note on the self came from William James, in his famous *Principles of Psychology* (1890). Burns (1979) says, 'His writing marks the change between older and newer ways of thinking about self. He was strikingly objective in his treatment of the problem and hurled stinging criticism at earlier philosophic notions.' James conceived the self to be composed of two elements: the Me and the I. The distinction is that 'Me' is the self as an object (a body, a voice, a set of abilities and so on), and 'I' is the judging thought. The individual can be aware of his body, his actions and even his personality in a removed, quasi-objective sense. The central viewer, the self of selves, is the I in James's theory. This distinction proves to be a major influence in self theory. James went on to argue that the object self (Me) has four components: the spiritual self, the material self, the social self and bodily self. These cluster around the I to form a global self. Certainly the self is multi-faceted, and comprises a number of judgements on different criteria. Erikson (1956) says that to have formed a good 'ego-identity' is to have a feeling of 'being at home in one's body, a sense of knowing where one is going, and an inner assurance of anticipated recognition from those who count'.

It is generally agreed that the first aspect of the self to develop is an appreciation of its physical boundaries, the body. In the first few months of life, the child does not distinguish himself from his environment: as he sees his hand on the cot rail and they appear visually linked, he does not conceptually differentiate them. Gradually, however, the youngster comes to recognize the independence of his own existence – eventually in terms of recognition of the control he has over his actions, though initially he differentiates only between his body and the rest of the world, the body being 'self' and everything else 'non-self'. Allport (1955) says, 'The first aspect we encounter is the bodily me. It seems to be composed of streams of sensations that arise within the organism.' Thus by feeling and being affected by our own body we first come to separate our self from the outside world.

Body image is often an important aspect of self in adult life. Are we too thin, too fat, too tall, too short, ugly or attractive? In a society such as ours where a considerable emphasis is placed upon physical appearance, and especially the social desirability of certain body shapes, it is easy to understand why a person's perception of his own body can assume quite disproportionate importance. 'Body fashions' change over the years: Jourard and Secord reported in 1956 that males were most pleased when their bodies were large, whereas women liked their bodies to be small but with large busts, but quite a different picture would probably emerge today. In our society in recent years the illness anorexia nervosa has greatly increased in incidence, especially amongst adolescent girls. In this condition girls starve themselves in order to become slim, attractive and liked by others. The cause of the illness is not fully understood; in fact, it appears unlikely to be attributable to any one single factor. It seems to be a combination of a need for genuine love and support (hence the need to look slim and attractive), and an instrumentally conditioned response in which the hunger pangs associated with not eating become highly valued and rewarding. Anorexia nervosa involves all three self areas listed by Secord and Backman: a girl may see herself as being fat (cognitive), regard this as undesirable, thinking that others will find her unlovable (affective), and be obsessed with losing weight (behavioural). One of the central features of the illness is the distortion of the body image that afflicts the sufferer. Advanced cases, who have starved themselves down to a skeletal five stones, tragically still see themselves as fat and so continue 'slimming'.

Hardy and Heyes (1979) discuss the importance of the body image as a part of the self-concept. It appears to be particularly heavily weighted by adolescents. They cite an experiment by Arnhoff and Damiaopoulos (1962), showing that twenty-year-olds had a more definite body image than forty-year-olds. They took photographs of individuals dressed only in shorts and blotted out their faces; the younger subjects were better at recognizing their own photographs from a group of six than were the forty-year-olds.

Studies carried out at the University of California suggest that the time at which the adolescent growth-spurt occurs may have an important effect on the self-concept. A boy who matures late will find that his peers start to race ahead of him in size and strength, that their voices change and that they start to grow body hair. Suddenly a boy who has compared favourably with his contemporaries may feel immature in comparison.

Social theories of the self
As Kuhn (1960) has shown, as we grow older the self-image becomes less physically oriented and increasingly referred to social considerations. When asked to answer the question 'Who am I?' in twenty statements, seven-year-olds used few social categories (only approximately 25% of total descriptions given), whereas the profiles of

twenty-four-year-olds studied showed 50% of the categories used were social ones. After the young child comes to recognize his inner, bodily sensations and 'claim' these as belonging to himself, the self has begun to grow and becomes increasingly based in the outside, social world. He realizes that he has a means of social reference, his name, and has become treated as an individual who is held responsible for his actions.

Cooley (1902) was the first writer to emphasize the importance of the socialized self. He said, 'The self that is most important is a reflection, largely from the minds of others.' It is as if we project ourselves into the minds of people watching us to see how they perceive us. He goes on, 'A self-idea of this sort seems to have three principal elements: the imagination of our *appearance* to the other person; the imagination of his *judgment* of that appearance; and some sort of *self-feeling*, such as pride or mortification' (our italics).

An illustration of the power of social feedback in affecting self-perception and consequent behaviour is given by Guthrie (1938), who tells a story about one of his students – a girl who was considered generally to be dull and unattractive. Some of her classmates decided to play what was initially a rather cruel joke on the girl by treating her as though she were the most attractive and interesting girl in the college. They drew lots to decide who should ask her out first, who second and so on. Guthrie noticed that by the time the fifth or sixth boy came to ask her out he did not consider it such a chore; by the end of term the girl had become an interesting and confident type. She had changed her behaviour. The girl's new self-esteem meant that people came to really find her interesting.

Cooley's so-called '*looking glass theory*' clearly influenced the thinking of G.H. Mead (1934), who argued that the self-concept arises as a result of the individual's concern about how others regard him. To enable himself to anticipate the responses of other people, he learns to see and interpret the world in the same way that they do. This leads to what he called 'a *generalized other*'. Mead says,

The self arises in conduct, when the individual becomes a social object in experience to himself. This takes place when the individual assumes the attitude or gesture which another individual could use and responds to it himself or tends to so respond.... The child gradually becomes a social being in his own experience, and he acts towards himself in a manner analogous to that in which he acts toward others.

He learns through play, interaction and observation. He may, for example, play out the parts of mother and father as they talk to each other, and consequently come to see himself, indirectly, as a social object that is talked to and responded to.

Mead goes on to suggest that the self which has developed in this way has two elements: a set of inner, individual drives and capacities – that is, what sets him apart from others (the I); and a social self – what he has in common with others (the Me). Mead argues that all actions begin as I – individual needs and demands – and end up as Me – socially moderated and acceptable behaviours. As Burns puts it, 'I provides propulsion, Me the direction.' We are talking, therefore, about the socialization of the self, as the individual learns to behave in a social way which will ultimately maximize his drive satisfaction. But we must emphasize the *gradual* nature of the shift into the world of social models and considerations. The difficulty of developing a self-identity in childhood is shown by the ease with which a child depersonalizes himself in play and speech. It is not until the age of about four or five that the child's self-image becomes fairly stable; but thereafter it becomes an individual's surest proof of his own existence.

One problem which the individual faces as he grows older is that beyond childhood and adolescence we provide and receive much less honest evaluative comment from others. Children tend to speak directly and bluntly, but this can be hurtful and distressing, so as adults we become 'tactful' and diplomatic in what we say to others. The problem is then, that as social discretion increases, accuracy of feedback often dwindles. However, to naïvely suggest that as adults we should be more frank and forthright in the information we provide would be likely to produce other problems, for experience with T-groups (see Chapter 13) has shown that such direct feedback can be very distressing.

A different way of looking at social influences upon behaviour is that of *role theory*. As Argyle says, 'Roles provide an easy solution to the problem of ego-identity – there is a clear public identity to adopt.' The fact that we choose to be seen as an academic, a vicar or a shop-steward speaks volumes for how we see ourselves. Goffman (1961) says:

It is important to note that in performing a role the individual must see to it that the impressions of him that are conveyed in the social situation are comparable with role-appropriate personal qualities imputed to him: a judge is supposed to be deliberate and sober; a pilot, in a cockpit, to be cool; a book-keeper to be accurate and neat in doing his work. These personal qualities, effectively imputed and effectively claimed, combine with a position's title, when there is one, to provide a basis of self-image for the incumbent and a basis for the image that others will have of him. A self, then, virtually awaits the individual entering a position; he need only conform to the pressures on him and he will find one ready-made for him.

The most interesting part of Goffman's theory, however, concerns the way in which the individual plays his roles. He sees us as actors playing parts; that is, however convincing our behaviour is, we are aware that it is not 'us', but merely a social position or presentation. The parts are used as social identities to tell people 'who we are' at any particular moment, and how we wish to be treated. Goffman emphasizes that we maintain a distance between our 'self' and the part being played: it is as if we put a mask over our face. He thus talks of the 'management' and 'presentation' of the self.

What happens if the feedback from others is negative or threatening? A superficial reading of the social theories of self might suggest that the self is 'reality-adjusted' and so the individual would see himself as less worthy and valued. However, the contributions from psychiatry and depth psychology give us a different picture. One of the most dramatic statements of the outcome of social rejection comes from Laing (1960), writing about the origins of schizophrenia. He talks of the existence of a true, inner self and a social, performed self which is constructed in early childhood to please and gain parents' favour. In certain cases the child feels unable to display the true, inner self, either because it is rejected by the parents, or because he feels it would be rejected if he were to show it. The embryonic schizophrenic then hides the inner self away from danger (it is 'disembodied'), and the division between this self and the performed self becomes total. We thus see the model of the schizophrenic as portrayed by the popular media – the classic display of the split personality. The social self becomes a satirical caricature – more extreme, and reflecting the behaviour of others. The schizophrenic wants to be his true self but is fearful of the consequences. Eventually the desire to 'be himself' and reject the artificial social self becomes too strong, and the outer self is ripped away. This decision is frequently sudden and dramatic. One man ran naked into the sea to baptize the emergence of the new self! For many, however, the effects are not liberating, and the sufferer withdraws into himself.

With the killing of the social self the catatonic schizophrenic becomes totally removed from the real world, and his behaviour shows
no form of social influence at all.

We should emphasize that acceptance of Laing's theory that the
family is the causal agent in cases of schizophrenia is far from
universal; many writers, for example, believe that the illness is genetically transmitted. However, Laing does provide a powerful picture
of the disintegration of the self, and the rift between the self as
viewer and the self as object which was first coherently identified by
James.

Contributions from depth theorists

We have just seen how one consequence of powerful negative feedback may be the disintegration of the self as we know it. Less
dramatically, but more typically, the response to such threat may be
denial, repression and the invocation of other psychological defence
mechanisms. The individual denies the validity of *reality checks*.

The greatest protagonist of unconscious influence was, of course,
Freud (see also Chapter 8). The closest we come to the self-concept
in his writings is the ego. Mead's concept of the I and Me, for
example, is very similar to the Freudian id-ego relationship, discussed earlier. As we have seen, Freud stressed the importance of the
unconscious, as the roots of the ego lie in this part of the mind. We
can see how this conceptualization of the self is in marked contrast
to the earlier theories of self that we have examined. You may recall
our initial definition of the self by Murphy ('The self is the individual
as known to the individual'); it is evident that Freudian theory views
the self in a markedly different way. This different perspective provided by the writings of Freud has given us many insights. Burns
says, 'His material allowed him to see more clearly than others that
irrational unconscious determiners of behaviour had to be reckoned
with.'

Not all psychoanalysts agree with Freud, the founding father; for
example, Adler (1927) views the self as being almost exclusively
governed by conscious factors. He believes that our behaviour is
motivated by the goal of 'self-assertion'. We wish to engineer our
lives so that our inferior positions are minimally important and
influential, and activities in which we excel (whether they be practical, emotional, academic or whatever) are maximized. Our inferiori-
ties and shortcomings, whether real or imagined, lead to what Adler

384 Understanding Psychology

called 'our life style'; our 'life plans' aim to overcome or compensate for them.

We thus see opposition between the ideas of Freud and Adler – the former suggesting that the drive system behind behaviour is the unconscious id and the latter suggesting that it is the conscious drive system of perceived superiority. Perhaps, however, part of the difference may be attributed to semantics, for whereas we can classify Adler as a self theorist, Freud did not talk directly of the self, but, as we pointed out, only of the ego. In what senses do the terms differ? Symonds (1951) says that the distinction is chiefly one between perception and process. The ego is a balancing process which aims by expediency and diplomacy to gratify the drives of the id, whereas the self (at least the self that Adler talks about) is concerned with the way the individual sees himself and his world, and evaluates them.

The brief psychoanalytic picture presented here is completed by Jung (see Chapter 8), who believes that the self is a total of both conscious *and* unconscious elements. He argues that it represents our striving for unity and wholeness – an equilibrium between the conscious and unconscious levels.

One interesting development is that Jung believes the self does not emerge until middle age, when all the elements of personality are fully developed. This is in contrast to his earlier colleague, Freud, who thinks that personality development is completed by adolescence. The difference is chiefly due to Freud's total emphasis upon sexuality as the driving and moulding force of the personality. Consequently, for Freud, once sexual development is complete, so is the personality. Many years later, Erikson (1950) adapted psychoanalysis from Freud's psychosexual model to his own psychosocial one. He said that our 'ego-identity' is shaped by our interactions with significant social others, beginning with the mother and generalizing out through the family to the relevant micro-society, including school, work and loved ones. Because the nature of this shaping and the relevant others changes in an orderly and structured manner (there are eight 'basic ages of man' beginning in the first year of life and going through into old age), Erikson argues that static theories of the self are misleading: identity changes and evolves with age. Like Freud, however, Erikson believes that the most influential factors are for the most part unconscious. He goes on to claim that an optimal sense of identity is a sense of knowing where one is going and of inner assuredness.

One of the most influential personality theorists, G.W. Allport, suggested (1955) that since terms such as 'self', 'I' and, previously 'soul' arouse such emotional involvement, a new, neutral term should be introduced: he suggested *'proprium'*. He said that the centre of the proprium is 'self as knower', that is, the core self which sees and evaluates. The full propriate functions are:

Bodily sense: sensations and the sense of self-boundary or enclosedness
Self-identity: the realization of autonomy and the ability to affect the environment
Ego enhancement: the value of self-preservation and achievement
Ego extension: the extension of the self into the outside world (for example, through possessions and interest- or political-group membership)
Rational agent: the ego function
Self-image: the perceived self, comprising two elements – the current evaluation of self and the ideal self
Propriate striving: our pursuit of the ideal self
The knower

The aspects of the proprium are what make us different from others, and it is our perceptions of these which comprise the cognizing self, 'the knower that transcends all other functions of the proprium and holds them in view'. He says:

> The self as knower emerges as a final and inescapable postulate.... We not only know things, but we know (i.e., we are acquainted with) the empirical features of our own proprium. It is I who have bodily sensations, I who recognize my self-identity from day to day, I who note and reflect upon my self-interests and strivings. When I thus think about my own propriate functions I am likely to perceive their essential togetherness, and feel them intimately bound in some way to the knowing function itself.

Allport, in a later work (1961), developed the model into a developmental structure, and argued, like Jung, that the self is not complete until middle age.

Stability and change in the self-image
In our considerations of the various theories of the self we have noted that some writers view it as relatively static and fixed whereas others regard it as changing and flexible. We now turn our attention to a consideration of the factors which make for stability and those which cause change in the self-image.

The self may sometimes be highly resilient to change. We have noted Laing's work with schizophrenics which led him to contend that the patient withdraws behind a social performance because he fears for the existence of his 'true' self (which he locks away in order to ensure its preservation). Many works of fiction of the 'one person versus the system' concentrate upon the prime integrity of the self and the need to protect its existence *in toto*. A television series which gathered a cult following in the late seventies, *The Prisoner*, concentrates upon the dilemma of reality and self: is the character a prisoner of a mysterious society or a prisoner of his own distorted mind? As he seeks escape from an exotic, oppressive environment, the only certain reference-point he has is the solidity of his own 'inner' self. As long as he has this unchanging and stable point of reference he is strong; but could it be that the 'society' is the production of his own (paranoid) mind?

We would probably all agree that self-concept should be modified against reality, but over-flexibility is just as characteristic of mental disorder as over-rigidity, as Bannister (1962) has shown.

Maintaining and stabilizing the self-image
The findings below, by Secord and Backman, indicate the ways in which the individual is able to maintain and stabilize his self-image.

Misperception External events are not received 'directly'; we perceive and interpret them. The Phenomenologists claim that it is not reality but our perception of it which influences us. Therefore one of the ways the individual protects the self is to misperceive incoming negative evaluation. We may actually deceive ourselves that valued others like or admire us when in fact they may hold us in disdain. Many a tearful love story has been woven around this theme.

Selective interaction A person elects to interact with those persons with whom he can most readily establish a 'congruent state'; for example, if he regards himself as especially intelligent, he interacts frequently with persons who respect his intelligence, or who allow him to exercise it.

Response evocation A person can, by behaving and dressing in a particular way, evoke particular responses. The modern-day Teddy

Boy who dresses in the rock-and-roll fashion of the fifties will, by his appearance, increase the likelihood of people responding to him in a manner which will reinforce his self-image.

Selective evaluation of the other person A number of studies have shown that when a person is negatively evaluated by another the former reduces the status and liking of that person, thereby negating the person's opinions and averting possible damage to the self-image or to self-esteem. Thus the views of 'unimportant' others offer no threat to the self-image, even if their views are at odds with it.

Selective evaluation of the self We weight the importance of various aspects of our selves, so that if we are regarded as physically weak we may downgrade the importance of 'muscle power' and concentrate upon other, more positive features. In this example, we would not change our low estimation of our strength: it would simply be seen as unimportant.

Affective congruency In several investigations a variety of defence mechanisms were employed by individuals in response to unfavourable reactions from others. Such people were, for example, ignored, disliked, discredited, distorted or not believed.

Social factors
Roles The adoption and playing of certain roles is a stabilizing factor because roles make behaviour more stereotyped, uniform and predictable. By occupying certain positions individuals are both consistently defined by others and reinforced in their own self-perception.

Constancy of interaction We tend to spend most of our social lives in the company of a relatively unchanging group of friends and colleagues. This means that we tend to receive fairly stable feedback on ourselves, since the source of feedback is constant. Even if the actual people we interact with change, the *positions* usually do not, for we tend to stay in certain socio-economic classes, occupations and so on.

Changes in the self
Age
Self-image changes with age. The adolescent loses a lot of his rebelliousness when he leaves his teens because he has a changing view of

himself, and the self-image continues to evolve and 'mature' as he becomes more worldly and experienced with age. Sometimes the old, inappropriate self will not die without a struggle: middle-aged men may try to rejuvenate themselves with sports cars, fashion clothes and an eye for young girls. Sadly, the end result is often ridicule, although delusion may mean that the individual does not himself perceive the reaction he evokes.

Occupation

A change of job, a promotion or demotion can greatly influence our self-image, for a major aspect of a self-definition is usually determined by a person's occupation. The nature of the influence was shown by Kuhn. He found that only one-third of first-year trainee nurses identified themselves as nurses, whereas more than seven out of ten did so by the end of their junior year. Job changes can also involve major personal and social upheaval, and this again may greatly affect an individual's image of himself. If, for example, a person is suddenly moved into a new community, his new associates may respond quite differently to him, and, as Cooley and Mead have emphasized, changes in the responses of others are extremely influential in the shaping of the self-image.

Highly significant others

Common sense tells us that during our lives we may meet certain highly respected, admired or loved others who greatly change our self-image and help us to see ourselves in a new light. Close friends, lovers, colleagues and therapists can all bring about such changes. It is the changes that may be brought about by therapists to which we now turn.

Self-actualization and the integrity of the self

As we saw in Chapter 8, Maslow (1954) postulated a set of hierarchically ordered needs (Fig. 71). The individual is only able to progress up the pyramid when each succeeding level has been satisfied. In other words, people are only able to concern themselves with self-fulfilment and self-advancement when the basic needs of subsistence, personal safety and so on have been satisfied. It is therefore hardly surprising that whereas middle-class America, probably the most widely affluent society in the world, has been preoccupied with self-enrichment and 'coming to terms with oneself' in recent years, these considerations have hardly constituted the major concerns of the inhabitants of the Third World. It is only when all other considerations have been met that the individual is able to turn his attention inwards and address himself to the ultimate need – the need 'to realize his full and highest potential'. Few people ever achieve this ideal state. Maslow gives examples including Beethoven, Einstein and William James. He says that such self-actualizers are characterized by a realistic orientation to life; positive self-acceptance; positive acceptance of others in general; spontaneity of thinking and emotions; a lack of self-centredness; independence of thought; and a sense of identity with the whole of mankind. How many of us can claim such an achievement?

One of Maslow's main qualifications for self-actualization, the need for self-acceptance, has been the cornerstone of the 'client-centred therapy' of Carl Rogers. The present state and formulation of self theory owes much to his work; indeed, in a recent poll of American psychologists, Rogers was rated the third most influential theorist in contemporary psychology (after only Freud and Skinner). Rogers' definition of good mental health was self-actualization; unconditional self-esteem; congruence between the perceived self and the real organism; openness to experience; and personal growth.

The concept of self, then, is clearly central to mental health. Its importance was forced upon Rogers, who originally regarded it as a vague, scientifically meaningless construct, by his clients' continual talk about their 'selves' and especially about trying to be their real selves. For Rogers the *perceived* self is a phenomenological event (remember that phenomenologists contend that we are affected not by reality but by our own perception of it). Rogers says (1959), 'Man lives essentially in his own personal and subjective world.' We can thus see the self as a selective barrier, letting in acceptable perceptions and excluding others. Only under conditions of great security can the individual afford to drop the screen and let in *all* experiences. One of the chief aims of Rogerian therapy is to give the client the confidence to be able to do this.

Rogers believed that the main reason for clients coming to counsellors is an unsatisfactory feeling that there is a discrepancy between the perceived self, how the person sees himself, and the 'real organism', or reality. Certain parts of the self appear not to be in consciousness, or to be incorrectly perceived or interpreted. This discrepancy gives rise to feelings of tension, anxiety, 'not being one-self', an uncomfortably low level of self-esteem and, viewed socially, inappropriate behaviour. Rogers developed a therapeutic procedure for helping the client to alter his perceived self. When this is achieved, he argued, the symptoms will disappear. The counsellor is trained in two techniques: *empathy* (adopting the same subjective viewpoint as the client; seeing his problems as the client sees them himself) and *unconditional regard* (treating the client as an individual worthy of respect). The technique is directed at encouraging the client to see himself more honestly and to accept himself. It is his self-esteem which has to be improved (which Argyle defines as 'the extent to which a person approves of and accepts himself, and regards himself as praiseworthy, either absolutely or in comparison with others').

The strategy of client-centred therapy is that if the client can recognize that the counsellor sees him and his world as he sees it himself, and has respect ('unconditional regard') for him, then he will develop a positive regard and acceptance of himself.

Measuring the self-concept
The self-concept has not only been of theoretical and therapeutic interest to psychologists. A large number of clinical and psychometric techniques and scales have been devised to measure the self. The most widely used approaches reflect the different theoretical orientations that we have been examining. Burns classifies them as follows.

The interview
An example of this approach in operation would be Rogers' client-centred therapy.

Rating scales
This is by far the most widely used technique and takes three forms – questionnaires, inventories and attitudes-to-self scales. Typically, a number of statements are made, and the subject has to indicate how well each one applies to him. Figure 88, Rosenberg's *scale of self-esteem*, illustrates the procedure.

This instrument is not typical of most rating scales, which are usually more descriptive of the self than evaluative, tend to have far more response items, and adopt the Likert five-point response system (with a middle neutral or uncertain category). However, the

88. *Rosenberg's scale of self-esteem* (excerpts from D-1: Self
Esteem Scale, in Morris Rosenberg, *Society and the Adolescent
Self-Image* (Princeton University Press, 1965; Princeton
paperback, 1968), pp. 305–7. Reprinted by permission of
Princeton University Press)

	Strongly agree	Agree	Disagree	Strongly disagree
1 I feel that I am a person of worth, at least on an equal plane with others				
2 All in all, I am inclined to to feel that I am a failure				
3 I feel that I have a number of good qualities				
4 I am able to do things as well as most other people				
5 I feel that I do not have much to be proud of				
6 I take a positive attitude towards myself				
7 On the whole, I am satisfied with myself				
8 I wish I could have more respect for myself				
9 I certainly feel useless at times				
10 At times I think I am no good at all				

Rosenberg scale, which is designed for use with students and adolescents, is easy to follow and use, takes little time to administer and is
unusually high on measures of both validity and reliability.

We should note of rating scales in general that since the final self-
image is usually a total score obtained by summing all the component item scores, the uniqueness of individual components is lost,
and hence important clues to certain aspects of self-perception are

missed. In addition, the technique assumes the equal importance of all the items; this is unlikely to reflect the phenomenological reality, for each individual will see certain attributes and qualities as very important, and others as insignificant, yet they will be equally weighted by the scale.

The checklist

The subject is given a list of adjectives or statements, and has to indicate which of them apply to him. An example of such a tool is the *interpersonal checklist* devised by Leary (1957). The list comprises 128 items listed serially, and the subject is asked to describe both his perceived self and his ideal self by ticking as many as he wishes. The major shortcoming of the test, in common with all checklists, is that it does not provide any information on the degree of applicability; for example, if a person ticks 'I am of a jealous nature', we cannot tell whether he sees himself as an extremely jealous or just a mildly jealous type. With the Likert scale we are given values of applicability.

Q-sorts

This technique stimulated a great deal of interest and research in the 1950s, and represents one of psychology's most notable attempts at defining a concept in terms of its measurement tool. In a typical form (for example, Butler and Haigh, 1954) the subject is given a hundred statements (such as 'I am hard-working', 'I am likeable') and the following instructions: 'Sort these cards to describe yourself as you see yourself today, from those that are least like you to those that are most like you.' The subject is required to sort the cards into nine piles covering one extreme – 'Most like me' – through to the other extreme – 'Least like me' – with the important constraint that the number of cards that he is allowed to place in each pile is fixed, so that the final allocation produces a 'normal curve'. This procedure is shown in Figure 89. Although subjects apparently find this an inter-

89. A typical Q-sort

Pile

	1	2	3	4	5	6	7	8	9	
Least like me	4	9	16	26	40	26	16	9	4	Most like me

Number of cards

esting task, it is very time-consuming, rigid and, as Wylie points out (1961), poorly validated.

Unstructured and free-response methods
These methods adopt a phenomenological approach and differ markedly in rationale from the technique of Q-sorts. The subject is asked to complete an open-ended task such as writing an essay entitled 'Myself', complete a series of statements such as 'I am happy when ...', 'I fear ...', 'I can ...', or, as in Kuhn's (1960) test, to which we have previously referred, provide twenty answers to the question 'Who am I?'

Despite the freedom and flexibility accorded by this technique, it is reported that it is not well liked by subjects, who seem to prefer more structure and guidance. In addition, it is difficult to score objectively, for it necessitates the assessor's categorizing the responses. Even with the employment of a classification system, the onus still falls upon his personal judgement. Assessment is not only prone to bias by the experimenter, but is also complex and time-consuming.

Projective techniques
These techniques are in direct theoretical opposition to free-response techniques. The workers in this field stress the importance of unconscious factors, which, by definition, cannot be admitted by phenomenologists, and claim that projective techniques are necessary to reveal them. Such an approach is adopted by Adams and Caldwell (1963), who developed the *somatic apperception test* for seven- to fourteen-year-olds.

A child is presented with ten wooden model bodies and required to select the one which he thinks is most like him (his perceived self) and the model which best corresponds to the body he would like to have (his ideal self). A number of spare parts (hands and limbs) are available, and in a second task the child is required to construct his ideal body. The test, which would be useful in the analysis of anorexia nervosa, enables the researcher to correlate perceived self and actual self, and perceived self and ideal self (that is, how the child sees himself compared with his actual proportions and measurements, and a comparison between what he sees himself to be and what he would like to be). This is one of a relatively small number of projective techniques that have been developed.

Readers interested in examining a larger sample of the tests and tools used to measure the self-image should consult Burns (1979), Chapter 5.

Interpersonal perception

Having looked at self-perception, we now turn our attention to examining the way in which we perceive other people, and how they perceive us. This is not the simple matter that it may initially appear to be. How do we judge when someone is 'in a good mood' so that we can ask a favour of them? How can we tell if our feelings of attraction towards another person are mutual (without the embarrassment of asking them)? How successful are we at hiding our feelings of anxiety and apprehension in tense situations? The phenomena that are studied in the field of interpersonal perception are indeed complex, but their analysis can often be particularly illuminating and rewarding.

Interpersonal perception, which Cook defines (1971) as 'the study of the ways people react and respond to others, in thought, feeling and action', covers a wide variety of judgements and responses, from simple communication through to the most complex evaluations that we make about people. Moreover, it appears that we differ in our ability to perceive and respond to others accurately and appropriately. There are some people who seem to have an almost unerring ability to weigh up situations and judge others, whereas some seem to be embarrassingly 'insensitive' on many occasions. Most of us probably fall between these two extremes: most of the time our judgements are sound, but occasionally we totally misinterpret a situation, usually with uncomfortable consequences.

Why, then, is interpersonal perception so difficult? One reason is that we have to distinguish between permanent and temporary facets of a person's behaviour and character, for example, when a person is interviewed for a job, the interviewer makes an assessment of his intelligence and assumes that it is a fairly stable attribute of the candidate. On the other hand, we may judge one of our friends to be 'fed up', but realize tht this is not a permanent disposition, simply a temporary one. Thus we have to differentiate between *dynamic* (changing) and *static* (relatively fixed) *attributes* in interpersonal perception – though in fact very few factors are totally permanent:

even our physical appearance changes with age. It is consequently safer to talk of factors which are fixed or transitory *in the short term.*

Interpersonal perception is made more difficult because in most communications we are not absolutely honest. We often learn by painful experience in childhood or adolescence that it is not wise to 'wear our hearts on our sleeves', and our parents encourage us to be tactful in the things we say to people – not to ask upsetting or indiscreet questions, or make embarrassing comments in our conversation. Consequently we learn a polite, social language, which has the effect of reducing emotional content and communicational accuracy. Because of this we have to learn to read 'between the lines' in social situations, and behave accordingly. When students in a psychology class were asked how they would communicate their feelings to someone they felt attracted to, none of them said that they would *tell* the person (this would be too direct and 'frighten the person off', or it might lead to a severe loss of face if the feelings were not reciprocated).

Another confounding factor is that we do not behave typically to all people, in all situations. We tend to select certain aspects of ourselves to put on view. There are three main reasons for this. The first motivating factor is social synchronization. We tend to make safe conversation when dealing with strangers to enhance social synchronization, that is, to enable us to have interactions which are not emotionally disturbing (for example, arguments) or too demanding. We therefore talk about neutral, non-emotive subjects like the weather, the latest sports results or last night's television programmes. Such topics are unlikely to strongly agitate or arouse the listener: they will probably facilitate smooth, safe conversation. In the film *Bob and Carol and Ted and Alice*, two of the characters visit a therapy session which places great value upon frank communication. When they next see their friends they visit a restaurant and apply their new values. The waiter tells Carol that he hopes the meal is satisfactory. She asks if he really means this: is he genuinely concerned about her meal? She goes on to say that she has been dining at the restaurant for years and yet feels that she does not really know the waiter, although he has always attended her. She now feels that she wishes to communicate meaningfully and honestly with him. The waiter and her friends are clearly embarrassed, because the social rules of role playing are being flagrantly disregarded.

Secondly, Argyle has said that most of us have a real need to be liked by other people. Because of this we seek to maximize our social attractiveness, and are thus careful initially not to reveal too much of ourselves and our beliefs when dealing with others for fear that we may be rejected. Only with close friends do most of us feel able to 'let our hair down', be ourselves and speak openly and frankly.

Thirdly, there is a *response bias*: a person will often adjust his behaviour according to the perceived status or acceptability of the recipient. A classic authoritarian personality might react quite differently to a black African from how he would behave to a white African, even if the former was higher in real status and power. A rebellious adolescent might view all people over the age of twenty as out-of-touch OAPs; he would certainly behave quite differently to members of his own age-group, who would see quite a different facet of his behaviour.

Having said all this, it is vital that we do perceive others accurately. On the basis of our perceptions we decide whom we can trust, whom we can love, whom we marry. An interviewer, on the basis of perhaps twenty-five minutes' interaction, will decide whether a person is suitable for a job or promotion; a teacher will decide how capable a pupil is; and a psychiatrist may decide whether or not an individual will be institutionalized. Interpersonal perceptions are thus not only complex and hazardous: they are also crucially important and influential in all our lives.

The majority of textbooks which deal with interpersonal perception are content merely to present the findings of some of the most interesting experiments in the field in a shopping-list fashion. We feel that such an approach may well excite the reader's interest, but will hardly help him to understand how we perceive others. A useful contribution has been made by Cook, who says that the research may be classified into two theories: the *intuition model* and the *inference model*.

The intuition model
This viewpoint may be summarized under three contentions.

Innate perception
The intuition writers believe that we are *born* with the ability to perceive other people – to read their facial expressions, to recognize displays of emotion and so on, and to react appropriately. Although

Ekman (1969) has shown that some emotional displays are universal (that is, found in all known cultures), and that blind children, who have no opportunity to learn by imitation, display many recognizable non-verbal cues (such as smiling when happy), the findings of anthropologists such as La Barre (1964) leave us in little doubt of the cultural diversity and, hence, of the socialized acquisition of interpersonal communication and perception. For example, social kissing is a sign of platonic affection in most European countries but is seen as more affiliative and sexual in Britain; and this is reflected in the far lower incidence of men kissing each other in public in this country. In Japan, kissing is an act of private love-making and hence considerable censorship of western films is necessary there. So our interpretation of interpersonal behaviour depends largely upon the values of our particular culture. We can confidently say that there are as many, or more, variations in social language between different cultures as there are variations in their spoken languages.

'Global' perception

The intuition theorists adopt the same stance towards interpersonal perception as the Gestalt psychologists do towards object perception, that is, that we perceive in terms of meaningful wholes rather than in elements or parts. Thus we perceive and judge other people as whole entities, rather than as tall and nice and middle-class and intelligent and sexy, for example. We have an overall or *global*, rather than a piecemeal, judgement of others. The evidence suggests that this contention is essentially correct, but the way in which the separate traits are combined into the 'whole' has been the subject of much disagreement. There are three alternative explanations. The first is that the separate judgements are simply added up, with all the 'units' being seen as equally important. According to this view, someone may be judged as, for example, intelligent if more of his characteristics support than refute this. The fact that he has a first-class honours degree is judged as only equally important as any other one attribute (such as the ability to dominate intellectual conversations – which would hardly have reflected the brilliance of history's many introverted, withdrawn or eccentric geniuses).

According to a second viewpoint, some factors are judged to be of greater importance, or value than others. These are seen as *Central*, the less important ones as *Peripheral*. Thus one aspect of a person (perhaps his sincerity) may outweigh several other factors (for exam-

398 Understanding Psychology

ple, a slow mind or carelessness). This was demonstrated experimentally in a classic investigation by Asch (1946). He presented a group of subjects with the following list of adjectives relating to a fictitious individual: 'intelligent', 'skilful', 'industrious', 'warm', 'determined', 'practical', 'cautious'. A second group of subjects was presented with a list which differed only in that the fourth word, 'warm', was replaced by 'cold'. The groups were presented with a list of eighteen trait words (different from the original list) and were asked to underline the ones which described the person. Asch found that the selections differed markedly and consistently between the two groups. Apparently, the change from 'warm' to 'cold' produces a totally different picture of the individual. In contrast, if the varying adjectives are 'polite' and 'blunt' (the other words, as before, remaining constant) almost identical pictures emerge. In other words, the warm–cold is a central dimension, the changing of which produces large-scale changes in judgement, and the polite–blunt dimension is peripheral, being less influential and having no effect on other judgements.

The central dimension that is most heavily weighted (that is, which affects other judgements more than any other factor) is the evaluative one – whether a person is liked or disliked. If a person is liked he will be judged positively, as more intelligent, capable and so on than he really is; conversely, if a person is disliked he will be judged unrealistically negatively: we often see people we dislike as totally objectionable, without any redeeming features at all, though objectively no one can really be so bad. The characteristic that liking and disliking affects all our judgements about a person has been termed the *'halo effect'*, and many counsellors ruefully verify its influence in courting and marriage behaviour – hence the adage 'Love is blind'.

The third explanation of how 'unit' perceptions are combined to form our global judgements also emphasizes weighting (that is, that some factors are more influential than others), but states that the bias is determined solely by the *order* in which we learn things about a person, with first impressions being most important. This was experimentally established by Luchins (1959). Subjects, who had been matched on personality measures, were allocated into four groups and each group was read a different description of a character called Jim. The first group (the E group) received a straightforward description of an extravert:

Jim left the house to get some stationery. He walked out into the sun-filled street with two of his friends, basking in the sun as he walked. Jim entered the stationery store, which was full of people. Jim talked with an acquaintance while he waited for the clerk to catch his eye. On his way out, he stopped to chat with a school friend who was just coming into the store. Leaving the store, he walked toward school. On his way out, he met the girl to whom he had been introduced the night before. They talked for a short while, and then Jim left for school.

The second group (group I) were given a description of an introvert:

After school Jim left the classroom alone. Leaving the school, he started on his long walk home. The street was brilliantly filled with sunshine. Jim walked down the street on the shady side. Coming down the street toward him, he saw the pretty girl whom he had met on the previous evening. Jim crossed the street and entered a candy store. The store was crowded with students, and he noticed a few familiar faces. Jim waited quietly until the counterman caught his eye and then gave his order. Taking a drink he sat down at a side table. When he had finished the drink he went home.

These two were 'base-line' groups to establish that subjects were able to accurately identify extraverts and introverts. The result for groups E and I below show that approximately three-quarters of the subjects were successful. The interesting feature of the study was that the remaining two groups received split descriptions: group EI received the first half of the E description and the second part of the I, while for the IE group this was reversed. The results in Figure 90 clearly show that the initial elements of the description were most influential. Luchins termed this phenomenon the *primacy effect*: it confirms another well-known adage, 'First impressions count.' Kahn and Cannell (1957) studied tape-recordings of interviews and

90. Luchin's results

	Percentages of groups			
	E	**EI**	**IE**	**I**
Extraverted	79	52	34	16
Introverted	14	36	56	73

found that after a brief 'judgement' period, the interviewer acted as though he had made up his mind about the interviewee's capabilities and attributes, and interrupted him or 'corrected' him if he contradicted this initial impression. The moral for the job interview is clear: give your all in the first ten minutes or so!

We should note, however, that Luchins found that although the order of presentation of information is important in all situations, for friends and close acquaintances the *latest* information received is the most influential. If we have known someone for quite a long time and then discover something previously unknown about them (perhaps something that happened to them a long time ago, or an unexpected leisure interest), this new information has a disproportionate effect upon our overall perception of the person. This has been called the *recency effect*, and applies only to people we are familiar with; with strangers the primacy effect applies.

We thus see that while many psychologists believe that interpersonal perception is global, there is disagreement concerning how the global perceptions are built up. To this extent the second contention of the intuition model is supported; however, and this should be clearly understood, the support does not totally uphold the model, because the intuition model theorists believe that the global percept is a single simple physical entity, or Gestalt. The evidence above does not support this aspect of the model.

Immediate perception

The idea that interpersonal perception is direct (that is, that it is not mediated by mental processes) has received practically no validation. In Chapter 2 we saw how the apparently straightforward and simple act of object perception necessitates a process of cognitive activity (hypothesis testing); so it seems extremely unlikely that the more hazardous and socially influenced activity of interpersonal perception could be direct, and without mediation.

Cook concludes, 'We have seen that three unrelated claims are being made. These three claims all have some degree of truth, although two of them – that perception is direct and that it is innate – apply only to judgements of emotional states. The third – that perception is global – is true of many judgements, but is not a necessary feature of perception.' Clearly, as an explanation of interpersonal perception, the intuition model is not satisfactory.

The inference model
As an alternative to the above, Cook offers the inference model. He emphasizes that strictly speaking it is not a theory but rather 'an explanatory model using an analogy with symbolic logic'. It states that we recognize or *identify* certain attributes in an individual; we *associate* these factors with other attributes; and we then *infer* that the individual in front of us possesses these additional qualities, though they cannot be judged directly. For example, we may believe that Americans are materialistic; we identify an individual in front of us as American; and we then infer that he is likely to be materialistic. As another example, we may believe that people who avoid eye contact are shy and insecure; a person to whom we are talking is conspicuously averting his gaze; and we consequently assume that he is shy and insecure. We shall now consider the experimental evidence for these processes under the headings of 'Associations' and 'Identifications'.

The inference model, clearly, should be adopted. As Cook concludes, 'The inference model has given rise to much research already and could inspire much more. It is also reasonably clear and logically sound; the intuition model, on the other hand, inspires little or no research, and is obscure and logically unsatisfactory.'

Associations
The beliefs about certain factors 'going together' are not limited to *encounter situations* (that is, when we are interacting with someone): we carry them around in our heads all the time, ready to apply them when necessary. They sometimes take the form of prejudices (see p. 359): the racial bigot is always predisposed to identifying racial and ethnic minorities so that he may bring his own associations into play. If the inference model is correct, we *all* hold associations which we apply to infer additional characteristics about the people we meet, however; but the difference is, of course, that normally they are not of a prejudiced nature, and do not concern attitudes to ethnic or social groups: they frequently concern the inference of psychological states from physical cues. Allport has listed some common associations of this kind: fat people are seen as being jolly; women as less practical than men; faces with wrinkles at the corners of the eye are seen as friendly, humorous and easy-going; people whose eyebrows meet are seen as untrustworthy; and those with high foreheads are seen as more intelligent and dependable.

Let us examine in rather more detail one example of associations, to illustrate their nature. If you were asked to judge the intelligence of a stranger, how would you do it? (You could, of course, ask him. However, this would be no guarantee of accuracy. He might not know himself or he might lie.) Such a task was given to subjects by Wiggin, Hoffman and Taber (1969); they were presented with biographies and general descriptions about practically all aspects of a person except his IQ, which they had to estimate. The question was, which details from the list would be used by the subjects to this end? Two-thirds of the subjects used vocabulary and scholastic achievement as the main indicators, and in a real-life situation would probably have been reasonably accurate, for both of these are positively correlated with intelligence. However, a substantial minority inferred intelligence from social status and industriousness, and these are actually poor indicators. A few subjects used highly illogical criteria; for example, one assumed that the sole criterion of high intelligence was emotional instability. Psychologists are unsure about the way in which we acquire our associations. Sarbin, Taft and Bailey (1960) suggest four different sources, listed below.

Induction This means experience. If we observe that people who work hard at school do well, we will come to equate industriousness with success.

Construction These are associations which are invented by the individual, perhaps as defence mechanisms. A student who believes that his colleagues who do well are all 'swots' who totally sacrifice their social lives may be rationalizing his own academic failure. While this may be true of some of his colleagues, it is unlikely to be true of them all: clearly a perceptual bias has been introduced.

Analogy We reason that because something is true of one person whom we know well, it will be true of others too. Models for analogy include our family, friends, teachers and, most important of all, ourselves. For example, if we become withdrawn and sad when disappointed, rather than angry or resentful, we reason that others will respond similarly in the same situation.

Authority We are sometimes told that certain things go together. Our parents may tell us as youngsters that it is wrong to be selfish and mean, and that such people will have no friends. Our teachers tell us about relationships in the world, and our friends are a great source of our knowledge. In early adolescence, our thirst for knowledge about our development and change into adulthood is almost insatiable. For all of us, the school playground may have made a greater contribution to our beliefs and attitudes than we will acknowledge.

Identifications

The application of the associations that we have considered, necessitates the identification of certain characteristics before they can be used. A person who believes that students are politically left-wing must identify an individual as a student before his associations can operate; someone who believes that trustworthiness is associated with certain amounts of eye contact must be able to differentiate between abnormal and normal amounts of eye contact and so on.

The information which we examine and consider in making our identifications may be classified under three headings.

Content Content refers to what might be called 'direct' information – the subject's statements and behaviour. We have referred already to the fact that we cannot necessarily take at face value what people tell us: they may wish to present themselves in a flattering light; they may feel that we are not entitled to an honest answer; they may wish to deceive us for their own ends (for example, the 'con man'); or they may not, as a result of Freudian defence mechanisms, mental disturbance or an unrealistic self-image, be fully aware of certain aspects of themselves. But is their behaviour any more reliable than their speech? A well-known study by Kutner, Williams and Yarrow (1952) would suggest not. Restaurant owners in the southern states of America were asked if they would serve black customers. Their answers were later put to the test as Negroes entered their premises and requested service. The investigators found no correlation between the owners' stated policy and their actual behaviour.

Furthermore, Argyle has pointed out that there may be a taboo upon the direct communication of many emotions; in consequence, these are coded into non-verbal communication, to which we shall turn shortly.

Context The second source of information is the context of behaviour. A person who talked endlessly about politics might be considered rather dull and boring at a high-spirited party, whereas the same behaviour might be considered outrageous during a funeral

404 *Understanding Psychology*

service. Clearly, the context in which a piece of behaviour occurs has a considerable bearing upon our interpretation of it.

Holmes and Berkowitz (1961) found a context effect in our judgements of others. When asked to judge the 'pleasantness' of people, it was found that higher ratings were given to those people following clearly 'unpleasant' and objectionable ones: the influence of the contrast demonstrates the power of context.

Non-verbal communication The final source of information to which we look in judging others, and the one which has attracted considerable research in recent years, is *non-verbal communication*. It has been considered in many different theoretical perspectives (for example, Hardy and Heyes examine it as a functional alternative and addition to speech), but in our framework we shall look at NVC as an information channel which contributes greatly to the process of interpersonal perception.

If you watch a television programme with the sound turned down, you will notice the stream of information that the actor provides to the viewer and to his fellow performers – facial expressions, gestures, shifts of posture, movement, touching and so on. Moreover, under the umbrella term non-verbal communication we also include what is called 'para-language' – vocal factors other than the actual words used (for example, grunts, sighs, laughter, pauses and stutters). Taken together, body and para-language are extraordinarily influential sources of information. Argyle *et al.* (1970) found that if a person's non-verbal communication contradicts his utterances, we generally believe the NVC.

An essential distinction in considering the different elements of NVC is that between static and dynamic cues. As before, we mean that the static factors are fixed in the short term, whereas the dynamic ones are manipulated and change during the course of an interaction. Thus although a person's hairstyle, for example, can be changed without too much difficulty, it rarely varies during the course of a single interaction.

The face is a static factor when it is at rest, rather than being used as an aid to communication. What can we tell from an examination of, say, a photograph of a face? We can probably judge age, race and possibly sex reasonably accurately. Most importantly, however, the face communicates the unique identity of the person: in recognizing people, it is the face which is almost always the focus of recognition.

A sexist myth was laid by a study which filmed the eye-direction and gaze of members of a nudist camp. The analyses were quite clear: the unclothed members still looked to faces for identification despite the availability of other sources of information.

Secord (1968) has shown that certain types of faces do elicit strong stereotypes – the lean, anxious face, the hard, criminal face, the seductive, promiscuous face. The only accuracy that emerges is that of a self-fulfilling prophecy: if the owner of such a face is constantly and consistently treated in a particular way then he may well adopt appropriate behaviours as appeasement, or to 'make life easy'. Thus the person with the 'jolly, fat' face may act in a jolly, happy-go-lucky way because everyone expects it of him.

Physique can also be a static factor. In Chapter 8 Sheldon's theory of somatypes was outlined, in which personality predictions are made from body shape. It is unlikely that physique does have any validity as an indicator of psychological dispositions, but a study by the aptly named Strongman and Hart (1968) revealed that people react *as though* it was a true indicator.

As with the face, the voice also contains certain valuable information. From listening to someone speaking on a telephone we may often be able to identify the speaker's age, sex and national or regional origin reasonably well. One early study found class and occupation could also be successfully judged from voice (actors and clergymen were those most accurately identified). But what about 'inner' characteristics such as personality and intelligence? Allport and Cantril (1934) found that certain personality traits, such as the ascendance–submission dimension, were identified successfully by a considerable number of their subjects, but, most importantly, that the voices (as with the faces) were associated with certain stereotypes. The subjects in the study, even if in error, gave similar answers: apparently, certain voices arouse consistent, even if inaccurate, responses in listeners.

The voice, however, does provide more accurate information than the face. This is because whereas a person cannot fundamentally change his face, he can, by education, elocution and imitation, modify and mould his voice as he wishes.

A number of studies have shown that teenage girls are particularly influenced by further factors such as style and fashion of dress, hair-style, make-up and so on. The judgement extends beyond evaluation to predictions of behaviour. This is clearly related to the emphasis of youth culture upon fashion demarcation whereby groups differentiate themselves (for example, Mods and Rockers), and they also differentiate their age-group from adults. Because of the total control that can be exercised over this medium, it is by far the most useful predictor of the static cues.

Dynamic cues, on the other hand, are those which are varied and manipulated by interacting individuals *during* an interaction. They are sometimes deliberate, as when a listener raises his eyebrows in mock admonition and amazement to show the speaker that he finds his story difficult to believe, and sometimes unconscious, as when our pupils dilate in the presence of a person we find attractive. We frequently put more trust in NVC cues than in what a person says; this may well be because we feel that a person is less able to control or falsify the information his body and para-language communicates. Thus the material we now consider is given a high weighting in our judgements of other people. There are three chief areas: the face, the voice and the body.

Facial expression is the most complex of the non-verbal cues. Its subtlety and enormous diversity have made it almost impossible to study systematically and accurately. Because of this, research has tended to concentrate on micro-units of the face, such as Eibl-Eibesfeldt's work on the 'eyebrow flash' (the automatic and unconscious raising of our eyebrows when we meet someone we know). Argyle says, 'the eyebrows provide a continuous running commentary', and summarizes this as follows:

Fully raised: disbelief
Half raised: surprise
Normal: no comment
Half lowered: puzzled
Fully lowered: angry

At the end of interactions, we tend to look at the other person and smile – as if we feel an obligation to end a conversation in a pleasant manner.

Emotional tension and stress can be identified from the face, for example by perspiration on the forehead and dilation of the pupils.

The micro-face unit which has attracted the most research is eye contact. In the normal course of events we do not engage extensively in this activity; for example, if we are sitting in a train compartment and 'catch someone's glance' we usually quickly look away. This aversion may well have its origins in childhood, when our parents frequently told us that it was rude to stare; but it appears also to go beyond this. It seems to be a strong, intimate channel of communication, a regulator of intimacy, which we reserve for a small number of others. Thus eye contact is considerably reduced, or even becomes non-existent, when the topic of conversation becomes too personal, when there is too much smiling or when interpersonal distance is too small. In a crowded lift the occupants stare at the floor, the ceiling or anywhere else rather than into the eyes of the other people; and we regard someone standing close to us, looking into our eyes and smiling, as a strong interpersonal cue.

To communicate intimacy and liking is only one of the reasons we engage in eye contact. We do so also to gain someone's attention (we try to 'catch their eye'); to show that we agree or disagree with them; or to enhance credibility (we are more likely to believe someone who can 'look us in the eye' as he talks to us).

The tone of the voice is another non-verbal cue. Ostwald (1965) used an objective device for measuring the voice (a *speech spectrograph*) and found that in mental patients certain kinds of voice patterns indicate the type and the severity of mental illness. More subjective studies (for example, Davitz, 1964) have tested the ability of listeners to differentiate between emotions such as admiration, affection, amusement, disgust, fear, joy, impatience and surprise in the voices of actors. Up to 70% accuracy was found in the studies.

The rate and fluency of speaking are also non-verbal indicators. A large number of hesitations and pauses (especially when they occur within phrases) are seen as indicating that the speaker is having difficulty with his material. A more general tension and anxiety, perhaps relating to the situation or the audience rather than to the material, is thought by subjects to be indicated by speech disturbances – errors in articulation and changes in sentence structure. Studies have shown that these disturbances do indicate anxiety, and thus subjects are correct in interpreting them in this way.

The distances at which we stand as we interact with others are not usually chance-determined. It is likely that we may stand quite close when talking to someone we are fond of, but at a noticeably greater distance when we interact with a formal business colleague or stranger. Interpersonal distance has been systematically studied by the American anthropologist E.T. Hall (1964). As a result of his investigations he suggested that we can reliably identify four different interacting distances:

Intimate friends: 0 to 18 inches
Casual friends: 30 to 48 inches
People in social or consultative encounters: 4 to 12 feet
People in public encounters: greater than 12 feet

It should be emphasized that there are marked cultural differences in preferred interacting distances. One of the reasons why Continental men are seen as particularly friendly or amorous by British girls abroad is that they prefer to interact at far closer proximity than most British males. Lott (1969) found that Arabs and Latin Americans stand closest during interactions, while Swedes and Scots are the most distant.

Body contact provides another non-verbal cue. In all societies there is a very strict code regulating permissible touching and body contact, which usually indicates intimacy. There are, however, considerable differences between cultures. In Britain very little touching is tolerated in normal interaction: if accidental body contact is made there is an apology and a rapid withdrawal of the offending limb.

Jourard (1966) produced a picture of how frequently American students are touched, where, and by whom (see Fig. 91).

The area of posture and gesture can be seen as a microcosm of interpersonal perception research. Accounts tend to be fragmentary, and descriptive rather than explanatory, concentrating upon listing the nuances and varieties of body language and stopping short of any functional analysis. One of the most promising classifications has been made by Ekman and Friesen (1969), who distinguish five types and functions of cues.

The first category is *emblems*. These are the signals which can be directly translated into spoken language. Examples would include shaking and nodding of the head to show affirmation and negation, shaking the fist to indicate anger and thumbing the nose to show disrespect. These signs are directly related to the content of the spoken communication. The second type, *affect displays*, consists of the emotional cues. Ekman and Friesen argue that the face is the main channel for such display but that it may be identified in body language too. We can identify relaxed or tense postures (whether the subject is seated or standing), as well as a number of other emotional states which are mirrored in body posture and gestures. Thirdly,

91. Male and female 'bodies-for-others', as experienced through the amount of touching received from others (after Sidney M. Jourard, 'An exploratory study of body-accessibility', *British Journal of Social and Clinical Psychology*, 1966, 5, p.229)

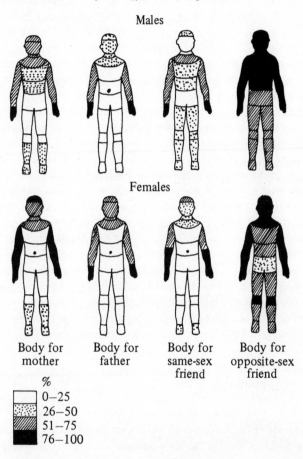

Males

Females

| Body for mother | Body for father | Body for same-sex friend | Body for opposite-sex friend |

%
0–25
26–50
51–75
76–100

illustrators, as the name suggests, give the visual commentary to supplement a speaker's spoken message. Speakers use their hands and a number of postural shifts to emphasize certain points, to expand and clarify others, such as by drawing objects in the air, and to act as a form of visual punctuation. The fourth kind, *regulators*, are the reciprocals of illustrators: they are the cues the listener gives the speaker during a conversation. By head nods, facial expressions and a number of gestures the listener can communicate that he is interested, bored, surprised, pleased, disgusted and so on by what the speaker is saying. He can inform him that he wants him to carry on, stop, speed up, repeat or clarify a point. One of the most interesting studies on the use of regulators was carried out by Kendon (1970), who analysed film recordings and found that when there is a strong affiliative attraction or bond between the speaker and the listener, the listener tends to mirror the behaviour of the speaker as he talks, in postures, gestures, and especially, facial expressions. The fifth and final type, *adaptors*, are the idiosyncratic behaviours that individuals display in certain situations. These individual characteristics may be seen as mannerisms, either endearing or annoying, and can only really be understood by close acquaintance with the subject. Many adaptors outlast any usefulness they may have had.

Ekman and Friesen's classification system has proved useful in the scientific study of NVC, for it concentrates on the functions served by the various cues. It puts some order into the rather chaotic jumble of apparently unrelated cues which have been identified so far.

It is hoped that by looking at the above material you now have a reasonable picture of how we perceive other people. The process is complex, and we do make mistakes. Only by understanding the underlying nature of the process as well as the units of the language with which it works can the 'insensitive' people referred to at the beginning of this section be offered guidance and training. This is because we can help only if we ourselves understand the process.

Further reading

Allport, G.W. (1961), *Pattern and Growth in Personality*, Holt, Rinehart and Winston

Argyle, M. (1972), *The Psychology of Interpersonal Behaviour* (2nd ed.), Penguin

Burns, R.B. (1979), *The Self Concept*, Longmans

Cook, M. (1971), *Interpersonal Perception*, Penguin

Morris, D. (1977), *Manwatching*, Jonathan Cape

15 The psychology examination

This final chapter has much general advice which will be of considerable benefit to all students taking an examination course in psychology, at whatever level; but it also presents material which will be especially applicable to the GCE A-level psychology examination.

The format of practical reports

For many students the practical component of the course is the most interesting, but some difficulties are often encountered when the time comes to 'write up'. Practical work which might otherwise be commendable may be spoiled by a student's inability to write an acceptable account of the work.

Writing up an experiment in a practical notebook takes up valuable time, and errors can easily be made unless sufficient care is taken. In spite of this, a carefully constructed account is essential, for it allows others to replicate the experiment or to conduct it again with modifications. It is important, therefore, that each stage of the experiment should be reported accurately and systematically. Examiners cannot fail to be impressed by a neatly reported experiment, and they are usually able to assess how much time has been devoted to the work.

The following suggestions provide an outline for writing up experimental reports, and the headings should always be tackled in the order shown. Examiners like to see students' material clearly presented in a logical sequence.

The title

This should be as short as possible and must indicate the main theme or topic of the experiment. This can usually be achieved if the title aims to reflect the hypothesis. While it is always politic to pay attention to correct spelling, this is particularly desirable in the title. As the title is one of the first things a reader notices, it is most disconcerting to find a careless error at the beginning of what may later develop into a competent piece of work.

The summary

In research papers this is usually called an abstract. Its purpose is to provide readers with an overview of the design and content of the experiment. It helps a reader to decide quickly whether the experiment is relevant to his own research interests, and whether it would be worth his while reading through the whole report.

The summary is an extension of the title, for titles by themselves cannot always give sufficient details to make the nature of an experiment clear. Researchers are frequently attracted to a report as a result of seeing a title listed in the contents page of a learned journal, but lose interest when they have read the abstract.

One paragraph is sufficient for a summary, which should contain only the essentials of the experimental design; the results of the experiment concisely expressed; and the major conclusions derived from the results. It will have become obvious that, while the summary is placed at the beginning of the report, it cannot in fact be written until all the other sections have been completed.

The aim of the experiment and its background

This part of the report should give the rationale of the experiment, relating it to appropriate, relevant research in the same area. The names of authors should be accurately quoted along with short references to their work, and the year of publication of the research paper or book (in brackets) should appear immediately after the author's name. The section should conclude with a statement of the hypothesis (or, in some cases, hypotheses) to be tested, bearing in mind what was mentioned about the types of hypothesis in Chapter 1.

The conditions

The conditions under which the experiment was conducted must be described in detail, because these could affect the results and lead to incorrect conclusions. A number of factors may be included in this section, such as time of day, place, room temperature and various environmental conditions which operated during the progress of the experiment.

Depending on the type of experiment, time of day, for example, could be very important. Thus in a memory or learning experiment the results could differ considerably between morning and afternoon trials. Subjects might be more receptive earlier in the day, and more fatigued later on.

Noisy surroundings, too, might cause the subject to lose his powers of concentration, though it is very difficult to escape certain kinds of noise in today's world. What the experimenter has to decide is whether this variable could have influenced the results of the experiment in any way. Room temperature could be another critical factor - if it is either too hot or too cold.

There is no need to mention the conditions in any detail if they appear to be trivial, but a full account must be given of factors which could have affected the results. Examiners realize that it is usually difficult to secure ideal conditions in most instances, but the experimenter has a duty to record any adverse conditions which might have affected the outcome of the experiment.

The subjects and experimenters
The report should include the number of subjects involved in the experiment. Sometimes it may be necessary to elaborate on the kind of subjects used if this is not obvious; for example, it may be useful to mention their sex, age-ranges, occupations and so on. There should be some reference to the experimenter(s) - whether known to the subjects, the same age or older and so on.

The apparatus
Sometimes no apparatus is needed for an experiment, in which case the title of this section should still be included in the report, and the word 'Nil' written underneath. There is no need to describe standard equipment, such as a tachistoscope or a memory drum. It is necessary, however, to give a full description of all equipment and material constructed specially for the experiment.

It is always helpful, too, to have examples of the material appended to the report for reference. It would not be sufficient, for instance, to mention word lists without including specimens to indicate the number of words, length, difficulty, whether they all have the same meaning for all subjects, and so on. Such material also provides a good basis for discussion in the oral examination.

The method

An extremely important part of the report is concerned with the method used for conducting the experiment. Here, clear and concise information has to be given on *how* the various stages of the experiment were undertaken. This will require a great deal of patience and care, and may need to be rewritten several times before the final version is acceptable.

This section will include precise details about the experimental design, the way in which the apparatus was used, the rate at which the material was presented to the subjects, the number of trials and time intervals, and instructions to subjects. This latter point requires further comment. Since it is important that the same instructions are given to each subject, they should be set out clearly - perhaps underlined, arranged in a block, or placed in inverted commas.

The results

The raw data will be recorded as they are produced by the subjects. No attempt should be made to 'treat' the results by applying statistical procedures; this will be the concern of the next section. The results will appear in concise tables with suitable, meaningful headings, unless it is considered that the data might be more aptly presented by means of graphs, diagrams and so on. Detailed comments on the results should be reserved for the 'Discussion' section, though this does not preclude short introspections, such as 'Males scored significantly better than females'.

The treatment of results

Raw results can often be misleading, and conclusions drawn from them may be erroneous. For example, it may *appear* that the difference between the means of two sets of data is significant, or that there *is* a relationship between two sets of scores. While it is interesting to speculate, subjective evaluation is not sufficiently accurate to be useful, hence the need to make a statistical analysis of the raw data.

This will require the correct use of statistical tests (see Miller, *Experimental Design and Statistics*). Great care must be taken to select the correct procedure suited to the experimental design chosen. All mathematical functions should be carefully checked before writing up this section to avoid serious errors.

The discussion of results and the conclusion
This section calls for an assessment of the results of the experiment; any implications and conclusions should be carefully drawn out. Failings in the experimental design or in the conduct of the experiment should be discussed, though it is not necessary to explain away all discrepancies. It is customary to refer to aspects of the experiment which point to ideas for further development. The section should end with a recapitulation of the main results and conclusions of the experiment, and it is sound practice to re-state the hypothesis, indicating whether or not it was supported.

References
A list of references should conclude the report. The list should include only those works cited earlier in the report and no others, and they should be recorded accurately. There is an accepted format for writing the references, and the following are examples:

Paivio, A. (1974), 'Language and knowledge of the world', *Educational Research*, 3, pp. 5–12

Yates, F. A. (1966), *The Art of Memory*, Routledge and Kegan Paul

Here are three important points to note:

1 The references are listed in alphabetical order according to authors' names.
2 When the reference is to an article in a learned journal, the name of the journal is underlined.
3 When the reference is to the title of a book, the title is underlined.

An example of a practical report
The following experiment was conducted by sixth-formers in a boys' grammar school as part of their A-level psychology course. It has been reproduced here to illustrate the points made above.

The title
School stereotypes.

The summary
It was hypothesized that sixth-form students would attribute certain characteristics to people in different types of schools according to preconceived and therefore biased notions. Forty-eight sixth-formers, randomly assigned to three groups, were each given a data sheet containing six items describing an imaginary girl. Item four differed slightly for each group. Subjects were then presented with twenty pairs of alternative extreme statements and asked to underline the statement from each pair which best suited, in their opinion, the girl described on the data sheet. It was found that certain statements showed significant differences in responses between groups; other statements revealed interesting directional responses.

The aim of the experiment and its background
The aim of the experiment was to investigate school stereotypes of first-year sixth-form students. There is a tendency for people to make generalized statements, unsupported by sufficient factual information, about the characteristics which supposedly relate to certain kinds of people, objects or institutions. This is known as stereotyping. Stereotyping is not necessarily an undesirable process, for it helps people to make provisional inferences which may be modified, retained or dismissed at a later stage when further information becomes available. On the other hand, the process of stereotyping can be harmful if judgements of a more permanent kind are made on the basis of too few facts.

Research has been undertaken to examine how people perceive others as individuals and in groups. For example, a study concerning ethnic and racial groups in South Africa was carried out by Pettigrew, Allport and Barnett (1958). A similar study was undertaken by Hovland and Sherif (1952) in connection with the social problem of desegregation in the United States. The public have always tended to hold strong views about conscientious objectors in time of war, and a study relating to this topic was reported by Crespi (1945).

Where the views of people are particularly strong, that is, where they feel reasonably involved in a situation, they tend to hold relatively extreme views, and therefore to pass extreme judgements. An instance of this is mentioned by Tajfel and Wilkes (1963) in which they used photographs of youngish men in order to elicit from their subjects free descriptive statements about other people.

Over forty years ago, Katz and Braly (1933) asked students to describe ethnic groups by ticking adjectives on a list, and similar investigations were conducted years later by Gilbert (1951) and Karling, Coffman and Walters (1969). Stereotyping has also been extended to drivers of different makes of cars (Wells, Goi and Sender, 1958). Interesting studies into name stereotypes have been conducted, including those of Razran (1950) which dealt with surnames, and Harari and McDavid (1973) which examined first names of people.

This research background provided a basis for a discussion of stereotyping in a school situation – especially in different types of schools, such as a grammar school, a comprehensive school and a boarding school. The discussion gave rise to the hypothesis for the present experiment: 'That first-year sixth-formers will attribute certain characteristics to people in different types of schools, according to preconceived notions'.

The conditions
The experiment was conducted in a school classroom with groups of first-year sixth-formers during general studies periods. The environmental conditions were normal.

The subjects and experimenters
Forty-eight sixth-formers acted as subjects for the experiment. There were approximately equal numbers of arts and science students. In all, there were seven experimenters who shared the conduct of the experiment at various times. All the experimenters were A-level psychology students.

The apparatus
1 Three sets of biographical data sheets were produced (see sheets A1, A2 and A3 [Fig. 92]). These were compiled by first-year sixth-form psychologists, and were based on similar ones in Brown, Cherrington and Cohen (1975). Each sheet contained six statements giving factual information about a fictitious female (Miss X). The statements on each of the sheets were identical, with the exception of item 4, where the variation was as follows: (1) Attends a girls' grammar school, (2) Attends a mixed comprehensive school, or (3) Attends a girls' boarding school.
2 A personality inventory was produced containing twenty pairs of alternative statements relating to the personality of the fictitious

92. Biographical data sheets

Sheet A1: Miss X	Sheet A2: Miss X	Sheet A3: Miss X
Is a fifth-year pupil	Is a fifth-year pupil	Is a fifth-year pupil
Has lots of friends	Has lots of friends	Has lots of friends
Has an active social life	Has an active social life	Has an active social life
Attends a girls' grammar school	Attends a mixed comprehensive school	Attends a girls' boarding school
Enjoys music	Enjoys music	Enjoys music
Plays hockey at school	Plays hockey at school	Plays hockey at school

93. Personality inventory of Miss X (sheet B)

Consider the 20 pairs of alternatives below. For each pair, underline the *one* statement which you feel best applies to the person described on your small sheet. If you are not sure, make a guess. Please do not omit any item.

1 Mainly optimistic	Mainly pessimistic
2 Regards her work lightly	Conscientious in her work
3 Gets on well with her family	Does not get on well with her family
4 Tends to be thrifty	Rather reckless with money
5 Dislikes domestic chores	Likes domestic chores
6 Lives mainly in the present	Plans for the future
7 Attentive to friends	Apt to take friends for granted
8 Unopposed to gambling	Opposed to gambling
9 Self-reliant	Dependent on others
10 Somewhat untidy	Meticulous in her habits
11 Largely self-centred	Shows great concern for others
12 Active Church member	Not bothered about religion
13 Loud and boisterous	Quiet and reserved
14 Wears fashionable clothes	Not influenced by fashion
15 Interested in politics	Not interested in politics
16 Slow and deliberate	Quick and impulsive
17 Somewhat ambitious	Has few ambitions
18 An interesting person	A boring person
19 On friendly terms with her teachers	Tends to remain aloof from teachers
20 Scrupulously honest	Not averse to petty dishonesty

94. Responses to statements on the personality inventory

Items	Sheet 1		Sheet 2		Sheet 3	
	L	R	L	R	L	R
1	18	0	16	0	14	0
2	9	9	12	4	11	3
3	15	3	12	4	6	8
4	5	13	2	14	3	11
5	16	2	16	0	9	5
6	17	1	13	3	10	4
7	12	6	10	6	8	6
8	16	2	14	2	10	4
9	17	1	11	5	8	6
10	8	10	13	3	8	6
11	8	10	9	7	5	9
12	10	8	2	14	6	8
13	16	2	15	1	13	1
14	15	3	16	0	14	0
15	7	11	2	14	2	12
16	1	17	1	15	0	14
17	17	1	11	5	10	4
18	18	0	15	1	12	2
19	14	4	14	2	13	1
20	7	11	4	12	3	11

Miss X (see sheet B [Fig. 93]). Some of the twenty statements remained in their original form as in Brown *et al.* The rest were compiled by the first-year sixth-form psychologists.

3 There was a response sheet relating to each of the three data sheets (see Fig. 94). This was divided into three sets of two columns headed 'L' and 'R', indicating responses to statements in the left-hand and right-hand columns of sheet B. The left-hand side of the sheet was numbered from 1 to 20 to identify each pair of statements.

The method

The experiment was conducted with different groups of sixth-formers during one week's general study periods. The nature of the experiment (investigation into stereotyping, etc.) was not discussed with the subjects at this stage, in order to avoid bias in the results.

Subjects were given biographical data sheets at random (1, 2 or 3), and also the personality inventory of Miss X. They were instructed to read the description on the data sheet and then to underline whichever one of each pair of personality statements they considered to be most appropriate to the Miss X described on their sheet.

They were requested to work through the items as quickly as possible, since first impressions were required, and they were also asked not to discuss the experiment with other subjects. The subjects were instructed to hold up the data sheet and the completed personality inventory as soon as they had finished. The actual instructions read as follows:

> We would like you to read a description of a Miss X which is given on the small data sheet. Then, look at the larger sheet – a personality inventory. This inventory has twenty pairs of statements. We want you to underline *one* statement from each pair which you feel is most appropriate to the Miss X about whom you have been reading. Please work through the items as quickly as possible as your first impressions are required. When you have finished, hold up both sheets for collection. Please do not discuss the experiment with other subjects. Thank you for your help.

The data sheets and inventories were then collected by the experimenters, who later transferred the subjects' responses to the response sheet (Fig. 94).

The results
The table (Fig. 94) shows the responses to the personality items made by subjects in each of the three conditions – grammar school (sheet 1, N = 18), comprehensive school (sheet 2, N = 16), and boarding school (sheet 3, N = 14).

The treatment of results
As frequency data were being used, a chi-squared (χ^2) test was employed. The computation of the χ^2 has been given in full for statement 18 on the personality inventory. The remaining nineteen statements were treated in exactly the same way.

Step 1

L	18	15	12
R	0	1	2

Step 2

L	18	15	12	45
R	0	1	2	3
Total	18	16	14	48

Step 3

(1) $E = \dfrac{45 \times 18}{48} = 16.87$ (4) $E = \dfrac{3 \times 18}{48} = 1.12$

(2) $E = \dfrac{45 \times 16}{48} = 15.00$ (5) $E = \dfrac{3 \times 16}{48} = 1.00$

(3) $E = \dfrac{45 \times 14}{48} = 13.12$ (6) $E = \dfrac{3 \times 14}{48} = 0.87$

Step 4

L	16.87 18	15.00 15	13.12 12
R	1.12 0	1.00 1	0.87 2

O	E	Step 5 (O−E)	Step 6 $(O-E)^2$	Step 7 $(O-E)^2/E$
18	16.87	1.13	1.27	0.08
15	15.00	0.00	0.00	0.00
12	13.12	−1.12	1.25	0.10
0	1.12	−1.12	1.25	1.12
1	1.00	0.00	0.00	0.00
2	0.87	1.13	1.27	1.46
				2.76

Step 8

$$\chi^2 = \Sigma \frac{(O-E)^2}{E}$$
$$= 0.08 + 0.10 + 1.12 + 1.46$$
$$= 2.76$$

Step 9

Table value of χ^2 with 2 degrees of freedom (d.f.) = 5.99 at the 5% level of significance. As the χ^2 obtained (2.76) is less than the table value, it is concluded that there is no significant difference in the responses between the school groups.

The χ^2 values for all twenty personality items are shown in the table below.

Item	X^2 value	Item	X^2 value
1	0.00	11	1.29
2	3.63	*12	6.94
*3	8.34	13	0.28
4	1.12	14	5.33
*5	6.77	15	4.17
6	3.26	16	0.85
7	0.30	17	4.07
8	2.90	18	2.75
*9	6.34	19	1.52
10	4.88	20	1.36

Table value of X^2 = 5.99 at the 5% level of significance.
*Significant at the 5% level

The discussion of results and the conclusion

Item 3. Grammar-school girls and comprehensive-school girls are thought to get on well with their families, whereas this was not seen as especially true in the case of boarding-school girls. A possible explanation may be that a boarding-school girl seldom sees her family, so she does not have as much time or opportunity to develop a strong relationship with her parents or her brothers and sisters. The fact that she is in a boarding school may suggest a poor relationship between herself and her family, or alternatively, she might resent being separated from her home and therefore attach some blame for this to her parents, finding it harder to get on well with them.

Item 5. It would seem that grammar-school girls and comprehensive-school girls dislike domestic chores more than boarding-school girls. Chores, for a boarding-school girl, are part of her routine and she can possibly see the reason for them. If she does not perform certain chores, she knows that nobody else will do them, as they are assigned to her alone. At home, however, a girl may not see the purpose quite so clearly, especially as there are others in the family to come to the rescue. The chores she does at boarding school may be more for her own benefit, whereas at home she would have to do more for other people in the family. It was also felt that the obedience factor might enter into it: a girl might be more willing to obey a teacher than a parent.

Item 9. There is a tendency for grammar-school girls and comprehensive-school girls to be more self-reliant, according to these results, while boarding-school girls are likely to be more dependent on others. A boarding-school girl may not have to rely upon herself too much, since all aspects of her daily routine are carefully planned by teachers, ancillary staff and others. On the other hand, it was thought that girls in the other types of schools have to be more resourceful, and to use their initiative to a greater degree. It was suggested, too, that girls in boarding school might be more dependent on each other on account of a community spirit which such schools try to encourage. It was further considered that boarding-school girls would receive much financial support from their parents, whereas other girls might have to work at week-ends and in holidays to earn sufficient pocket money to meet their needs.

Item 12. Comprehensive-school girls appeared to be far less interested in religion than other school girls. Many boarding schools may be pictured as linked to Church foundations, where the pupils are usually obliged to attend religious services. In this case, the pupils would belong mainly to the same denomination, whereas comprehensive-school pupils generally come from a variety of religious backgrounds or none. Perhaps, too, there would not be so much encouragement given at home for the practice of religion amongst comprehensive-school girls. The grammar-school girl, in this context, was seen as identical with the boarding-school girl, receiving her education in a Church environment and attending its services.

Although they failed to reach the required level of significance, two other items, 10 and 14, deserve some comment on account of their directional responses.

Item 10. It was expected that this item might bring out the stereotype of a comprehensive-school girl as being rather untidy, and the responses in the table (Fig. 94) confirm this impression. Nevertheless the results just failed to be significant ($\chi^2 = 4.88$).

Item 14. In constructing this item, the experimenters felt that fashionable clothes would be readily associated with comprehensive-school girls, but this was not borne out statistically ($\chi^2 = 5.33$).

In retrospect, the experimenters were in total agreement that they supposed that personal knowledge of someone in any one of the three categories would influence the subjects' responses and lead to generalizations about the group as a whole. As far as the outcome of the experiment was concerned, it was concluded that the hypothesis was supported in that sixth-form students did attribute certain characteristics to people in different types of schools according to preconceived and therefore biased notions.

References

Brown, G., Cherrington, D.H. and Cohen, L. (1975), *Experiments in the Social Sciences*, Harper and Row

Crespi, L.P. (1945), 'Public opinion towards conscientious objectors: intensity of social rejection in stereotype and attitude', *Journal of Psychology*, 19, pp. 251–76

Gilbert, C.M. (1951), 'Stereotype persistence and change among college students', *Journal of Abnormal and Social Psychology*, 46, pp. 245–54

Harari, H. and McDavid, J.W. (1973), 'Teachers' expectations and name stereotypes', *Journal of Educational Psychology*, 65, pp. 222–5

Hovland, C.I. and Sherif, M. (1952), 'Judgment phenomena and scales of attitude measurement: item displacement in Thurstone scales', *Journal of Abnormal and Social Psychology*, 47, pp. 822–32

Karling, M., Coffman, T.L. and Walters, G. (1969), 'On the fading of social stereotypes: studies in three generations of college students', *Journal of Personality and Social Psychology*, 13, pp. 1–16

Katz, D. and Braly, K.W. (1933), 'Racial stereotypes of 100 college students', *Journal of Abnormal and Social Psychology*, 28, pp. 280–90

Pettigrew, T.F., Allport, G.W. and Barnett, E.O. (1958), 'Binocular resolution and perception of race in South Africa', *British Journal of Psychology*, 49, pp. 265–78

Razran, G. (1950), 'Ethnic dislikes and stereotypes', *Journal of Abnormal and Social Psychology*, 45, pp. 7–27

Tajfel, H. and Wilkes, A.L. (1963), 'Salience of attributes and commitment to extreme judgment in the perception of people', *British Journal of Social and Clinical Psychology*, 2, pp. 40–9

Wells, W.D., Goi, F.J. and Sender, S. (1958), 'A change in a product image', *Journal of Applied Psychology*, 42, pp. 120–1

The oral examination

We have just looked at the way in which the student will be expected to write up a typical practical. It is important that each report is as complete and considered a statement as he feels able to make at the time, for under the present AEB syllabus 20% of the overall marks for the psychology examination is allocated for assessment of the practical notebook and the understanding of the work contained in it.

Examiners visit schools and colleges to talk about the practicals that have been carried out and look at the notebooks. This is normally the student's own school or college, unless it is entering a small number of candidates for psychology (less than five), or is geographically remote. In either of these instances, the student may have to travel to another centre nearby. The interview is an essential part of the AEB examination and candidates who merely sit the two written papers and do not have an interview with a visiting examiner will automatically fail the A level. Another easy way to fail the examination is to turn up for the interview without a set of reports. The rule is simple: no notebook – no interview; no interview – no A level.

Students sometimes feel anxious about the oral examination, as they do for any form of examination assessment, but it is particularly unfortunate in this context, for the interview gives the candidate the opportunity to discuss practicals with an interested outsider. The interview is not designed to test the candidate's memory of what he has written, merely to see if it has been understood. Examiners will not expect candidates to be able to recall the small details of each experiment from memory, such as exactly how many subjects were used in a particular study and precisely what instructions were given to them. However, they will be interested in whether or not the candidate can explain why a particular set of subjects were used, why the instructions were so phrased, and so on. Candidates are not expected to be able to recite the formulae for the tests that have been used, but they are expected to be able to say why a particular test was used and what its limitations are. To summarize: the interview aims to assess understanding of what the candidate has done, not necessarily his memory of its small details.

What can be done to maximize a student's chances of doing well in this part of the examination? The answer is that over the duration of the course he should complete a good set of experimental study reports and make sure that he understands all the relevant concepts of experimentation and analysis, so that he is able to convey his knowledge to the assessor. The advice that we may offer covers three stages: carrying out practicals and writing them up in the notebook, preparation for the interview and the interview itself.

The practical notebook

Over the duration of his course the student will carry out a number of practicals. We have already discussed at the beginning of this chapter how they should be written up, but here it may be useful to talk about the types of studies that may be regarded as legitimate for a psychology practical notebook. The only criteria of acceptability are, first, that the subject matter of the study must be broadly psychological, and, secondly, that the student should have participated in the practical himself, either as the designer or as one of the experimenters or subjects. Little can be added to the second criterion; it would not be acceptable, for example, for a student to re-write a report of an experiment he had merely read about in a book or journal, but it would be acceptable if he had taken part in a replication study of the experiment.

What, then, constitutes a psychological study? In practice, this is a difficult question to answer; let us say that any investigation or observation of a structured nature concerning the behaviour or experience of organisms should be acceptable. Thus although a coin-tossing experiment counting the occurrence of heads and tails may demonstrate a number of important statistical laws, it hardly qualifies as a study in psychology. However, the choice behaviour of a rat or gerbil in a T-maze (where the animal has a two-option choice, between left and right) would be acceptable. Examiners frequently make the plea that they would like candidates to carry out studies in a variety of different areas, for example perception and memory, animal studies, developmental processes, social psychology and physiological aspects of behaviour. A large number of books are available which suggest experiments and studies which are easy to carry out. The following may be particularly helpful:

DeBold, R.C. (1968), *Manual of Contemporary Experiments in Psychology*, Prentice Hall

Fernald, L.D. (1965), *Experiments and Studies in General Psychology*, Houghton Mifflin

Gardiner and Kaminska (1975), *First Experiments in Psychology*, Methuen

Humphrey and Argyle (1962), *Social Psychology Through Experimentation*, Methuen

It is important to emphasize that we are not talking exclusively about experiments. A-level students should try to take a wide-ranging perspective of the large number of techniques that psychologists employ. The notebook should not necessarily be a 'lab. book'. The survey, the case study and the structured observation are all legitimate alternatives to the experiment, and will introduce a greater flexibility and contrast into the notebook. The variety also makes life a little unpredictable and interesting for the examiner, and this can only be beneficial.

Students sometimes worry that non-experimental studies are more difficult to analyse and interpret, or that they do not facilitate statistical treatment of data. This does not constitute a problem as long as there are write-ups in the notebook which *do* cover the relevant statistical tests and design procedures. A notebook containing no statistical analyses or recognized design procedures would put its owner in a difficult position in the interview, for the examiner is required to talk about these, even if they are not dealt with in the reports. However, this does not mean that *every* report needs to be appended with sophisticated statistical analysis. If numerical treatment is appropriate it should be included, but a study which satisfies other criteria should not be omitted just because it does not produce data which can be subjected to statistical treatment.

Another widely held fallacy is that practicals should utilize sophisticated equipment; furthermore, that the more sophisticated the apparatus, the better the experiment. This is nonsense; in fact, advanced hardware often has a besotting effect upon the experimenter: he becomes so obsessed with the equipment, its performance and handling that he loses sight of the psychological effects that he is studying. Centres vary greatly in the amount of equipment that they possess, but the only 'sufferers' are the staff of the impoverished schools and colleges, who have to rely largely upon their own ingenuity and inventiveness in the structuring of practicals which require little or no apparatus.

In the course of the interview, opportunity is often given to candidates to discuss any work that they may have carried out on their own, or have had a hand in designing. It should immediately be said that the student who has not been involved in any such original work will not be penalized: it is not prescribed, and a sound pass may perfectly well be secured by a candidate who has followed a set of class practicals and written them up competently. However, the student who *has* carried out some individual work, either on his own or with a small number of other students, may well benefit from his originality. Teachers should be able to offer advice and guidance.

What about the number of reports in the notebook? The syllabus talks of a minimum number of ten reports unless any of them are unusually extensive. However, it should be realized that the figure quoted is a minimum one, and students should aim to exceed the basic prescription if possible. Credit will be given for additional write-ups. In collating reports into his folder at the end of the course a student may look back on his first few write-ups and see them in retrospect as relatively poor and unsophisticated. Consequently, he may decide to omit them from the final selection. This is a mistake, for the examiner is aware that the ability to write up a practical well develops only with time and practice, and will not deduct marks for early inexperience, as long as the candidate can, if necessary, identify and discuss any deficiencies in the light of what he now knows.

Finally, we come to the presentation of the reports. As indicated earlier in the chapter, the work should be laid out in the accepted format, with clear headings and divisions. Write neatly and legibly, and make intelligent use of diagrams and tables where appropriate. Use a good-quality ring-folder, and dividers to separate the reports and to facilitate easy location of any particular practical. Always include a full table of contents at the front of the folder. The candidate who presents a set of grubby, coffee-stained reports housed in a war-weary, battered envelope folder or one with fold-down metal strips which prevent the examiner keeping it open at any one place is unlikely to get the best of starts in his interview. First impressions are important, and students should aim to do all they can to maximize initial impact.

Preparation for the interview
Make sure that plenty of time is allowed to complete the notebook well before the date of the interview. It is often all too evident to examiners that some students' final two or three reports have been written up in a great hurry and do not do them justice. A student is particularly at risk of this happening if he is taking the A-level course in one year, instead of the recommended two; if he is a part-time student and hence has less class-time in which to carry out the practical work; if his teacher does not take in and assess each write-up as it is completed over the duration of the course but asks to see them only in their collected final form just a few weeks before the oral; or if he is one of life's procrastinators, always putting off until tomorrow what should be done today.

In the days immediately before the oral, read through the reports thoroughly and be absolutely clear why things were done in a certain way, why a particular test was used, what the results tell us and so on. Try to anticipate the questions that the examiner may ask; for example, were there any other ways that the subjects could have been allocated to the experimental conditions; could the instructions have been improved; could any other procedural improvements have been made? Students should try to look at their practicals anew, with the eyes of an outsider. Above all, they should ensure that they know what lies behind the jargon. What is meant by a correlation coefficient? What exactly is the difference between a one-tailed and a two-tailed hypothesis? What do we really mean by two sets of scores being significantly different at the 0.05 level of confidence? Candidates must be able to answer these and similar questions in their own words. The examiner will be able to tell immediately if they really understand the concepts or have merely learned the 'right words' to impress. The assessment of candidates' understanding and comprehension is the main aim of these interviews.

Read and re-read the books that have been used on design and statistics thoroughly. Books such as Robson, Miller and Anderson are invaluable. However, assimilation of material is one thing, its resurrection and reproduction often entirely another. A person does not prepare for a driving test by simply sitting at home and reading the Highway Code. Just as the driving instructor will give the test applicant practice in the skills that he will need in his actual test, so the student should have undergone some simulation exercise similar to the interview before the real event – in short, a 'practice oral'. If the first time the candidate has to discuss his work with someone else is in the actual interview he will almost inevitably encounter some difficulties in coping because the situation will be completely novel and he will have no past experience to call upon. Thus students should practise 'trial runs' with both their teachers and their contemporaries. In fact, student–student orals can be more valuable, especially for the one playing the role of examiner. Role-playing techniques are well known for their success at giving players insight into, and empathy with, the values and expectations of others. To have played the part of examiner in simulation may well help in the all-important performance as student in the real interview.

One final suggestion: if there is another school or college in the area which enters candidates for the AEB Psychology A-level examination, ask if it is possible to swop teachers for practice sessions. The novel perspective, different questions and social strangeness of the newcomer will probably be a good indicator of the situation the candidate will have to deal with in the real interview.

The interview
The day of the oral examination arrives. By this time the candidate should have a sound understanding of the practical work and be confident that he has produced a good notebook. If this is not the case then it is clearly too late on the day itself to put things right, so be well prepared. Follow the advice already given in this chapter.

Each school or college will draw up a timetable of candidates for the examiner to see. If the centre is entering more than ten or twelve psychology candidates, two or three examiners will probably visit, and possibly for more than one day. Although examiners are 'standardized' (the Examining Board holds meetings and practical sessions to ensure that all examiners are equally fair and would agree upon the mark given to any particular oral performance and notebook), they may differ slightly in their interview techniques. This is, of course, due to individual differences in personality, background and so on. But candidates can be sure that although the techniques of appraisal may vary between examiners, standards do not. There are no 'hard' or 'soft' markers, so it makes no real difference which examiner carries out each assessment. It does, however, greatly affect the usefulness of the advice that we can offer concerning the interview, for not only are there personality differences between examiners, but no one particular examiner will be constant when viewed over a series of interviews. Flexibility of approach is stressed to examiners; consequently they will alter their approach and questioning in accordance with the capability and needs of each candidate. For example, some candidates perform well when the interviewer takes a 'chatty', easy line; others respond better to a more direct academic approach. So the oral examination that each student receives will be unique, unlike the written papers that he will sit, in which he is given exactly the same questions and with the same choice of alternatives as all the other candidates taking the A level. Because of this we cannot say which questions the examiner will ask, what answers should be given and what overall format the interview will take. The nature of the assessment, with each interview being unique, makes the answering of such questions quite impossible; clearly, there can be no such answers. However, we can give advice on what could conceivably be encountered bearing in mind that we shall only be able to talk about generalities rather than specifics.

The first information about the interview that the candidate will probably be given will be his appointment time. It should be clearly emphasized that the timetable drawn up by the teacher is only a rough guide, to give candidates some idea of what time they can expect their interview if everything goes according to plan. But students may be ill, or delayed by transport problems, or decide to withdraw at the last minute; the examiner may be a little early or late, or may want to take a longer or shorter lunch break than the one scheduled for him by the teacher; there may be some unforeseen event like the interview room being double-booked. Therefore if a candidate is told that his interview is at, say, 2.30 he should be aware that this is only an approximate guideline so that he will not feel the need to sit outside the interview room for eight hours waiting to be called in. Be prepared, then, to be flexible and adapt to the needs of the situation. If someone fails to turn up in the morning the teacher may ask a candidate to step in at short notice so that the examiner does not have to sit twiddling his thumbs for thirty minutes waiting for the next scheduled candidate to appear. Remember, the timetable is a very approximate guideline, and may not accurately correspond to what happens on the day itself. Unless there are some exonerating circumstances, like having a full-time job and not being able to take both the morning and the afternoon off work, a candidate should be available for interview at any time during the day.

As we have said earlier, candidates will need to have their notebooks with them on the day of the interview, otherwise they cannot be considered for assessment. Some examiners ask for all the notebooks to be brought to them collectively upon their arrival; others are happy for candidates to bring their own notebooks with them at the time of their interview. Again, some will permit notebooks to be taken away at the end of the interview, while others may wish to keep them until the end of the day so that they can compare different students' work and check out other factors that concern them. The examiner will assess the notebook during the interview, which will last approximately twenty-five to thirty minutes. He will probably also check through it, and read samples of the material either immediately before or (most likely) after each interview when the candidate is not in the room. He is guided by a written report that teachers are required to make on every notebook. Examiners value these teacher reports very highly.

In the time that candidates are actually in interview, it will not be possible to discuss all the practicals in which they have been involved. It could be done if the studies were considered in a very superficial manner, but this would be of little use to the examiner in trying to map out a candidate's understanding of the important concepts in design, analysis and general methodology. The studies are really a means to an end: by discussing the work that has been carried out, the examiner will be able to form a picture of the candidate's capability as a practical psychologist. So do not worry about being unable to discuss *all* the practicals, for it is not the studies themselves that are being assessed in this part of the examination, but the ability to write them up and to appreciate their strengths and weaknesses.

The typical examiner will allow discussions of three studies. But there are differences in examiners' preferences here, and candidates should not be surprised if any one particular examiner wishes to discuss more or less than this figure. Also, the means of selecting the reports for discussion will vary. A typical pattern is for the examiner to choose one, for one to be selected at random and for the choice of the third to be left to the candidate. (Again, we must emphasize that this is only a guideline. The examiner is, of course, at liberty to nominate all the areas for discussion himself if he so wishes.) There will be a number of motives affecting the examiner's selection of studies to be discussed. For example, if he wishes to see if a candidate appreciates the concept of association he may well select a study which is concerned with finding relationships between a number of variables and which possibly uses a correlation statistic to measure the degree of co-variance. This selection would then give the examiner a structure for his enquiry and help put the candidate at ease by enabling the examiner to relate his questions, which may be of a theoretical nature, to work which the candidate will have been involved in personally. Another, perhaps less altruistic, motive for selection is variety. The examiner will probably want to ring the changes and discuss different practicals with successive students: it can become rather predictable and even a little boring spending a whole day discussing the same study with every candidate.

What about the candidate's choice of report to discuss? If given the opportunity, which practical should he select? Three criteria tend to dominate candidates' choices. Many select the 'best' write-up, perhaps the one to which the teacher has given the highest mark; others select the most 'successful' practical (invariably, one which 'worked' and produced sound support for the experimental hypothesis); and others opt for a study which has fairly straightforward analysis, with no complicated statistical treatment involved. While these are, in their own different ways, understandable, only the second one has the potential for significantly affecting the examiner's judgement. Consider the other two. The first criterion is not likely to be particularly successful as a technique for securing a high grade because the examiner will not only have his own reading of a reasonable sample of a candidate's studies to guide him, but also the teacher's assessment, which will give an overall evaluation of the reports. It is wishful thinking to pick out an untypically good write-up and hope that the examiner will believe all the others are of the same standard. The final criterion mentioned, which we may call 'avoiding the statistics', is also mistaken. If the examiner wishes to talk about measures of dispersion, or tests of significance, he will, and such tactics will only make him take a different route. By continually trying to avoid any discussion of statistics the student will only succeed in alerting the examiner to any lack of confidence which he may have.

How valid, then, is the remaining rationale – selection of the 'best' or 'most successful' practical? The answer is that it is valid, but possibly not for the reasons students may initially suppose. Selection of 'good' experiments may be beneficial and illuminating not because the examiner will be impressed by the 'successful' practical that has been carried out (for this is, if anything, more likely to reflect the ability of the teacher if he has been the designer and supervisor): of greater value is why the candidate sees it as a good study. What actually constitutes the difference between a good study and a bad one? This is an important question.

It may well be apparent that the same benefit would accrue if the opposite approach were taken, that is, selecting a 'bad' study, so that design flaws in control and operation (for example) could be pointed out. Paradoxically, it may almost be in the candidate's interest to select his worst study for discussion if given the opportunity.

Incidentally, do not continually make excuses to the examiner about small disturbances or occurences which crop up from time to time in a study. Students rarely have highly sophisticated equipment at their disposal which could introduce more stringent control; in any case, people do not behave in a homogeneous fashion when used as subjects. It does not help the candidate's cause if he is unable to see beyond these nuisance-value 'noise effects' when trying to explain why things worked out as they did.

Having talked about the structuring of the interview, about the brief given to examiners and how the sample of reports that are discussed may be selected, it only remains for us to consider the type of questions examiners ask. It must be reiterated that there is no set format, no list of 'approved' questions. Flexibility of approach is constantly stressed to examiners so that they will match their approach to the particular student and particular notebook they are assessing. The best preparation for the student is to begin by considering the function of the interview. As we have stated previously, the examiner's task is to assess the competence of each student as a practical psychologist: how adequately can he write up a study, and how well does he understand what he has done? Candidates will be assessed on their knowledge, use and understanding of experimental methods in psychology as shown in their practical reports and in the interview. The assessment is divided into two categories: (1) the notebook, and (2) an understanding of design and statistics. The two parts are usually equally weighted and judged concurrently. Study the current syllabus very carefully, item by item, for this will largely govern the range of possible areas that the examiner may cover. *Remember that the questions asked may be on any part of the syllabus, even if it has not been covered in the notebook.* In fact, the item listing given in the syllabus serves as a guide to the questions that could be asked. In preparation for the oral use it as a checklist, going through each individual item. Tick those which are understood and then see the teacher about the remainder. By the time of the oral the candidate should have a sound understanding of all the following. It must be noted that this represents only part of the total syllabus (copies of the complete syllabus may be obtained from the AEB, Aldershot), and is correct at the time of going to press and for the foreseeable future.

Design
Hypothesis testing. The null hypothesis. One- and two-tailed hypotheses.
Independent and dependent variables. Control of variables.
Control and experimental groups: selection and function.
Randomization and random sampling. Appropriate size of samples.
Matching: purpose and use.
Independent and related measures designs; differences and relative merits.
Confounding; counterbalancing.
Standardized instructions; avoidance of experimenter effects.
Concepts of validity, reliability and standardization.

Statistics
The normal distribution and its use in psychological investigations.
Measures of central tendency and dispersion, particularly mean and standard deviation. Aptness of standard deviation as a descriptive/inferential measure.
Concept of statistical significance.
Two-sample tests of difference for related and unrelated samples, parametric and/or non-parametric (T-test, Mann–Whitney, Wilcoxon, Sign, binomial).
Assumptions of parametric tests.
Chi-squared test.
Correlation: rank and/or product-moment method. Significance and interpretation of a correlation coefficient.

Remember that design characteristics and statistical analysis are not really separate entities; it is simply convenient to consider a study in terms of two procedures – carrying out the study and then assessing the outcome. It should hardly need saying at this stage that the two parts are really one. In an experiment, once the data are in it is often too late to make changes; consequently design and analysis should be considered together at the outset. It is important that a candidate's discussion does not create the impression that statistics are something to be 'tagged on' to the end of a study as an afterthought.

The written examination

It is possible to analyse examination and study skills in the same way that we look at the performance of any other skill. The student should aim to isolate and identify the component parts of the skills that examinations measure, so that he can practise them, and, with the guidance of accurate feedback, gain in competence at the performance of the skills in order to put them into operation in the examination situation. Just as an individual can learn to trace around a star shape while looking only at a reflection of his performance in a mirror, or, with practice and guidance, to control and drive a car, so the student can learn to perform the skills that examinations require. Limitations of space and the specialist nature of this book prevent us from discussing some of the more general study skills that the student should be aware of. There are a number of excellent study skills books ranging from the classic texts such as Mace (1962) to the newer programmed-unit books, for example, Rowntree (1976). Fundamental skills such as processing and recording information, organizing and timetabling study time and writing essays are clearly crucial to scholastic success and the student should ensure that he is well grounded and competent in these areas, which form the foundation of the more specialized skills which we shall discuss in this section. It should be borne in mind that what we have to say – the processes that we examine and the advice that follows – is only the first part of the programme outlined above. The identification of examination skills is only the starting-point for action on the part of the student. Practice and modification are obviously vital.

A few basic points should be made before we consider the actual examination. One error that is made by many students is to rely upon too few sources of information in building up their knowledge of the subject. In psychology a large number of students use only one particular textbook or, even worse, do not read any books at all, simply relying upon their class notes. No single book can cover all aspects of a topic, and general textbooks in particular have to be highly selective, being able to consider only a very small proportion of the research in any field. The student should consult as large a number of sources as he can; not only will he amass more information as a result but he will also become aware of particular writers' biases, whether intentional or accidental. Students should also try and avoid having books in front of them when they are writing course essays: the temptation is all too great to copy out large chunks of the material. It is preferable to translate the ideas into one's own words, for this exercise greatly increases understanding of the material. It is all too easy to pretend that an idea has been understood, when in fact only a few jargon words and a phrase or two have been learned.

Let us now consider the examination itself. Remember, we are identifying and discussing examination skills so that they may be practised and, hopefully, perfected during the period of study. A candidate's fate is rarely decided on the day of the examination; it is the knowledge he has acquired and the skills that he has gradually learned that will be most influential. Despite what many say, examinations are not lotteries: much can be done in advance to ensure success.

Selecting the questions

What can the student do to minimize his shortcomings in the examination? The first major task that he will need to deal with is the selection of questions that he will answer. When he is allowed to look at the question paper the candidate should ensure that he does not panic and race through looking for 'trigger' words: where is the Piaget question? Where is the conditioning question? All the questions should be read carefully and slowly – a 'good' question may be missed because it does not contain a trigger word, and difficult ones attempted because they do. How often are students heard to say, after an examination, 'If only I'd known that question meant that' or 'I wish I'd done question four rather than six; I can see now how much better it was'? It is not that questions usually go unnoticed because of particularly heavy disguise – rather that the candidate has rushed through his reading of them and not considered them sufficiently carefully. With regard to each question he should ask himself, 'What does the examiner want here?', 'Do I have the information to write such an answer?' The time spent considering the questions, and selecting the ones to be attempted, is one of the most important parts of the whole examination, and should be recognized as such. Mock examination and essay-writing practice in the months before the examination will reduce the amount of time that the exercise requires.

One thing that a candidate should never do is 'bend' a question or pretend that it is worded slightly differently to how it actually is. He must answer the question set rather than the ones that he might have preferred. The candidate who answers his own versions of questions rather than the ones on the paper will receive practically no marks, irrespective of length or quality of answer. Sometimes this may be an oversight on the part of the candidate, an accident, but the end product will be the same as if it were deliberate. This is another reason for ensuring that the questions are carefully scrutinized. If a question specifically asks for an evaluation of Freud's contribution to psychology and a candidate merely describes, say, his stages of psychosexual development, he will not receive many marks for he will not have answered the question. It may be useful to note that many questions can be categorized as requiring either description or evaluation: practice will help the student to quickly discriminate between the two.

One way in which a candidate can decide whether or not he would be able to answer a question is to ask himself whether he could offer a single-sentence or, at most, single-paragraph answer to it. If he could, it is likely that he has a good understanding of the material and issues involved and could cope well with the question.

Strategy and technique

We have just emphasized the importance of selecting the right questions to answer. It is also vital to the candidate's chances of success that he attempt the required number of questions. It is surprising how frequently examiners encounter papers where the candidate has attempted, say, three instead of the stipulated four questions. The consequences are extremely serious because, in this case, the candidate's mark will now be out of a maximum of 75 rather than 100: he will have completely written off 25% of his potential marks. Teachers and examiners obviously recognize that there are reasons for such omissions. The candidate probably either ran out of time or 'couldn't answer another question'. Let us consider this last point. It is not particularly uncommon for candidates to find it difficult to select a last question that they feel able to answer, especially if their revision has been inadequate and rushed or if they have tried 'question-spotting' and come to grief. In this unfortunate eventuality the candidate should always make an attempt at a last question, because it is relatively easy to pick up the first few marks that are available on each question (some credit will be given for a reasonable attempt at an answer), and these marks may well make a difference between a pass and a fail. The selection of such questions is again important. Candidates should try to find a general, discussion-type of question rather than one requiring specific experimental knowledge, for an intelligent, reasoned argument which may nonetheless lack evidence will probably pick up more marks in the former than the latter.

Running short of time at the end of the examination for the last question, or having to severely rush it, can never be condoned. The candidate knows in advance how much time he will have in the examination and how many questions he will be required to answer. He should then ensure that he gets lots of practice at writing essays under examination conditions, for this will greatly aid his ability to assess how much he can write in forty minutes. He should also concentrate upon writing essays of equal duration. It is a serious mistake for an examinee to spend a disproportionate amount of time, say sixty or seventy minutes, writing an outstanding answer to his best question. A simple calculation will demonstrate the folly. Let us allow a total of ten minutes for reading the questions and planning the answers. This leaves two hours fifty minutes. If sixty-five minutes are spent on one answer, and forty-five minutes on the second and third questions, only fifteen minutes are left at the end for the final essay and reading through the answers. This is clearly inadequate, and illustrates the need for candidates to discipline and train themselves in writing strictly equal essays.

Let us examine the consequences of writing a relatively poor last answer. A typical A-level grading table might perhaps read as follows.

Grade	Mark range (%)
A	70–100
B	60–9
C	55–9
D	50–4
E	40–9
'O'	35–9
F	0–34

Perhaps the most interesting feature is the fact that the range between the top of the E grade and the bottom of the B grade is only 11 points. If one realizes that a good answer to a question might pick up, say, 16 points out of 25 and a poor one 5, we can see that such a difference on a last question could possibly mean a difference of three grades. It is not unreasonable to say that a good candidate's grade may well be determined by his final answer on each paper.

Candidates sometimes fail to appreciate that writing essays is an exercise in communication. They should always remember that their work will actually be read by another person and they need to convey their knowledge and ideas to him. Obviously if the candidate's handwriting is totally illegible he cannot be awarded any marks, for it will be impossible to judge the essay's worth. It is rare for handwriting to be absolutely unreadable, although examiners do encounter such work occasionally. However, untidy and messy scrawl is quite common and can hardly enhance a candidate's chances of impressing the examiner.

Just as legibility of handwriting is vital to the communication of ideas from candidate to examiner, so clarity and accuracy of expression are also extremely important. As we have said previously, students should practise putting concepts and theories into their own words; it is all too easy to shield one's ignorance behind empty jargon. Candidates should use specialized and technical terminology where it is appropriate and adds to the quality of the text, but generally they should concentrate upon straightforward and precise English.

Sometimes an idea or argument can be better understood from a diagram or flow-chart than textual explanation, and candidates should not hesitate to include diagrams and drawings if they add to a passage and enhance communication from candidate to examiner. However, a candidate should not waste precious examination time by sketching out diagrams which merely repeat what has already been said in the text, or adds nothing to it; for example, a drawing of Pavlov's dog in harness tells us very little about classical conditioning. Another kind of redundancy of information can occur if the candidate produces a worthwhile diagram but then wastes time by going over the same area in words. This doubling-up is unnecessary and inefficient: once a piece of information has been registered by the examiner and credited it will not be counted again, no matter how often it is repeated. Let us be quite clear about this: in GCE psychology examinations at least (for we are not qualified to speak about others) probably the single most influential factor in determining the mark which an examiner will award to an essay is the number of different relevant points that are made and related to answering the question. This works differently according to the phrasing of the question. In the case of a question such as 'Discuss the evidence that experimental studies have produced on the importance of early experience', the candidate who could articulately and accurately discuss, say, nine or ten different studies would probably receive more credit than a colleague who only knew of one or two. If, however, the question read 'Describe and critically evaluate any one study of early experience' the candidate would clearly be precluded from considering a plurality of studies: the high marks would be awarded to the examinee who could offer an intelligent and informed evaluation of a study with a large number of different criticisms and contributions, rather than to the candidate who talked around a single point, constantly repeating it. Quantity of production is not only or always the prime consideration; but the student who works on the assumption that in order to do well he needs to present a good volume of relevant material, intelligently presented and continually referred to, answering the question set is unlikely to be misguided.

Finally, candidates should pitch their answers at the 'intelligent layman'. It is worth pausing for a moment to consider what is meant by such a description. We mean that the writer should assume no psychological knowledge in the reader (that is, nothing can be taken for granted); but he should assume that he will be able to readily comprehend and appreciate information and arguments without going into unnecessary detail or repetition; and the logically obvious should not have to be pointed out. In short, the candidate should write as though to a man who is intelligent, but does not have specialist knowledge in the area.

Writing the answers

Having talked about the preparatory examination exercises we now turn to what is the most important aspect of the candidate's performance – the writing of the essays.

It should be emphasized at the outset that many vital activities occur between the selection of the questions and the writing of the answers. First there is the planning of the answers; secondly, the questions of style and technique. We are saying nothing new in emphasizing the need for the candidate to plan his answers: there are a number of reasons why he should do so. And if it is practised in normal essay-writing and mock examinations it can be reduced to a matter of a few minutes. In any case, the time is well spent. It is a dangerous fallacy that candidates should spend every possible minute of the examination writing: a little time spent in thought and preparation will pay dividends. For the candidate who does not plan his essays, the examination tends to be a three-hour exercise in recall and reproduction: he writes things down as and when they come to mind. As a consequence too much emphasis is placed upon straight regurgitation of learned material (at the expense of intelligent application and interpretation); essays tend to wander and lack direction, and usually do not answer the question very well, for the candidate is preoccupied with recall rather than usage of knowledge. If the non-planning candidate does attempt to draw his essay together with a conclusion he often finds it an impossibly difficult task, because he discovers on re-reading the essay that it lacks structure, purpose and integrating logic.

Having tried to convince the reader of the need for and value of planning, how should it be done? Probably the most common approach is simply for the candidate to ask himself what broad area the question is interested in and quickly jot down all the ideas as they come, without critical appraisal. The candidate then tries to match the specific demands of the question with the information he has listed down and crosses out the points which cannot be considered strictly relevant. Once this is done the candidate then organizes the material into meaningful categories (items that can be logically related), and decides upon his overall plan of attack to answer the question. As we have said, the length of time this exercise takes may initially be quite long, but with continual practice can be reduced to just a few minutes.

Little can be added to what we have already said about the first stage of the procedure; if the student's problem is one of recall then he should look to the books on basic study skills for advice. This is not to make light of the problem, for we know from the experience of our own students how common it is for examination candidates to 'go blank': it is simply that remedies are well detailed in other books. Let us then examine the second half of the process – relating the recalled material to the specific question and planning the strategy of the answer.

It should be repeated that the material must be organized in such a way that the question is actually answered. A question such as 'Discuss some of the factors that can cause us to forget' cannot be identified as 'the memory question' and then treated as though it said, 'Write down everything you know about memory.' Candidates must realize that questions require essays that actually answer them, not rigid, 'blanket' information. With regard to the content of answers, examiners state that they should be psychological in nature. This sounds a banality, but sociological, biological and even totally anecdotal answers are not particularly uncommon. Clearly, the examination is one in psychology, and therefore a candidate should not pass if he is unable to present evidence of having acquired a reasonable amount of knowledge in psychology. What is meant by psychology in this context? Given the perspective in which the current GCE examining boards view psychology (generally a science of behaviour and experience), experimental evidence is most likely to gain credit. For example, the syllabus of the AEB A level says that the main emphasis is on 'Experimental approaches to human behaviour'. This is not to say, of course, that observational data, case histories and other material will not be acceptable – simply that experimental data are preferred.

If being able to cite relevant psychological information is one of the major characteristics of a good candidate, then so is the ability to construct and communicate an intelligent, logical line of argument. In some essays (the more general, 'debate' questions like 'Should psychology be considered an arts or a science subject?'), this ability is of particular importance. Here again, candidates can help themselves by practising writing essays on the debate topics such as nature/nurture and science controversies, which tend to crop up frequently in past examination papers. The arguments can effectively be rehearsed in advance so that the well-prepared candidate will not have to work out difficult lines of thought under examination conditions. The prepared debate will, of course, have to be modified and adapted to the particular question that is set. That these two abilities are of primary importance is emphasized by the founding father of GCE psychology, John Radford, in one of his Chief Examiners' Reports, when he says, 'A really outstanding answer should show a clear grasp of relevant and up-to-date evidence, coupled with the ability to present a reasoned argument.'

Let us finally look at the structuring of the essay. Essays should usually comprise three distinct sections: an introduction, the main text in which the evidence and arguments are presented, and a conclusion which is a summary of the most important issues raised in the essay.

The main value of the introduction is that it presents a programme to the examiner so that he can see at the outset how the candidate intends to tackle the question and what kind of material is to be presented. It should be noted that the candidate who does not plan his essays before he writes them will be unable to do this. The introduction should be a brief orientation to the question and a list of 'contents' which are to follow. This will show the examiner that the candidate is well organized, and has a sound overview of the field and a systematic approach to answering the question. It can also provide a valuable perspective for the examiner, and can help justify the long-term, eventual relevance of a piece of material which, if first encountered in the main text, may be regarded as unnecessary. Do make sure, however, that introductions are kept as 'tight' and brief as possible – this is not the place for elaboration.

In the text of the essay, the candidate should ensure that key terms are defined (remember that our intelligent layman does not possess specialist psychological knowledge). For example, when answering the question 'Outline any one theory of the socialization of the child', a candidate should not launch straight into an exposition of the Piagetian view of social learning theory: he should ensure that he gives a working definition of 'socialization' to justify the answer that will follow. It is surprising how often candidates appear to be uncertain and confused about central concepts (what do we mean in essence by the term 'conditioning', for example?). Uncertainty or error in dealing with central concepts will create a poor impression in an examination. A good preparation for candidates to minimize the likelihood of such an occurrence is to check through problematic terms in the glossaries that can be found at the back of many widely used textbooks. As we have emphasized, comprehension and understanding are vitally important: examiners can invariably discriminate between the candidate who has genuine understanding and the one who has merely learned the right words to impress.

At the end of an essay, there should be a concluding paragraph which draws the material together, relates it to the question and provides a summary answer. It is not necessary to finish with a categorical statement, such as 'Yes, perception is learnt'; this is clearly inappropriate in many areas of psychology. As Hudson has observed, Humpty Dumpty would have made a fine psychologist, as he spent so much time sitting on the wall.

Further reading

Dobson, C.B. (ed.) (1976), *Schools Council General Studies Project*, Psychology Collection, Longman Resources Unit

Miller, S. (1975), *Experimental Design and Statistics*, Methuen

Bibliography

Abelson, R.P. and Lesser, G.S. 'The measurement of persuasibility in children', in C.I. Hovland and I.L. Janis, *Personality and Persuasibility* (1959), Yale University Press.

Adams, N.M. and Caldwell, W. (1963), 'The children's somatic apperception test,' *J. Gen. Psychol.*, 68, pp. 43–57.

Adler, A. (1927), *The Practice and Theory of Individual Psychology*, Harcourt Brace.

Adler, A. (1930), *Practice and Theory of Individual Psychology*, Bergmann.

Adorno, T.W., Frenkel-Brunswik, E., Levinson, D.J. and Sanford, R.N. (1950), *The Authoritarian Personality*, Harper.

Ainsworth, M. (1973), 'Anxious attachment and defensive reactions in a strange situation and their relationship to behaviour at home', *Paper presented to Society for Research in Child Development*.

Alfert, E. (1960), 'Comparison of responses to a vicarious and a direct threat', *J. Exp. Res. Personality*, 1, pp. 179–86.

Allport, F.H. (1955), *Theories of Perception and the Concept of Structure*, Wiley.

Allport, G.W., 'Attitudes', in C.M. Murchison (ed.) (1935), *Handbook of Social Psychology*, Clark University Press.

Allport, G.W. (1937), *Personality: A Psychological Interpretation*, Holt, Rinehart and Winston.

Allport, G.W. (1947), *The Use of Personal Documents in Psychological Science*, Holt, Rinehart and Winston.

Allport, G.W. (1955), *Becoming*, Yale University Press.

Allport, G.W. (1961), *Pattern and Growth in Personality*, Holt, Rinehart and Winston.

Allport, G.W. and Cantril, H. (1934), 'Judging personality from voice', *J. Soc. Psychol.*, 5, pp. 37–55.

Allport, G.W. and Odbert, H.S. (1936), 'Trait names: a psycho-lexical study', *Psychological Monographs: General and Applied*, 47.

Allport, G.W., Vernon, P.E. and Lindzey, G. (1960), *Study of Values Manual* (3rd. ed.), Houghton Mifflin.

Alpern, H.P. and Crabbe, J.C. (1972), 'Facilitation of the long-term store of memory with strychnine', *Science*, 177, pp. 722-4.

Ames, A. - *see* Ittelson, W.H. (1952), *The Ames Demonstrations in Perception*, Princeton University Press.

Amsel, A. (1962), 'Frustrative non-reward in partial reinforcement and discrimination. Some recent history and theoretical extension', *Psychol. Rev.*, 76, pp. 306-28.

Anastasi, A. (1958), *Differential Psychology* (3rd ed.), Macmillan

Anastasi, A. (1961), *Psychological Testing*, Macmillan.

Anderson, B.F. (1966), *The Psychology Experiment: An Introduction to the Scientific Method*, Brooks/Cole.

Anderson, L.D. (1939), 'The predictive value of infant tests in relation to intelligence at five years', *Child Dev.*, 10, pp. 202-12.

Antelman, S.M., Szechtman, H., Chin, P. and Fisher, A.D. (1975), 'Tail-pinching induced eating, gnawing and licking behaviour in rats: dependence on the nigrostriatal dopamine system', *Brain Research*, 99, pp. 319-77.

Argyle, M. (1967), *The Psychology of Interpersonal Behaviour*, Penguin.

Argyle, M., Salter, V., Burgess, P., Nicholson, N. C. and Williams, M. (1970), 'The communication of inferior, and superior attitudes by verbal and non-verbal signals', *Psychol. Bull.*, 23, 540-8.

Aronson, E. (1968), 'The process of dissonance', in N. Warren and M. Jahoda (1973), *Attitudes* (2nd ed.), Penguin.

Asch, S.E. (1946), 'Forming impressions of personality', *J. Abnorm. Soc. Psychol.*, 41, 258-90.

Asch, S.E., 'Effects of group pressure upon the modification and distortion of judgments', in H. Guetzkow (ed.) (1915), *Groups, Leadership and Men*, Carnegie Press.

Asch, S.E. (1952), *Social Psychology*, Prentice-Hall.

Atkinson, R.C. and Shiffrin, R.M. (1971), 'The control of short-term memory', *Scientific American*, 225 (2), 82-90.

Ball, S., Wood, C., and Smith, E.E. (1975), 'When are semantic targets detected faster than acoustic ones?' *Perception and Psychophysics*, 17, pp. 1-8.

Bandura, A. (1965), 'Influences of a model's reinforcement contingencies on the acquisition of imitative responses', *J. Pers. Soc. Psychol.*, 1, pp. 589-95.

Bandura, A. (1972), in *Encyclopaedia of Psychology*, Search Press.

Bandura, A., Grusec, J.E. and Menlove, C. (1965), 'Vicarious extinction of avoidance responses' (unpublished).

Bandura, A., Ross, D. and Ross, S.A. (1961), 'Transmission of aggression through imitation of aggressive models', *J. Abnorm. Psychol.*, 63, pp. 575-82.

Bandura, A. and Walters, R.H. (1959), *Adolescent Aggression*, Ronald.

Bannister, D. (1962), 'The nature and measurement of schizophrenic thought disorder', *J. Ment. Sci.*, 108, pp. 825-30.

Barber, P.J. and Legge, D. (1976), *Perception and Information*, Methuen.

Barnard, C. (1979), 'Birds of a feather', *New Scientist*, 13 August.

Bartlett, F.C. (1932), *Remembering*, Cambridge University Press.

Baumrind, D. (1964), 'Some thoughts on the ethics of research after reading Milgram's "Behavioural study of obedience"', *Am. Psychol.*, 19, pp. 4211-23.

Bayley, N., 'The development of mental abilities', in P.H. Mussen (ed.) (1970), *Carmichael's Manual of Child Psychology*, Wiley.

Bereiter, C. and Engelmann, S. (1966), *Teaching Disadvantaged Children in the Pre-school*, Prentice-Hall.

Bernstein, I.S. and Gordon, T.P., 'The function of aggression in primate societies', in I.L. Janis (ed.) (1977), *Current Trends In Psychology*, W. Kaufmann Inc.

Bettelheim, B. (1943),. 'Individual and mass behaviour in extreme situations', *J. Abnorm. Soc. Psychol.*, 38, pp. 417-52.

Bidney, D. (1953), *Theoretical Anthropology*, Columbia University Press.

Birch, H.G. (1945), 'The relation of previous experience to insightful problem-solving', *J. Comp. Psychol.*, 38, pp. 367-83.

Bitterman, M.E. and Kniffin, C.W. (1953), 'Manifest anxiety and perceptual defense', *J. Abnorm. Soc. Psychol.*, 48, p. 248.

Blank, M. and Solomon, F. (1968), 'A tutorial language programme to develop abstract thinking in socially disadvantaged pre-school children', *Child Dev.*, 39, pp. 379-89.

Blundell, J. (1975), *Physiological Psychology*, Methuen.

Borger, R. and Seaborne, A.E.M. (1966), *The Psychology of Learning*, Pelican.

Bower, G.H. (1970), 'Organizational factors in memory', *J. Cog. Psychol.*, 1, pp. 18-46.

Bower, G.H., 'Mental imagery and associative learning', in L. Gregg (ed.) (1972), *Cognition in Learning and Memory*, Wiley.

Bower, G.H., Clark, M.C., Lesgold, A.M. and Winzenz, D. (1969), 'Hierarchical retrieval schemes in recall of categorized word lists', *J. Verbal Learning and Verbal Behaviour*, 8, pp. 323-43.

Bower, T.G.R. (1966), 'The visual world of infants', *Scientific American*, 215 (6), pp. 80-92, offprint no. 502.

Bower, T.G.R. (1977), *The Perceptual World of the Child*, Fontana/Open Books.

Bowlby, J. (1965), *Child Care and the Growth of Love*, Pelican.

Braud, L.W. and Braud, W.G. (1972), 'Biochemical transfer of relational responding', *Science*, 176, pp. 942-4.

Brehm, J.W. (1966), *A Theory of Psychological Reactance*, Academic Press.

Brehm, J.W. and Cohen, A.R. (1962), *Explorations in Cognitive Dissonance*, Wiley.

Broadbent, D.E. (1958), *Perception and Communication*, Pergamon.

Broadbent, D.E. (1964), *Behaviour*, Methuen.

Broadbent, D.E. (1973), *In Defence of Empirical Psychology*, Methuen.

Broca, P. – *see* Geschwind, N. (1979), 'Specializations of the human brain', *Scientific American*, September.

Brown, H. and Stevens, R. (eds.) (1975), *Social Behaviour and Experience*, Hodder and Stoughton Educational/Open University Press.

Brown, R. (1965), *Social Psychology*, Free Press.

Brown, R. (1965), *Social Psychology*, Collier Macmillan International.

Brown, R. and Hernstein, R.J. (1975), *Psychology*, Methuen.

Bruce, R.W. (1933), 'Conditions of transfer of training', *J. Exp. Psychol.*, 16, pp. 343–61.

Bruner, J.S., in J.S. Bruner, J.J. Goodnow and G.A. Austin (1956), *A Study of Thinking*, Wiley.

Bruner, J.S., Busiek, R.D. and Minturn, A.L. (1952), 'Assimilation in the immediate reproduction of visually perceived figures', *J. Exp. Psychol.*, 44, pp. 151–5.

Bruner, J.S. and Goodman, C.C. (1947), 'Value and need as organizing factors in perception', *J. Abnorm. Soc. Psychol.*, 42, p. 33.

Bruner, J.S., Goodnow, J.J. and Austin, G.A. (1956), *A Study of Thinking*, Wiley.

Brunswik, E. (1952), *Conceptual Framework of Psychology*, University of Chicago Press.

Brunswik, E. (1956), *Perception and the Representative Design of Psychological Experiments*, University of California Press.

Bryant, P.E. (1972), 'The understanding of invariance by very young children', *Canadian J. Psychol.*/Rev. *Canadian Psychol.*, 26, pp. 78–96.

Bryant, P.E. (1974), *Perception and Understanding in Young Children*, Methuen.

Burks, B.S. (1928), 'The relative influence of nature and nurture upon mental development', in *Twenty-seventh Yearbook of the National Society for the Study of Education (Part 1)*, University of Chicago Press.

Burns, R.B. (1979), *The Self Concept*, Longmans.

Burns, R.B. and Dobson, C.B. (1981), *Experimental Psychology*, M.T.P.

Butler, J.M. and Haigh, G.V., 'Changes in the relation between self-concept and ideal concepts consequent upon client-centred counselling', in C.R. Rogers and R.F. Dymond (eds.) (1954), *Psychotherapy and Personality Change*, University of Chicago Press.

Calhoun, J.B. (1962), 'Population density and social pathology', *Scientific American*, 206 (2), pp. 139–48.

Campbell, D.T. (1963), 'Social attitudes and other acquired behavioural dispositions', in S. Koch (ed.), *Psychology: A Study of a Science*, McGraw-Hill.

Campbell, H.J. (1973), *The Pleasure Areas*, Methuen.

Cannon, W.B. (1927), 'The James–Lange theory of emotions: a critical examination and an alternative theory', *Am. J. Psychol.*, 39, pp. 106–24.

Cannon, W.B. (1929), *Bodily Changes in Pain, Hunger, Fear and Rage: An Account of Recent Researches into the Function of Emotional Excitement*, Appleton-Century-Crofts.

Cantril, H. (1944), *Gauging Public Opinion*, Princeton University Press.

Carlson, N.R. (1977), *Physiology of Behaviour*, Allyn and Bacon Inc.

Carmichael, L. (1927), in R.C. Birney and R.C. Teevan (eds.), *Instinct*, Van Nostrand.

Carmichael, L., Hogan, H.P. and Walter, A.A. (1932), 'An experimental study of the effect of language on the reproduction of visually perceived forms', *J. Exp. Psychol.*, 15, pp. 73–86.

Carpenter, B., Wiener, M. and Carpenter, J. T. (1956), 'Predictability of perceptual defense behaviour', *J. Abnorm. Soc. Psychol.*, 52, p. 380.

Carroll, J.B. (1964), *Language and Thought*, Prentice-Hall.

Cattell, R.B. (1965), *The Scientific Analysis of Personality*, Penguin.

Cavanagh, P. (1963), 'The autotutor and classroom instructions', *Occupational Psychol.*, 37, pp. 44–9.

Chapanis, N.P. and Chapanis, A. (1964), 'Cognitive dissonance five years later', *Psychol. Bull.*, 61, pp. 1–22.

Chapman, R.N., in R. Brown (1965), *Social Psychology*, Collier MacMillan International.

Chomsky, N. (1968), *Language and Mind*, Harcourt Brace.

Cohen, A.R. (1959), 'Communication discrepancy and attitude change: a dissonance theory approach', *J. Personality*, 27, pp. 386–96.

Cohen, B.D., Noblin, C.D. and Silverman, A.J. (1968), 'Functional asymmetry of the human brain', *Science*, 162, pp. 475–7.

Cohen, J. (ed.) (1968), *Psychology: An Outline for the Intending Student*, Routledge and Kegan Paul.

Cohen, S.A. (1966), 'A classification of LSD complications', *Psychosomatics*, 7, pp. 182–6.

Collins, A.M. and Quillian, M.R., 'Experiments on semantic memory and language comprehension', in L.W. Gregg (ed.) (1972), *Cognition in Learning and Memory*, Wiley.

Conrad, R. (1964), 'Acoustic confusions in immediate memory', *Brit. J. Psychol.*, 55, pp. 75–84.

Conrad, R. and Hull, A.J. (1964), 'Information, acoustic confusion and memory span', *Brit. J. Psychol.*, 55, 429–32.

Cook, M. (1971), *Interpersonal Perception*, Penguin.

Cook, S.W., Hicks, L.H., Kimble, G.A., McGuire, W.J., Schoggen, P.H. and Smith, M.B. (1972), 'Ethical standards for research with human subjects', *Amer. Psychol. Assoc. Mon.*, 3, pp. 1–19.

Cook, S.W. and Selltiz, C. (1964), 'A multiple indicator approach to attitude measurement', in N. Warren and M. Jahoda (eds.) (1973), *Attitudes*, Penguin.

Cooley, C.H. (1902), *Human Nature and the Social Order*, Scribner.

Cooper, R.M., and Zubeck, J.P. (1958), 'Effects of enriched and restricted early environments on the learning ability of bright and dull rats', *Canadian J. Psychol.*, 12, pp. 159-64.

Craik, F.I.M. (1971), 'Primary memory', *Brit. Med. Bull.*, 27, pp. 232-6.

Craik, F.I.M. and Lockhart, R.S. (1972), 'Levels of processing: a framework for memory research', *J. Verbal Learning and Verbal Behaviour*, 11, pp. 671-84.

Craik, F.I.M. and Watkins, M.J. (1973), 'The role of rehearsal in short-term memory', *J. Verbal Learning and Verbal Behaviour*, 12, pp. 599-607.

Craik, F.I.M. and Tulving, E. (1975), 'Depth of processing and the retention of words in episodic memory', *J. Exp. Psychol.*, 104, pp. 268-94.

Crocker, A.C. (1969), *Psychology for the Teacher or how to put Figures in their Place*, Penguin.

Crow, T.J. (1979) – *see* Iversen, L.L., 'The chemistry of the brain', *Scientific American*, September.

Crutchfield, R.S. (1954), 'A new technique for measuring individual differences in conformity to group judgment', *Proc. Invitational Conf. on Testing Problems*, pp. 69-74.

Darwin, C. (1859), *Origin of Species*, Murray.

Davitz, J.R. (1964), *The Communication of Emotional Meaning*, McGraw-Hill.

DeFleur, M.L. and Westie, F.R. (1958), 'Verbal attitudes and overt acts: an experiment on the salience of attitudes', *Am. Sociol. Rev.*, 23, pp. 667-73.

Deutsch, J.A. (1960), *The Structural Basis of Behaviour*, Cambridge University Press.

Disch, T.M. (1980), *The Prisoner*, New English Library.

Dixon, N.F. (1958), 'The effect of subliminal stimulation upon autonomic and verbal behaviour', *J. Abnorm. Soc. Psychol.*, 57, p. 29.

Dodwell, P.C. 'Studies of the visual system', in B.M. Foss (ed.) (1966), *New Horizons in Psychology, 1*, Penguin.

Dollard, J. and Miller, N.E. (1950), *Personality and Psychotherapy*, McGraw-Hill.

Dulit, E. (1972), 'Adolescent thinking à la Piaget: the formal stage', *J. Youth and Adolescence*, 1 (4), pp. 282-301.

Ebbinghaus, H. (1885), *Memory*, Teachers' College.

Ebling, F. and Highnam, K.C. (1969), *Chemical Communication*, Edward Arnold.

Ehrlich, D., Guttman, I., Schonbach, P. and Mills, J. (1957), 'Post-decision exposure to relevant information', *J. Abnorm. Soc. Psychol.*, 54, pp. 98-102.

Eibl-Eibesfeldt, I., 'Similarities and differences between cultures in expressive movements', in R. Hinde (ed.) (1972), *Non-Verbal Communication*, Cambridge University Press.

Ekman, P. (1969), 'Studies in non-verbal behaviour', *Paper read at NATO Symposium on Non-Verbal Communication, Oxford.*

Ekman, P. and Friesen, W.V. (1969), 'Origin, usage and coding: the basis of five categories in non-verbal behaviour', *Semiotica*, 1, pp. 49-98.

Elkind, D. (1971), *Children and Adolescents: Interpretative Essays on Jean Piaget*, Oxford University Press.

Elms, A.C. (1969), 'Role playing, reward and attitude change', in N.Warren and M. Jahoda (eds.) (1973), *Attitudes*, Penguin.

Elms, A.C. (1976), *Attitudes*, Open University Press.

Engel, E. (1956), 'The role of content in binocular resolution', *Amer. J. Psychol.*, 69, p. 87.

Eriksen, C.W. (1951), 'Some implications for TAT interpretation arising from need and perception experiments', *J. Person.*, 19, p. 282.

Eriksen, C.W. and Brown, C.T. (1956), 'An experimental and theoretical analysis of perceptual defense', *J. Abnorm. Soc. Psychol.*, 52, p. 224.

Erikson, E.H., 'Ego identity and the psychosocial moratorium', in H.L. Witner and R. Kosinsky (eds.) (1956), *New Perspectives for Research in Juvenile Delinquency*, US Children's Bureau, no. 356.

Erikson, E.H. (1956), 'The problem of ego identity', *J. Amer. Psychoan. Assoc.*, 4, pp. 58-121.

Erikson, E.H. (1963), *Childhood and Society*, Norton.

Erikson, E.H. (1965), *Childhood and Society* (2nd ed.), Penguin.

Erlingmeyer-Kimling, L. and Jarvik, L.F. (1963), 'Genetics and intelligence: a review', *Science*, 142, pp. 1477-9.

Escalona, S.K., 'The use of infant tests for predictive purposes', in W.E. Martin and C.B. Stendler (eds.) (1954), *Readings in Child Development*, Harcourt Brace.

Estes, W.K. (1970), *Learning Theory and Mental Development*, Academic Press.

Eysenck, H.J. (1957), *Sense and Nonsense in Psychology*, Penguin.

Eysenck, H.J. (1965), *Fact and Fiction in Psychology*, Penguin.

Eysenck, H.J. (1971), *Race, Intelligence and Education*, Maurice Temple-Smith.

Eysenck, H.J. (1977), *Psychology is about People*, Penguin.

Fantz, R.L., 'The origin of form perception', in W.T. Greenough (ed.), (1961), *The Nature and Nurture of Behaviour; Developmental Psychobiology*, W.H. Freeman and Co.

Festinger, L. (1957), *A Theory of Cognitive Dissonance*, Row, Peterson.

Festinger, L. and Carlsmith, J. (1959), 'Cognitive consequences of forced compliances', *J. Abnorm. Soc. Psychol.*, 58, pp. 203-10.

Festinger, L., Riecken, H. and Schachter, S. (1956), *When Prophecy Fails*, University of Minnesota Press.

Fields, H. (1979), reported at Second World Congress of Pain, Montreal.

Fillmore, C.J. 'The case for case,' in E. Bach and E.T. Harmes (eds.), (1968), *Universals in Linguistic Theory*, Holt, Rinehart and Winston.

Fischer, B. and Poggio, G., quoted in M. Robertson (1978), 'There's more to seeing in depth than meets the eye', *New Scientist*, 18 Mayo.

Fishbein, M. and Ajzen, I. (1975), *Belief, Attitude, Intention and Behaviour*, Addison-Wesley.

Fisher, A.E. (1956, 1962), quoted in P.M. Milner (1971), *Physiological Psychology*, Holt.

Flavell, J.H. (1963), *The Developmental Psychology of Jean Piaget*, Van Nostrand.

Fransella, F. (1975), *Need to Change?*, Methuen.

Franksenberg, R. (1957), *Village on the Border*, Cohen and West.

Freedman, J.L. and Sears, D.O., 'Selective exposure', in L. Berkowitz (ed.) (1965), *Advances in Experimental Social Psychology*, vol. 2, Academic Press.

Freeman, F.N., Holzinger, K.J. and Mitchell, B.C. (1928), 'The influence of environment on the intelligence, school achievement and conduct of foster children', *Twenty-seventh Yearbook of the National Society for the Study of Education*, 27, pp. 103–217.

Friedman, M.I., Rowland, N., Saller, C.F. and Stricker, E.M. (1976), 'Homeostasis during hypoglycemia', *Science*.

Friedman, M.I. and Stricker, E.M. (1976), 'The physiological psychology of hunger', *Psychol. Rev.* 83 (6), pp. 409–31.

Freud, S. (1940), in J. Strachey (ed.) (1964), *An Outline of Psychoanalysis*, vol. 23.

Fromm, E. (1956), *The Art of Loving*, Harper and Row.

Fuller, J.L. and Thompson, W.R. (1960), *Behaviour Genetics*, Wiley.

Gainotti, G. (1972), 'Emotional behaviour and hemispheric side of the lesion', *Cortex*, 8 (1), pp. 41–55.

Gahagan, J. (1975), *Interpersonal and Group Behaviour*, Methuen.

Galton, F. (1869), *Hereditary Genius*, Fontana, 1962.

Galton, F. (1893), *Inquiries into Human Faculty and its Development*, Macmillan.

Gardner, A.R. and Gardner, B. (1969), 'Teaching sign language to a chimpanzee', *Science*, 165, pp. 664–72.

Gates, A.I. (1931), *Elementary Psychology*, Macmillan.

Gazzaniga, M.S. (1970), *The Bisected Brain*, Appleton-Century-Crofts.

Gibson, E.J. and Walk, R.D., 'The visual cliff', in W.T. Greenough (ed.) (1960), *The Nature and Nurture of Behaviour: Developmental Psychobiology*, W.H. Freeman and Co.

Gibson, W.E., Reid, L.D., Sakai, M. and Porter, P.B. (1965), 'Inter-cranial stimulation compared with sugar–water reinforcement', *Science*, 148, pp. 1357–9.

Gilchrist, J.C. and Nesberg, L.S. (1952), 'Need and perceptual change in need-related objects', *J. Exp. Psychol.*, 44, p. 369.

Glanzer, M. and Cunitz, A.R. (1966), 'Two storage mechanisms in free recall', *J. Verbal Learning and Verbal Behaviour*, 5, pp. 351-60.

Goddard, H.H. (1912), 'How shall we educate mental defectives?', *The Training School Bull.*, 9, p. 43.

Goffman, E. (1961), *Asylums*, Penguin.

Gold, R.M. (1973), 'Hypothalamic obesity: the myth of the ventro-medial nucleus', *Science*, 182, pp. 488-90.

Gordon, E.W., 'Introduction', in J. Hellmuth (ed.) (1969), *Disadvantaged Child*, vol. 2, Brunner-Mazel.

Gottschaldt, K. (1926), 'Uber den Einfluss der Ehrfahrung auf die Wahrnehmung von Figuren', *Psych. Forsch.*, 8, p. 261.

Gray, J.A. (1971), *The Psychology of Fear and Stress*, Weidenfeld and Nicolson.

Gray, S.W. and Klaus, R.A. (1970), 'The early training project: a seventh-year report', *Child Dev.*, 41, pp. 909-24.

Gregory, R. (1977), *Eye and Brain*, Weidenfeld and Nicolson.

Gregory, R.L. and Wallace, J.G. (1963), 'Recovery from early blindness: a case study', *Exp. Psychol. Soc. Monogr.*, 2.

Gross, C.G., Rocha-Miranda, C.E., and Bender, D.B. (1972), 'Visual properties of neurons in the inferotemporal cortex of the macaque', *J. Neurophysiology*, 35, pp. 96-111.

Grossman, S.P. (1960), 'Eating or drinking elicited by direct adrenergic or cholinergic stimulation of hypothalamus', *Science*, 132, pp. 301-2.

Guilford, J.P. (1967), *The Nature of Human Intelligence*, McGraw-Hill.

Guthrie, E.R. (1938), *Psychology of Human Conflict*, Harper.

Haber, R.N. and Haber, R.B. (1964), 'Eidetic imagery: 1. Frequency', *Perceptual and Motor Skills*, 19, pp. 131-8.

Hailman, J.P. (1969), 'How an instinct is learned', *Scientific American*, 22 (6), 98-106.

Hall, E.T. (1963), 'Silent assumptions in social communication', *Res. Pub. Assn. Nerv. Ment. Dis.*, 42, pp. 41-55.

Hammond, K.R. (1959), *Teaching Comprehensive Medical Care: A Psychological Study of a Change in Medical Education*, Harvard University Press.

Hardy, M. and Heyes, S. (1979), *Beginning Psychology*, Weidenfeld and Nicolson.

Harlow, H.F. (1949), 'The formation of learning sets', *Psychol. Rev.*, 56, pp. 51-6; also in *Scientific American*, 181 (2), 36-9.

Harlow, H.F. (1958), 'The nature of love', *Am. Psychologist*, 13, pp. 673-85.

Harlow, H.F. (1959), 'Love in infant monkeys', *Scientific American*, 200 (6), pp. 68-74.

Harlow, H.F. and Harlow, M.K. (1962), 'Social deprivation in monkeys', *Scientific American*, 207 (5), pp. 136-46.

Harrobin, D. (1980), 'A singular solution for schizophrenia', *New Scientist*, 28, February.

Heather, N. (1976), *Radical Perspectives in Psychology*, Methuen.

Hebb, D.O. (1949), *The Organization of Behaviour*, Wiley.

Hebb, D.O. (1958), *A Textbook of Psychology*, Saunders.

Heider, F. (1946), 'Attitudes and cognitive organizations', *J. Psychol.*, 21, pp. 107–112.

Heiligenberg, W. (1963), quoted in A. Manning, *An Introduction to Animal Behaviour*, Edward Arnold.

Held, R. (1965), 'Plasticity in sensory-motor systems', *Scientific American*, 213 (5).

Henderson, N.D. (1970), 'Genetic influences on the behaviour of mice can be obscured by laboratory rearing', *J. Comp. Physiolog. Psychol.*, 72, pp. 505–11.

Hess, E.H. (1956), 'Space perception in the chick', *Scientific American*, 195, pp. 71–80.

Hess, E.H. (1972), 'Imprinting in a natural laboratory', *Scientific American*, 227 (2), pp. 24–31.

Hetherington, A.W. and Ranson, S.W. (1939), 'Experimental hypothalamohypophyseal obesity in the rat', *Proc. Society Exp. Biol. and Medicine*, 41, pp. 465–6.

Hetherington, E.M. and Frankie, G. (1967), 'Effects of parental dominance, warmth and conflict on imitation in children', *J. Personality and Social Psychol.*, 6, pp. 119–25.

Hildum, D.C. and Brown, R.W. (1956), 'Verbal reinforcement and interviewer bias', *J. Abnorm. Soc. Psychol.*, 53, pp. 108–11.

Hilgard, E.R., Atkinson, R.C. and Atkinson, R.L. (1975). *Introduction to Psychology*, Harcourt Brace Jovanovich Inc.

Hinde, R.A. (1970), *Animal Behaviour* (2nd ed.), McGraw-Hill.

Hinde, R.A., 'The nature of aggression', in N. Chalmers, R. Crawley and S. Rose (eds.) (1971), *The Biological Bases of Behaviour*, Open University Press.

Hockett, C.F. (1958), *A Course in Modern Linguistics*, Macmillan.

Hohmann, G.W. (1966), 'Some effects of spinal cord lesions on experienced emotional feelings', *Psychophysiology*, 3, pp. 143–56.

Hollander, E.P. and Willis, R.H. (1967), 'Some current issues in the psychology of conformity and nonconformity', *Psychol. Bull.*, 68, pp. 62–76.

Holmes, D.S. and Berkowitz, L. (1961), 'Some context effects in social perception', *J. Abnorm. Soc. Psychol.*, 62, pp. 150–12.

Holway, A.H. and Boring, E.G. (1941), 'Determinants of apparent visual size with distance variant', *Am. J. Psychol.*, 54, pp. 21–37.

Honzik, M.P. (1957), 'Developmental studies of parent–child resemblance in intelligence', *Child Dev.*, 28, pp. 215–28.

Honzik, M.P., MacFarlane, J.W. and Allen, L. (1948), 'The stability of mental test performance between two and eighteen years', *J. Exp. Education*, 17, pp. 309–24.

Horney, K. (1937), *The Neurotic Personality of Our Time*, Routledge.

Horowitz, E.L. (1936), 'Developing attitudes towards negroes', in H. Proshanky and B. Seidenberg (eds.) (1936), *Basic Studies in Social Psychology*, Holt, Rinehart and Winston.

Hovland, C.I. (1959), 'Reconciling conflicting results derived from experimental and survey studies of attitude change', *Am. Psychol.*, 14, pp. 8-17.

Hovland, C.I. and Janis, I.L. (1959), *Personality and Persuasibility*, Yale University Press.

Hovland, C.I., Lumsdaine, A.A. and Sheffield, F.D. (1949), *Experiments in Mass Communication*, Princeton University Press.

Hovland, C.I. and Mandell, W. (1952), 'An experimental comparison of conclusion drawing by the communicator and the audience', *J. Abnorm. Soc. Psychol.*, 47, pp. 581-8.

Hovland, C.I. and Weiss, W. (1951), 'The influence of source credibility on communication effectiveness', *Public Opinion Quarterly*, 15, pp. 635-50.

Hubel, D.H. (1963), 'The visual cortex of the brain', in N. Chalmers *et al.* (eds.), (1971), *The Biological Bases of Behaviour*, Open University Press.

Hubel, D.H. and Wiesel, T.N. (1962), 'Receptive fields of cells in the striate cortex of young, visually inexperienced kittens', *Journal of Neurophysiology*, 26, p. 994.

Hubel, D.H. and Wiesel, T.N. (1962), 'Receptive fields, binocular interaction and functional architecture in the cat's visual cortex', *J. Physiol. Psychol.*, 160, pp. 106-54.

Hughes, J. and Kosterlitz, H. (1975), quoted in L. Iversen, 'The chemistry of the brain', *Scientific American*, September, 1979.

Hull, C.L. (1943), *Principles of Behaviour*, Appleton-Century-Crofts.

Hunt, J.McV. (1961), *Intelligence and Experience*, Ronald Press.

Hunt, J. McV. (1969), 'Has compensatory education failed? Has it been attempted?', *Harvard Educational Rev.*, 39, pp. 278-300.

Hunt, J. McV. (1972), 'Early childhood education and social class', *The Canadian Psychologist*, 13, pp. 305-28.

Hyman, H. (1959), *Political Socialization: a Study in the Psychology of Political Behaviour*, Free Press.

Hyman, R. (1964), *The Nature of Psychological Inquiry*, Prentice-Hall.

Illingworth, R.S. (1961), 'Predictive value of developmental tests in the first years', *J. Child Psychol. and Psychiatry*, 2, pp. 210-15.

Irwin, W. and Benuazizi, A. (1966), 'Pentylenetetrazol enhances memory function', *Science*, 152, pp. 100-2.

James, W. (1890), *The Principles of Psychology*, Holt.

Janis, I.L. and Feshback, S. (1963), 'Effects of fear-arousing communications', *J. Abnorm. Soc. Psychol.*, 48, pp. 78-92.

Janis, I.L. and Field, P., 'Sex differences and personality factors related to persuasibility', in C.I. Hovland and I.L. Janis (eds.) (1959), *Personality and Persuasibility*, Yale University Press.

Jensen, A.R. (1969a), 'How much can we boost IQ and scolastic achievement?', *Harvard Educational Review*, 39, pp. 1-123.

Jensen, A.R. (1969b), 'Reducing the heredity-environmental uncertainty', *Harvard Educational Review*, 39, pp. 203-43.

Jensen, A.R. (1973), *Educability and Group Differences*, Harper and Row.

Jones, E. (1964), *The Life and Work of Sigmund Freud*, ed. L. Trilling and S. Marcus, Penguin.

Jourard, S.M. (1966), 'An exploratory study of body accessibility', *Brit. J. Soc. Clin. Psychol.*, 5, pp. 221-31.

Jourard, S.M. and Secord, P.F. (1955), 'Body-cathexis and personality', *Brit. J. Psychol.*, 46, pp. 130-8.

Juel-Nielsen, N. (1965), 'Individual and environment: a psychiatric-psychological investigation of monozygotic twins reared apart', *Acta Psychiatrica et Neurologica Scandinavica*, Monograph Supplement, p. 183.

Kahn, R.L. and Cannel, C.F. (1957), *The Dynamics of Interviewing*, Wiley.

Karnes, M.B., Teska, J.A., Hodgins, A.A. and Badger, E.D. (1970), 'Educational intervention at home by mothers of disadvantaged children', *Child Dev.*, 41, pp. 925-35.

Kasting, N. and Cooper, K. (1979), 'Antipyresis following perfusion of brain sites with vasopressin', *Experientia*, 35, 208.

Katz, D. (1942), 'Do interviewers bias poll results?', *Public Opinion Quarterly*, 6, pp. 248-68.

Katz, D. (1960), 'The functional approach to the study of attitudes', *Public Opinion Quarterly*, 24, pp. 163-204.

Kaufman, E.L., Lord, M.W., Reese, T.W. and Yolkmann, J. (1949), 'The discrimination of visual number', *American Journal of Psychology*, 62, pp. 498-525.

Kaufmann, H. (1973), *Social Psychology: The Study of Human Interaction*, Holt, Rinehart and Winston.

Kelly, G.A. (1955), *The Psychology of Personal Constructs*, vols. 1 and 2, Norton.

Kelman, H.C. (1953), 'Attitude change as a function of response restriction', *Human Rltns.*, 6, pp. 185-214.

Kelman, H.C. (1961), 'Processes of opinion change', *Public Opinion Quarterly*, 25, pp. 57-78.

Kelman, H.C. and Hovland, C.I. (1953), 'Reinstatement of the communicator in delayed measurement of opinion change', *J. Abnorm. Soc. Psychol.*, 48, pp. 327-35.

Kelvin, P. (1969), *The Bases of Social Behaviour*, Holt, Rinehart and Winston.

Kimble, G.A. (1948), 'Reminiscence in motor learning as a function of length of interpolated rest', *J. Exp. Psychol.*, 38, pp. 239-44.

Kinder, E.F. (1927), 'A study of the nest-building activity of the albino rat', *J. Exp. Zoology*, 47, pp. 117-61.

Kinsey, A.C., Pomeroy, W.B. and Martin, C.E. (1948), *Sexual Behaviour in the Human Male*, Saunders.

Kinsey, A.C., Pomeroy, W.B., Martin, C.E. and Gebhard, P.H. (1953), *Sexual Behaviour in the Human Female*, Saunders.

Kirby, R. and Radford, J. (1976), *Individual Differences*, Methuen.

Klaus, R.A. and Gray, S.W. (1968), 'The early training project for disadvantaged children: a report after five years', *Monographs of the Society for Research in Child Development*, 33, p. 4.

Kohler, I. (1962), 'Experiments with goggles', *Scientific American*, offprint no. 465.

Kohler, W. (1925), *The Mentality of Apes*, trans. E. Winter, Harcourt Brace.

Koluchova, J. (1972), 'Severe deprivation in twins: a case study', *J. Child Psychol. and Psychiatry*, 13, pp. 107–14.

Krebs, C. and Boonstra, R. (1979), 'Viability of large and small sized adults, in fluctuating vole populations', *Ecology*, 60 (3), pp. 567.

Kretschmer, E. (1948), *Physique and Character*, Kegan Paul.

Kuffler, S.W. (1953), quoted in D.H. Hubel (1963), 'The visual cortex of the brain', in N. Chalmers *et al.* (eds.) (1971), *The Biological Bases of Behaviour*, Open University Press.

Kuhn, H.H. (1960), 'Self attitudes by age, sex and professional training', *Sociol. Quarterly*, 1, pp. 39–55.

Kuhn, H.H. and McPartland, T.S. (1954), 'An empirical investigation of self attitudes', *Amer. Sociol. Rev.*, 47, pp. 647–52.

Kuhn, T.S. (1970), *The Structure of Scientific Revolutions*, University of Chicago Press.

Kulpe, O. (1904), 'Versuche uber Abstraktion', *Ber. I Kongress exp. Psychol.*

Kuo, Z.Y., in R.C. Birney and R.C. Teevan (eds.) (1924), *Instinct*, Van Nostrand.

Kutner, B., Williams, C. and Yarrow, P.R. (1952), 'Verbal attitudes and overt behaviour involving racial prejudice', *J. Abnorm. Soc. Psychol.*, 47, pp. 647–52.

LaBarre, W., 'Paralinguistics, kinesics and cultural anthropology', in T.A. Sebeok, A.S. Hayes and M.C. Bateson (eds.) (1964), *Approaches to Semiotics*, Mouton.

Laing, R.D. (1960), *The Divided Self*, Penguin.

Lambert, W.W., Solomon, R.L. and Watson, P.D. (1949), 'Reinforcement and extinction as factors in size estimation', *J. Exp. Psychol.*, 39, p. 637.

LaPiere, R.T. (1934), 'Attitudes and actions', *Social Forces*, 13, pp. 230–7.

Lashley, K.S. (1963), *Brain Mechanisms and Intelligence*, Dover Pub. Inc.

Lassen, N., Ingvar, D. and Skinhoj, E. (1978), 'Brain function and blood flow', *Scientific American*, October.

Lazurus, R.S. and McCleary, R.A. (1951), 'Autonomic discrimination without awareness', *Psychol. Rev.*, 58, p. 113.

Leahy, A.M. (1935), 'Nature–nurture and intelligence', *Genetic Psychology Monographs*, 17, pp. 235–308.

Leary, T. (1957), *Interpersonal Diagnosis of Personality*, Ronald Press.

Lehrman, D.S. (1953), 'Problems raised by instinct theory', *Quarterly Rev., Biology*, 28, pp. 337–65.

Leventhal, H.R., Singer, P. and Jones, S. (1965), 'Effects of fear and specificity of recommendation upon attitudes and behaviour', *J. Personality and Soc. Psychol.*, 2, pp. 20-9.

Lewis, M. and Johnson, N. (1971), 'What's thrown out with the bath water: a baby?', *Child Dev.*, 42, pp. 1053-5.

Lewis, M. and McGurk, H. (1972), 'Education of infant intelligence', *Science*, 178, pp. 1174-7.

Liebelt, R.A., Bordelon, C.B. and Liebelt, A.G., 'The adipose tissue system and food intake', in E. Stellar and J. Sprague (eds.) (1973), *Progress in Physiological Psychology*, Academic Press.

Lieberman, S. (1956), 'The effects of changes in roles on the attitudes of role-occupants', *Hum. Rltns.*, 9, pp. 385-402.

Likert, R. (1932), 'A technique for the measurement of attitudes', *Archives of Psychol.*, 22, pp. 1-55.

Linden, E. (1974), *Apes, Men and Language*, Penguin.

Lindsay, P.H. and Norman, D.A. (1973), *Human Information Processing: An Introduction to Psychology*, Academic Press.

Lorenz, K.Z. (1937), in W. Sluckin (1972), *Imprinting and Early Learning* (2nd ed.), Methuen.

Lorenz, K.Z. (1966), *On Aggression*, Methuen.

Lorge, I. (1930), 'Influences of regularly-interpolated time intervals on subsequent learning', *Teachers' College Contributions to Education*, no. 438.

Lott, A.J. (1969), 'The potential power of liking as a factor in social change', *Paper presented at the Meeting of the South-Western Psychological Association*.

Lovell, K., 'Some aspects of the work of Piaget in perspective', in A. Floyd (ed.) (1978), *Cognitive Development in the School Years*, Croom Helm.

Luchins, A.S., 'Primacy-recency in impression formation', in C.I. Hovland (ed.) (1959), *The Order of Presentation in Persuasion*, Yale University Press.

Lupton, T. (1963), *On the Shop Floor: Two Studies in Workshop Organization and Output*, Pergamon Press.

Luria, A.R. (1973), *The Working Brain*, Penguin.

Mace, C.A. (1962), *The Psychology of Study*, Penguin.

Le Magnen, (1956), quoted in J. Boddy, *Brain Systems and Psychological Concepts*, J. Wiley.

Mann, L. (1969), *Social Psychology*, Wiley.

Manning, A. (1979), *An Introduction to Animal Behaviour* (3rd ed.), Edward Arnold.

Maslow, A.H. (1954), *Motivation and Personality*, Harper and Row.

Maslow, A.H., 'Some basic propositions of a growth and self-actualization psychology', in G. Lindzey and C. Hall (eds.) (1965), *Theories of Personality: Primary Sources and Research*, Wiley.

Masters, W.H. and Johnson, V.E. (1966), *Human Sexual Response*, Little, Brown and Co.

Maynard-Smith, J. (1978), 'The evolution of behaviour', *Scientific American*, September.

McClelland, D.C. and Liberman, A.M. (1949), 'The effect of need for achievement on recognition of need-related words', *J. Person.*, 18, p. 236.

McConnell, J.V., Jacobson, A.L. and Kimble, D.P. (1959), 'The effects of regeneration upon retention of a conditioned response in the planarian', *J. Comp. Physiol. Psychol.*, 52, pp. 1–5.

McDougall, W. (1921), 'The use and abuse of instinct in social psychology', *J. Abnorm. Soc. Psychol.*, 16, p. 310.

McGeoch, J.A. and Irion, A.L. (1952), *Psychology of Human Learning*, (2nd ed.), Longmans.

McGinnies, E. (1949), 'Emotionality and perceptual defense', *Psychol. Rev.*, 56, p. 244.

McGuire, W.J. (1964), 'Inducing resistance to persuasion: some contemporary approaches', in L. Berkowitz (ed.), *Advances in Experimental Social Psychology*, vol. I., Academic Press.

McGuire, W.J. and Papageorgis, D. (1961), 'The relative efficacy of various types of prior belief defense in producing immunity against persuasion', *J. Abnorm. Soc. Psychol.*, 62, pp. 327–37.

McGuire, W.J., 'Theory of the structure of human thought', in R.P. Abelson *et al.* (eds.) (1968), *Theories of Cognitive Consistency: A Sourcebook*, Rand-McNally.

McGuire, W.J., 'Personality and susceptibility to social influence', in E. Borgatta and W. Lambert (eds.) (1968), *Handbook of Personality Theory and Research*, vol. 3, Rand-McNally.

McKellar, P. (1957), *Imagination and Thinking: A Psychological Analysis*, Cohen and West.

McVicker-Hunt, J. 'Intelligence and experience,' in S. Wiseman (ed.) (1967), *Intelligence and Ability*, Penguin.

Mead, G.H. (1934), *Mind, Self and Society*, University of Chicago Press.

Medawar, P.B. (1963), 'Is the scientific paper a fraud?' *The Listener*, 10, pp. 377–8.

Milgram, S. (1963), 'Behavioural study of obedience', *J. Abnorm. Soc. Psychol.*, 67, pp. 371–8.

Milgram, S. (1974), *Obedience to Authority*, Tavistock.

Miller, G.A. (1966), *Psychology: The Science of Mental Life*, Penguin.

Miller, N.E. (1948), 'Theory and experiment relating psycho-analytic displacement to S–R generalization', *J. Abnorm. Soc. Psychol.*, 43, pp. 155–78.

Miller, N.E. and Dollard, J., (1941), *Social Learning and Imitation*, Yale University Press.

Miller, S. (1975), *Experimental Design and Statistics*, Methuen.

Milner, B., 'Amnesia following operation on the temporal lobes', in C.W.M. Whitty and O.L. Zangwill (eds.) (1966), *Amnesia*, Butterworth.'

Milgram, S. (1964), 'Issues in the study of obedience', *Amer. Psychol.*, 19, pp. 848-52.

Milgram, S. (1965), 'Some conditions of obedience and disobedience to authority', *Human Rltns.*, 18, pp. 57-76.

Milner, P.M. (1966), *Physiological Psychology*, Holt, Rinehart and Winston.

Moreno, J.L. (1953), *Who Shall Survive?*, Beacon House.

Morgan, C.T. and King, R.A. (1971), *Introduction to Psychology*, McGraw-Hill.

Morris, C.D., Bransford, J.D. and Franks, J.J. (1977), 'Levels of processing versus transfer of appropriate processing', *J. Verbal Learning and Verbal Behaviour*, 16, pp. 419-533.

Morris, P.E. and Gruneberg, M.M. (1978), *Aspects of Memory*, Methuen.

Morton, J., 'A functional model for memory', in D.A. Norman (ed.) (1970), *Models of Human Memory*, Academic Press.

Murphy, G. (1947), *Personality: A Biosocial Approach to Origins and Structure*, Harper and Row.

Murray, H.A. (1938), *Explorations in Personality*, Oxford University Press.

Mussen, P. and Rutherford, E. (1963), 'Parent-child relations and parental personality in relation to young children's sex-role preferences', *Child Dev.*, 34, pp. 359-607.

Newcomb, T.M. (1943), *Personality and Social Change*, Dryden.

Newcomb, T.M. (1963), 'Persistence and regression of changed attitudes: long range studies', *J. Soc. Issues*, 19, 3-14.

Niemark, E. (1975), 'Longitudinal development of formal operational thought', *Genetic Psychol. Monographs*, 91, pp. 171-225.

Novin, D., Sanderson, J.D. and Vander Weele, D.A. (1974), 'The effect of isotonic glucose on eating as a function of feeding condition and infusion site', *Physiology and Behaviour*, 13, pp. 3-7.

Olds, J. and Milner, P. (1954), 'Positive reinforcement produced by electrical stimulation of the septal area and other regions of rat brain', *J. Comp. Physiol. Psychol.*, 47, pp. 419-27.

Ora, J.P. (1965), 'Characteristics of the volunteer for psychological investigations', *Office of Naval Research Contract 2149(03)*, Technical Report 27.

Orne, M.T. (1962), 'On the social psychology of the psychological experiment: with particular reference to demand characteristics and their implications', *Amer. Psychol.*, 17, pp. 776-83.

Osgood, C.E. and Tannenbaum, P.H. (1955), 'The principle of congruity in the prediction of attitude change', *Psychol. Rev.*, 62, pp. 42-55.

Osgood, C.E., Suci, G.J. and Tannenbaum, P.H. (1957), *The Measurement of Meaning*, University of Illinois Press.

Ostwald, P.F. (1965), 'Accoustic methods in psychiatry', *Scientific American*, 212, pp. 82–91.

Patrick, J. (1973), *A Glasgow Gang Observed*, Eyre Methuen.

Patterson, F. (1979), 'Conversations with a gorilla', *National Geographic*, 154(4), pp. 438–65.

Pavlov, I.P. (1911), *Conditioned Reflexes*, Oxford University Press, 1927.

Penfield, W. and Jasper, H. (1954), *Epilepsy and the Functional Anatomy of the Human Brain*, Little, Brown.

Penfield, W. and Roberts, L. (1959), *Speech and Brain Mechanisms*, Princeton University Press.

Peterson, J. and Peterson, J.K. (1938), 'Does practice with inverting lenses make vision normal?', *Psychological Monograph*, vol. 50, no. 12.

Peterson, L.R. (1966), 'Short-term memory', *Scientific American*, 215 (7), pp. 90–5.

Peterson, L.R. and Peterson, M. (1959), 'Short-term retention of individual items', *J. Exp. Psychol.*, 58, pp. 193–8.

Pettigrew, T.F. (1958), 'Personality and socio-cultural factors in intergroup attitudes: a cross-national comparison', *J. Conflict Resolution*, 2, pp. 29–42.

Pettigrew, T.F., Allport, G.W. and Barnett, E.O. (1958), 'Binocular resolution and perception of race in S. Africa', *Brit. J. Psychol.*, 49, p. 265.

Piaget, J. (1932), *The Moral Judgment of the Child*, Routledge and Kegan Paul.

Piaget, J., in P. Adams (ed.) (1972), *Language in Thinking*, Penguin.

Popper, K. (1945), *The Open Society and its Enemies*, Routledge and Kegan Paul.

Popper, K. (1959), *The Logic of Scientific Discoveries*, Hutchinson.

Popper, K. (1972), *Conjectures and Refutations: The Growth of Scientific Knowledge* (4th ed.), Routledge and Kegan Paul.

Powley, T.L. and Keesey, R.E. (1970), 'Relationship of body weight to the lateral hypothalamic feeding syndrome', *J. Comp. Physiolog. Psychol.*, 70, pp. 25–36.

Premack, A.J. and Premack, D. (1972), 'Teaching language to an ape', *Scientific American*, 222 (4), pp. 92–9.

Quillian, M.R. (1969), 'The teachable language comprehender: a simulation programme and theory of language', *Communications of the Assoc. for Computing Machinery*, 12, pp. 459–76.

Reeves, A.G. and Plum, F. (1969), 'Hyperphagia, rage and dementia accompanying a ventro-medial hypothalamic neoplasm', *Arch. Neurol.*, 20, pp. 616–24.

Reisen, A.H. (1950), 'Arrested vision', *Scientific American*, offprint no. 408, July.

Restle, F. (1957), 'Discrimination of cues in mazes', *Psychol. Rev.*, 64, pp. 217–28.

Robson, C. (1973), *Experiment, Design and Statistics in Psychology*, Penguin.

Rogers, C.R., 'A theory of therapy, personality and interpersonal relationships, as developed in the client-centred framework', in S. Koch (ed.) (1959), *Psychology: A Study of a Science*, McGraw-Hill.

Rogers, C.R., 'The process of the basic encounter group,' in J. Bugental (ed.) (1967), *Challenges in Humanistic Psychology*, McGraw-Hill.

Rokeach, M. (1960), *The Open and Closed Mind*, Basic Books.

Rokeach, M. (1968a), *Beliefs, Attitudes and Values*, Jossey-Bass.

Rokeach, M. (1968b), 'The Nature of Attitudes', in *International Encyclopaedia of the Social Sciences*, vol. I. The Macmillan Co. and The Free Press.

Rokeach, M. (1973), *The Nature of Human Values*, Free Press.

Rosenthal, R. (1966), *Experimenter Effects in Behavioural Research*, Appleton-Century-Crofts.

Rosenthal, R. and Jacobson, L. (1968), *Pygmalion in the classroom*, Holt, Rinehart and Winston.

Routtenberg, A. (1978), 'The reward system of the brain', *Scientific American*, November.

Rowland, N.E. and Antelman, S.M. (1976), 'Stress induced hyperphagia and obesity in rats: a possible model for understanding human obesity', *Science*, 191, pp. 310–12.

Rowntree, D. (1976), *Learn How to Study* (2nd ed.), MacDonald and Jane's.

Rundus, D. and Atkinson, R.C. (1970), 'Rehearsal processes in free recall: a procedure for direct observation', *J. Verbal Learning and Verbal Behaviour*, 9, pp. 99–105.

Russeck, M., 'Hepatic receptors and the neurophysiological mechanisms controlling feeding behaviour', in S. Ehrenpreis (ed.) (1971), *Neurosciences Research*, vol. 4, Academic Press.

Rutter, M., *Maternal Deprivation Re-assessed*, Penguin.

Sarbin, T.R., Taft, R. and Bailey, D.E. (1960), *Clinical Inference and Cognitive Theory*, Holt, Rinehart and Winston.

Sargent, S.S. (1939), 'Emotional stereotypes in the *Chicago Tribune*', *Sociometry*, 2, pp. 69–75.

Satinoff, E. (1964), 'Behavioural thermoregulation in response to local cooling of the rat brain', *Am. J. Physiol.*, 206, pp. 1389–94.

Schacter, S. (1971), 'Some extraordinary facts about obese humans and rats', in P. Mussen *et al.* (eds.), *Concepts in Psychology*, D.C. Heath and Co.

Schachter, S. and Singer, J.E. (1962), 'Cognitive, social and physiological determinants of emotional state', *Psychol. Rev.*, 69, pp. 379–99.

Schafer, R. and Murphy, G. (1943), 'The role of autism in a visual figure–ground relationship', *J. Exp. Psychol.*, 32, p. 335.

Schaffer, H.R. (1974), 'Early social behaviour and the study of reciprocity', *Bull. BPS*, 27, pp. 109–16.

Schaie, K.W. and Strother, C.R. (1968), 'A cross-sequential study of age changes in cognitive behaviour', *Psychol. Bull.*, 70, pp. 671-80.

Schein, E.H. (1957), 'Reaction patterns to severe chronic stress in American Army prisoners of war of the Chinese', *J. Soc. Issues*, 13, pp. 21-30.

Schneider, G.E., quoted in P.H. Lindsay and D.A. Norman (eds.) (1969), *Human Information Processing: An Introduction to Psychology*, Academic Press.

Sears, D.O., 'The paradox of *de facto* selective exposure without preference for supportive information', in R.P. Abelson *et al.* (eds.) (1968), *Theories of Cognitive Consistency: a Sourcebook*, Rand McNally.

Sears, D.O., 'Political behaviour', in G. Lindzey and E. Aronson (eds.) (1969), *Handbook of Social Psychology* (2nd ed.), vol. 3, Addison-Wesley.

Sears, R.R., Maccoby, E.E. and Levin, H. (1957), *Patterns of Child Rearing*, Row Peterson.

Secord, P.F., 'The role of facial features in interpersonal perception', in R. Tagiuri and L. Petrullo (eds.) (1958), *Perception and Interpersonal Behaviour*, Stanford University Press.

Secord, P.F. and Backman, C.W. (1964), *Social Psychology*, McGraw-Hill.

von Senden, M. (1932), *Space and Sight*, Methuen/Free Press.

Shallice, T. and Warrington, E.K. (1970), 'Independent functioning of verbal memory stores: a neurophysiological study', *Quarterly J. Exp. Psychol.*, 22, pp. 261-73.

Sheldon, W.H. (1954), *Atlas of Men: A Guide for Somatotyping the Adult Male at All Ages*, Harper and Row.

Shepherd, G.M. (1965), quoted in G.M. Shepherd, 'Microcircuits in the nervous system', *Scientific American*, February 1978.

Sherif, M. (1935), 'A study of some social factors in perception', *Archives of Psychol.*, 27, no. 187.

Sherif, M. and Hovland, C.I. (1961), *Social Judgment: Assimilation and Contrast in Communication and Attitude Change*, Yale University Press.

Shields, J. (1962), *Monozygotic Twins brought up Apart and brought up Together*, Oxford University Press.

Shuey, A.M. (1966), *The Testing of Negro Intelligence*, Social Science Press.

Siipola, E. (1935), 'A group study of some effects of preparatory sets', *Psychol. Monogs.*, vol. 46, no. 210.

Singer, R.D. (1961), 'Verbal conditioning and generalization of pro-democratic responses', *J. Abnorm. Soc. Psychol.*, 63, pp. 43-6.

Skeels, H.M. (1966), 'Adult status of children with contrasting early life experiences', *Monographs of the Society for Research in Child Development*, 31, p. 3.

Skinner, B.F. (1938), *Science and Human Behaviour*, Macmillan, 1953.

Skinner, B.F. (1957), *Verbal Behaviour*, Appleton-Century-Crofts.

Skinner, B.F., 'Behaviourism at fifty', in T.W. Wann (ed.) (1964), *Behaviourism and Phenomenology*, University of Chicago Press.

Skodak, M. and Skeels, H.M. (1949), 'A final follow-up study of one hundred adopted children', *J. Genetic Psychol.*, 75, pp. 85–125.

Skolnick, P. (1979), reported in 'Body molecules fight stress', *New Scientist*, 28 June.

Smith, M.B., Bruner, J. and White, R.W. 'The adjustive functions of opinion', in H. Brown and R. Stevens (eds.) (1956), *Social Behaviour and Experience*, Hodder and Stoughton Educational/Open University Press.

Smith, P.B. (1969), 'Improving skills in working with people: the T-group', *Dept of Employment, Training Information Paper*, 4, HMSO.

Snygg, D. (1938), 'The relationship between the intelligence of mothers and of their children living in foster homes', *J. Genetic Psychol.*, 52, pp. 401–6.

Sokoloff, L. (1979), quoted in L.L. Iversen, 'The chemistry of the brain', *Scientific American*, September.

Solley, C.M. and Murphy, G. (1960), *Development of the Perceptual World*, Basic Books.

Sontag, L.W., Baker, C.T. and Nelson, V.L. (1958), 'Mental growth and personality development: a longitudinal study', *Monographs of the Society for Research in Child Development*, 23, p. 2.

Southwick, C.H., Beg, M.A. and Siddiai, M.R. (1965), 'Rhesus monkeys in North India', in I. De Vore (ed.), *Primate Behaviour: Field Studies of Monkeys and Apes*, Holt, Rinehart and Winston.

Spearman, C. (1904), ' "General intelligence" objectively determined and measured', *Am. J. Psychol.*, 15, pp. 201–93.

Sperry, R.W. (1943), 'The effect of 180-degree rotation in the retinal field on visuo-motor coordination', *Journal of Experimental Zoology*, 92, pp. 263–79.

Sperry, R.W., 'The great cerebral commissure', *Scientific American*, 210 (1), pp. 42–52.

Stanton, H.R. and Litwak, E. (1955), 'Toward the development of a short-form test of interpersonal competence', *Am. Sociol. Rev.*, 20, pp. 668–74.

Stein, D.G., in E. Eidelberg and D.G. Stein (eds.) (1974), 'Functional recovery after lesions of the nervous system', *Neurosciences Resource Program Bulletin*, vol. 12.

Stellar, E. (1954), 'The psychology of motivation', *Psychol. Rev.*, 61, pp. 5–22.

Stratton, G.M. (1897) – experiments described in Gregory, R.L. (1977), *Eye and Brain* (3rd ed.), Weidenfeld and Nicolson.

Strongman, K.T. and Hart, C.J. (1968), 'Stereotyped reactions to body build', *Psychol. Rep.*, 23, pp. 1175–8.

Swingle, P. (1973), *Social Psychology in Everyday Life*, Penguin.

Symonds, P.M. (1951), *The Ego and the Self*, Appleton-Century-Crofts.

Tanner, J.M. (1978), *Foetus into Man: Physical Growth from Conception to Maturity*, Open Books.

Teitelbaum, P. (1955), 'The encephalization of hunger', in E. Stellar and J.M. Sprague (eds.) (1971), *Progress in Physiological Psychology*, vol. 4, Academic Press.

Teitelbaum, P. and Epstein, A.N. (1962), 'The lateral hypothalamic syndrome', *Psychol. Rev.*, 69, pp. 74-90.

Teitelbaum, P. and Stellar, E. (1954), 'Recovery from the failure to eat produced by hypothalamic lesions', *Science*, 120, pp. 894-5.

Terman, L.M. (1916), *The Measurement of Intelligence*, Houghton Mifflin.

Thompson, R. (1972), *Psychology of Thinking*, Penguin.

Thompson, W.R. (1954), 'The inheritance and development of intelligence', *Proc. Assoc. Research in Nervous and Mental Disease*, 33, pp. 209-31.

Thorndike, E.L. (1911), 'The fundamentals of learning', *Teachers' College Bureau of Publications*, 1932.

Thorndike, R.L. (1948), 'Growth of intelligence during adolescence', *J. Genetic Psychol.*, 72, pp. 11-15.

Thurstone, L.L. (1930), 'A scale for measuring attitudes towards the movies', *J. Ed. Res.*, 22, pp. 88-94.

Thurstone, L.L. (1938), 'Primary mental abilities', *Psychometric Monographs*, no. 1, University of Chicago Press.

Tinbergen, N. (1952), 'The curious behaviour of the stickleback', *Scientific American*, 187 (6), pp. 22-6.

Tinbergen, N. (1968), 'On war and peace in men and animals', *Science*, 160, pp. 1411-18.

Tolman, E.C. (1930), *Psychology: A Study of A Science*, McGraw-Hill, 1959.

Tolman, E.C., 'Principles of purposive behaviour', in S. Koch (ed.) (1948), *Psychology: A Study of a Science*, McGraw-Hill.

Trevarthen, C. (1974), 'Conversations with a two month old', *New Scientist*, 2 May.

Triesman, A.M. (1960), 'Contextual cues in selective listening', *Quarterly J. Exp. Psychol.*, 12, pp. 242-8.

Triesman, A.M. (1969), 'Strategies and models of selective attention', *Psychol. Rev.*, 76, pp. 282-99.

Tulving, E. (1962), 'Subjective organization in free recall of "unrelated" words', *Psychol. Rev.*, 69, pp. 344-54.

Tulving, E., 'Episodic and semantic memory', in E. Tulving and W. Donaldson (eds.) (1972), *Organisation of Memory*, Academic Press.

Tulving, E. and Pearlstone, Z. (1966), 'Availability versus accessibility of information in memory for words', *J. Verbal Learning and Verbal Behaviour*, 5, pp. 381-91.

Tyler, L.E. (1965), *The Psychology of Human Differences*, Appleton-Century-Crofts.

Vernon, M.D. (1955), 'The functions of schemata in perceiving', *Psychol. Rev.*, 62, pp. 180-92.

Vernon, M.D. (1962), *Psychology of Perception*, Penguin.

Vygotsky, L.S. (1962), *Thought and Language*, MIT Press.

Walster, E. and Festinger, L. (1962), 'The effectiveness of "overheard" persuasive communications', *J. Abnorm. Soc. Psychol.*, 65, pp. 395-402.

Warren, N. and Jahoda, M. (1973), *Attitudes* (2nd ed.), Penguin.

Watson, J. (1913), 'Psychology as the behaviourist sees it', *Psychol. Rev.*, 20, pp. 158–77.

Werner, H. and Kaplan, E. (1950), 'Development of word meaning through verbal context: an experimental study', *J. Psychol.*, 29, pp. 251–7.

Weschler, D. (1958), *The Measurement and Appraisal of Adult Intelligence*, Williams and Wilkins.

Whiting, J.W.M., 'Resource mediation and learning by identification', in I. Iscoe and H.W. Stevenson (eds.), *Personality Development in Young Children*, University of Texas Press.

Whorf, B.L., in P. Adams (1941), *Language in Thinking*, Penguin.

Whyte, W.F. (1955), *Street Corner Society: The Social Structure of an Italian Slum*, University of Chicago Press.

Wickelgren, W.A. (1965), 'Acoustic similarity and retroactive interference in short term memory', *J. Verbal Learning and Verbal Behaviour*, 4, pp. 53–61.

Wickens, D.D., 'Characteristics of word encoding', in A.W. Melton and E. Martin (eds.) (1972), *Coding Processes in Human Memory*, Winston.

Wicker, A.W. (1969), 'Attitudes versus actions: the relationship of verbal and overt responses to attitude objects', in N. Warren and M. Jahoda (eds.) (1973), *Attitudes*, Penguin.

Wiggin, N., Hoffman, P.J. and Taber, T. (1969), 'Types of judges and cue utilization in judgments of intelligence', *J. Person. Soc. Psychol.*, 12, pp. 52–9.

Wilson, E. (1976), 'Sociobiology: a new approach to understanding the basis of human nature', *New Scientist*, 13 May.

Wittgenstein, L. (1953), *Philosophical Investigations*, Blackwell.

Wohlwill, J.F., 'Piaget's system as a source of empirical research', in I.E. Sigel *et al.* (eds.) (1968), *Logical Thinking in Children*, Holt, Rinehart and Winston.

Wrightsman, L.S. (1972), *Social Psychology in the Seventies*, Brooks/Cole.

Wynne-Edwards, V.C. (1962), *Animal Dispersion in Relation to Social Behaviour*, Oliver and Boyd.

Yarrow, M.R., Campbell, J.D. and Burton, R.N. (1968), *Child Rearing: An Inquiry into Research and Methods*, Jossey-Bass.

Yasuka, K. (1979), 'A fair advantage in animal confrontations', *New Scientist*, 1 November.

Zeiglar, H.P. and Karten, H.J. (1974), 'Central trigeminal structures and the lateral hypothalamus syndrome in the rat', *Science*, 186, pp. 636–7.

Index

nigro-striatal bundle, 183
nodes of ranvier, 145
Noirot, E., 286
non-conformity, 301
non-verbal communication, interpersonal perception, 404-10
noradrenalin, 158, 162
Norman, D.A., 191
normative conformity, 300
Novin, D., 181

obedience, 308-14
obesity, 180, 182-4
observation, 25-30; non-participant, 27-9; participant, 29-30; surveys, 25-7
occupations, and self-perception, 388
Odbert, H.S., 252
Oedipus complex, 261-2, 329, 356
oestrogen, 159
Olds, J., 184, 185
ontogenesis, 270
operant conditioning, 87, 91-109; applications, 101-9; avoidance learning, 97-8; behaviour therapy, 101, 107-9; continuous reinforcement, 94; escape learning, 97-8; extinction, 94, 98-101; fixed-interval reinforcement, 94; fixed-ratio reinforcement, 94; generalization, 96-7; negative reinforcement, 97; programmed learning, 101-7; reinforcement schedules, 94-5; secondary reinforcement, 98; variable-interval reinforcement, 95; variable-ratio reinforcement, 95
opiate drugs, 196-7
opinion polls, 344-7
opinions, attitudes and, 343-7
opsin, 187
optic chiasma, 170, 171
optic nerve, 146
Ora, J.P., 14
Orne, M.J., 11, 229, 350, 365

pain: centres, 184; chemical factors in, 196-7
Papageorgis, D., 375
paradigms, 40-1
Patrick, 273
Patrick, J., 29
Patterson, F., 244-5
Pavlov, I.P., 87, 88-9, 91
Pearlstone, Z., 128
pendulum fighting, 292
Penfield, W., 140, 163, 166-7

penis-envy complex, 329, 330
perception, 43-85; altruistic, 66; Ames distorted room, 70-2; attenuator theory, 58, 60-1; Broadbent's attention model, 58-61; Brunswik's model, 44-6, 47, 56, 61-2; contrast of stimulus, 57-8; definition, 61-73; deprivation effects, 65-6; deprivation studies, 74-7; depth perception, 49-57; distal analysis, 44, 45, 47-9; effects of rewards on, 67; emotion and, 66, 67-70; of emotion, 152-5; expectancy and, 66-7; framework of, 43-9; intensity of stimulus, 57; memory and, 125-6; motivation effects, 65-6; movement and, 58-61, 195-6; nature/nurture debate, 73-85; neonate studies, 79-85; perceptual constancies, 49; perceptual defence, 68-9; perceptual semitization, 68-9; perspective, 49-50; physiology of, 186-96; proximal analysis, 44, 45, 46-7; readjustment studies, 78-9; repetition of stimulus, 58; selective attention, 57-61; set as interpreter, 65-70; set in hypothesis testing, 70-3; set as selector, 63-5; set as umbrella, 62-3; social, see interpersonal perception; self-perception: three-dimensional, 194-5; Whorfian hypothesis, 231-6
peripheral nervous system, 151-5
personality, 247-64; attitudes and, 353-4; cardinal traits, 254; cluster analysis, 252; cognitive approach, 257-9; factor analysis, 250-4; Freudian themes, 259-64; learning theories, 256-7; manifest needs, 254-5; neo-Freudian theories, 263-4; non-Freudian theories, 247-59; personal constructs, 257-8; phenomenological theories, 254-6; psychosexual stages and, 260-2; Repertory Grid, 258-9; Role Construct Repertory Test, 258; Sixteen Personality Factor Questionnaire, 253; social learning approach, 257; types and categories, 247-9
perspective, 49-52; decreasing size and, 51-2; gradient of texture, 52; height in the horizontal plane, 52
Peterson, J., 78-9
Peterson, J.K., 78-9
Peterson, L., 122
Peterson, M., 122
Pettigrew, T.F., 64, 359
Pfungst, O., 267